Praise of *New Way to Care*

"John Goodman is a national treasure whose book *New Way to Care: Social Protections That Put Families First* should be national policy. It is pragmatic, knowledgeable, and accessible. Read it and help to accomplish John's wise advice."
   —**Regina E. Herzlinger**, Nancy R. McPherson Professor of Business Administration, Harvard Business School

"John Goodman is an extraordinarily deep, knowledgeable, and original architect of American domestic policy. His book *New Way to Care* provides a compelling path out of our terrible social insurance policy morass. It is a must read for anyone truly seeking to make America great again."
   —**Laurence J. Kotlikoff**, William Fairfield Warren Distinguished Professor and Professor of Economics, Boston University

"Long one of the nation's leading health policy experts, Goodman has a history of proposing the next big thing in market-based reforms. *New Way to Care* takes readers on a tour of federal entitlement programs in search for win-win policy changes that can leave everyone better off. Anyone alarmed that the safety net will not remain safe can find cause for hope here."
   —**Mitchel E. Daniels Jr.**, President, Purdue University; former Governor of Indiana; former Director, U.S. Office of Management and Budget; Co-Chair, Committee for a Responsible Federal Budget

"No one has worked longer and more effectively at creating a modern, people-oriented and affordable health system than John Goodman. He is an amazing pioneer and his book *New Way to Care* reflects his knowledge and his insights. In the book, he shows what's wrong with our antiquated system of social insurance. Other countries, he writes, have found better solutions that merit our attention."
   —**Newt Gingrich**, former Majority Leader, U.S. House of Representatives

"John Goodman is someone everyone should listen to when it comes to healthcare policy—with his book *New Way to Care*, the same can now be said for social insurance. While many misdiagnose the problems with our healthcare and social insurance systems, Goodman correctly identifies one of the most serious problems—inefficient regulations. While others propose more regulation to cure the ills caused by past regulations, Goodman proposes the types of market-based reforms that can make our social insurance system function better."
   —**Kevin M. Murphy**, George J. Stigler Distinguished Service Professor of Economics, University of Chicago; Member, American Academy of Arts and Sciences; MacArthur Fellow

"John Goodman is one of the most creative thinkers of our time in the complex world of health care policy. In his book *New Way to Care*, he puts forth important, thought-provoking ideas about the role of government in the personal lives of Americans. Read it!"

—**Scott W. Atlas**, M.D., Member, White House Coronavirus Task Force; Robert Wesson Senior Fellow in Scientific Philosophy and Public Policy, Hoover Institution

"In *New Way to Care*, John Goodman is consistently ahead of his time with market solutions which align incentives that respect the agency of individuals while ensuring there is a social safety net. What he writes today will be policy in the coming years."

—**Bill Cassidy**, M.D., U.S. Senator

"In his book *New Way to Care*, John Goodman again demonstrates the creativity that led to his invention of 'Health Savings Accounts.' John shows that the major risks of life—health, premature death, outliving one's assets, disability, unemployment—are made worse by inefficient government policies. John shows in detail how elimination of many government policies would enable people to use the private market to minimize these risks at a much lower cost. Under the right circumstances, this book could improve many areas of life in the same way that Health Savings Accounts have improved markets for health insurance."

—**Paul H. Rubin**, Samuel Candler Dobbs Professor of Economics and Law, Emory University

"Whether the topic is the FDA, Medicare, the VA or telemedicine, John Goodman uses his characteristic clarity and vast storehouse of knowledge in the book *New Way to Care* to shed light on the arcane technicalities and perverse rules that stand between all American families and the healthcare that they need, deserve and can afford."

—**Richard A. Epstein**, Laurence A. Tisch Professor of Law, New York University; Peter and Kirsten Bedford Senior Fellow, Hoover Institution; and James Parker Hall Distinguished Service Professor Emeritus of Law, University of Chicago

"For the last quarter century, John Goodman has been one of the nation's best and most original thinkers on the economics of health care. The book *New Way to Care* is more of his good and original thinking about how we can improve both the efficiency of the health care system and the quality of care that it provides. I commend this book to you because it contains a whole new way of organizing the American health care system—something that is desperately needed."

—**W. Philip Gramm**, former U.S. Senator; former Chairman, Senate Committee on Banking, Housing, and Urban Affairs; Senior Partner, US Policy Metrics; former Vice Chairman, UBS Investment Bank

"John C. Goodman's book, *New Way to Care*, should be mandatory reading for every politician in Congress and state legislatures. It is an instruction manual to escape the morass of the current stifling bureaucratic government-controlled healthcare system designed by politicians focusing on votes. Goodman clearly explains how to build a patient-centric medical system where the patient has choice, control, and responsibility for their medical insurance and physicians. Highly recommended for everyone in the USA!"

> —**Donald J. Palmisano**, M.D., J.D., FACS, former President, American Medical Association; Adjunct Professor of Surgery and Clinical Professor of Medical Jurisprudence, Tulane University School of Medicine

"John Goodman has kept up a high standard of commentary on social policy in America for several decades and *New Way to Care* is no exception."

> —**David G. Green**, Director, Civitas, United Kingdom

"In *New Way to Care*, once again John Goodman's clear and down-to-earth writing style has provided a clear and convincing argument for increasing individual freedom as a way to increase the population's well-being. This book covers a wide range of government infringements on the freedom of individuals to improve their wellbeing. Its discussion of the current COVID-19 pandemic is especially on point."

> —**Thomas R. Saving**, Director, Private Enterprise Research Center and University Distinguished Professor of Economics, Texas A&M University

"*New Way to Care* is a provocative book. Even those of us who don't fully share John Goodman's fundamental world view should carefully consider many of his arguments for making social programs more efficient."

> —**Susan Dentzer**, Senior Policy Fellow, Robert J. Margolis Center for Health Policy, Duke University; former Editor-in-Chief, *Health Affairs*

"In the innovative book *New Way to Care*, John Goodman takes the reader on a tour through the labyrinth of government-run social insurance programs—Social Security, Medicare, and other programs that are supposed to help those who are most in need. The book explains how even the most sophisticated individual can be caught up in contradictory program rules that can mean the devastating loss of benefits. Goodman argues that instead of uprooting the whole system, let Americans decide how much they want to rely on the government or on their own actions through the private sector to meet their families' needs. That's a reform we can live with."

> —**Joseph R. Antos**, Wilson H. Taylor Scholar in Health Care and Retirement Policy, American Enterprise Institute

"In his book *New Way to Care*, John Goodman, rightly credited with conceiving of the Health Savings Account, presents a series of practical suggestions to improve American social insurance programs such as Medicare and Social Security. His combination of analysis and proposals can help citizens understand the flaws in the current systems and help guide lawmakers who are serious about improving them."

> —**Howard A. Husock**, Senior Fellow and Director, Tocqueville Project, Manhattan Institute; author, *Who Killed Civil Society? The Rise of Big Government and Decline of Bourgeois Norms*

"In *New Way to Care*, John Goodman holds a mirror up to our emerging reality under government-designed and regulated social-protection programs. What we clearly see is an unsustainable economic reality, coupled with benefit delivery that falls short for everyone. He also reminds us of the power of individuality and creativity, suggesting that everyone would do better if we put families first, and let them secure their own futures. Unlike the current communications style, Goodman offers a fact-based, calm and respectful approach to negotiating the path to a better future."

> —**Stephen B. Bonner**, former President and CEO, Cancer Treatment Centers of America

"John C. Goodman's *New Way to Care: Social Protections That Put Families* is an essential guide to the shortcomings of politicized social insurance in the U.S., including the government's failure to deal with the COVID-19 crisis. Goodman gives Americans a path forward that will empower individuals. Drawing on careful research, and backed by compelling analysis, Goodman discusses lessons to be learned from such diverse real-world alternatives as Medi-Share, an innovative private cooperative health-care sharing plan, and Chile's tremendously successful private retirement plans which have brought ordinary people higher returns than were ever possible under the governmental system. Goodman has written a first-rate book that both reveals the flaws of the status quo and points the way to a better future."

> —**David T. Beito**, Professor of History, University of Alabama; author, *From Mutual Aid to the Welfare State: Fraternal Societies and Social Services, 1890–1967*; co-editor, *The Voluntary City: Choice, Community and Civil Society*

Principal Researchers Cited*

Courtney Collins
Mercer University

William B. Conerly
Conerly Consulting, LLC

Hans Fehr
University of Wuerzburg

John C. Goodman
Goodman Institute

N. Michael Helvacian
MNH Consulting

Devon Herrick
Goodman Institute,
Heartland Institute

Augusto Iglesias
PrimAmérica Consultores

Estelle James
State University of New York, Stony Brook

Sabine Jokisch
University of Wuerzburg

Laurence Kotlikoff
Boston University

Liqun Liu
Texas A&M University

Andrew J. Rettenmaier
Texas A&M University

Thomas R. Saving
Texas A&M University

Pamela Villarreal
University of Texas at Dallas,
Goodman Institute

*References to these researchers do not imply their agreement with the content of this book.

INDEPENDENT INSTITUTE is a non-profit, non-partisan, public-policy research and educational organization that shapes ideas into profound and lasting impact. The mission of Independent is to boldly advance peaceful, prosperous, and free societies grounded in a commitment to human worth and dignity. Applying independent thinking to issues that matter, we create transformational ideas for today's most pressing social and economic challenges. The results of this work are published as books, our quarterly journal, *The Independent Review*, and other publications and form the basis for numerous conference and media programs. By connecting these ideas with organizations and networks, we seek to inspire action that can unleash an era of unparalleled human flourishing at home and around the globe.

100 Swan Way, Oakland, California 94621-1428, U.S.A.
Telephone: 510-632-1366 • Facsimile: 510-568-6040 • Email: info@independent.org • www.independent.org

JOHN C. GOODMAN

New Way to
CARE

Social Protections that Put Families First

INDEPENDENT
I N S T I T U T E

OAKLAND, CALIFORNIA

Independent Institute
100 Swan Way, Oakland, CA 94621-1428
Telephone: 510-632-1366
Fax: 510-568-6040
Email: info@independent.org
Website: www.independent.org

Cover Design: Denise Tsui
Cover Image: Africa Studio / Adobe Stock

Library of Congress Cataloging-in-Publication Data Available

ISBN: 9781598133172

Contents

Introduction A New Approach to Public Policy   1

SECTION 1 **A Better Way to Manage Life's Risks**   11

    1 The Case for Change   13

    2 Balancing Individual and Societal Interests   23

    3 Alternatives That Offer Individual Choice   33

    4 Choice, Ownership, Responsibility   43

SECTION 2 **Taking a Closer Look at the Risks**   53

    5 The Risk of Growing Too Old and Outliving One's Assets   55

    6 The Risk of Dying Too Young and Leaving Dependent Family Members without Resources   101

    7 The Risk of Becoming Disabled and Facing Financial Ruin   103

    8 The Risk of Facing a Major Health Event and Being Unable to Afford Needed Medical Care   117

    9 The Risk of Becoming Unemployed and Finding No Market for One's Skills   157

    10 The Risk of Plagues, Pandemics, and Other Threats to Public Health   167

SECTION 3 Taking a Closer Look at Some Solutions   175

    11   Addressing the Risks of Old Age   177

    12   Opting Out of Survivor Insurance   223

    13   Opting Out of Disability Insurance   225

    14   Addressing the Risk of Ill Health   239

    15   Opting Out of Unemployment Insurance   273

    16   Combatting the Coronavirus   277

Conclusion   Life under a Reformed System   287

Appendix 1   Ten Things You Need to Know about
Medicare for All   293

Appendix 2   What Socialized Medicine Looks Like   303

Notes   309

Index   357

About the Author   371

Introduction
A New Approach to Public Policy

AS THIS BOOK goes to press, the entire world is in the midst of an economic and health care crisis. No country seems untouched.

The prime minister of the United Kingdom was infected with the coronavirus. The chancellor of Germany was in quarantine. One of our most popular actors and his wife were in self-isolation in Australia. NBA basketball players, U.S. senators, TV anchors—the virus is no respecter of wealth, occupation, or social status.

Claims for unemployment compensation in the United States hit the highest weekly spike in the history of the program. The stock market endured the largest weekly crash in its history. Everybody is expecting a severe economic contraction. The only question is: how deep and how long?

There are two observations worth making. First, we weren't ready for this. That's not surprising. There has never been a time in the history of the world when a country was prepared for a pandemic. The second observation is less obvious. Social institutions that allegedly were designed to protect people in the face of unforeseen bad luck not only didn't work, they actually interfered with the ability of people to get the help they needed.

America's greatest strength is that it is a place where inventors, creators, entrepreneurs, and just about anybody with a new idea on how to meet other people's needs are free to try out their ideas. If their ideas work, they might become very, very rich. We've seen that happen time and again.

But when the coronavirus hit our health care sector, entrepreneurs faced roadblocks, no matter where they looked. Health care is the most regulated sector in our economy. Those regulations comprise what I call a huge "social insurance" system, shaped and molded by public policy. It is defended on the theory that we want people to get care when they need it. And we want the care they get to be safe and based on the best treatments medical science has to offer.

Yet the very system we created to insure people against bad health outcomes turned out to be the patient's biggest obstacle. To echo Ronald Reagan, in 2020 we discovered that in health care, more often than not, government is not the solution; it is the problem.

A little over sixty years ago, Earl Bakken invented the pacemaker in his garage. The value of this life-saving product was soon recognized, and his company Medtronic grew rapidly from its humble beginnings to a multinational medical technology corporation. By the time he retired, he was a multimillionaire.

Today, no one could do what Earl Bakken did. The reason: the heavy hand of government regulation.

Think about everything that is involved in treating a patient with the coronavirus: testing kits, masks, gloves, gowns, respirators, ventilators, hospital beds, etc. Three months into 2020, there was a nationwide shortage of all of these. But you couldn't make any of them in a garage, or anywhere else, without the government's permission. Entrepreneurs knew that. They also knew that getting permission would be a long, arduous, and possibly unsuccessful process.

The private sector was more than ready to do the job. For example, there were tests approved in Europe that could be administered anywhere—in schools, airports, homes, etc.—and give results in only a few minutes. But when the coronavirus hit the United States, the only place allowed to conduct a coronavirus test was the Centers for Disease Control and Prevention (CDC); and it could only do a few tests a day, with results expected several days (and maybe weeks) later.

When the CDC finally realized it was being overwhelmed by a pandemic, it bent its own rules. The agency sent testing kits out to about one hundred labs and facilities around the country so that more testing could be done in a shorter amount of time. Unfortunately, half the kits didn't work.

Think about that. While our health care bureaucracy was fumbling around and making error after error, people in other countries had access to tests at the drop of a hat.

We learned quickly that the private sector stood ready to fill the shortage gap in all kinds of creative ways. For example, masks designed for industrial use can be retrofitted for hospital use. The same is true for ventilators. Not only was this not allowed under existing regulations, there was an additional threat. In health care, every time a patient dies, there is a potential lawsuit. What company wants to step outside the established regulatory system and send medical supplies around the country, knowing that there is a potential lawsuit every time a patient doesn't make it? Hospital beds were also regulated. Medicare even told hospitals how many beds they could have.

As city after city went into total "lockdown," think how many hotel rooms were completely empty. In theory, that's an opportunity for supply to meet demand. A lot of coronavirus patients in hospitals don't actually need to be there. If hotels could be used as intermediate facilities, patients who were less severely ill could be bedded there and monitored and cared for by nurses. Yet that was another opportunity blocked by excessive regulation.

One reason American health care is so expensive is that we don't allow inexpensive care.

It gets worse. As everyone knows, in the middle of a pandemic you should avoid other people as much as possible. With that in mind, about the worse place to be is in a doctor's office or in a hospital emergency room—where not only are you around other people, but they are people likely to be sick.

By mid-March, President Trump and the health care experts on the White House COVID-19 team began stressing in their daily briefings the desirability of telemedicine—including phone, email, and video conferencing.

There was only one problem. When Donald Trump took office, in most cases it was illegal (by law of Congress!) for a doctor to charge Medicare for a consultation with a patient that was not face to face, except in rare circumstances. It was also illegal for a Medicare doctor to charge a patient a monthly fee for round-the-clock access to primary care, including nights and weekends. Ditto for Uber-type house calls.

In other words, everything that the health care sector could do to improve patient care and minimize exposure for the most at-risk population (senior citizens) was against the law!

Employers were shackled as well. When Donald Trump took office, it was illegal for private employers to put money in an employee account that allowed workers to choose a doctor who would provide 24/7 primary care, including telemedicine. It was also illegal (under penalty of heavy fines) for an employer to buy insurance for employees that they would own and take with them if they left the firm.

In other words, the kind of insurance that would have been most helpful to the millions of workers who lost their jobs because of COVID-19 was against the law! In the first quarter of 2020, some of these regulations were rescinded by emergency executive orders. Others were rescinded by acts of Congress.

But almost none of these reforms are permanent. A new president could reverse Trump's executive orders—just as Trump reversed the executive orders of President Obama. And most of the congressional legislative changes were restricted to the duration of the coronavirus threat. Once the threat from the virus is gone, the old system will be back in place.

We live in a world in which I am free to do all kinds of risky things. I can jump out of an airplane with a parachute. I can scuba-dive in caves. I can go into the sea in a metal cage and interact with great white sharks. I can parasail off mountain tops. I can drop out of a helicopter and extreme-ski. I can try to scale a vertical mountainside, without a net. I can join Cirque du Soleil and hang upside down on a rope, thirty feet in the air. I can get on a surfboard and see if I can survive an eighty-foot wave. I can climb Mount Everest, where the mortality rate is 10 percent. I can abuse my body with liquor, tobacco, and fatty foods.

So if the government allows me to do all those things, why does it tell me how I can communicate with my doctor? Or dictate what kind of hospital bed I can lie in? Or what kind of mask my caregiver wears?

This book is concerned with risk. As we go through life, we face all kinds of risks. As noted, government is only involved in some of them. But why some and not others?

Perhaps more fundamentally, why is government involved in any of them?

What we call "social insurance" is insurance provided by government. It is an alternative to all the various ways people can avoid risk and insure against it through private action alone. As we look around the world, we find that insurance against risk has been socialized almost everywhere in certain key areas. They include: retirement, disability, premature death, medical care, and unemployment.

Our look at these institutions will be critical. Like the government's lack of preparation for the coronavirus, social insurance often does not work well.

For elderly entitlement programs, for example, we have made promises to future retirees that far exceed the revenue that will be there to fund them. In fact, the unfunded liability in elderly entitlement programs alone is about six times the size of the entire economy. Even when a social insurance program is reasonably funded, individuals invariably face perverse incentives to behave in ways that undermine the purpose of the program and increase the costs for others.

Can social insurance be reformed in ways that make it work better? Can the failures of government administration be reformed through privatization? Are there ways of returning responsibility back to individuals—so that society as a whole doesn't need to be involved at all?

Let's find out.

Origins of Social Insurance

Human beings have always faced the risks of growing too old and outliving their assets—or dying too young and leaving their families without resources. They have worried about the financial impact of disability or major sicknesses. Today's political climate is impacted by the frustration of the long-term unemployment for those whose skills are no longer attuned to the job market.

Societies have wrestled with these issues and come up with different solutions in different times and places. In America prior to the twentieth century, nuclear families and extended families served as the principal form of insurance against these risks. In fact, it was not uncommon for parents to view their children as a retirement plan.

As we moved from the nineteenth to the twentieth century, a very important social change took place. For the first time in the history of the human race, nuclear families and extended families ceased becoming reliable means of insuring against life's most important risks. Whether it was the risk of old age, premature death, ill health, disability, or unemployment, government began to fulfill the role that had been performed by kin for eons.

The reason for the growth of government in the twentieth century was the growth of programs that provided middle-class families with insurance they could not easily acquire on their own in the private marketplace.[1] Many people incorrectly assume that governments expanded in the twentieth century, both here and abroad, to take care of the poor and the unfortunate. Even the term "welfare state" suggests that way of thinking. But modern governments in developed countries are not principally focused on welfare for the poor. They are focused on insurance and other benefits (such as public education) for the middle class. More than one commentator has loosely characterized our federal government as an insurance company connected to an army. That insurance is "social insurance."

But whereas families were typically sensible caregivers, all too often governments have done things that were not sensible. Our elderly entitlement programs are collecting taxes from twenty-year-olds and making promises to provide them with income, medical care, and nursing home care six or seven decades into the future. Yet no money is being saved or invested to cover these costs. In order for these promises to be honored, future twenty-year-old taxpayers must be willing to pay the tab. These are taxpayers who are not yet born. Yet today's politicians have no idea what the fertility rate will be decades from now. Therefore, they have no idea how many taxpayers there will be or what burden they will be expected to bear. These facts will only come to light long after today's decision-makers are out of office and departed from the earth.

Precisely because they do not have to bear the costs of their own bad decisions—or even witness the consequences—our political representatives have perverse incentives to overpromise. If they sold private insurance that way, they would be committing a crime. But our political system has decided that elected officials and government employees can get away with statements that would land a garden-variety Wall Street hustler in prison.

Based on approximate intergenerational accounting, Social Security and Medicare have unfunded liabilities of $119 trillion—about six times the current size of our entire economy. If we followed sound principles of pension finance, we would have that much money in the bank right now, drawing interest. In fact, there is nothing in the bank.

Just as substance abusers have to dry out and face reality before they can get on the road to recovery, people addicted to unfunded government benefits have to face accounting reality before we can begin generational bargaining. Once young people realize that our trust funds set aside for entitlement spending contain no real assets, it will be far easier to make sensible reforms. Every year the trustees of Social Security and Medicare release reports documenting that we are trillions of dollars in debt. Yet the documentation is buried deeply and is ignored in almost all news accounts. This is by design. These reports are accompanied by administration press releases and briefings designed to convince reporters that, if there is a financial problem, it is decades in the future.

This is true for both Republican and Democratic administrations. Even though George W. Bush advocated privatizing Social Security with individual accounts, every single trustees report issued during the eight years of his administration was accompanied by a press release that completely ignored the unfunded liability in Social Security and suggested that any financial problems were far away.

Those who recognize the problem are likely to propose a draconian remedy: since our elderly entitlement programs are spending more than they are taking in, putting them on a sound financial footing would seem to require tax increases, benefit cuts, or both. That's what I call the zero-sum approach, under which there are always losers and maybe a few winners.

I think there is a better way.

Policy Changes That Make Everybody Better Off

A typical government social program is funded by taxpayers. It provides goods, services, or money to a group of beneficiaries. Imagine that you could make a change in that program that reduces the cost to the taxpayers and enhances the value of the program for the beneficiaries—at the same time. Who could possibly object to that?

In this book I'm suggesting that thousands of opportunities exist to make policy changes like this in the political system.

Here is an example. Many veterans see private doctors—because of the long waits to see Veterans Affairs (VA) doctors, because of convenience, and perhaps for other reasons. Yet they frequently turn to VA pharmacies to have their prescriptions filled because of the lower cost of drugs in the VA system. Unfortunately, VA pharmacies can only fill prescriptions ordered by VA providers. So the veteran has to get in line with other patients who really need care in order to get a VA provider to give a second approval to a prescription that a private doctor already has written. The same rule applies to refills.

According to one estimate, *VA waiting lists could be reduced by one-third* if VA pharmacies could do what every other pharmacy in the country can do: fill prescriptions ordered by private doctors.[2] This should be a no-brainer. Right?

Well, let's play devil's advocate for a moment—if for no other reason than to understand how Capitol Hill's bean counters think about things. Like everyone else, veterans face a trade-off between time costs and money costs. Right now, they can reduce their out-of-pocket money cost of drugs if they are willing to wait to see a VA doctor. If we get rid of the waiting, however, more veterans will likely get their prescriptions filled in VA pharmacies. To meet the greater demand, the VA might have to hire additional staff or stay open longer hours. That might increase the VA's costs. Even more important, without the prescription fillers clogging up the access lines, other veterans would find it easier to get their needs met. And meeting more real medical needs also costs more money.

Now, many readers might think these are acceptable burdens for the rest of us to bear. After all, the veterans did their part; we taxpayers should step up to the plate and do ours. But this book is not about fairness. It's also not about optimal policy. It's about making all stakeholders in all important policy changes better off.

How can we solve problems for the veterans in a way that wins for the taxpayers as well? Veterans in the current system are able to lower their out-of-pocket costs of care if they are willing to incur waiting costs. Since we know that a trade-off is involved, why not try something in between? That is, we could charge veterans with private doctor prescriptions, say, 10 percent more in return for not waiting as long. The veteran who accepts the deal still comes out ahead. And the new revenue the VA system collects could offset some of the other cost increases we expect to incur.

Whenever two policy extremes exist such that one kind of cost falls and another rises as we move back and forth between them, there is almost always some intermediate point where everyone gains. We can't find that point by armchair theorizing, however. We must be willing to experiment and adapt—the trial-and-error method. That is, we must be willing to do the kind of experimentation that private markets do every day.

Why do I think there are thousands of opportunities for win/win public policy changes? Because so many government programs are so visibly inefficient. They labor under archaic rules and regulations (like the one we just described)—obstacles that any private entrepreneur would jettison in a second. Further, they inevitably leave all of us with perverse incentives. When we act on those incentives, we do things that make social costs higher and social benefits lower than otherwise.

Economists define inefficiency as a state of affairs in which everyone could potentially be better off by doing things differently.[3] If government programs are inefficient, we know that in principle everyone could be better off through some sort of policy change.[4] But are those policy changes practical? In this book, we will look at numerous cases where everything suggests the answer is "yes."

I am advocating new policies that give individuals more choice and control over their lives and resources, while protecting the important social goals that led to the program's creation in the first place. See if you agree.

A Better Way to Manage Life's Risks

IN MOST COUNTRIES around the world, government is deeply involved in protecting people against certain kinds of risk. These include the risk of growing old and lacking the income and assets needed for everyday living. They also include the risk of getting sick, needing medical care, and not having the funds to pay for it.

But why does government typically insure people against some risks and not others? And when social insurance is created, why does it function so differently from private insurance? If we think private pension funds should be funded (with real assets to pay expected claims), why doesn't government insurance have to follow the same rules? If private insurance charges people actuarially fair premiums (reflecting the enrollee's expected costs), why doesn't government insurance do the same thing?

In this section, our goal is to understand social insurance—why it exists, how it works, and why reform is so urgently needed. In the next section we will show how reform can be successfully accomplished.

I

The Case for Change

THE UNITED STATES, like many developed countries in the world today, faces a common problem: we have promised more than we can deliver. Faced with the risky business of life, particularly as they age, Americans as consumers of government benefits have come to expect payments for which, as taxpayers, they may be unwilling or unable to pay. Studies suggest that tax increases to pay for social insurance are going to take a larger and larger portion of their income. The cost might seem less burdensome if the outlays truly resolved the problems they were intended to fix. Sadly, social benefits that government provides are all too often delivered inefficiently, impersonally, and inflexibly, failing to meet the needs of the individuals they are intended to help. Indeed, the system at times encourages behavior that works against the intended goals.

In the United States, the national debt (held by the public) now equals about 100 percent of gross domestic product (GDP), and it will grow even larger in the next few decades.[1] With the retirement of the baby boomer generation, seventy-eight million additional people have been turning to the federal government for Social Security, Medicare, and Medicaid benefits—at a rate of ten thousand per day and at a cost of roughly $30,000 per beneficiary per year, on the average.[2] If we continue on the current course, the federal government will need to more than double the tax revenues it now collects by the time we reach the mid-twenty-first century, according to the Congressional Budget Office.[3] At the same time the government prepares to take more of our income, it is also making it increasingly difficult to earn that income. Despite some improvements under the Trump administration, taxes and regulations raise the cost of labor, reduce the rewards for working, and make the economy less productive than it could be.[4]

European countries have made even more generous promises to their citizens. Although government spending there recently averaged 40 percent of GDP, by 2050 the average EU country will have to spend more than 60 percent of its national income to meet its entitlement spending obligations.[5]

Before we can attempt to address this situation, we must understand the underlying historical and social causes.

The Philosophy of Social Insurance

Although social insurance addresses some risks, citizens generally take personal responsibility for insuring against other risks. Individuals purchase their own life insurance, homeowners insurance, and automobile collision insurance, for example. Why is government involved in some of these risks and not others? There's a good economic reason for these decisions. Most of us essentially are indifferent to whether other people insure to protect their own assets. We have good reasons to care, however, about risks that could create costs for the rest of us.

Through Social Security, we force people to pay for survivors' insurance that will benefit dependent children, who might otherwise become wards of the state, but not for working-age spouses. All but three states force people to have auto liability insurance (covering harm to others) but not casualty insurance (covering their own cars). We basically don't care whether people insure their own homes or automobiles, but we force them to contribute to retirement and disability schemes to prevent them from becoming dependent on all the rest of us.

Here is the principle: Government intervenes in those insurance markets where people's choices to insure or not insure impose potential costs on others. Because of our basic human generosity, we're not going to allow people to starve or live in destitution. So when people don't insure for retirement, for example, society will step in if the need is great enough. Implicitly, we have a social contract in which society as a whole takes responsibility for the downside of certain risks. If we allow the upside to be left to individual choice, we will have privatized the gains and socialized the losses. When people don't bear the social cost of their risk-taking, they will take more risks than they would otherwise, a behavioral response known as "moral hazard."

One way to think about the problem is in terms of the opportunity to become a "free rider" on other people's generosity. If people are free to make their own (uncoerced) choices, some will choose to have no life insurance covering dependent children, no disability insurance, and no retirement savings. Because they are not paying premiums or saving for retirement, they can consume all of their income and enjoy a higher standard of living than their cohorts. But if they bet wrong (die too early, become disabled, reach retirement with no assets), they are counting on everyone else to help them out.

A free society allows people to have a wide range of choices. At the same time, social insurance prevents them from becoming free riders on the rest of society if their choices turn out to be wrong.

How Social Insurance Works

At the federal level, social insurance includes Social Security, Medicare, Medicaid, and federal survivors and disability insurance. Under the provisions of the Affordable Care Act (Obamacare), it also subsidizes private and public health insurance for the nonelderly population. At the state level, social insurance includes the state-financed portion of Medicaid, unemployment insurance, and workers' compensation insurance.

Although many of these programs include the word *insurance* in their names, they are very different from traditional indemnity insurance. In many respects, they are not insurance at all but merely thinly disguised vehicles for redistributing income. These programs have been insulated from private-sector competition. People who find a better way of insuring on-the-job injuries or health or disability expenses or providing for retirement income are normally not able to take advantage of that knowledge. For the most part, we are all forced to participate in monopoly insurance schemes, regardless of potentially better alternatives. Even where and when competition is allowed (as in health insurance), it is regulated so tightly that no one ever sees a real premium. Government insurance and government-regulated insurance are also subject to special-interest political pressures that undermine rational decisions about their provision.

As a result:

- Social insurance is almost always more expensive than it needs to be. Disability insurance in the United States and Europe, for example, is twice as expensive as private disability insurance in Chile. Medicare's health insurance for the elderly and the disabled and Medicaid's long-term care insurance both cost about twice as much as well-designed private insurance should cost.

- Social insurance is impervious to consumer needs. Medicare, for example, covers many small expenses that the elderly could easily afford to pay for out of pocket, while leaving seniors exposed for thousands of dollars in catastrophic costs. Both Medicare and Medicaid prevent patients from adding out-of-pocket expenses to the government's fees in order to purchase timelier, higher-quality care. Obamacare is forcing millions of Americans to buy mandated packages of benefits, regardless of individual preferences.

- Social insurance is almost always one-size-fits-all, ignoring important differences in individual needs. Social Security, for example, completely ignores other sources of retirement income and prevents seniors from trading some or all of their government annuity in return, say, for assisted living.

- Social insurance is almost never accurately priced. Because unemployment insurance premiums fail to reflect the true probability of unemployment, the program actually encourages employers to provide seasonal, rather than year-round, jobs. Because workers' compensation insurance is not accurately priced, employers face highly imperfect incentives to make their workplaces safer. Because insurance in the (Obamacare) health insurance exchanges is community rated, sicker enrollees are encouraged to overinsure and healthy enrollees are encouraged to underinsure.[6]

Three additional problems are also disconcerting. First, social insurance is often poorly designed. Many seniors, for example, pay three separate premiums to three separate health plans and yet still lack the comprehensive coverage that many nonseniors take for granted. As a result of poorly designed social insurance programs, the cost of hiring labor is higher and the take-home pay of workers smaller than what they might otherwise be.

Second, in the United States and in most other countries around the world, social insurance schemes almost always leave individuals with perverse incentives. For example:

- Social Security's early retirement program and its survivorship benefits discourage work by imposing an implicit marginal tax rate of 50 percent—on top of all the other taxes workers face.
- Our unemployment insurance and disability insurance programs literally are paying people not to work.
- Both Social Security and Medicare have substantially altered the lifetime consumption and saving behavior of most people.
- Both Medicare and Medicaid encourage the overuse of health care and long-term care services.
- Obamacare's regulations are encouraging employers to hire part-time rather than full-time workers, to use contract labor, and to outsource work rather than hiring more staff. Small firms are discouraged from becoming larger.

Finally, social insurance arrangements that are intergenerational often adopt a chain-letter approach to finance—making promises to the current generation of beneficiaries that have to be financed by future taxpayers. Long-term social insurance is rarely funded by existing resources. Rather than saving to pay for future benefits, elected officials are tempted to use payroll tax revenues that aren't needed for current benefits to pay for other politically popular programs. As a result, social insurance is almost always operated on a pay-as-you-go basis, with no money saved for the future. Both here and abroad, this strategy has created huge unfunded liabilities. According to a Social Security trustees report, the unfunded liability in Social Security and Medicare is $119 trillion, or six times the size of the entire US economy. If the implicit, unfunded promises in Medicaid, Obamacare, and other programs are included, the government's total implicit debt is $165 trillion.[7]

The Cost of Social Insurance

If the federal government continues to fulfill all of its current spending obligations, marginal income tax rates will have to increase dramatically for all taxpayers. According to a Congressional Budget Office estimate, by 2050 (see figure 1.1):

- The lowest income earners will see their marginal rates more than double from the current 10 to 26 percent.

- The highest income earners will face marginal tax rates of 92 percent (from the current 35 percent).

- And the US corporate income tax rate, will skyrocket to 92 percent.[8]

The expert who later became President Obama's chief economist made these projections before the passage of the Affordable Care Act (ACA), creating Obamacare. However, the ACA envisions large cuts in Medicare spending as well as reductions in federal spending under Medicaid and in subsidies for private insurance. If these reductions occur, the financial picture will look better. How likely is that?

Figure 1.1 Tax Rates Needed to Pay for Existing Federal Programs

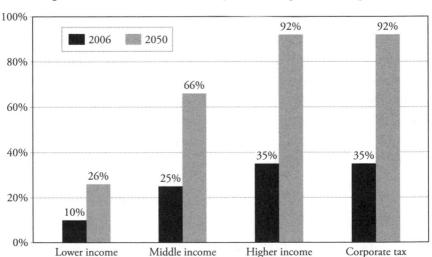

Source: Peter Orszag, "Financing Projected Spending in the Long Run," letter to Honorable Judd Gregg, Congressional Budget Office, July 9, 2007.

Case Study: Behind the Medicare Numbers?

Prior to 2010, projecting Medicare's health care spending was a fairly straight-forward exercise.[9] Each year, the trustees of the Medicare Trust Fund issued a report projecting the program's expenditures for the next seventy-five years and a separate projection that extended indefinitely into the future. The Affordable Care Act changed all that. The act not only creates a new entitlement program, but also changes how the actuaries forecast health care spending.

In recent decades, real Medicare spending has been growing at a rate roughly equal to the rate of growth of real gross domestic product (GDP) plus two percentage points, meaning that Medicare has been growing at twice the rate of growth of national income—an obviously unsustainable path. The ACA seeks to limit Medicare's growth rate to the rate of GDP growth plus 0.5 percent.

This is the growth path assumed by the Centers for Medicare and Medicaid Services (CMS), and it has been incorporated into all subsequent Medicare trustees reports. It is also the ultimate spending path assumed by the Congressional Budget Office (CBO), although both the CBO and the Medicare Actuaries Office also publish an "alternative estimate," showing what just about everyone believes to be more accurate predictions of future spending.

One way to think about this is to observe that if per capita Medicare spending is growing no faster than the economy as a whole, it will ultimately grow no faster than the dedicated payroll and income taxes and premiums that fund it. In other words, if the ACA can resist future legislative changes, once the baby boom generation works its way through the system, the problem of Medicare spending will effectively be solved!

The table on the next page shows what the ACA means in terms of Medicare's unfunded liability. Prior to the passage of the ACA, Medicare's spending obligations minus expected premiums and dedicated taxes equaled almost $90 trillion—looking indefinitely into the future. Yet on the day that Barack Obama signed his health care reform bill, that figure was more than cut in half (see table 1-1). President Obama wiped out $53 trillion of unfunded liability with pen and ink![10]

To get an idea of who the winners and losers are under reform, the graph below shows where the spending cuts will occur (see figure 1.2):

Table 1-1. Medicare 75-Year Unfunded Obligations

	2009 Trustees Report Trillions	2010 Trustees Report Trillions	Percent Change
Part A	$13.77	$2.68	-81
Part B	$17.20	$12.90	-25
Part D	$7.20	$7.20	0
Total	$38.17	$22.78	-40

Medicare Infinite Horizon Unfunded Obligations			
	2009 Trustees Report Trillions	2010 Trustees Report Trillions	Percent Change
Part A	$36.72	-$0.30	-101
Part B	$37.00	$21.10	-43
Part D	$15.50	$15.80	2
Total	$89.22	$36.60	-59

Source: Andrew J. Rettenmaier and Thomas R. Saving, "Medicare Trustees Reports 2010 and 2009: What a Difference a Year Makes," National Center for Policy Analysis, NCPA Policy Report No. 330, October 2010.

- By 2065, Medicare spending on hospital Part A services will be half of what it would have been under the old law.

- Medicare spending on doctors (Part B services) will be 61 percent of what it would have been under the old law.

- Yet remarkably, Medicare spending on drugs (Part D) will barely have changed at all.

How does the ACA accomplish the projected reduction in future Medicare spending? The Obama administration's Plan A assumed that health care providers will increase their productivity at the same rate as the non–health care sector, indefinitely into the future. However, this has never happened in the past, largely because health is a labor-intensive industry. To assist in the goal of productivity improvements, the administration has funded pilot programs and demonstration projects designed to find more efficient ways

Figure 1.2 Medicare Spending from the 2010 Trustees
Report as a Percentage of Spending from the 2009 Trustees Report

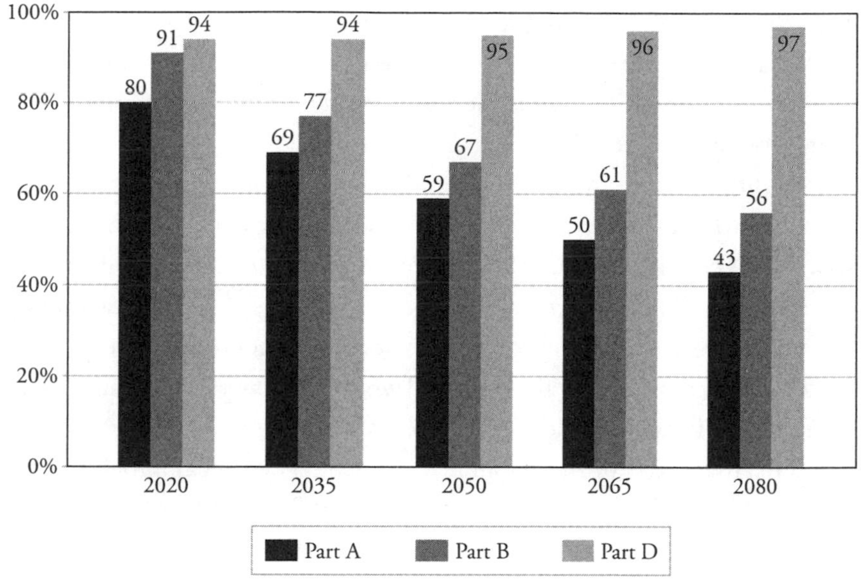

Source: Table III.A2, 2009 and 2010 Medicare Trustees Report. Percentages reflect the 2010 report's shares of GDP as percentages of the 2009 estimates.

of delivering medical care. However, three different CBO reports concluded that these experiments did not produce the hoped-for gains.[11]

Plan B was to reduce the fees Medicare pays to doctors and hospitals, relative to what they would have been. Those fees were already well below what the private sector pays, however. For example, Medicare pays doctors almost 20 percent less than what private payers pay. It pays hospitals almost 30 percent less. Under the Obamacare spending cap, that discrepancy would grow wider with each passing year.

To achieve the necessary targets, the ACA gave an Independent Payment Advisory Board the power to recommend cuts in reimbursement rates for providers of health care. Congress was required either to accept these cuts or propose its own plan to cut costs by as much as, or by more than, the board's proposal. If Congress failed to substitute its own plan, the board's cuts were to become effective. In this way, the growth rate for Medicare spending was officially capped. Moreover, the advisory board was barred from considering just about any cost control idea other than cutting fees to doctors, hospitals, and other suppliers. According to the Medicare actuaries, if we follow this scenario, Medicare will be paying less than half of what private payers pay and only 75 percent of Medicaid rates by midcentury.

What would these reductions in payments to health care providers mean to Medicare patients? A reasonable assumption is that to get the same care, seniors would have to offset some or all of Medicare's spending reductions with additional spending of their own. On the plus side, a slowdown in the growth of Medicare would make senior income somewhat higher than otherwise. That's because a smaller Medicare means lower Medicare premiums and lower taxes. Beyond that, seniors may have to choose between medical care (or the amenities they have come to expect with their care) and other expenses.

The Medicare actuaries also projected what these low payment rates would mean for the financial health of the nation's hospitals. Overall, the actuaries predicted that by 2030, one in four facilities would become unprofitable and probably be forced to leave the Medicare program. That number was projected to grow to 40 percent of all facilities by 2050.[12] Basically, on this spending path, hospitals would not be able to provide seniors with the same kind of services they provide younger patients. We might see an end to private rooms for Medicare patients and an end to gourmet meals. There might even be reduced access to expensive technology.

Will any of this actually happen? One negative indication is the fact that President Obama never appointed any members to the Independent Payment Advisory Board. Then, during the Trump administration, Congress abolished the enforcement mechanism altogether.

Another thing to consider is that the federal government tried to impose a very similar growth path on physicians' fees—and it failed. In 1989, Congress stipulated that after 2003, physicians' fees under Medicare could grow no faster than GDP. The CMS was instructed to maintain that growth path by refusing to increase those fees or even by cutting them. Yet in every single year that followed, Congress intervened—seventeen times in all—to prevent Medicare from doing what is was statutorily required to do![13]

Presidential budgets and the Social Security Trustees are still publishing forecasts that assume Medicare spending in future years will be held to the cap Congress legislated back in 2010. But almost no one else in Washington thinks that the growth of Medicare can be held substantially below the growth of the rest of the health care system.

2

Balancing Individual and Societal Interests

SOCIAL INSURANCE PROGRAMS should not be regarded as ends in themselves. They are instead a means to an end: protecting society's members against life's risks. If individuals can find better ways to accomplish this, I argue, they should be allowed to take advantage of those discoveries. If they are willing to take responsibility for their own needs and relieve others of that burden, they should be encouraged to do so. Wherever possible, the goal should be to maximize choices and opportunities for individuals, leaving to government the minimum role of insuring that the needs of the most vulnerable continue to be met.

Why is Amazon creator Jeff Bezos paying into the Social Security system? Why is he paying into Medicare? The technical answer is that the law requires everyone to participate. But is that good public policy? In 2019, *Forbes* listed Bezos as America's richest man, with an estimated net worth of $114 billion. While no one argues that he is in danger of becoming destitute during his retirement years, you could argue that his taxes will help pay benefits to other current beneficiaries. But remember: every time Bezos pays a dollar in Social Security taxes, he accumulates a claim for additional benefits during his retirement years. The same considerations apply to Bill Gates, worth an estimated $106 billion.

Warren Buffett raises another set of questions. *Forbes* ranks Buffett as the third-richest individual in America, with an estimated net worth of $81 billion. Why are taxpayers paying his medical bills under Medicare? Again, the answer is that Buffett paid into the system when he was young and, therefore, is entitled to collect benefits. But is this a good way to run a retirement system?

When Social Security was established more than seventy-five years ago, proponents argued that without a compulsory retirement program, too many people would fail to save for their own retirement needs. They would reach retirement age destitute and impose a financial burden on everyone else. So a compulsory pension program, they said, was needed in order to force people to save for their own retirement. Fifty-five years ago the same argument was made about the compulsory health care program we call Medicare.

Of course, we know that these programs did not do what they promised. Social Security did not result in any personal savings. It simply took money from workers and gave it to retirees. The same thing is true of Medicare. Still, it is clear that we don't need Social Security or Medicare for people like Bezos, Gates, and Buffett—or their spouses and children and other family members. They are in no danger of ever being destitute. They can take care of their own retirement needs. So why not let them?

If we do nothing to reform our nation's entitlement programs, we will eventually be forced to cut off high-income individuals. They will not receive any Social Security checks, or if they do get them, the government will take the money back through higher taxes. Instead of getting subsidized Medicare, they will be forced to pay the full (unsubsidized) premium—and then some. Yet these changes will amount to no more than a drop in the bucket for Uncle Sam. Before it's over, most people will find that they are getting less than what was originally promised. In fact, it's likely that *everyone* will face higher taxes, smaller benefits, or both. Such a zero-sum outcome is one in which almost everybody loses. And because everyone will lose, these reforms will be difficult and painful to enact.

Is there an alternative to that? Is there a way to step in now to reconstruct a policy in which everyone gains? Is there a way for people to exit the existing systems to benefit themselves and at the same time leave everyone else better off, too?

Potential Trade-Offs Derived from Risk Differences

Different people have different attitudes toward risk.[1] They also have different financial needs. Reverse mortgages, widely advertised on TV, promise to turn the value of an elderly person's house into an income stream. Many corporate severance packages allow executives who are leaving to choose between a pension benefit payable in the future or a lump sum they can invest as they choose. In general, the financial world stands ready to convert an asset into an income stream or an income stream into an asset. But remember, individuals stand on either side of these transactions. The agreements are possible only because different people have different needs.

Our entitlement programs generate a stream of taxes and a stream of benefits. Looking forward, a young male worker can expect a steady stream of payroll tax payments for as long as he earns wages. What if he made a lump sum payment today in order to avoid all future payroll taxes? Would that be good for him? Would it be good for the rest of us? On the benefit side, what if we could offer him a lump sum amount today in return for his forgoing any future Social Security or Medicare benefits? Or, what if we allowed young workers to pay a lower lifetime payroll tax, provided they make private provision for their future retirement needs?

Are there substantial opportunities for such deals to be struck? There are at least four reasons to believe so.

Differences in Discount Rates. When the Social Security and Medicare trustees calculate the unfunded liabilities in those two programs, they discount future taxes and future benefits at a rate of interest equal to the federal government's long-term borrowing rate. Historically that has been about 3 percent. But when individuals borrow, they typically pay a much higher rate. Some people, for example, are paying double-digit rates on their credit card debt. If individuals evaluate Social Security's promised benefits at a discount rate higher than the one the government (on behalf of taxpayers) uses, then they will place a lower value on those benefits.

Take a man who has just reached retirement age and has a life expectancy of about twenty more years. If he evaluates his expected Social Security benefits using a discount rate of, say, 6 percent, he will value a twenty-year stream of expected benefits at about 60 percent of what the government calculates as its cost. If the retiree's discount rate is 9 percent, he will value the benefits at only one-third of the government's estimated cost.

Continuing with that last example, let's say the government offers the retiree a lump sum, upfront cash payment equal to half the present value of his expected future benefits (evaluated at a 3 percent real rate of interest). Since the offered sum is substantially more than the value the retiree places on the income stream it will replace (evaluated at 9 percent), the retiree is much better off. And the government will have cut its liability in half!

Differences in Portfolios. One reason people have different attitudes toward Social Security income streams is that the other assets they hold may vary. Some people have a private annuity or a government pension. If these assets are viewed as highly secure, a rational individual might wish to trade in his Social Security income stream for investments that would round out a more diversified portfolio.

Differences in Attitudes toward Economic Risk. Looking back over a long period of time, the stock market has always generated a higher return than the bond market. For example, over the whole of the twentieth century, the stock market generated a real rate of return more than twice that of the bond market (6.4 percent versus 2.48 percent). Moreover, there never has been a thirty-five-year period in which stocks failed to outperform bonds. In some particular years, however, investors were better off if they were invested in bonds.

Different people respond differently to this information. If you have a reasonable tolerance for risk, you will be the kind of person who wants to get out of bonds and into stocks in making long-term retirement decisions. If you have strong risk aversion, you will have the opposite preference.

One way to think about Social Security is to see it as similar to a government bond. It's not actually a bond. You can't buy or sell Social Security benefits; and future Congresses can renege on Social Security promises without creating the kind of financial crisis that would ensue if the Treasury failed to pay interest on US government debt. Still, Social Security's promises are promises of the US government. In the short run, the right to receive a Social Security check is just as secure as the right to receive interest on a Treasury bill.

Now, suppose we gave people the opportunity to get out of Social Security and into investments that carry a higher risk, but also promise a higher return. Some people would pay for that privilege, just as some people would pay for the opportunity to get out of an investment in government bonds and into other assets.

Of course, in the long run, Social Security isn't very safe at all, because of its huge unfunded liability. As more and more of the baby boom crosses into retirement age, proposals to alter Social Security are coming faster and growing louder, and the payouts to current beneficiaries are threatened.

Differences in Attitudes toward Political Risk. More than 90 percent of all lawsuits are settled without ever going to trial. The reason: most people are risk averse, especially when it comes to something as variable and hard to predict as jury verdicts. Parties to lawsuits are willing to settle for less than they think they may have gotten in court because they are willing to "pay" something to avoid uncertainty. A similar principle may apply to the looming battle over what to do about elderly entitlement programs. Interested parties may be willing to settle for less than they might have gotten simply to avoid the uncertainty over what some future Congress might do.

Clearly, the US government has promised what it cannot afford. But how confident are you about how you will personally fare when politicians are forced to change the entitlement programs? What if you received an offer to forgo future benefits in return for a cash settlement today? Just as parties to a lawsuit may find it in their self-interest to make an agreement today in order to avoid an uncertain future outcome, everyone who has a stake in our elderly entitlement systems may come to a similar conclusion.

Political risks, incidentally, can be positive or negative. For most of the history of Social Security—times when payroll tax revenues exceeded expenses and politicians had money to spend—Congress increased benefits beyond what was initially promised. In 1983, however, a bipartisan agreement led to a substantial reduction in the expected return from Social Security, authorizing a large increase in the payroll tax; a phased-in increase in the normal retirement age (from sixty-five to sixty-seven); and a tax on Social Security benefits that eventually will affect all retirees.

Viewing Trade-Offs in the Long Term

To be weighed against the considerable advantages to individuals of alternatives to government social insurance, we must look at the impact on the overall society.[2] Remember: the goal of social insurance originally was to protect *all* citizens against poverty due to old age or catastrophic health expenses.

In 1935, very few people had a retirement pension provided by their employer. No one had an Individual Retirement Account (IRA) or any of the other savings vehicles that have subsequently been added to the tax law. Life expectancy fell far short of age sixty-five anyway. So for the vast majority of people, Social Security was seen not as a replacement for private retirement savings but as something new—an additional source of income for the minority of people who would outlive their labor market participation and grow old enough to have to rely on it. Similarly, in 1965, very few workers had an employer promise of health care benefits after retirement or any other kind of postretirement health care plan.

Today things are different. According to the Department of Labor, almost sixteen million workers are in a defined-benefit pension plan and more than seventy-five million are building retirement assets in 401(k), 403(b), and other defined-contribution accounts.[3] More than eleven million people have an IRA account, and the assets in those accounts total more than $1 trillion.[4] About twenty-seven million workers have a promise of postretirement health care benefits from an employer,[5] and millions of veterans have access to VA health care benefits. All of these programs are potential substitutes for promises made under Social Security and Medicare.[6]

Also, the theoretical argument for postretirement social insurance is entirely focused on a *minimum benefit*. We don't want the elderly to live out their remaining years of life in extreme poverty. Most of us don't care very much, however, if seniors fail to live out their remaining years in luxury. That is important to remember because Social Security benefit payments are actually highly regressive.[7] The largest checks are cashed by the richest senior citizens. Medicare benefits also tend to be regressive—not because of the benefit formula, but partly because of little-understood features of the sociology of medical care. Zip codes where Medicare spending per beneficiary is highest also tend to be the zip codes where the largest Social Security checks are cashed.

In thinking about acceptable substitutes for Social Security and Medicare, therefore, our goal should not be to find alternatives that replace them entirely. Instead, we should focus on identifying acceptable alternatives that achieve a minimum level of retirement benefits.

Take the forty-four million workers who have private pension plans insured by the federal Pension Benefit Guarantee Corporation (PGBC).[8] Their plans are invested in stocks, bonds, and other assets. However, should the investments fail to pan out or (a much greater risk) should the employers who sponsor these plans go bankrupt and become unable to keep making the required contributions, the PGBC promises a minimum benefit to the retirees. Could this minimum benefit serve as an acceptable substitute for whatever we hope to accomplish through Social Security? If the answer is yes, then we should consider making a lump sum payment to these workers today in return for their agreement to forgo Social Security benefits in the future. Alternatively, we could consider a permanent reduction in their payroll tax rates.

Could health care coverage from the Veterans Health Administration serve as an acceptable substitute for the minimum health insurance we want people to have under Medicare? Would an annuity from a major financial institution or a promise of pension or health care benefits from a state or local government count as acceptable alternatives? Again, if the answer is yes, then we could consider making these workers a financial offer to buy them out of their right to receive some or all of their Social Security and Medicare benefits.

What about private savings? If they are to serve as acceptable substitutes, there would probably have to be some assurance that the funds would not be squandered or gambled away. Part of the requirement might be that the funds be held by reputable financial institutions and that they be managed according to prudent investment rules. There would also have to be rules governing the rate of withdrawal during the retirement years and a general prohibition against putting the asset up as collateral for loans or other indebtedness.[9]

Earlier we considered the possibility of allowing Bezos, Gates, and Buffett to exit the system in a way that made their tax burdens smaller and at the same time created no risk for the rest of us.

But why limit ourselves to Bezos, Gates, and Buffett? Aren't there tens of thousands of high-income retirees who would do just fine without Social Security or Medicare benefits? Shouldn't we consider whether they too could find a way to exit the system and leave taxpayers with a lighter burden than they had before? And why limit ourselves to the wealthy? There is a more general principle here: any time anyone—rich or poor—can find a way to solve the social problems Social Security and Medicare were designed to address and leave the taxpayers with a smaller burden in the process, we should welcome the change.

Case Study: Social Security and Young Workers

Texas A&M University economists Thomas Saving, Andrew Rettenmaier, and Liqun Liu have produced a first-of-its-kind calculation of the value of Social Security to young people in light of the political uncertainty about its future. They conclude that twenty-one-year-olds earning the average wage with a moderate degree of risk averseness would be better off if they could completely opt out of the system by paying a 4.5 percent payroll tax for the remainder of their work life. That means *both* forgoing all future Social Security benefits *and* avoiding, the current 12.4 percent Social Security tax they are copaying with their employers.

The exit fees they would pay would be enough to keep the system solvent, and they could invest their payroll tax savings—the difference between their share of the 12.4 and 4.5 percent—as they choose. When they retire, their privately financed benefits would be better than what Social Security would have provided. Privatization, in other words, would work for both the individuals and society. There do not have to be any losers.

Research by some of the same scholars offers a different array of opportunities we could offer young workers in lieu of the Social Security tax. If all young workers took full advantage of these opportunities, our entitlement spending programs could be brought under control by the time they reach the age of retirement. In particular:

- If employees and their employers set aside 4 percent of wages every pay period to be invested in a diversified portfolio and if Social Security's indexing formulas were subjected to modest reform, not only would a young, average-wage worker receive all the benefits they would have derived, but the Social Security payroll tax could be substantially lower than it is today.[10]

- If employees and their employers set aside an additional 4 percent of wages, and if some additional modest reforms were made to Medicare, a young, average-wage worker would receive all the postretirement health care benefits they would have derived from the old plan, and the Medicare payroll tax at that time would be lower than it is today.[11]

- For an additional 2 percent of wages, young workers would be able to securely replace the risk protection promises made by (Social Security's) disability insurance and by (Medicaid's) long-term care insurance.

In total, I believe that all of these federal programs could be replaced by an annual deposit equal to 10 percent of wages throughout a worker's work life.[12]

Ten percent of wages is not a small sacrifice. It reflects three features of our current dilemma. First, providing for even a modest retirement is expensive. In fact, meeting most people's retirement expectations will probably require an additional 4 or 5 percent investment in an IRA or 401(k) account. Second, this sacrifice must be on top of taxes needed to pay the retirement expenses of the current generation of retirees, including the 15 percent payroll tax. Third, even these two sacrifices do not solve the problem of what to do about the baby boomer retirees, since current tax rates will produce revenues far short of promised benefits.

At the state and local level, replacing unemployment and workers' compensation insurance with better, cheaper alternatives will cost from 1 to 2 percent of wages. But this will not be an additional burden. These funds will replace money that is currently being spent on less-efficient, dysfunctional systems.

3

Alternatives That Offer Individual Choice

IN CHOOSING AMONG policies with different kinds of costs, the ideal social objective would not be to minimize the money cost of policy choices to government. Ideally, it would minimize total social costs. We are seeking policy changes for which taxpayers as well as beneficiaries both come out ahead.

As it happens, we have some examples both national and international that we can look to for ideas.

The Experiences of Other Countries

What rational person would choose a system that makes promises to pay young people benefits five or six decades into the future without making any provision to save and invest the funds needed to pay those benefits?[1] What rational person would devise a system that encourages young people to believe they will get benefits five or six decades into the future, knowing all along that the payment of benefits depends on future taxpayers—but without knowing how many future taxpayers there will be or what tax burden they will be expected to bear? In short, what rational person would devise an entire retirement system, using the same techniques that Bernie Madoff used to scam his investors?

The short answer is that no one would do that and to my knowledge no rational person ever did. That is, wherever leaders had discretion, wherever they were not compelled by the pressures of democratic voting, they devised entirely different systems.

After World War II, about twenty-one former British colonies were governed by individuals appointed by the Crown. In these countries, the systems adopted were provident funds to which workers were required to contribute, the funds were invested, and the workers' retirement benefits were dependent on worker contributions and market returns—much like the 401(k) system today in our country.[2]

The most notable of these was the Singapore system—which is probably the most successful social security system in the world. The second most successful system in the world is the Chilean system—which subsequently was copied by a number of other countries including (nondemocratic) Hong Kong. Although Chile was never a British colony, its system was adopted under a dictatorship. Let's take a look at how those systems worked out over time.

Singapore is a country that has no government-run social security system, and it has also avoided most other welfare-state institutions of developed countries. Yet no one in Singapore is starving. It has the highest rate of home ownership in the world, and the vast majority of people reach the retirement age with substantial assets. Indeed, Singapore has the highest percentage of millionaires (17 percent) in the world.[3]

How do they do it? In Singapore, people are required to save a substantial part of their income to meet basic needs.[4] But they have considerable discretion over how the funds are invested, and they have a very wide range of choices over how they use their savings to meet their needs.

Chile is another country that has been exceptionally innovative in liberating people from social insurance institutions. Chileans are required to save in individual retirement accounts. But once they have saved enough to purchase an annuity to provide a minimum retirement income, they have complete discretion over what they do with the remaining funds—even if they are only middle-aged.[5]

Chile also has the world's most innovative disability insurance system and the world's most innovative unemployment insurance system.[6] Both systems involve substantial individual control over resources and leave individual workers with considerable freedom to make their own decisions.

Closer to Home: Social Security in Galveston, Texas

Prior to 1983 in the United States, local governments and nonprofit institutions were allowed to opt out of Social Security and establish their own retirement plans instead. In 1979, Galveston, Texas, and two neighboring counties did just that. The plan was voluntary in the beginning, and 70 percent joined. Later it became mandatory, and now there is full participation.

The results have been impressive. In 1979, a typical worker could expect to receive more benefits from Social Security than he expected to pay in Social Security taxes. So when Galveston decided to opt out, the US taxpayer gained. But the employees also gained.[7]

A 2005 assessment by one of the creators of the plan explained that it has provided substantially better benefits in all three Social Security categories: retirement, survivorship, and disability.[8] For example, benefits to retirees are at least 50 percent higher than they would have been under Social Security (see figure 3.1). As for survivorship and disability:

Figure 3.1 Retirement Benefits: Galveston Plan vs. Social Security

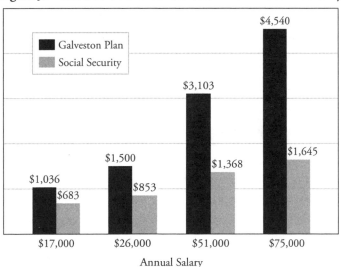

Source: Ray Halbrook and Alcestis Oberg, "Galveston Country: A Model for Social Security Reform," National Center for Policy Analysis, April 26, 2005.

Galveston County's survivorship benefits pay four times a worker's annual salary—a minimum of $75,000 to a maximum $215,000—versus Social Security, which forces widows to wait until age sixty to qualify for benefits, or provides 75 percent of a worker's salary for school-age children. In Galveston, if the worker dies before retirement, the survivors not only receive the full survivorship, but also get generous accidental death benefits, too. Galveston County's disability benefit also pays more: 60 percent of an individual's salary, better than Social Security's.

A 2011 update of that analysis by Merrill Matthews found that the plan still beats government benefits in every category for just about every worker at every income level.[9] The earlier assessment noted:

> We sought a secure, risk-free alternative to the Social Security system, and it has worked very well for nearly a quarter century. Our retirees have prospered, and our working people have had the security of generous disability and accidental death benefits. Most important, we didn't force our children and grandchildren to be unduly taxed and burdened for our retirement while these fine young people are struggling to raise and provide for their own families. What has been good for Galveston County may, indeed, be good for this country.[10]

The Trial-and-Error Approach

We have already considered how the VA health system could benefit by trial-and-error improvements. The medical marketplace provides other examples as well. Walk-in clinics are an alternative to appointments with individual doctors or visits to the emergency room for primary care. However, a study by the RAND Corporation found that walk-in clinics actually raise overall health care spending. In other words, when primary care is more convenient, people obtain more of it.

Does this mean that walk-in clinics are a bad idea?

As we have seen, in obtaining medical care there are typically two kinds of costs: money costs and time costs. Most people in health policy tend to believe that the ideal money price for a health services is zero and that if demand exceeds supply, the least burdensome solution—especially for low-income families—is rationing by waiting. As it turns out, that belief is not supported by evidence.

In the market for most consumer goods, we end up paying with both time and money. Most of us prefer price certainty to price uncertainty, other things being equal. This is especially true where highly volatile price changes may be needed to clear the market. At the other extreme, if the price never changes (and especially if it is fixed at zero), people will likely face waiting costs, and waiting times may themselves also be highly variable.

Price rationing makes patients bear one kind of cost. Rationing by waiting makes them bear another kind of cost. As we move between options A and B, one cost falls as the other rises.

The *trial-and-error principle* says that a solution in which all parties benefit is likely to lie somewhere between the policy extremes. If you graphed the change in these costs as you move from A to B or vice versa, the two cost lines will almost certainly cross. We can't know where this happens by armchair reasoning. But with trial and error, we should be able to find it.

The trial-and-error approach seems to emerge naturally in unfettered markets. If we look at real markets, we find that money costs as well as waiting costs typically are part of most normal transactions. It's rarely one extreme or the other. That's also true of medical markets where Medicare and Medicaid (and most other third-party insurers) are not involved at all.

Teladoc, for example, provides telephone consultations for roughly twenty million Americans. The cost of a typical consultation is about thirty-five dollars. A patient must wait, however, between placing a call to the company and getting a return call from the doctor. The company says the average callback time is sixteen minutes.[11] Uber-type house calls in selected cities around the country allow patients with a smartphone app to request a doctor visit in their home.[12] This involves a money cost (typically one hundred dollars) as well as a time cost (typically less than an hour). MinuteClinics in CVS pharmacies don't guarantee that you will be seen within a minute. But while you shop, they will text you to let you know when the nurse is available.[13]

Markets tend to find an optimal balance between time costs and money costs. There is no reason why public policy cannot do the same. Those who worry that money prices in health care place an undesirable burden on low-income families may be surprised to learn that the time cost of care is typically a greater deterrent than the money cost of care for these families.[14]

Let's apply the trial-and-error approach to telephone consultations. The cost tends to be about one-tenth of the cost of a typical emergency room visit and nearly one-third the cost of a visit to a doctor's office.[15] So other things being equal, allowing Medicare patients free access to the services of a firm like Teladoc should greatly reduce the cost of a doctor consultation. But if it's easy to get access to doctors, seniors are likely to do so more often. With trial and error, we may find that the cost to Medicare is minimized somewhere in between—with seniors, for example, paying some portion of the money cost in order to take advantage of the convenience that telephone consultations offer.

Similarly, with walk-in clinics, Uber-type house calls, and other services, the cost to Medicare is almost certainly minimized by allowing seniors access to the service but requiring them to pay some portion of the fee.

Case Study: Finding Opportunities for Individual Choice in Obamacare

These days, everyone seems to have a plan for reforming Obamacare. In general, positive changes would allow people to experience lower costs of care, higher quality of care, and better access to care if they are willing to make some trade-offs.

For example, lower premiums might be tied to reducing risky behavior like smoking, forgoing benefits of marginal value, and accepting higher self-insurance costs (e.g., out-of-pocket minimums and copays). Buyers might choose to waive coverage for low-probability events in return for better coverage for high-probability issues. They might give up the right to move among insurance plans at community-rated premiums in return for a market that promises lower costs, higher quality, and better access to care.

Let's look briefly at how some features of Obamacare could be altered to provide more individual choice and control overall health care costs.

Mandated Coverage. Under the Affordable Care Act, most people were initially required to obtain a package of health insurance benefits every year until they became eligible for Medicare. Although the mandate for buyers has since been repealed by Congress, it still exists on the seller side. Obamacare insurance is the only insurance sellers can sell. The problem is that the cost of the mandated benefits package is expected to grow faster than income so that health insurance will take a larger and larger share of every family's budget. Health economist Stephen Parente estimates that the cost of family coverage will rise from $13,000 in 2015 to almost $21,000 in the next eight years, to $30,000 eight years after that, and more than $42,000 after another eight-year interval.[16] It's easy to see how these costs will force more and more families out of the market, unless they qualify for subsidies. For unsubsidized families, Obamacare in the individual market will more or less wither on the vine as an ever-increasing number of them are stuck with no health insurance at all.

How could things be different? One possibility is to allow insurers to sell insurance that substantially restricts largely futile end-of-life care. As Atul Gawande writes in his book *Being Mortal: Medicine and What Happens in the End*, we could easily provide better care and less expensive care for those who are about to die.[17] In the Medicare program, about 28 percent of all spending is on patients in the last six months of life.[18] We might allow plans to adopt a cost-benefit standard in deciding what care to withhold. To take an extreme example, a terminally ill cancer patient would not get a liver transplant.

Another possibility would be to allow insurance contracts to offer smaller premium increases over time if people make substantial lifestyle changes. We could imagine insurance contracts that allow premium reductions in return for success in weight and diabetes control. No one would have to buy any of these plans. The idea is to get rid of the mandate and allow insurers to offer people reasonable alternatives to Obamacare's current mandated benefits.

Tailoring Insurance to Individual and Family Needs. Under Obamacare, millions of families are forced to obtain inappropriate insurance. People need health insurance to protect assets and to gain better access to care. But what about young, healthy employees of fast-food restaurants, who probably have no assets at all? Most likely, they are living paycheck to paycheck. A Bronze plan offered to these workers by an employer in 2020 can have a deductible of $8,150. It's double that for family coverage. With this type of plan, the family will still have to pay almost all its expected medical bills out of pocket. From the family's perspective, having this kind of insurance is not much better than being uninsured.[19]

If there were no government interference, what kind of health insurance would these employees want? Prior to Obamacare, employers of low-income workers often provided "mini-med" plans in lieu of taxable wages. These plans paid for expenses the employees were most likely to incur, with a cap, say, of $25,000. Let's call this "limited-benefit insurance."[20] A useful change to Obamacare would allow this option, giving people who select it a partial tax credit.

Community Rating. Insurers in the health insurance exchanges cannot discriminate among enrollees on the basis of health status. Essentially every one of the same age and in the same location pays the same premium for any plan offered on the market. However, this type of community rating creates perverse incentives that encourage insurers to attract the healthy and avoid the sick.[21] One way they do that is by excluding access to the best doctors and the best hospitals.

How can we improve on this outcome?

Under the Medicare Advantage program, which has enrolled more than one of every three seniors, health plans must charge all enrollees the same premium, but Medicare pays the insurer an additional sum, depending on the enrollee's expected costs. Using the most extensive risk adjustment formula found anywhere in the world, Medicare makes a significant effort to ensure that the overall premium received by the insurer is actuarially fair. Under this system, all enrollees are equally financially attractive to insurers, regardless of health status.

What we call "health-status insurance" would begin with the Medicare Advantage risk adjustment formulas; however, the extra premium adjustments would be paid by insurers to each other—not by Medicare.[22] Furthermore, the insurers would be able to improve on Medicare's formulas as they learn of better methods, and they could adjust the payments through time when they discover that the originally estimated expense was too high or too low.[23] The risk adjustment we are describing here is an adjustment produced by the marketplace, not by a bureaucracy.

Health-status insurance would radically improve the incentives faced by the sellers of health insurance. It would end the race to the bottom and the trend toward narrow provider networks with inferior-quality care. We will have more to say about it in the pages that follow.

4

Choice, Ownership, Responsibility

PEOPLE OF ANY age should have the opportunity to opt out of social insurance in favor of alternatives that better meet their individual and family needs. In particular, they should be able to substitute assets and arrangements that they have voluntarily chosen and that they own and control, for the government systems they are now forced to be part of. In particular:

- People should be able to substitute private savings, private pensions and annuities, and private insurance for participation in Social Security.

- They should be able to substitute private insurance and private health savings for participation in Medicare and for participation in the federalized health care system sometimes called Obamacare.

- They should be able to substitute private disability insurance for participation in the federal disability program.

- They should be able to substitute private savings, private pensions and annuities, and private insurance for participation in Medicaid's long-term care insurance.

- At their places of work, employees and their employers should be free to choose private unemployment insurance arrangements, private disability insurance, and private alternatives to workers' compensation.[1]

Furthermore, the choice does not have to be all or nothing. People should also be free to opt out partially and to opt out progressively over time.[2] What would make these options possible? Public policy reforms that honor individual choice and at the same time support goals that underlie social insurance in the first place.

Philosophy of Reform

The reform agenda proposed in this book would maximize individual free-dom and minimize the role of government. Under our proposals, individuals would have the opportunity to choose the insurance options that best meet their individual and family needs. They would own the assets and the finan-cial contracts that protect them without having to depend on the unreliable promises of politicians. And individuals and their families would be allowed to take responsibility for their own lives. In an ideal system:

- Each generation should pay its own way.
- Each family should pay its own way.
- Each individual should pay his own way.

Only after passing through these three filters should anyone ever turn to government for any remaining needs.

There is only one general condition that must govern the choice to opt out. It must not increase the expected burden for other taxpayers. This means that there must be a reasonable expectation that (1) the direct tax burden for others will not rise as a result of an individual's opting out and (2) the individual will not try to return to the government program (thus creating an additional burden for everyone else) if the private option turns out to be disappointing.[3]

Pareto-Optimal Change

Opting out must be good for the individual who exercises choice as well as for everyone else. Such a change has been given a formal name by economists. A Pareto-optimal change is a change that leaves at least one person better off and no one worse off. It is precisely that kind of change that is the focus of this book.[4]

At first glance, you would think that Pareto-optimal changes in public policy would be a politician's delight. Most changes in laws and policies cre-ate winners and losers. When politicians endorse such changes, they have to worry that the losers might get mad enough to defeat them in the next elec-tion. If there are no losers, the problem disappears.

Despite this almost self-evident fact, Pareto optimality is ignored in most proposals to change our social insurance programs. Politicians in both political parties almost always take a zero-sum approach. For every gain they promise, someone else must bear a loss. For example, some Democrats are proposing more generous Social Security benefits. But those benefits would be paid for by imposing new burdens on the young, either in the form of higher payroll taxes or a larger public debt. Some Republicans propose to solve future deficit problems by reducing future benefits. But this would create a burden for the young without any corresponding gain. From time to time, both parties have considered cutting elderly entitlement benefits. They did that in 1983.[5] And they have seriously discussed doing it again.[6] This, of course, is good for taxpayers but bad for seniors.

Ideally, we would like a system in which individuals have an alternative to government programs that are not working. When they exercise that alternative, the results should be win/win. There should be no losers. How can those alternatives be created? We need a distinct strategy for each of four kinds of social insurance.

A New System of Social Insurance

Governments at the federal and state level are currently providing various kinds of social insurance: Social Security retirement benefits, Medicare and Medicaid health plans, unemployment and disability coverage for workers, and insurance to provide for workers' families in the event of death. Each would require a somewhat different approach.

When the Benefit Is Proportional to Income and Each Age Group Is Paying Its Own Way. This essentially describes the structure of unemployment insurance, disability insurance, and survivors' insurance. In each case, there is a straightforward remedy: instead of paying taxes to a government monopoly insurance plan, give individuals the opportunity to privately insure against these risks. People who opt out of the government's insurance program would have to demonstrate a minimum level of private coverage so that neither they nor members of their families will become dependent on society as a whole.

For example, rather than pay taxes for (Social Security's) survivors' insurance, people could purchase term life insurance. Rather than pay taxes for (Social Security's) disability insurance, individuals and their employers could purchase private disability policies. We probably will want to keep workers' compensation for workplace injuries, rather than revert to common-law remedies. But even this can be done privately. In fact, Texas allows employers to privately insure for workers' compensation, and the system is apparently superior to the experiences of other states.

Insuring against unemployment is a more complex problem. But given the opportunity, employees and their employers can find private alternatives that are much more efficient than our unemployment insurance system. For example, instead of paying unemployment insurance taxes, Chilean workers contribute a small percentage of their wages into an individual account they control. During a spell of unemployment, they can use the funds in these accounts to cover living expenses and the cost of job searches and retraining.

When the Benefit Is Not Proportional to Income, but Each Age Group Is Paying Its Own Way. This essentially describes health insurance for the pre-Medicare population. Under the Affordable Care Act (Obamacare), most people were initially required to have health insurance, and although that mandate has been repealed, federal and state regulations dictate what kind of insurance people have the opportunity to buy. These regulations, in turn, heavily influence where people can get insurance, when they can get it, and how much they must pay for it.

The alternative: if all government tax and spending subsidies for health insurance were combined, we believe the government could afford to give every family a very generous refundable tax credit, which they could use to purchase health insurance tailored to their own needs. In their own hands, these resources would give almost everyone access to a health plan comparable to a well-managed, privately administered Medicaid plan. Why not allow individuals and families to get this amount if they agree to obtain acceptable private coverage on their own? If they and their employers add additional (after-tax) dollars, they will have more options.

When the Benefit Is Proportional to Income, but Each Age Group Is Not Paying Its Own Way. This essentially describes Social Security. Because of intergenerational transfers, two problems must be solved here, not just one. To eliminate the unfunded liability will require raising taxes, reducing benefits, or some combination of the two. However, we can give individuals an option: they can avoid higher taxes and lower benefits, provided they can make a minimum private provision for a retirement income on their own.

The option of a private alternative to Social Security should be open to people at any age, not just young people. Many opportunities are available that will be good deals for the beneficiary and for taxpayers. In theory, the government could write a check to an individual who reaches retirement age for an amount much smaller than the cost (to the government) of the annuity and still leave the individual better off. In return, the beneficiary would have to guarantee that provision has been made for a minimum income that will not leave him dependent on society as a whole for postretirement financial needs.

We should also think in terms of partial privatization. This means that individuals could give up some future benefits in return for some private provision. Moreover, partial privatization translates into total privatization, given enough time. In general, a 4 percent private savings rate over an average person's work life should be sufficient over time to completely replace Social Security's promised benefits.

After one generation of workers completes a life cycle, traditional Social Security would be needed only as a welfare program for the very lowest-income retirees.

When the Benefit Is Not Proportional to Income and Each Age Group Is Not Paying Its Own Way. This essentially describes Medicare (for the elderly), long-term care for the elderly under Medicaid, and health care for low-income seniors under Medicaid. As in the case of Social Security, we have the additional problem of a large unfunded liability plus a third problem: the benefit is largely independent of income and therefore cannot easily be expressed as a percentage of payroll.

Some of the same principles apply, however. To solve the problem of the unfunded liability, we need (a) fundamental health reform, (b) higher taxes, and/or (c) lower benefits. Given this initial step, four types of privatization could be considered.

First, the current generation of Medicare beneficiaries should have the option of receiving a "risk-adjusted" payment to be applied to private insurance premiums and deposits to Roth-type Health Savings Accounts. More than one out of every three Medicare beneficiaries is doing something like this already—through the Medicare Advantage program. However, the current program is way too restrictive. Seniors should have the same private-sector options currently available to nonseniors, including any plan offered to federal employees through the Federal Employee Health Benefits Program. The same principle should apply to the disabled individuals who qualify for Medicare and to seniors covered by both Medicaid and Medicare (the "dual eligibles"). Medicaid enrollees, for example, should at least have the opportunity to enroll in any private health plan offered to state employees.

Second, people of any age should have the opportunity to opt out of long-term care under Medicaid. If they opt out completely, they should receive a tax reduction, representing the government's expected reduced liability. If they opt out partially, they should be able to integrate private long-term care insurance with Medicaid. For example, if a family insures for $100,000 of nursing home costs, it should be able to "shield" $100,000 of assets and have them excluded from Medicaid's asset threshold test. (Without the shield, the family would have to "spend down" the $100,000 before becoming eligible for Medicaid.)

Third, individuals of any age should be able to completely opt out of traditional Medicare, so long as they are able to make adequate private health insurance provision for themselves. As in the case of Social Security, we can think of Medicare as a program that provides a stream of benefits through time. If the individual and the government evaluate their stream of benefits differently, there will be an opportunity when both parties can gain from a transaction.

Finally, we should allow partial opting out of Medicare for people of working age. As in the case of Social Security, workers would be allowed to make deposits to an account that would grow tax-free through time. As the value of the account grows, it would substitute for the government's benefit promises.

For the average worker, an annual deposit of about 4 percent of wages over a full work life should be sufficient to fully opt out of Medicare by the time of retirement. An amount equal to 2 percent of wages should be sufficient to completely opt out of the disability program (both the income and the medical care components) and Medicaid's long-term care program.

The general principles governing this type of privatization are the same as they are for Social Security. Individuals could avoid higher taxes and lower benefits if they are willing to make private provisions for themselves. The structural difficulty created by a medical benefit is that individuals will be making deposits that are a percentage of income, while the annual post-retirement benefit is largely independent of income. However, we believe that a properly structured privatization plan will—over the working lives of one generation of workers—leave the great majority of retirees with adequate private insurance. Like Social Security, traditional Medicare would largely become a welfare program for very low-income families.

Is Reform of Social Insurance Politically Possible?

Many people tend to think public policy could be very different if only we elect the right leaders.[7] Certainly, presidential candidates often campaign on that idea. And it's reinforced by historians and political scientists who focus on people in leadership positions—on their personalities and even their political parties. It wouldn't be unusual, for example, to hear one give Franklin Roosevelt credit or blame for our Social Security system. Many economists also tend to view the world in this way.

However, by the last decade of the twentieth century, 95 percent of all the countries in the world had a social security system that looked structurally identical to ours. If you stop and think about that for a moment, it's hard to conclude that social security owes much to the personality or leadership of any one politician in any particular country. It would appear that forces are at work that are independent of individual leaders.

Individual politicians are important only insofar as they play an entrepreneurial role. Just as entrepreneurs disrupt the equilibrium and lead us to a new equilibrium in the economic sphere, political entrepreneurs find opportunities to lead us to a new equilibrium in the political system. But once this new equilibrium is reached, it will be one from which politicians cannot deviate very far without the risk of being ousted.

Until the last decade or two of the twentieth century, every democracy that established a social security system set it up as a pay-as-you-go system with no saving, no investment, and no way to ensure benefit payments in the future.

What is it about democratic voting that creates pay-as-you-go social security? First, as we have already seen, it meets a need. Second, politicians can appear to meet the need without really paying for it. That means they can confer benefits on some without appearing to impose costs on others. This works because people tend to be rationally ignorant about how government programs work.[8] Political systems everywhere allow politicians to make promises that would land a garden-variety Wall Street fund manager in prison.

Third, pay-as-you-go social security generates revenues in the early years that are much larger than the required payouts. This means that (like a chain letter) politicians can give retirees in the early years more than what was promised. They can also spend the extra revenue on other programs that confer benefits on their constituencies. The incentives to do these things seem to be irresistible. Politicians who don't do them lose elections.

Finally, as more people are brought into the system, the taxpayer base expands. As the years go by, the beneficiary base also expands. This creates a "ratchet effect," making it harder and harder for a future group of politicians to undo what has been done. Franklin Roosevelt put it this way:

> We put those payroll contributions there so as to give the contributors
> a legal, moral, and political right to collect their pensions and their
> unemployment benefits. With those taxes in there, no damn politician
> can ever scrap my social security program.[9]

Why, then, do pay-as-you-go systems get privatized? Because at some point, countries realize they can't afford to fulfill the promises they have made. This realization may be reinforced by foreign creditors. Once the realization filters down to voters, the political cost-benefit calculations begin to change.

We need political entrepreneurs to discover and take advantage of what I believe are literally thousands of opportunities to make Pareto-improving changes. Those changes will take us down a new path. Moreover, once you make a change that makes everybody better off, it's hard to reverse that decision. The longer the new policy remains in place, the more people benefit from it and the more their benefits grow—making reversal harder and harder, as time passes.

As we entered the twenty-first century, thirty countries were either fully or partially privatizing their social security systems.[10] That suggests that countervailing forces were at work—again, independent of individual personalities. At the same time, countries around the world were privatizing, deregulating, lowering marginal tax rates, and turning to free markets.

Yet by the time we got to the second decade of this century, a counterrevolution had set in. Governments seized, temporarily seized, or threatened to seize private pension funds in France, Ireland, Hungary, Poland, Cyprus, Russia, Argentina, and other countries.[11] In many cases the pensions were individual accounts, set up as an effort to create a funded alternative to pay-as-you-go social security. In fact, a 2011 report by the Adam Smith Institute, published in the *Christian Science Monitor*, noted that at least eleven countries had rolled back or abandoned efforts to privatize their retirement systems:

> The most striking example is Hungary, where last month [December 2010] the government made the citizens an offer they could not refuse. They could either remit their individual retirement savings to the state or lose the right to the basic state pension (but still have an obligation to pay contributions for it). In this extortionate way, the government wants to gain control of more than $14 billion of individual retirement savings.
>
> The Bulgarian government has come up with a similar idea. Three hundred million dollars of private early retirement savings was supposed to be transferred to the state pension scheme. The government gave way after trade unions protested, and finally only about 20 percent of the original plans were implemented.
>
> A slightly less drastic situation is developing in Poland. The government wants to transfer one-third of future contributions from individual retirement accounts to the state-run social security system.[12]

It's not clear what makes these seizures possible. I cannot imagine a situation in which the U.S. government could ever seize IRA or 401(k) accounts successfully. The political resistance would be overwhelming. The same would be true in Singapore, Chile, Britain, and other places. Where backsliding is occurring, what makes it politically possible?

It may be that the ratchet effect is somewhat weak in countries without a strong tradition of individual investments in financial markets. Perhaps the idea of ownership of investment funds has to be sold as part of a marketing campaign to the general public—just as pay-as-you-go social security had to be sold to voters by Roosevelt and other leaders. In any event, these developments are a clear warning that nonreversibility cannot be taken for granted.

SECTION 2

Taking a Closer Look
at the Risks

IN THIS SECTION we will take a closer look at the five risks that give rise to social insurance and the economic problems that each of these create. We will also look at the social insurance programs themselves—their unfunded liabilities, their perverse incentives, and their inefficiencies. Along the way we will identify a number of win/win opportunities for public policy changes—changes that are good for almost everyone. Then, in the next section we go after the big prize: using the win/win approach to reform entire social insurance systems.

The Risk of Growing Too Old and Outliving One's Assets

THE BABY BOOMERS have been reaching the age of sixty-five at the rate of ten thousand per day. By the time they are finished, seventy-eight million of them will claim Social Security, Medicare, and Medicaid benefits. On the average, each retiree will cost taxpayers about $30,000 at today's prices.[1] Because benefits for the baby boomer generation have not been funded, there is a cash flow deficit, and it will get larger and larger with each passing day.

Social Security and Medicare

According to a recent Gallup poll, the largest financial worry for American adults is running out of money in retirement. But most people nearing retirement are wealthier than they think. Take a sixty-year-old couple, earning an average income for most of their work life. If this couple retires at age sixty-two, the present value of their expected Social Security benefits will be $1.2 million! If the couple waits to draw benefits until they reach the age of seventy, their Social Security wealth will be $1.6 million.[2]

The value of Medicare is a little harder to calculate. The "young" elderly tend to have modest medical expenses, while the "old" elderly tend to have a lot. Also, what Medicare spends is not necessarily the value seniors place on it. For example, about 10 percent of Medicare spending is lost to fraud.[3] This contrasts with less than 1 percent for credit card companies.[4] Another 28 percent of Medicare spending is on patients in the last year of life.[5] It is reasonable to think that, if families were spending their own money, they would be more judicious about spending on end-of-life care. With those caveats, a reasonable estimate for a couple reaching the age of sixty-five is that Medicare's health insurance coverage for the rest of their life is worth about $720,000.

The average senior, therefore, is actually a millionaire in terms of entitlement spending wealth—even if they don't have a penny in their bank account.

In the future, the cost of entitlement programs will significantly rise, largely because of increases in health care spending. In fact, by the time today's young workers retire, Medicare will spend more on them than they get from Social Security. The reason: health care spending is expected to rise more rapidly than wages. The two programs combined will replace more than 100 percent of their preretirement wages.

Think about that. In terms of overall spending, government benefits will more than replace the previous wages of average workers, even if they haven't saved a dime.

A study by Texas A&M University economists Andrew Rettenmaier and Thomas Saving concludes that an eighty-five-year-old today is the recipient of Medicare spending equal to about 27 percent of preretirement wages, on the average, based on the Medicare trustees' "alternative" projection. For people turning sixty-five today, Medicare spending will equal about 35 percent of their preretirement wages. For workers entering the labor market today, Medicare will equal 53 percent.[6]

There is just one problem with all of this. The "entitlement wealth" of the retirees is only as sound as the willingness and ability of taxpayers to pay for those benefits. The single biggest problem of Social Security and Medicare is that we have promised future benefits without saving the funds needed to pay for those benefits. In the future, we will need very large increases in tax rates, or we will need very large benefit cuts, or we will need to move to a funded system in which each generation pays its own way.

Problem: Unfunded Liabilities. As of the 2019 Social Security and Medicare trustees report, these two programs have an unfunded liability of more than $119 trillion (see table 5-1), roughly six times the size of the entire economy. This is the excess of promises we have made over and above expected dedicated taxes and premiums. To avoid draconian benefit cuts or tax increases in future

Table 5-1. Social Security and Medicare Trustees Reports: Unfunded Liabilities ($ Trillions)

75-Year Forecast	2019
Social Security	13.9
Medicare	42.8
Total	56.7

Infinite Horizon Forecast	2019
Social Security	43.2
Medicare	76.4
Total	119.6

Source: The 2019 Annual Report of the Board of Trustees of The Federal Old-Age And Survivors Insurance and Federal Disability Insurance Trust Funds and 2019 Annual Report of the Board of Trustees of the Federal Hospital Insurance and Federal Supplementary Medical Insurance Trust Funds.

years, we would need to have that $119 trillion in the bank, earning interest today. But of course we do not.

As noted, the $76.4 trillion unfunded liability in Medicare is based on the assumption that Medicare will grow no faster than the economy as a whole. This assumption was embedded in the Affordable Care Act; and all of the Treasury's federal budgets and all of the trustees reports assume that this growth rate will be adhered to—even though real per capita health care spending has been growing at twice the rate of real per capita income. On the basis of more realistic assumptions, the unfunded liability in Social Security and Medicare is much higher.

These numbers are based on looking indefinitely into the future. But there is a different way of assessing this debt: to use the accounting techniques that private companies and many state and local governments use. On that approach, we ask: what do we owe as of today—assuming we could stop the entire program right now? If we halted these programs today, collecting no more taxes and allowing no more benefit accruals, how much do we owe people for benefits they have already earned? Answer: $52 trillion. That is, even if we took the draconian measure of closing down the entire enterprise and settling up on who owes who what this very minute, we still have a deficit that is more than twice the size of the annual output of the US economy![7]

Problem: No Saving or Investing. Both Social Security and Medicare are based on pay-as-you-go financing rather than a funded system in which each generation saves and invests and pays its own way.[8] Pay-as-you-go means every dollar collected in payroll taxes is spent on current beneficiaries. Nothing is saved. Nothing is invested. The payroll taxes contributed by today's workers pay the benefits of today's retirees. When today's workers retire, their benefits will have to be paid by future taxpayers.

Like other government trust funds (highway, unemployment insurance, and so forth), the Social Security Trust Fund exists purely for accounting purposes: to keep track of surpluses and deficits, and the inflow and outflow of funds. The accumulated Social Security surplus actually consists of paper certificates (nonnegotiable bonds) kept in a filing cabinet in a government office in West Virginia. (Medicare avoids the paperwork by doing the accounting electronically.) These bonds cannot be sold on Wall Street or to foreign investors. They can only be returned to the Treasury. In essence, they are IOUs the government writes to itself.

Every payroll tax check signed by employers is written to the US Treasury. Every Social Security benefit check comes from the US Treasury. The trust funds neither receive money nor disburse it. Moreover, every asset of the trust funds is a liability of the Treasury. Summing over both agencies, the balance is zero. For the Treasury to write a check, it must first tax or borrow.

Problem: Cash Flow Deficits. Since Social Security and Medicare are set up on a pay-as-you-go basis, the immediate concern is the cash flow problem these programs are creating.[9] The two programs combined are paying out more than they are taking in. As the baby boomers retire, this deficit will grow dramatically. Currently, we are using about one in every five general revenue dollars to cover the deficits in Social Security and Medicare. By 2030, we will need about one in three.

That implies that in order to fund Social Security and Medicare benefits at their current levels and at the same time balance the budget, the federal government needs to stop doing about one out of every five other things it is currently doing. In just ten years, the government will need to stop doing about one out of three other things it is currently doing. Clearly, elderly entitlements are on a course to crowd out all other federal programs.

Although the trust funds do not hold valuable assets that can be used to pay benefits, they are useful for another reason. As figures 5.1 and 5.2 show, trust fund accounting keeps track of the inflow and outflow of funds related to our entitlement programs over time. As reflected in figure 5.1, up until sometime in the first decade of the twenty-first century, Social Security (OASI), Medicare Part A (HI), and the disability (DI) trust funds were collecting more in taxes and premiums than they were paying out in benefits. Today, all three programs are paying out more than they are taking in. Figure 5.2 shows how Social Security's negative cash flow is affecting the overall federal budget.

Figure 5.1 Trust Fund Balances as a Percentage of Annual Expenditures

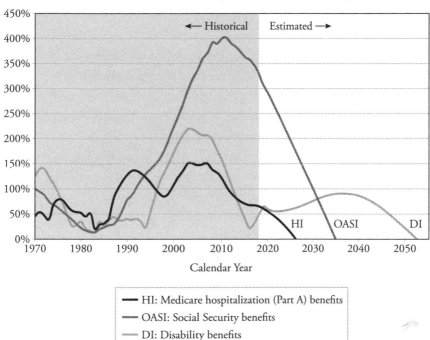

Source: Social Security and Medicare Boards of Trustees, *A Summary of the 2019 Annual Reports*, Chart E.

Figure 5.2 Social Security Trust Fund Reserves

(Present value in trillions)

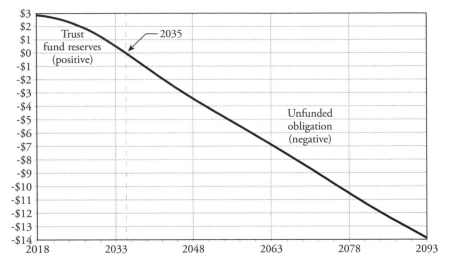

Source: 2019 OASDI Trustees Report, Figure II.D5.

In conventional media accounts, the trust funds will "run out of money" when the lines on the graph in figure 5.2 cross the x-axis and become negative. This will occur in 2052 for the disability program. For Medicare Part A, it will occur in 2026. For Social Security retirement, it will occur in 2034. Of course, there is no "money" to run out of. But those are the dates on which Congress and the president must act. If they fail to act, the Treasury will be required to reduce benefit payments to the point where they equal the income (taxes and premiums) of each of the programs.

Problem: Regressive Taxes and Benefits. Although Social Security is broadly popular in the academic community, Nobel laureate Milton Friedman pointed out years ago that it combines two features that would command disapproval if proposed in isolation: regressive taxes and regressive benefits.[10]

Social Security payroll taxes are regressive for two reasons: they apply only to wage income, not capital income, and they are capped. The maximum taxable wage was $132,900 in 2019. As a result, the Social Security payroll tax (12.4 percent) takes a larger share of the income of low-wage workers than of high-wage workers.

Table 5-2. Social Security Monthly Benefit in 2019

Maximum benefit:	$2,861
Average benefit:	$1,397
Minimum benefit:	$849

Source: Social Security Administration. For an explanation of the minimum benefit, see https://finance.zacks.com/there-minimum-monthly-social-security-payment-regardless-retirement-earnings-6330.html.

Social Security benefits are also regressive. Higher preretirement wages result in a higher retirement benefit. As table 5-2 shows, a retiree earning the maximum taxable income gets a monthly benefit that is more than three times greater than the benefit received by someone at the bottom of the income ladder.

All of this would be understandable if the worker's contributions and benefits were connected—the way they are in a private pension, where today's contributions "pay for" tomorrow's benefits. But, as we have seen, under Social Security, they are not connected. In a pay-as-you-go system, regressive taxes collected from workers make it possible for the wealthiest seniors to cash the largest checks.

That said, the benefits formula itself is very progressive. Social Security replaces a much higher percentage of preretirement earnings for a low-wage worker than it does for a high-wage earner.

Medicare taxes originally were just as regressive as the Social Security payroll tax. But beginning in 1994, the income cap was removed on the Medicare payroll tax (2.9 percent) and, with passage of the Affordable Care Act in 2010, the tax was applied to capital income as well. Also, high-income seniors now pay steeply higher (Medicare Part B) premiums. Additionally, Medicare gets a large infusion of money from general revenue taxes, and the income tax has become increasingly progressive over time.

On the benefit side, the system is surprisingly regressive, however. Even though all seniors participate in the same Medicare health system and even though benefits are supposed to be completely independent of income, those zip codes where the largest Social Security checks are cashed are the same zip codes where Medicare spends the most money. A 1996 study by Jonathan Skinner and Mark McClellan found that:

- Among male seniors at every age level, Medicare spent more on those with higher incomes.
- Among enrollees who were eighty-five years of age and older, for example, Medicare spent 33 percent more on those in the top 10 percent in terms of income than it spent on the bottom 10 percent.
- Among women above age seventy, Medicare again spent the most on those with the highest incomes.
- Among women who were eighty-five and older, Medicare spent 15 percent more on those at the top than it did on those at the bottom.
- For Medicare Part B spending (mainly doctor's care), eighty-five-year-old males at the top of the income ladder received 51 percent more benefits than those at the bottom.
- Among women, the corresponding figure was 25 percent.[12]

Skinner and McClellan also found that Medicare is regressive over the lifetime of workers. Although higher-income individuals paid more taxes during their working years, the extra benefits they received more than offset those taxes. In addition to spending more Medicare money in any given year, higher-income retirees have longer life expectancies, so they enjoy more time as beneficiaries.

With the higher taxes and higher premium payments described above, Medicare has become more progressive than it was at the time of the Skinner/McClellan study. However, another development is making it more regressive: changes in life expectancy.

Researchers have long known that there is a positive relationship between income and health. But it has never been entirely clear why. Take a look at the graph below. It shows that the gains in life expectancy among women in the past thirty years have been concentrated in the top 20 percent of the income distribution. The bottom 40 percent of the population actually has seen a decline in life expectancy. A similar life expectancy gap exists for men.[13]

For people on the political left, this could be taken as evidence that only the rich can afford good medical care. However, a life expectancy gap is occurring worldwide. It is even occurring in Britain,[14] where everyone supposedly is entitled to free health care from the National Health Service.

Figure 5.3 Inequality in Life Expectancy Widens for Women

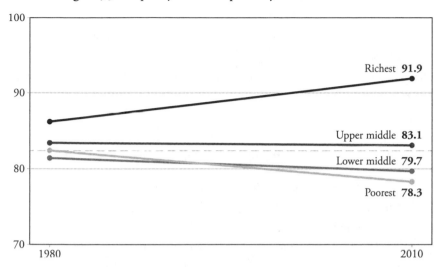

Note: Life expectancy for 50-year-olds in a given year, by quintile of income over the previous ten years. Wealthier women can expect to live longer than their parents did, while life expectancy for poor women may have declined.

Source: National Academies of Sciences, Engineering and Medicine.

It may well be that an important connection exists between the demand for health and income earned. Exploring that connection means confronting some unresolved issues in the economics of human capital (see Grossman and Gardner) and the economics of time (see Goodman).[15] To the best of my knowledge, this type of serious research is not now being done.

Problem: Social Security's Perverse Incentives Not to Work or Save. For most of its history, the full retirement age under Social Security was sixty-five. However, a higher retirement age is being phased in. It's currently sixty-six, and it's scheduled to rise to sixty-seven in the future. Individuals can claim early retirement and receive a smaller benefit. But if they do so and if they continue working, they will be in for a nasty surprise.

Starting at age sixty-two, through age sixty-five, for every dollar of wages a senior earns above $17,640, Social Security reduces the benefit by fifty cents. This is a whopping 50 percent marginal tax rate. And it falls on top of a 15.3 percent payroll (FICA) tax and income taxes as well. If a senior works full time and earns little more than the minimum wage, he will sacrifice two-thirds of his earnings as a result of doing so.

Between age sixty-five and the full retirement age, another monster tax is lurking. For every dollar of wages a senior earns above $46,920, Social Security will reduce the benefit by thirty-three cents. This is a 33 percent marginal tax rate, and when other taxes are added in, it means that middle-income seniors face higher rates than the very rich.

This "earnings penalty" affects labor market behavior. In a *New York Times* editorial, Laurence Kotlikoff and Robert Pozen write:[16]

> Without the earnings test, low-wage earners would work 50 percent more, and middle earners 18 percent more, according to a 2000 study by Leora Friedberg, an economist at the University of Virginia. A 2008 study by Steven J. Haider, at Michigan State University, and David S. Loughran, at the RAND Corporation, found that the earnings test significantly reduced the labor supply of early retirees.[17]

But here is what is really odd. Retirees actually get the earnings penalty money back. What? That wasn't a misprint. Seniors who work get taxed and then untaxed. Kotlikoff and Pozen explain:

> The earnings penalty is actually a sheep in wolf's clothing. Under an arcane provision known as the adjustment of the reduction factor— ARF, for short—if you earn too much between sixty-two and sixty-six, the loss of benefits will be made up to you, at sixty-six, in the form of a permanent benefit increase.[18]

But if seniors get the money back, what's the point? And if the reduction in benefits is only temporary, why does it have such a big labor market effect? Kotlikoff and Pozen speculate that millions of elderly citizens are actually confused by all of this. As we explain below, Social Security does a miserable job of explaining its rules to ordinary citizens.

So here is an opportunity for a win/win policy change. Getting rid of the earnings test would cost the government almost nothing—perhaps a small loss since some people die before they get fully "untaxed." But this small loss would be completely swamped by the additional revenue gained, as millions of seniors would be liberated from a job-killing restriction on their right to work.

Kotlikoff and Pozen make another recommendation that probably also is win/win. They advocate eliminating the Social Security payroll tax for anyone who is over seventy years of age. This would cause some loss of payroll tax revenue. But as seniors worked and earned, they would pay income taxes. If they spent their earnings, they would pay sales taxes. If they saved them, they would pay taxes on investment income. And the nation as a whole would have a larger economic pie.

Another impediment to work is the Social Security benefits tax. Although the name suggests this is a tax on Social Security income, it really isn't. Seniors don't pay it if their only income is from Social Security. The tax is actually a hidden tax on other income. Here's how it works for wage earners.

Beyond a certain threshold, seniors must pay income taxes on fifty cents of Social Security benefits for each dollar they earn. That means that when they earn a dollar, they have to pay taxes on a dollar and fifty cents. At this point, the marginal tax rate paid by the senior is 50 percent more than what it is for nonseniors with the same income!

And it gets worse. If senior workers earn even more income, they will reach a point where they must pay income taxes on eighty-five cents of Social Security benefits for each dollar they earn. This means that when seniors earn a dollar, they have to pay taxes on $1.85. At this point, the marginal tax rate paid by the senior worker is 85 percent more than what it is for nonseniors with the same wage income!

When the Social Security benefits tax is added to the income tax, the payroll tax, and the earnings penalty, middle-income senior workers can lose as much as ninety-five cents of every dollar of wages—the highest income tax rate in the nation (see figure 5.4).[19]

It is worth noting that these very high tax rates only hit the middle class. If your income is low enough, the tax doesn't apply. If your income is high enough, Social Security benefits become completely "taxed," and your marginal tax rate falls back to normal.

Although many seniors are unaware of it, the Social Security benefits tax is also a tax on nonwage income. That means that seniors on Social Security face double taxation.[20] They must pay the ordinary income taxes that others pay, say, on their IRA withdrawals, and then pay an additional tax just because they are on Social Security.

Figure 5.4 Marginal Tax Rate on Wages

Income = $40,000; Age = 62

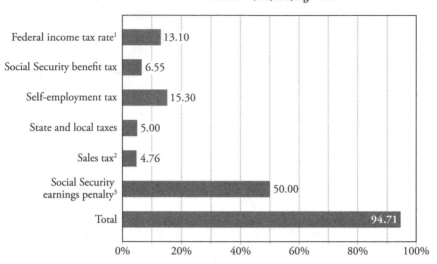

[1] Nominal bracket of 15% times (1–.0785–.05) accounts for employer portion of FICA not being taxable and state and local taxes being deductible.

[2] Effective rate for a nominal sales tax of 5%.

[3] This assumes worker doesn't comprehend adjustment of the reduction factor at full retirement age.

Source: Laurence J. Kotlikoff, "Some Older Workers Face Astronomical Tax Rates," Goodman Institute, Brief Analysis No. 115, October 5, 2016, http://www.goodmaninstitute.org/wp-content/uploads/2016/10/BA-115.pdf.

As figure 5.5 shows:

- Seniors in the 15 percent income tax bracket can face a tax rate of 27.8 percent on pension income, IRA withdrawals, and 401(k) withdrawals if they are on Social Security.

- Seniors who would ordinarily pay no taxes on capital gains and dividends (because of their low incomes) can be forced to pay a 12.8 percent tax on that income if they are on Social Security.

- Seniors who own tax-exempt bonds may be surprised to learn that their income isn't tax exempt at all, but subject to a 12.8 percent tax if they are receiving Social Security.[21]

There may be an argument for taxing some portion of Social Security benefits as ordinary income. But there is no good argument for double-taxing savings.

Figure 5.5 Marginal Tax Rate on Savings

The Effects of the Social Security Benefits Tax
Income = $40,000; Ordinary income tax rate = 15%

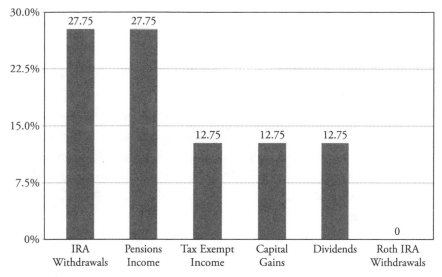

Source: Laurence J. Kotlikoff, "Some Older Workers Face Astronomical Tax Rates," Goodman Institute, Brief Analysis No. 115, October 5, 2016, http://www.goodmaninstitute.org/wp-content/uploads/2016/10/BA-115.pdf.

Problem: Medicare's Impossible Task—Setting Six Billion Prices. As Congress faces mounting pressure to keep health care from crowding out all other discretionary public spending, two sides seem to be squaring off.[22] The don't-touch-a-thing-other-than-squeezing-provider-fees position seems to appeal mainly to Democrats, while eat-your-spinach reforms, including more cost sharing and higher premiums, seem to appeal mainly to Republicans. Neither position is very appealing to voters, however. Nor should they be.

Is there a third way? To see how it might work, we first have to understand that what Medicare is currently trying to do is virtually impossible.

Consider that Medicare has a list of about 7,500 separate tasks that it pays physicians to perform. For each task there is a price that varies by location and other factors. Of the eight hundred thousand practicing physicians in this country, not all are in Medicare, and no doctor will be a candidate to perform every task on Medicare's list.

Still, Medicare is potentially setting about six billion prices at any one time all over the United States, as well as in Guam, Puerto Rico, the Mariana Islands, American Samoa, and the Virgin Islands.

Each price Medicare pays is tied to a patient with a condition. And of the 7,500 things doctors could possibly do to treat a condition, Medicare has to be just as diligent in not paying for inappropriate care as it is in paying for procedures that should be done. Medicare isn't just setting prices. It is regulating whole transactions.

Let's say that the fifty million or so Medicare enrollees average about ten doctor visits per year, and let's conservatively assume that each visit gives rise to only one procedure. Then considering all of the ways a procedure can be correctly and incorrectly coded, Medicare is regulating three quadrillion potential transactions over the course of a year! (A quadrillion is a one followed by fifteen zeroes.)

Is there any chance that Medicare can make the right decisions for all these transactions? Not likely.

What does it mean when Medicare makes the wrong decisions? It often means that doctors face perverse incentives to provide care that is too costly, too risky, and less appropriate than the care they should be providing. It also means that the skill set of our entire supply of doctors will become misallocated, as medical students and even practicing doctors respond to the fact that Medicare is overpaying for some skills and underpaying for others.

To pick one example, a post at the *Health Affairs* blog compared a twenty-five-minute office visit with a primary care physician (PCP) to a ten- to fifteen-minute cataract removal by an ophthalmologist. The authors note that in examining such symptoms as a persistent cough, the PCP must draw on the whole of medicine in order to diagnose the condition and treat the patient. By contrast, cataract removal is a fifty-year-old procedure, and many of the doctors who do it operate in assembly-line fashion in focused factories designed to maximize their income.[23]

Medicare pays $111.36 for the PCP visit, while the ophthalmologist is raking in $836.36 (including the patient copayment). Basically, Medicare is paying 7.5 times more for cataract removal than for primary care. Per time spent to earn the fee, Medicare is paying the specialist fifteen times what it pays the PCP!

Is there any wonder why the shortage of primary care is reaching crisis proportions in many parts of the country, while cataract removal is available at the drop of a hat?

Unfortunately, the authors of the *Health Affairs* piece think the solution is for Medicare to do a better job of setting the six billion prices. But, if Medicare's two-decades-old experiment in price setting has worked so poorly in the past, why would anyone expect it to work any better in the future?

A more sensible approach is to quit asking for the impossible. Instead, let's begin the process of allowing medical fees to be determined the way prices are determined everywhere else in our economy—in the marketplace.

In trying to do that, we face two problems. First, we have completely suppressed normal market forces in medical care for many years. How can you have market prices where no real market exists? Second, many people believe that Medicare is using monopsony (single-buyer) power to push fees below market levels. However, economic theory predicts that monopsony not only results in lower input prices, but also results in less output. In this case, that means less medical care.

Without government acting as a monopsony buyer, patients might end up paying more for the services they currently get, but they could also get more care and better access to care. In the next section we will look at ways to do this.

Problem: Medicare Has Not Entered the Twenty-First Century. One of the biggest hassles doctors face today is federal government pressure to adopt electronic medical records. Doctors are living in a pen-and-paper age, we are told. They need to step into the new century. Yet of all the sectors of the health care system, it is Medicare itself that has been the slowest to take advantage of modern technology. Until the coronavirus hit, Medicare missed out on the use of the phone, email, Skype, Zoom, and hospital-based telemedicine. It still doesn't pay for Uber-type house calls and other services that modern technology is making possible for the rest of the population. Consider that:

- About twenty million Americans are customers of Teladoc. By phone they can talk to a doctor who has access to their electronic medical records and can fill a prescription or meet other medical needs—at a fraction of the cost of a doctor visit or emergency room care.[24] Until it was pressured by the coronavirus threat in 2020, Medicare didn't pay.

- The Mayo Clinic uses telemedicine to help care for stroke victims in rural hospitals—saving lives and reducing costs at the same time.[25] Until recently, Medicare did not pay.

- People living in New York, Los Angeles, San Francisco, and other cities can use a smartphone app to summon a doctor to their home in less than an hour. The cost is $100—one-fifth of the average cost of an emergency room visit.[26] Medicare still doesn't pay.

Even when Medicare does pay, it rarely pays the market price. Take walk-in clinics. These clinics provide convenient medical services at a price that is well below the cost of a doctor visit or a trip to a hospital emergency room. Nurses who keep their records electronically operate the clinics and can prescribe drugs electronically and treat conditions they are capable of treating by using computerized protocols. Studies show that the nurses in these clinics follow best-practice medicine more often than traditional primary physician care.[27]

We could greatly expand access to care for the elderly and the disabled on Medicare and low-income patients on Medicaid if these two government health programs paid the same market prices everyone else is paying for walk-in clinic services. Instead, both programs pay prices set in Washington, DC, and in the state capitols—often miles away from the market to which they are dictating.

Medicaid's fees are so low that most walk-in clinics won't take them. Many do take Medicare, but because Medicare patients are paying below market, the clinic has no incentive to open in locations near places where seniors live or provide services that seniors uniquely need. In short, Medicare is not taking advantage of the opportunity to expand low-cost, high-quality medical care.

Problem: Perverse Incentives in Health Care. There are two additional factors driving Medicare's troubles:

- Since Medicare beneficiaries are participating in a use-it-or-lose-it system, patients can realize benefits only by consuming more care; they receive no personal benefit from consuming care prudently, and they bear no personal cost if they are wasteful.

- Medicare providers are trapped in a system in which they are paid pre-determined fees for prescribed tasks. They have no financial incentives to improve outcomes, and physicians often receive less take-home pay if they provide low-cost, high-quality care.[28]

On the patient side, studies show that the price of a mammogram can vary by $1,000 or more in some localities.[29] But if patients are insulated from the cost, they have no incentive to make cost-effective choices in selecting a provider. They are likely to choose a provider based on convenience instead. Or, they may choose higher-priced providers under the assumption that a higher price means higher quality.

From the doctor's perspective, consider a routine office visit. Five different billing codes might apply. For the simplest problems, requiring only five minutes or so of the doctor's time, Medicare might pay about $20. However, for more complex problems that require forty minutes of face-to-face contact between doctor and patient, Medicare pays about $140. That creates an obvious incentive for doctors to "up code," charging Medicare for level-five visits, instead of level one.

As one report noted:

[D]octors and hospitals have increasingly abandoned the lower-level codes for better-paying ones. Medicare officials have largely failed to challenge these surges in billing across a broad spectrum of medicine, from doctors working in hospital emergency departments and nursing homes to family physicians and specialists seeing patients in their offices.[30]

Take Michigan obstetrician-gynecologist Obioma Agomuoh. He charged for the most complex—and expensive—office visits for virtually every one of his 201 Medicare patients in 2012. In fact, Medicare paid Agomuoh for an average of eight such visits per patient that year, a staggering number compared with his peers. A ProPublica analysis of Medicare data found that Agomuoh was one of more than 1,800 health professionals nationwide who billed Medicare for the most expensive type of office visits at least 90 percent of the time.

Medicare's new "wellness exam" illustrates how perverse incentives on both sides of the market combine to fleece the taxpayer. Expert opinion is virtually unanimous: these procedures have no medical value. They were made available to the elderly free of charge because the politicians who gave us Obamacare wanted even healthy seniors to see some tangible benefits from the program.

But since it is free, millions of seniors are taking advantage of the service. Why not? And physicians are billing Medicare for providing the service. Again, why not?

What Difference Do Government Health Care Programs Make? Medicare and Medicaid reached their fiftieth anniversary in 2015.[31] It's a perfect time, therefore, to evaluate what these two programs have done and what they haven't done.

For starters, we know that the creation of these programs marked a turning point in health care cost inflation. Prior to 1965, health care spending bore a reasonable relationship to national income. People didn't generally talk about it being unaffordable, and a great many people avoided health insurance altogether—choosing to pay medical bills out of pocket instead.

Yet, as we have seen, for the past fifty years real per capita heath care spending has been growing at twice the rate of growth in real per capita income. As a result, health care spending is crowding out more and more other consumption items with each passing day.[32]

This should have come as no surprise, by the way. Medicare added millions of elderly and disabled citizens to the ranks of the insured, and Medicaid did the same thing for the poor. Yet nothing was done to increase the supply of medical services. If you increase the demand and do nothing to increase supply, the inevitable result is higher prices in any market. Also, with no expansion in supply, one person's increased consumption of medical care is likely to come at someone else's expense.

What about the health of people who were newly insured? A careful study of this question was conducted by MIT economist Amy Finkelstein. The answer: Medicare apparently has had no impact on the mortality of the elderly. What Medicare did was shift a lot of money around. But there is no evidence that the elderly got better care because of that effort.[33]

As for Medicaid, there have been conflicting studies through the years, including studies suggesting that people on Medicaid have more difficulty getting access to care and have worse health outcomes than the uninsured. (See the summary of the literature by Avik Roy.[34]) Yet all of these studies had critics who found one thing or another to complain about. (See Austin Frakt, for example.[35])

That was before Oregon gave us a one-of-its-kind test: a randomized, controlled trial in which researchers could compare the outcomes of people with similar characteristics who were selected for Medicaid enrollment at random. The results: Medicaid is apparently having no impact on the physical health of the enrollees or on emergency room visits for treating nonurgent health problems.[36]

Although these results may seem surprising, they are consistent with research on other types of health insurance. For example, a recent study of the Medicare Part D program for prescription drugs concludes:

> Five years after implementation, and contrary to previous reports, no evidence was found of Part D's effect on a range of population-level health indicators among Medicare enrollees. Further, there was no clear evidence of gains in medical care efficiencies.[37]

New evidence suggests that people who are newly insured because of Obamacare are not getting more care or better care as a result.[38] And despite a lot of propaganda on the left, it appears that health insurance generally has almost no detectable effect on population mortality.[39]

Could it be that Medicare and Medicaid have other valuable benefits, apart from their effects on health? The original Finkelstein study did show that Medicare reduced the exposure of the elderly to financial risk. But how much is that worth? Another study by Amy Finkelstein and her colleagues addressed that question. They found that the typical Medicaid enrollee values Medicaid at between 20 and 40 percent of its actual cost. That is, every time taxpayers spend a dollar, they are creating a value for the beneficiaries as low as twenty cents.

So what do the programs' apologists and defenders have to say about all this?

Writing in the *New York Times,* Paul Krugman reflected a leftwing view of health care by making these brash assertions: (1) Medicare controls costs better than the private sector, (2) Obamacare's pilot programs designed to discover new ways to control costs are working even better than expected, and (3) calls for privatization are "zombie" proposals made by people who are "living inside the conservative information bubble, whose impervious shield blocks all positive news about health reform."[40]

All three assertions are demonstrably false:

- There is not one Medicare program but two: conventional Medicare and Medicare Advantage; under the latter, one-third of all Medicare beneficiaries have chosen to enroll in private health insurance plans.

- In the opinion of health economists who have looked at the subject seriously, the most innovative and successful attempts to lower cost, raise quality, and improve access in the entire country are found in Medicare Advantage plans—particularly those run by independent doctor associations, managed by entrepreneurs.[41]

- Probably the worst-run insurance plan in the entire country is conventional Medicare, which (as we have seen) on any given day is setting about six billion prices—without any regard to supply and demand conditions and (for the most part) without any regard to how its administered prices affect quality of care or access to care.[42]

- The results of the Affordable Care Act's pilot programs and demonstration projects have been almost uniformly mediocre—although some of these very same techniques are actually working and working quite well in the best-run Medicare Advantage plans.[43]

- The Obama administration's attempt to encourage medicine to be practiced in Accountable Care Organizations (ACOs) is largely a failed experiment to duplicate what the Medicare Advantage plans are already doing. For example, of thirty-two "pioneer" ACOs participating in a demonstration project, the nineteen that remained in the program performed no better that the thirteen that dropped out.[44]

- It appears that the only real hope for the ACOs is deregulation—allowing them to copy what the Medicare Advantage plans are doing.[45]

Far from being a threat to Medicare, privatization appears to be the only way it can work well.

Problem: The Cost of Collecting Payroll Taxes. Social Security, Medicare, and disability insurance are largely funded by the FICA (Federal Insurance Contributions Act) tax.[46] It is already the largest tax most American families pay. In the future, it will claim even more of workers' wages if the current system remains in place. From its current level of 15.3 percent (combining the employer and employee shares), the payroll tax will need to rise above 25 percent by the middle of the century. Adding this tax to other taxes on labor income results in a surprisingly high marginal tax rate for average-income families. When all taxes on labor income are combined, the average American family faces a 44 percent marginal tax rate, implying that, on the average, families get to keep only fifty-six cents out of each additional dollar they earn.[47]

By 2050, when today's teenagers reach retirement age, the marginal tax rate the average family faces will be 53 percent. By the time today's newborns retire, taxpayers will keep only about forty cents of every additional dollar they earn. These very high tax rates will cause economic harm. The current system encourages people to work fewer hours and produce fewer goods and services, relative to an efficient tax system. In a study for the National Center for Policy Analysis, Liqun Liu and Andrew J. Rettenmaier estimate that:

- The cost to society as a whole from the Social Security payroll tax alone is between eleven and eighteen cents for every dollar of tax revenue collected.

- This implies a loss of between $110 billion and $180 billion in 2015, an amount equal to as much as $1,800 a year for every household in America.

Looking to the future, the burden will be even heavier:

- By the time today's teenagers reach the retirement age in 2050, the nation will be sacrificing as much as thirty cents for every dollar collected in payroll taxes.

- By the time today's newborns retire in 2070, the cost to society as a whole will be as much as thirty-four cents for every dollar collected.[48]

Other costs must also be taken into account. For example, the payroll tax encourages employers and employees to substitute nontaxed fringe benefits for taxable wages. It also induces workers to save less than they otherwise would because (a) Social Security's promises are a substitute for private savings and (b) the payroll tax leaves them with less income from which to save.[49] These distortions reduce the size of the nation's capital stock and result in less output than otherwise would have been the case.

When all costs are considered, Liu and Rettenmaier estimate that *for every four dollars the system pays out in benefits, society as a whole bears as much as three dollars in social cost.*[50]

Problem: Complicated Benefits Structure. Every senior citizen who has applied for benefits under Social Security or Medicare immediately becomes aware of a striking feature of these programs: they are incredibly complicated and complex.[51] Further, failure to master their complexity may mean forgoing important health benefits and failing to claim thousands of dollars of retirement income to which beneficiaries are entitled.

Social Security, for example, is so complicated that even PhD economists are losing tens of thousands of dollars because they don't know how to maximize the benefits the system owes them. As for ordinary mortals, the complexity is almost insufferable. The vast majority of people are missing out on enormous sums of money because they don't know how to navigate Social Security's complex rules.

Get What's Yours: The Secrets to Maxing Out Your Social Security is a book by Laurence Kotlikoff, Philip Moeller, and Paul Solman. In it, the authors identify just about every mistake you are likely to make and tell you how to avoid it. Along the way, they make a number of important public policy observations. Referring to "Social Security's thousands of rules and thousands upon thousands of explanations of its rules," the authors explain that it is probably the most complicated system with which you will ever have to deal:

> The Social Security system has 2,728 rules and thousands upon thousands of additional codicils in its Program Operating Manual, which supposedly clarify those rules. In the case of married couples alone, the formula for each spouse's benefit comprises ten complex mathematical functions, one of which is in four dimensions.[52]

Social Security spends only 1 percent of its budget on administration, and economics writer Paul Krugman at the *New York Times* thinks that is evidence of efficiency. In fact, the amount it spends is nowhere near what is needed to deal with the confusion, bewilderment, and need for advice on the part of the beneficiaries. The system gets three million requests for information every week. In 2012, the agency was forced to cut operating hours at more than 1,200 field offices at a time when more than 180,000 people were visiting these offices and another 430,000 phone calls to field—every day.

Worse, the advice people get from Social Security's employees is often bad advice. The staff are trained insufficiently, or they are too beleaguered to dispense information or advice about the system's ins and outs.

Let's take a relatively straightforward decision: when should you start drawing benefits? The full retirement age today is sixty-six. But in return for a smaller monthly check, people can start drawing as early as age sixty-two. Or they can get larger monthly checks if they delay retirement as late as age seventy. Say you are due $1,000 a month if you start drawing at age sixty-six. Your benefit would drop to $750 if you start at age sixty-two. It will rise to $1,320 if you delay until age seventy. The difference between early and late retirement is a whopping 76 percent larger benefit.

Delaying retirement until age seventy is the most sensible choice for the vast majority of retirees. Suppose a retiree is entitled to an annual benefit of $20,000 at age sixty-two. By exercising eight years of patience, the retiree will see that benefit grow to $35,200 by age seventy. If he then lives to be one hundred, his net benefit from waiting will be $296,000 (extra benefits of $456,000 minus $160,000 for the eight years of benefits that were not claimed).

One way to think about this choice is to consider that between ages sixty-six and seventy the benefit grows by 8 percent for each year of delay. About 5 percent of that is an adjustment for mortality (the older you are, the fewer are the remaining years of life). But the remaining 3 percent is an inflation-adjusted real rate of return. Where else these days can you get a risk-free real rate of return of 3 percent?

Despite this virtual gift from the federal government, only 1.1 percent of men and 1.7 percent of women wait until age seventy to begin drawing benefits! Worse still, the Social Security Administration has actually been encouraging people to opt for early retirement!

Now let's consider a slightly more complicated decision. Suppose you and your spouse are age sixty-six. In most cases, the optimal decision here is for one of you to file for retirement benefits, but then suspend their collection (so that the benefit grows by 8 percent per year for the next four years). Then the other spouse can file for spousal benefits for the next four years and choose to draw a benefit in his/her own right thereafter.

Here is a bad-news gotcha: if you are entitled to two benefits (say spousal and retirement) you can claim only one of them at any one time. If you are not careful, you may lose thousands of dollars as a result. And if you are not careful, odds are that the Social Security employee processing your claim won't be careful either. A study by Alicia Munnell estimated that Americans are losing $10.6 billion a year by failing to make the right choices on decisions like this.[53] How does Social Security affect the family? The authors write:

> Social Security has incentives for some people to marry, for others to divorce, for others to wait to get married, for others to wait to divorce, and for others to live in sin. Timing is everything. If you get divorced a day too soon or get married a day too soon, you can lose tens of thousands of dollars in benefits.[54]

Privacy rights—or at least the Social Security Administration's view of them—have strange implications:

> The agency won't permit the divorced person access to their ex-spouses' earnings records or automatically let widows and widowers have access to their late spouses' earnings records. Optimal claiming decisions are hard enough even when you know all the numbers. They become impossible when you can't get the information you need.[55]
>
> What began as a Model T Ford program—one size fits all—has been expanded, amended, reformed, and socially engineered into a fully loaded Rube Goldberg mobile. It has a driver's manual a mile thick that we bet most of Social Security's own representatives can't follow.[56]

What makes all of this complexity possible, however, is that year after year, for decade after decade, politicians handed out benefits to people that had never been earned.

Case Studies: Victims of Social Insurance Complexity

Professor Kotlikoff has compiled a long list of what can go wrong for ordinary people when they try to deal with the complexities of Social Security and Medicare. The following are some examples.

Case One. Sue knew that you need to sign up at age sixty-five for Medicare Part A (hospital care) and Part B (outpatient care) if you don't have employer-provided health insurance. She also knew that if you aren't covered by such an employer and don't sign up immediately, you face a penalty in the form of a higher Part B premium for the rest of your life once you do sign up. From the Medicare website, she learned that Medicare provides an eight-month special enrollment period after one job ends to apply penalty-free.

Between the ages of sixty-five and sixty-eight, Sue had several jobs with employers who provided health insurance, but she was never between jobs for more than eight months. Altogether, Sue was out of work for twenty-five months between age sixty-five and sixty-eight, during which she wasn't enrolled in Medicare.

Unfortunately, Sue got it wrong. In determining if you need to permanently pay a Medicare Part B penalty, Medicare counts all the months between age sixty-five and the month you first enroll in Part B.

For every twelve months that you're not covered by Medicare Part B, the penalty is an additional 10 percent. In Sue's case, the twenty-five months encompass two twelve-month periods, so she was hit with two 10 percent penalties for a total penalty of 20 percent.

Kotlikoff writes:

Sue has learned an extremely painful lesson, which ... will materially lower her living standard for the rest of her life.... You can't trust that you are getting the real story from Social Security and Medicare websites. Medicare could have easily provided on its site an example of how someone like Sue would be treated. It could also have sent a warning message to everyone at, say, age sixty-two about its Part B penalty. It does not.[57]

Case Two. Mrs. Jimmy Rogers of Houston, Texas, was disabled in 1996 in an aircraft accident while working for American Airlines. Starting in 2007, she received shareholder distributions from her ownership of stock in her husband's company. That same year, Social Security misinstructed Jimmy, telling her to revise her tax return and report these shareholder distributions as taxable labor earnings. Jimmy did as she was ordered but filed an appeal.

Kotlikoff writes:

> Compliance with Social Security's incorrect order triggered an unbelievable bureaucratic nightmare that is surely causing Franz Kafka to writhe in his grave.
>
> Over the past thirteen years, Jimmy and her husband, Larry, have, thanks to Social Security's acknowledged mistake, been deprived of tens of thousands of dollars in Social Security disability and spousal benefits. Jimmy has been forced to pay extra Social Security payroll taxes she didn't owe. Jimmy has been forced to pay extra federal income taxes she didn't owe. Jimmy and Larry's company has been forced to pay extra FICA taxes they didn't owe. Jimmy retroactively lost her Medicare health care coverage and is now being told to pay for years of health care treatment coverage. But the icing on the cake is that Social Security has been and is still, *to this day*, sending Jimmy and her husband a bill for over $120,000 for disability and spousal benefits that they rightfully received (before their benefits were incorrectly terminated), but were falsely told they shouldn't have received.[58]

Case Three. Jamie took her widow's benefit at age sixty and then waited ten years to take her own retirement benefit at age seventy. This should have meant a monthly retirement check that is 76 percent higher than an early retirement benefit. But that didn't happen.

Here's why. When she filed for her widow's benefit at age sixty, the Social Security staffer told her to call the office when she reached sixty-two. She made the call but does not remember much about the details. Nor is there anything from Social Security in writing.

Nonetheless, Social Security now claims in that call eight years ago she took early retirement beginning at age sixty-two. That meant two benefits running at the same time, although Social Security only pays the larger of the two. Since the larger benefit was the widow's benefit, Jamie never learned that anything had gone wrong until she tried to "retire" at age seventy.

Kotlikoff writes:

> What she thought she'd be able to collect, now that she has just turned seventy, is $1,760 per month, that is, her highest possible retirement benefit.... [But] thanks to the secret behavior of one Social Security staffer eight years ago, Jamie is facing the prospect of spending the next thirty years (if she makes it to one hundred) receiving a check each month that is $1,001 per month instead of $1,760 per month.[59]

Case Four. Jamie is not alone. The Office of the Inspector General (OIG) estimates that more than eleven thousand widows have been cheated out of more than $130,000,000 — an average of more than $10,000 each.[60]

Kotlikoff writes:

> In the following two years, Social Security has generously paid out a grand total of $0.00 (i.e., zero, zilch, zip, nil, naught, nothing) to each and every one of them.
>
> A high-profile class action suit against Social Security would force the system to clean up its act. Every day I hear another horror story about people getting hit with enormous bills for benefits that Social Security says it overpaid them in the past. In too many cases, Social Security has the facts wrong, but has put its victims at the mercy of the system's outdated computer systems.[61]

Case Five. Richard called the Social Security office and asked to have his benefit payments started when he reached age seventy. The woman who answered tried to "bribe" him with this offer: if he started his benefits at age sixty-nine instead, she would send him a six-month retroactive payment. Richard was smart enough to realize something the woman did not say: by accepting her offer he would endure a lower monthly benefit for the rest of his life.

Richard declined the offer. But the Social Security employee implemented it anyway. Now he's trying to undo the mistake.

Kotlikoff, who suspects the woman's behavior may reflect official Social Security policy, writes:

Richard has spent over eighty hours trying to fix this problem. He has other concerns. His wife is seriously ill. The stress of Social Security's "mistakes" is taking a major toll on both him and his wife. Older people have enough to worry about these days. They shouldn't have to face bureaucratic torture at the hands of Social Security staff who should learn loud and clear that they'll be fired if they continue to make "minor" mistakes, which produce massive damage to the lives of people who pay their salaries.[62]

Is Social Security a Good Deal? Although Social Security taxes are not "invested," we can still compare the rate of return people get with returns they might have received had they been able to invest those same dollars in real assets.[63] The Social Security Administration actually does these calculations for us and makes them available online.[64] As financial columnist Scott Burns explains:

> The best time to be born or retire was long ago. Workers at medium earnings levels born in 1920 and retired at 65 in 1985 did well. A single male receives $1.37 for every $1 committed. The next generation, those born in 1943 and retired in 2008, gets only 74 cents on the dollar. Their children, born in 1964 and retiring in 2029, will do somewhat better, at 94 cents on the dollar.
>
> But that 94-cent figure depends on Social Security's paying full benefits after the trust fund is empty. This will happen, the actuaries say, in around 2033. If benefits are paid from available employment taxes, their money's worth will decline to 81 cents. . . .
>
> Women earners of medium income retiring in 2014 will receive 88 cents for every dollar paid into Social Security. Men will receive only 78 cents. The difference is the longer life expectancy of women—they pay in the same amount but can expect to collect benefits longer.[65]

Also, Social Security isn't like a pension plan. As we have seen, the program skews benefits upward for people with lower incomes. And it skews them downward for people with higher incomes. In pension plans, benefits are proportional to contributions. The progressive nature of Social Security means that it is looking more and more like a welfare program rather than a pension program, and that will become truer in the future.

Can Privatizing Social Security Be a Win/Win for All Generations? If we want to move to a financially sound retirement system under which each generation pays its own way, we have to answer this question: what kind of offer can we make to young people that will induce them to continue to pay some taxes to support current retirees, while at the same time forgoing future benefits for themselves and saving for their own retirement needs instead?[66]

Although scholars and policy wonks have been talking about this prospect for almost two decades, and although both Presidents Bill Clinton and George W. Bush developed serious policy proposals, no one has answered that question. Until now.

In an article published in the *Journal of Retirement*, Liqun Liu, Andrew Rettenmaier, and Thomas Saving emphasize that any calculation of the value of Social Security must confront three problems:[67]

- Uncertainty about the future. There is a growing gap between expected future revenues and promised benefits, totaling a $27.7 trillion deficit, if we project into the future indefinitely. How will that gap be dealt with? By higher taxes? By reduced benefits? Or by some combination of the two?

- Attitudes toward risk. Not everybody approaches risky decisions in the same way. Some people are very risk averse—especially when it comes to retirement decisions. Others are less so.

- Income. The structure of Social Security benefits is highly progressive. As a result, low-income workers will come out ahead, almost regardless of what we assume about the future.

Suppose I offer you a coin flip: for heads you get ten dollars, and for tails you get nothing. Averaging the two outcomes, the expected value of this gamble is five dollars. But before the coin flip, suppose I ask if you would accept a certain sum of money instead of the coin flip. If you are risk averse (and when thinking about retirement, almost everyone is), you will take an amount less than five dollars rather than accept a fifty/fifty chance of getting nothing.

Now let's turn the bet around. If the coin turns up heads, you pay me ten dollars. If tails, you pay me nothing. Your expected cost is five dollars. But before the coin flip, you are given the opportunity to buy out of the gamble. How much would you pay to avoid the coin toss? If you are risk averse, you will pay more than five dollars.

These examples show that in a certain sense, the evaluation of costs and benefits is asymmetrical. You would accept less than five dollars rather than participate in a risky bet with an average gain of five dollars, but you will pay more than five dollars to avoid a risky bet with an average cost of five dollars.

Now suppose we think about repeating this exercise over and over again—years into the future. We have a stream of uncertain outcomes, and we have a stream of amounts of certain money you would pay or accept to avoid each of the gambles. What is the present value of those streams? To obtain the value of the certain amounts, we would use a "risk-free" discount rate—since there isn't any risk. Then, we would like to find an interest rate that makes you indifferent between all of the gambles and the certain alternatives. That would give us the most accurate estimate of the present value of a series of gambles that stretch into the future.

Similarly, the right interest rate to use to evaluate the present value of uncertain future Social Security taxes and benefits is the one that makes us indifferent between these risky outcomes and their certainty equivalents.

However, as we have seen from above, people will accept less than one dollar as an alternative to uncertain benefits with an expected payoff of one dollar, and they will pay more than one dollar to avoid uncertain costs with an expected burden of one dollar. That means that in evaluating Social Security benefits, we must use a discount rate lower than the risk-free rate, and in evaluating Social Security taxes, we must use an interest rate higher than the risk-free rate.

It is this unique insight that allowed Liu, Rettenmaier and Saving to make the calculations reported here.

Table 5-3 shows a calculation of the value of Social Security to twenty-one-year-olds with different incomes and different attitudes toward risk. The risk adjustment variable $\propto$ is equal to zero if the individual is not risk averse at all, and in this case, both future costs and future benefits are discounted at the Treasury's borrowing rate. (This is the conventional approach.) At $\propto = 4$,

Table 5-3. Value of the Social Security Contract to Twenty-One-Year-Olds in 2014

Earnings	∝ = Attitude toward risk			
	∝ = 0	∝ = 2	∝ = 4	∝ = 6
	$20,757	$19,611	$18,420	$17,177
	$3,011	$950	-$1,192	-$3,427
	-$51,494	-$56,073	-$60,834	-$65,803
	-$123,825	-$131,158	-$138,776	-$146,726
Taxable Maximum	-$308,698	-$320,722	-$333,252	-$346,369

a moderate amount of risk averseness, almost everyone is worse off. What the Social Security Administration calls a "scaled medium" worker loses $60,834 and the highest-income earners lose $333,252.

What would people pay to opt out? Table 5-4 shows that twenty-one-year-old workers earning an average income would be at least as well off if they paid between 3 and 4 percent of payroll for the remainder of their working life to opt out of Social Security completely. Opting out means they do not have to continue to pay the tax rate required to fund Social Security, but would forgo all future Social Security benefits.

Table 5-5 combines retirement benefits with spousal benefits, survivors' benefits, and disability benefits for an average twenty-one-year-old. The cost is equivalent to a lifetime payroll tax between 3.68 and 4.80 percent. The rates rise for younger people and those not yet born. For an average nine-year-old, the tax rate is between 4.52 and 7.13 percent.

Making Privatization Practical. Three requirements are necessary for conversion to a successful, privately funded retirement system:

- Each generation must secure its own benefits. In return for opting out, we presume that workers would be required to use some of their payroll tax savings to provide for their own retirement, and these benefits likely would exceed what Social Security is promising for most workers.

- The winners must compensate the losers with respect to lifetime incomes. At the end of a work life, some will have earned incomes well below the average and others will be way above it. The former paid too

Table 5-4. Tax Rate Required to Make Foregoing Benefits Attractive, as a Percent of Lifetime Earnings

Earnings	$\alpha = 0$	$\alpha = 2$	$\alpha = 4$	$\alpha = 6$
	-4.96	-4.60	-4.24	-3.87
	-0.40	-0.12	0.15	0.43
	3.08	3.29	3.50	3.71
	4.63	4.81	4.99	5.17
Taxable Maximum	6.78	6.91	7.05	7.18

Table 5-5. Tax Rate Required to Make Foregoing Benefits Attractive, as a Percent of Lifetime Earnings (all family benefits included)

Earnings	$\alpha = 0$	$\alpha = 2$	$\alpha = 4$	$\alpha = 6$
Net Benefit	-$60,649	-$66,464	-$72,609	-$79,157
Certain Tax Rate	3.68%	4.03%	4.40%	4.80%

much to opt out. They would have been better off under the old system. The latter paid too little to escape. To make sure everyone is better off, we need some kind of redistribution during the retirement years to make sure people on the bottom rung of the income ladder are taken care of. This will be a form of welfare—but it will be a much smaller welfare program than what we have today.

- Everyone who remains in the current system must get their promised benefits. We calculate that if all young people and each generation of succeeding workers pays a lifetime payroll tax of about 4.5 percent, there will be enough revenue to ensure that everyone who is paying into Social Security today will get the benefits they have been promised.

Most proposals to reform Social Security have winners and losers—either seniors lose benefits, workers pay higher taxes, or both. These are eat-your-spinach reforms that arouse natural opposition. Fortunately, we have found that reform can be win/win: every generation can be better off.

Is Medicare a Good Deal? Unlike Social Security, people who enroll in Medicare today can expect to get back more in benefits than they pay in taxes and premiums—provided that each dollar the government spends is valued at a dollar.[68] As table 5.6 shows, people reaching the age of sixty-five today can expect $1.26 in benefits for every dollar they contribute. In 2030, the ratio will be 1.16 to 1. Of course if retirees value Medicare at seventy-five cents on the dollar, the average enrollee is worse off, regardless of the age of eligibility.[69]

Table 5.6 also shows the effects of the Affordable Care Act on individuals at different ages, in light of the overall Medicare spending cuts. What do these projected changes in aggregate Medicare spending mean for individual retirees? As previously noted, that's not clear. It's much easier to say how much Medicare spending will change than it is to say what these changes will mean in terms of access to care. The bullet points below show the changes in Medicare spending for individuals of different ages:

- For someone turning sixty-five and enrolling in Medicare in 2010, the present value of projected Medicare spending was reduced by $27,310 the day Barack Obama signed the health reform bill.
- For fifty-five-year-olds, the projected reduction in Medicare spending is $43,022 per person.
- For forty-five-year-olds, the loss totals $58,302.

One way to think about these changes is to compare them to the average amount Medicare currently spends on enrollees each year. For sixty-five-year-olds, the reduction in spending is roughly equal to three years of average Medicare spending. For fifty-five-year-olds, the loss expected is the rough equivalent of five years of benefits; and for forty-five-year-olds, it's almost nine years.

Consider other reforms that would have reduced Medicare spending by an equivalent amount of money. Rather than ratcheting down the amount that Medicare spends on the average beneficiary, suppose that Congress had raised the age of eligibility for the program instead.

The Medicare spending reduction called for in the health reform bill is the rough equivalent of raising the age of eligibility for sixty-five-year-olds from sixty-five to sixty-eight. It is the equivalent of making fifty-five-year-olds wait until they reach age seventy and forty-five-year-olds wait all the way to age seventy-four!

Fortunately for beneficiaries, there are two offsetting benefits of lower Medicare spending. When Medicare spending declines (relative to trend), so do the required premiums and taxes needed to support those benefits. As a result, beneficiaries will have more disposable income than otherwise. However, this extra income will equal only about one-quarter of the spending reductions for sixty-five-year-olds, about one-third for fifty-five-year-olds, and almost one-half of the spending reduction for forty-five-year-olds.

Consider other reforms that would have reduced Medicare spending by an equivalent amount of money. Rather than ratcheting down the amount that Medicare spends on the average beneficiary, suppose that Congress had raised the age of eligibility for the program instead.

The Overall Effect of Social Insurance on Work, Saving, and Investment. Calculations of "money's worth" for Social Security and Medicare (such as those reported above) are almost always isolated from other taxes and entitlement benefits. But that paints an incomplete picture. Here's what we really want to know: if I earn an extra dollar—at any age—what does that do to my eligibility for benefits under various entitlement programs and what does it do to my taxes—both now and in the future?

The answer: there are certain circumstances where an extra dollar of earnings can be extremely costly. We have already seen that seniors can lose more than ninety cents when they earn a dollar of wages. The penalties can be many times higher than that, however.

Medicare premiums abruptly rise by $694 for seniors who earn $1 too much. No, that's not a misprint. A senior who earns one additional dollar can suddenly owe Medicare almost seven hundred times that amount. A mother with a child can lose Medicaid benefits that cost more than $10,000 if she earns one extra dollar. Thousands of dollars in Supplemental Security Income can be forfeited if the beneficiary's assets are a dollar too high. One additional dollar of wage or capital income can trigger the loss of thousands of dollars in Obamacare subsidies.

These are the unfortunate effects of earning money in the current period. But the consequences of earning income this year do not stop this year. In earning wage income today, twenty-year-olds will be affecting their Social Security income and Medicare benefits four or five decades from now, to say nothing of a myriad of other entitlement benefits.

Table 5-6. Value of Lifetime Medicare Benefits Compared to Taxes and Premiums, Before and After the Affordable Care Act

2009 Before ACA	65 Today	65 in 2020	65 in 2030
Benefits	$192,421	$254,900	$345,237
Taxes and Premiums	-$132,305	-$200,651	-$298,362
Net Benefits	$60,116	$54,249	$46,875
2010 After ACA			
Benefits	$156,833	$192,585	$240,233
Taxes and Premiums	-$124,027	-$181,358	-$251,660
Net Benefits	$32,806	$11,227	-$11,427
Net Loss Due to ACA	$27,310	$43,022	$58,302

Source: Courtney Collins and Andrew J. Rettenmaier, "How Health Reform Affects Current and Future Retirees," National Center for Policy Analysis, NCPA Policy Report, No. 333, May 2011.

In addition to the federal income tax and all its special provisions—the Child Tax Credit, the Earned Income Tax Credit, the Saver's Tax Credit, Social Security taxes on wage income, Medicare taxes on labor and capital income—there are forty-two separate state income tax systems. Then there are more than thirty different federal entitlement programs (most of which are state specific), including Medicaid, Obamacare, TAFDC, SNAP, Housing Assistance, Child Care Assistance, and Energy Assistance, etc.

How can an individual know how the earning of a dollar will affect all the various taxes that the dollar might give rise to and all the various benefit reductions that the dollar might trigger over the course of a lifetime? It's not easy.

Fortunately, the task has already been accomplished for us by means of complex computer modeling by Laurence Kotlikoff and his colleagues in a National Bureau for Economic Research working paper.[70]

Here's the bottom line: the average household in this country can expect to keep about fifty-seven cents out of every dollar of earnings. When you earn a dollar, you are only earning a little more than half of that dollar for yourself. The rest of the dollar will go to the government.

Lifetime marginal tax rates tend to rise with income. But not as much as you might suppose (see figure 5.6). For households in the bottom fifth of the resource distribution, the tax rate is 44.2 percent. For those in the top fifth, it's 50.7 percent—the same as it is for the top 1 percent.

These numbers are only averages. Even more surprising is the dispersion. Depending on where people live and what entitlement programs they qualify for, federal and state government work disincentives vary widely. For example, one in four low-wage workers under age fifty face a marginal net tax rate higher than 70 percent. For all practical purposes, these households are effectively locked into poverty.

Across all households, the economists identify the very best and very worst of outcomes:

> The maximum [lifetime net marginal tax rate] is 1,326 percent and the minimum is −1,313. The household with the maximum rate experiences over a $13,000 increase in net taxes as a result of earning an extra $1,000. The household with the minimum rate … experiences over a $13,000 increase in net benefits from earning another $1,000.[71]

Figure 5.6 Median Lifetime Marginal Tax Rate, Ages 20–79

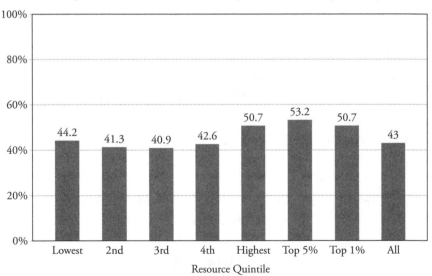

Source: David Altig, Alan Auerbach, Elias Ilin, Laurence Kotlikoff and Victor Ye, "Marginal Net Taxation of Americans' Labor Supply," National Bureau of Economic Research Working Paper, April 7, 2020.

Most people can improve their lot by moving to another state. In fact, the typical household can raise its total remaining lifetime spending by 7.9 percent by moving to some other state.

How Social Insurance Affects the Inequality of Income and Wealth

A typical study of the distribution of income compares people on the top and bottom rungs of the income ladder.[72] The problem: the entire population is on the ladder. That means these studies are comparing retirees with people who are working. They are comparing people who are at the peak of their career earnings with people who are just starting out.

Studies of the distribution of wealth typically have an even bigger problem. They count private savings (such as an IRA or 401(k) account) and private pensions as part of an individual's wealth. But they ignore Social Security and other entitlement benefits, even though people pay taxes to these programs.

A study by Alan J. Auerbach (University of California, Berkeley), Laurence J. Kotlikoff (Boston University), and Darryl Koehler (Fiscal Analysis Center) departs from previous studies in three important ways: (1) it recognizes that the only meaningful way to compare income and wealth is to do it for people of approximately the same age, (2) it chooses people's after-tax consumption (standard of living) as the best measure of well-being—not just at a point in time, but over the remainder of individuals' entire lives, and (3) it includes such government benefits as Social Security, Medicare, and Medicaid in calculating people's expected consumption.[73]

To appreciate what difference this approach makes, take people in their forties (see figure 5.7). Those in the top fifth of the distribution can expect to enjoy 55.3 percent of this age group's lifetime resources over the remainder of their lives. People in the bottom fifth can expect only 4 percent. That's a wealth difference of almost 14 to 1. But after government transfer programs do their redistribution, the wealth difference is cut in half: the difference in lifetime consumption drops to 7 to 1.

It is well known that inequality increases with age, with the greatest inequality existing among the elderly. Other studies have concluded that the main reason for this is differences in saving behavior, not some mysteri-

Figure 5.7 Wealth vs. Spending Inequality

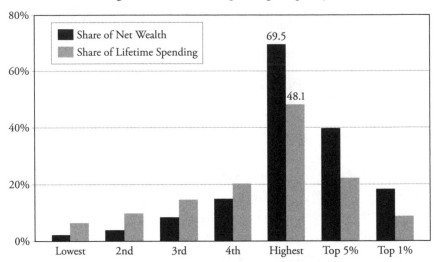

Note: This chart shows how wealth inequality of individuals aged 40 to 49 compares with spending inequality, which accounts for the impact of government taxes and benefits. The quintiles are divided based on the present value of future wages and net wealth.

Source: Alan Auerbach and Laurence Kotlikoff, "We've Been Measuring Inequality Wrong: Here's the Real Story," Goodman Institute for Public Policy Research, Brief Analysis No. 101, March 14, 2016.

ous Wall Street malfeasance imagined by Paul Krugman or Bernie Sanders. Those who save more when they are young accumulate more and have more when they retire. Those who save very little, will have a lot less in the retirement years.

This study finds that among twenty-year-olds, the wealth difference between the highest and lowest fifths is 7 to 1. But among seventy-year-olds, the difference in wealth is more than 70 to 1. That change over the life cycle of a group of cohorts is rather astonishing. Even so, after government redistribution takes its toll, the difference in remaining lifetime consumption falls all the way down to 8.6 to 1 for this age group.

And here is an interesting twist. The social insurance programs that tend to reduce inequality in one respect may increase inequality in another respect. In general, social insurance tends to redistribute resources from those who have more to those who have less. At the same time, the existence of very generous programs for the elderly reduce the incentive for people to save while they are young. Different responses to these incentives may, as we have seen, result in very unequal outcomes in the years of retirement.

This seems to be an international phenomenon. The United Sates saved 9 percent of national income in 1970, but only 2 percent in 2006. France and Italy saved over 17 percent of national income in 1970, but less than 7 percent in 2006. Japan saved 30 percent in 1970, but only 8 percent in 2006.[74]

Another important contributor to inequality of lifetime consumption is inequality in life expectancy. As we have seen, the gap in expected years of life for those in the top and bottom fifths of the income distribution has been growing for some thirty years. It has a big effect on lifetime consumption. Take people in their twenties. The authors estimate that if those in the bottom fifth lived as long as those in the top fifth, they would get one-third more benefits from government over their lifetimes.

Overall, our fiscal system is highly progressive. There is a price to be paid for this progressivity, however. The more redistribution that takes place, the smaller the rewards for working, saving, and investing and the larger the rewards for not working, not saving, and not investing. That has to be bad for economic growth.

What Difference Does Social Security Make? Our elderly entitlement programs have made workers and families of all income levels dependent on government for significant portions of their retirement savings. Consider that:[75]

- Social Security accounts for virtually all of the discretionary consumption of households with modest preretirement incomes (less than $50,000 a year for couples or $25,000 for singles).

- It is equal to about one-third of the consumption of high-earning households (couples with preretirement incomes of $500,000 and singles with $250,000).[76]

Currently, averaging a worker's thirty-five highest-earning years and putting that average wage through a complicated benefit formula determines Social Security benefits for all new retirees. Since the purchasing power of a dollar earned thirty-five years ago is not equal to the purchasing power of today's dollars, and because even without inflation real wages tend to rise over time, the worker's earnings are adjusted, or indexed, to the annual increase in average wages nationwide:

- In 2019, the average monthly Social Security benefit was $1,397.
- For a worker retiring in 2019 at age sixty-six, the maximum monthly benefit was $2,861.

Even with this steady flow of risk-free funds, a claim often heard is that most Americans are financially unprepared for retirement. Proposals have even been advanced to make Social Security more generous to meet this presumed inadequacy. Yet by international standards, America's retirees are doing quite well. Writing in the *Wall Street Journal*, Andrew Biggs and Sylvester Schieber note that:

> In a 2013 study, the Organization for Economic Cooperation and Development compared the incomes of a country's retirees with the average income in that country. The results are surprising. Despite a supposedly stingy Social Security program and ineffective retirement-savings vehicles, the average US retiree has an income equal to 92 percent of the average American income, handily outpacing the Scandinavian countries (81 percent), Germany (85 percent), Belgium (77 percent), and many others.[77]

The Social Security Administration's own modeling predicts that a typical retiree today will have a higher standard of living than they had during their working years. In a study by the RAND Corporation, 87 percent of retirees said their retirement years were "better" or "as good as" the years before they retired. Even following the Great Recession, 75 percent of retirees told Gallup in June 2013 that they have enough money to live comfortably.[78] Biggs and Schieber write:

> OECD data show a strong negative relationship between the generosity of public pensions and the income that retirees collect from work and private saving. *For each additional dollar of benefits paid by a country's government pension, that country's retirees themselves generate*

ninety-four cents less income from personal savings or employment during retirement. [Emphasis added.][79]

This is consistent with US studies showing that Social Security has a negative effect on overall national saving. Families who depend on Social Security for some or all of their retirement income reduce their own savings in response.[80]

Medicaid Long-Term Care

Medicaid is our nation's largest health insurance plan—larger even than Medicare. It has an enormous influence over many parts of our health care system:

- Medicaid and the Children's Health Insurance Program (CHIP) cover 72.6 million people, almost half of US births and approximately 40 percent of our nation's children.[81]

- Medicaid covers 51 percent of the country's long-term care expenses.[82]

- It is the largest provider of mental health care, paying for 25 percent of all behavioral health spending.[83]

- It is the single largest source of care for patients who rely on community health centers, which provide care for twenty-eight million individuals, 48 percent of whom are on Medicaid or uninsured.[84]

- Almost one in every five Medicare beneficiaries receives assistance from Medicaid for premiums or cost sharing or by receiving full coverage.[85]

- Medicaid also provides more than $150 billion annually to safety-net hospitals, which in our ten largest US cities provide more than 60 percent of the burn care and over 30 percent of the trauma care.[86]

Moreover, like Social Security and Medicare, Medicaid is incredibly complex. Writing at *Health Affairs*, Patricia Gabow and Thomas Daschle note that:

Medicaid actually comprises fifty-six programs. There is a separate program for every state, territory, and the District of Columbia. Moreover, the many waiver variations multiply by many times the functional number of programs....

Medicaid has approximately fifty to sixty eligibility pathways that are multiplied by state variations on many of them, making eligibility criteria extraordinarily complex. This variability creates issues for enrollment, payment, management, and transparency for patients, providers, states, and the federal government.[87]

Medicaid is both a welfare program for low-income families and a social insurance program for the middle class. It covers four distinct categories of beneficiaries: children, adults, the elderly, and the disabled. Although poverty programs potentially provide a safety net for anyone who might encounter a bit of bad luck, the disability and long-term care features of Medicaid are the ones that primarily serve as an enduring source of insurance for those who are solidly in the middle of the income distribution.

In this section, our focus will be on Medicaid as an insurer of long-term care. The analysis has been mainly provided by my colleague Pam Villarreal.

Medicaid is currently the largest funder of long-term care (see figure 5.8). About one-third of federal and state Medicaid dollars are spent on some type of long-term care—a combined total of about $133 billion a year.[88]

In general, middle-income seniors tend to enter nursing homes as private, paying patients. If the facility participates in Medicaid and the patient subsequently runs out of private funds during his stay, the patient cannot be evicted from the facility, even if it has no "Medicaid beds" available.[89]

Although most nursing homes accept Medicaid patients, a few of them do not. Once patients run out of private funds in these facilities, they can be discharged.

Problem: Inflexible Benefits. One of the fastest growing trends in living arrangements for the elderly is the phenomenon of assisted living. These facilities, which are growing by leaps and bounds, focus on integration: integrating living, health care, and long-term care expenses. In general, seniors buy a unit in a facility while they are healthy. This gives them access to all the amenities one would expect on a cruise ship: food, entertainment, companionship, and access to outpatient care, if needed. As they grow older and if their health

Figure 5.8 Long-Term Care Expenditures by Source, 2017

Total Spending = $235 Billion

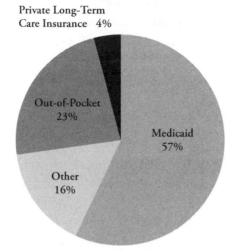

Private Long-Term
Care Insurance 4%

Out-of-Pocket
23%

Medicaid
57%

Other
16%

Note: "Other" includes private health insurance,
Veterans Affairs, the Indian Health Service, and
various state and local programs.

Source: AARP Public Policy Institute,
August 2019, https://www.aarp.org/content/
dam/aarp/ppi/2019/08/long-term-services-and-
supports.doi.10.26419-2Fppi.00079.001.pdf.

deteriorates, they are able to take advantage of the facility's long-term care services. If the need arises, the facility can become the senior's nursing home.

By contrast, our three most important entitlement programs for the elderly—Social Security, Medicare, and Medicaid—are largely compartmentalized. Social Security and Medicare, we have seen, are assets that are worth more than a million dollars at the time a typical senior reaches the age of eligibility. Potential Medicaid benefits are also an asset. Why can't seniors convert some portion of these assets into ownership and membership in an assisted living facility—sort of like a reverse mortgage? In a rational entitlements system they would be able to do so.

Bringing all of our entitlement programs into the twenty-first century ought to be a top priority for reformers. We need to get our entitlement programs in line with where the rest of the world is headed.

Currently, long-term care benefits administered through Medicaid are often inflexible with respect to the needs of the beneficiary. For instance, many states do not cover care outside of a nursing home. Federal law requires state Medicaid programs to cover health costs related to home care, but not custodial care, such as help with bathing and dressing. Because the program is not tailored to patient needs, it forces many individuals into expensive nursing homes for care that could have been delivered more economically in other settings.[90]

Problem: Inflexible Eligibility. The Medicaid long-term care system offers little in the way of options for seniors. Seniors in need of long-term care, who max out their Medicare coverage,[91] or those who need custodial care rather than medical treatment, must pay out of pocket unless they qualify for Medicaid.[92] It's all or nothing. Medicaid eligibility is governed by both federal and state regulations. Generally, in order to qualify for Medicaid nursing home coverage, an individual must have no more than $2,000 in "countable" assets. Assets that are not counted include a house and a car, with special provisions for houses:

- For single people, up to $585,000 of the value of a home is exempt from countable assets.

- However, states are allowed to exclude a maximum of $878,000 owing to regional differences in home prices.

- For married people, a house is excluded from countable assets regardless of value, provided that the spouse or a dependent relative continues to live in the home.

- In addition to a house, spouses also are permitted by federal regulations to keep half of a couple's "community resources"—from $25,284 to $126,420, depending on the state.[93]

States also limit the income a Medicaid long-term care patient can receive, within a range set by the Centers for Medicare and Medicaid Services.[94] Some states have an income limit of $2,199 a month, which is equivalent to 300 percent of the Supplemental Security Income (SSI) payment determined by Social Security, to qualify for Medicaid, although income above that can be paid into a "Miller trust," which will still allow the applicant to qualify.[95] Other states require the applicant to spend down income on their health care to no more than the state's income standard for eligibility, which can vary state by state, but often has been 100 percent of SSI in order to qualify for Medicaid long-term care.[96]

The applicant can spend the amount equal to that income standard for eligibility without restriction. But nursing home residents must pay all of their remaining income toward their health care, which can include medical costs not covered by Medicaid, such as Medicare or other health insurance premiums.

If a Medicaid applicant is married, an additional amount determined by each state is allowed for spousal income support or for any dependent children living at home. Any income earned in the healthy spouse's name is exempt from Medicaid's income eligibility standards.

The inflexibility of Medicaid can be problematic for families who must make the decision to put a loved one in long-term care. In areas with few nursing homes, one may be hard-pressed to find a good-quality facility that accepts Medicaid patients.

Problem: Incentives to Game the System. Several methods allow individuals legally to impoverish themselves and qualify for Medicaid. They can (1) transfer assets to their children, (2) divorce, or (3) set up irrevocable Qualified Income Trusts.[97] An entire industry of attorneys practicing "elder law" has sprung up in recent years to help seniors transfer assets in order to qualify. However, it is difficult to identify abuses because most asset transfers by seniors are not made to skirt Medicaid asset tests. According to the 2002 Health and Retirement Study of the National Institute on Aging, just over one in five elderly households (22 percent) transferred assets in the prior two years.[98]

A growing number of seniors have assigned their investment income to Qualified Income Trusts, which are designed to limit how the funds are distributed.[99] Trust funds can be used to make certain payments, including insurance premiums, support for a spouse, and sixty dollars per month for personal needs. A nursing home resident, for example, can assign to a trust the right to Social Security benefits or any other form of income, and that money does not count toward the eligibility limit. These trusts, therefore, effectively allow people temporarily to hide income that otherwise would reduce Medicaid's long-term care costs. A spouse's income is not included in the income eligibility test and is not included in the trust. Once the resident dies, however, Medicaid is reimbursed from the trust, based on the "patient responsibility" share of costs assessed by Medicaid.[100]

Problem: Other Perverse Incentives. Medicaid's long-term care system as a whole creates very little incentive for people to self-insure or to purchase long-term care insurance, for various reasons:

- The most valuable asset that people seek to protect, their home, is exempt from Medicaid's asset test.
- For married people, income in the spouse's name is exempt from income tests; this could amount to several thousand dollars a month.
- Long-term care insurance can be expensive and complicated, and premiums usually are not tax deductible.[101]

Low-income people with few assets have little incentive to purchase long-term care insurance, but they are the patients for whom Medicaid long-term care was intended in the first place.

6

The Risk of Dying Too Young and Leaving Dependent Family Members without Resources

THE UNITED STATES has changed significantly over the past six decades. When Social Security was created, two-thirds of all households consisted of a husband employed in the labor market while his wife worked at home. Social Security was designed to suit this 1930s single-earner household model. Today, however, single-earner couples no longer are the norm. They represent only one-fifth of American households. In contrast, dual-earner married couples represent 36.8 percent of households today, up from one in ten in 1940.[1]

The Government Solution: Social Security Survivors' Benefits. Social Security provides benefits to surviving spouses and children after the death of the family's primary wage earner if the marriage lasted at least nine months. It is useful to think of survivors' benefits in two parts. First are the benefits resulting from deaths prior to reaching the retirement age:

- In the case of a parental death, each surviving child under the age of eighteen is entitled to 75 percent of the benefit that the worker would have received based on his earnings history.
- A surviving spouse also is entitled to 75 percent of the decedent's benefit as long as a dependent child under the age of sixteen is in the household.
- The total family benefit is subject to a maximum that varies but is usually 150 to 180 percent of the decedent's benefit.

Second and more common are survivors' benefits resulting from death after retirement.

- A surviving spouse is entitled to 100 percent of the decedent's benefit if it is higher than the benefit to which the spouse would have been entitled based on his or her earnings history.

- A child under age eighteen is entitled to 75 percent of the benefit that the worker would have received.

- The total family benefit is subject to a maximum that varies but is usually 150 to 180 percent of the decedent's benefit.

Problem: Lack of Choice. Survivors' benefits suffer from many of the same problems as other government insurance schemes: premiums are unrelated to risks, benefits are unrelated to needs, and families have no alternatives. People must take the government's plan with the government's restrictions.

Problem: Penalties for Working. Spousal survivors' benefits (usually received by women) are predicated on the assumption that she will remain home with the children.[2] Should she work for wages, she will face a severe earnings penalty:

- A surviving spouse loses $1 of benefits for every $2 earned above $17,640 (the threshold for 2019), amounting to a 50 percent tax on her labor market income.

- She and her employer will also pay a combined 15.3 percent Social Security (FICA) tax. If she is in the 10 percent income tax bracket, this creates a total marginal tax rate of *75 percent* on work, not counting state and local income taxes.

A widow who wants to support herself until she reaches retirement will prudently enter the labor market and begin developing job skills well before her children are grown. High marginal tax rates discourage survivors from being self-supporting.

The Risk of Becoming Disabled and Facing Financial Ruin

WORKERS WILL COME into contact with a number of imperfect systems if they become disabled—workers' compensation if injured on the job, or disability insurance if a sickness or injury makes a person unable to work. In general, these systems are poorly designed and poorly managed. They create inefficiencies and perverse incentives for employers and employees and for individuals and their families.

Social Security Disability Insurance

The number of Americans collecting Social Security Disability Insurance has been rising at an alarming rate.[1] One person is now collecting disability benefits for every sixteen people in the workforce.[2] A steady increase over the past twenty years has been occurring despite the fact that, according to the Bureau of Labor Statistics, the American workplace is continually becoming safer, workplace accidents and injuries have been in long-term decline, and more employees are working at desk jobs than ever before.[3] Why is that?

One reason may be that unemployed workers see disability insurance as an alternative to working. A back pain, for example, can get an individual retired for life. Almost 18 percent of such claimants are under age forty and more than 40 percent are under fifty.[4] Another reason may be that disability payments are financially attractive: the average lifetime disability benefit is estimated at $300,000. Mental disorders are often difficult to pin down and open another door for people to game the system.

Then there is mismanagement. The Social Security Administration apparently has allowed hundreds of administrative law judges to more or less

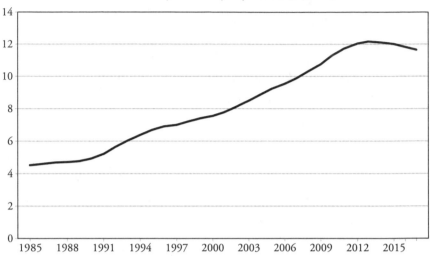

Figure 7.1 Number of Americans Receiving
Social Security Disability Payments, 1985–2017

Source: Social Security Administration.

rubber-stamp applicants into the program. One top-ranking administrative law judge told *60 Minutes* in 2013 that "if the American public knew what was going on in our [disability] system, half would be outraged, and the other half would apply for benefits."

How the Program Works. The Social Security Administration administers two large federal disability programs: the Social Security Disability Insurance (SSDI) program for people who have worked in the past and become disabled, and the Supplemental Security Income (SSI) program, for people who are disabled but have not worked enough (usually due to the severity of their disability) to qualify for SSDI insurance. Nowadays, about 17.9 million individuals collect over $200 billion in benefits through these two programs.[5] In addition to the direct cash benefit, individuals enrolled in the disability program for two years are automatically enrolled in Medicare. Those who are enrolled in the supplemental income program are automatically eligible for Medicaid. The addition of intellectual disability and mental disorder on the one hand and musculoskeletal disease on the other have led to significant expansion, especially among the younger population.

How do people become eligible for benefits? According to a staff report of the House of Representatives Committee on Oversight and Government reform:

> When an individual applies for disability benefits, their case is initially adjudicated by examiners in a State Disability Determination Service (DDS) office. In forty states plus most of California, an applicant may appeal to a different reviewer in the same office if they are denied benefits. If this second reviewer denies granting benefits, then the applicant can appeal to a Social Security Administrative Law Judge (ALJ). Therefore, a case typically only reaches an ALJ if it has already been denied twice. When an ALJ awards disability benefits, for all practical purposes, the decision is final, as awards are not appealable. If an ALJ denies benefits, the individual still has two levels of appeal for reconsideration—SSA's Appeals Council and the federal courts.[6]

Yet, prior to 2010, despite the fact that people appearing before the administrative law judges had been rejected on two previous occasions, 70 percent of the appeals were successful.

Problem: One-Size-Fits-All Benefits. Unlike the Veterans Administration disability system, Social Security disability determinations do not vary in degrees. No partial benefits for a partial disability are awarded, for example. Nor does the system differentiate between a treatable condition and a progressive, degenerative disease.

In a study for the National Center for Policy Analysis, Pam Villarreal notes that musculoskeletal and connective tissue disorders are the single largest diagnostic category for beneficiaries, accounting for about 30 percent of the cases. Osteoarthritis is the most common form of musculoskeletal disease and the most common cause of disability in the general population, affecting twenty-seven million people age twenty-five and older.[7]

Mental disorders are the second leading diagnosis category, including a variety of conditions ranging from mood disorders to schizophrenic/psychotic disorders.[8] Villarreal writes:

The prognoses for mental and musculoskeletal conditions are different. The majority of musculoskeletal diseases grow worse over time, even though treatments can stabilize symptoms; whereas most mental disorders, particularly mood disorders, can improve over time and in some instances, improve quickly.... But the Social Security disability system is a one-size-fits-all program.[9]

Problem: Eligibility Criteria That Are Not Family Friendly. In 2019, workers received one disability credit for every quarter in which they earned at least $1,360 in wages. To qualify for benefits, workers must have earned a minimum number of credits and the minimum number rises with age. Thus, a twenty-one-to-twenty-three-year-old worker needs only six credits, whereas a twenty-seven-year-old must have twelve credits. As figure 7.2 shows, older workers must have earned most of their credits within the recent past:

Figure 7.2 Total Years of Work Required for Disability Benefits

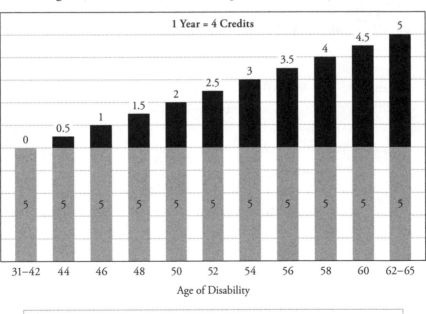

Source: Social Security Administration.

- A thirty-one-year-old disabled worker can claim benefits if he has earned at least twenty credits since age twenty-one.

- However, a fifty-year-old worker must have twenty-eight credits, twenty of which must have been earned in the ten years immediately preceding the disability.

- Finally, a sixty-two-year-old worker must earn forty credits (the maximum required)—twenty in the ten preceding years.

Since eligibility is based on credits earned in the years immediately before a worker becomes disabled, an individual who earned credits twenty years ago may find that not all of them count. Consider a forty-two-year-old woman who worked full time from age twenty-one to age thirty-one and earned forty credits. She has twice the number of credits required to receive benefits if she becomes disabled at age thirty-two. However, if this woman exits the workforce at age thirty-two to raise young children or attend school full-time:

- When she reenters the job market as a full-time worker at, say, age forty-two, she has no qualifying credits and will not receive benefits if she becomes disabled.

- As she ages, the bar is raised: if she reenters the workforce at forty-four, because she is older, she would need twenty-two credits, meaning that she would have to work at least five years more before regaining her eligibility.

- Any additional credits she needs can be drawn from the earlier years she worked, but the requirement for twenty credits in the ten previous years does not change.

Furthermore, a woman entering the workforce for the first time as an older adult—after raising a family and experiencing a divorce, for example—has to earn all her required credits in the current ten-year period. Thus, a forty-four-year-old woman who had not earned credits previously would not be eligible for disability benefits until age fifty-two.

Problem: Incentives Not to Return to Work. Currently, disability recipients can work and earn a minimum amount of income without losing their benefits.

(In 2019, the maximum monthly limit on labor income was $1,220.) As we shall see in section 3, this practice is in stark contrast to the Chilean system, where people can go back to work and earn an unlimited amount of income once the disability claim has been adjudicated.

According to Villarreal:

> The current SSDI system offers a voluntary "Ticket to Work" program in which beneficiaries can work for up to three years without losing their disability benefits. When the program began in 1999, the Congressional Budget Office estimated the program would generate savings beginning in fiscal year 2004.... However, the program had little effect on beneficiaries returning to work.[10]

Moreover, the Office of the Inspector General determined that those savings never materialized.

Bottom line: Fewer than 1 percent of beneficiaries ever go back to work, even if they are physically and mentally able to do so.[11]

Problem: Disability Insurance That Looks Increasingly Like Unemployment Insurance. Some economists see the recent increase in disability claims as evidence that many people now view the system as an extended unemployment program.[12] According to two recent studies, 10 percent of jobless workers aged fifty to sixty-five with access to less than $5,000 were likely to file for disability benefits when their unemployment benefits expired, while only 1 percent of such people sought benefits when they had fifty weeks of unemployed benefits left.[13]

A more recent study by economists at the Federal Reserve Bank of Atlanta concluded:

> As we noted in a previous *macroblog* post, from the fourth quarter of 2007 through the end of 2013, the number of people claiming to be out of the labor force for reasons of illness or disability increased almost three million (or 23 percent). The previous post also noted that the incidence of reported nonparticipation as a result of disability/illness is concentrated (unsurprisingly) in the age group from about fifty-one to sixty....

[O]nly about one-fifth of the decline in labor force participation as a result of reported illness or disability can be attributed to the population aging per se. A full three-quarters appears to be associated with some sort of behavioral change.

What is the source of this behavioral change? Our experiment can't say. But given that those who drop out of the labor force for reasons of disability/illness tend not to return, it would be worth finding out. [14]

John Merline makes an even more forceful case. After pointing out that there were more long-term unemployed at the official end of the Great Recession than at the beginning, he writes:

In just the first six months of 2012, almost 1.5 million workers applied to get into the SSDI program. That's more than applied in the entire year in 1998. Last year, SSDI received 2.9 million applications, which is nearly double the figure from a decade earlier. Since the economic recovery started, more than 8 million have applied for disability benefits. If recent history is any guide, more than a third of those who apply will get on the program within months. [15]

Problem: Waste, Fraud, and Abuse. On January 10, 2014, a *Wall Street Journal* editorial exclaimed:

New York tabloids are having a field day with the news that dozens of ex-cops have been charged with scamming as much as $400 million in Social Security disability benefits. The bigger outrage is that this grand taxpayer theft went undetected for two decades and is merely part of the national scandal that the disability program has become. [16]

The indicted retirees collected about $210,000 apiece in benefits, after paying a fee of $20,000 to $50,000 to the ringleaders, who coached them on how to answer questions and get through the maze in order to reach the court of an administrative law judge who apparently approved 99 percent of all the applications on which he ruled.

One ex-cop who claimed to suffer from post-traumatic stress syndrome posted a YouTube video of himself teaching karate.... Online photographs showed others riding motorcycles and jet skis.... [M]ost are still in their forties or early fifties.[17]

An investigation by Sen. Tom Coburn (R-OK) and Sen. Carl Levin (D-MI) found that one in every four cases randomly selected "should never have been approved" based on Social Security's own rules and procedures. A ten-year study[18] by the Social Security Administration's inspector general found that nearly half of the people receiving disability payments were overpaid.

Workers' Compensation

Each state has its own workers' compensation system.[19] When a worker is injured on the job or has a work-related illness, all states provide three basic types of benefits: (1) coverage of medical costs, (2) replacement of lost wages, and (3) payment for death or dismemberment.[20] Benefits under state workers' compensation systems interact with the federal Social Security disability system, with private, employment-based health insurance and public health care programs.

Employees often exercise discretion (even if they are not supposed to do so) in choosing whether to file a claim for a medical condition under workers' compensation or under group health insurance. Thus, employers who think they have achieved real savings after a significant change in their group health insurance plan often discover that their lower health insurance costs are at least partially offset by higher workers' compensation costs. When employers make health insurance coverage less attractive, often their workers' compensation claims rise instead.

Each state sets employee benefit levels and regulates insurance arrangements and premiums that cover benefit costs. Employers are obligated by law either to purchase insurance or to self-insure and pay claim costs.[21] Every state holds employers strictly liable for all costs of medical treatment and lost wages, with few exceptions. (Some state courts have held employers responsible even when an employee was drunk or high on drugs when the accident occurred!)

Ironically, although workplaces have become much safer in the last several decades and job-related injuries have declined, the cost of state-mandated workers' compensation insurance has not fallen in tandem. Instead, costs have soared. Costs are increasing because state systems provide incentives for employers, employees, and others to behave in ways that cause costs to be higher than they otherwise would be.

Although the goal of workers' compensation is to protect workers, employees ultimately bear the system's costs in the form of lower wages. Conversely, cost-reducing improvements in the system will eventually lead to higher wages.

Benefits to Replace Wages and Compensate Injured Workers. The maximum amount of wage replacement benefits and the length of time a worker can receive them vary considerably among the states.[22] There are three main types of wage replacement (or indemnity) benefits:

- Recuperating employees who are unable to work can receive temporary total disability payments.
- Workers who are permanently disabled and unable to work receive permanent total disability benefits.
- Employees who after treatment have an impairment that prevents them from continuing in their former occupations receive permanent partial disability payments.

However, the Social Security disability payments to workers are offset by any other public disability payments they receive—including workers' compensation. Monthly Social Security disability benefits, including benefits payable to any family members, are combined with workers' compensation or other public disability payments. If the total amount of these benefits exceeds 80 percent of a worker's average current earnings, the excess amount is deducted from the Social Security disability benefit.[23]

My colleague Michael Helvacian has done an exhaustive study of workers' compensation and has identified the following problems.[24]

Problem: Lack of Private Alternatives. Employers are held strictly liable for workers' compensation benefits.[25] In general, state statutes replaced the older, tort liability system, but not completely or in every state:

> Currently, Texas is the only state that allows employers to opt out of the statutory system, although Oklahoma has experimented with the idea,

and Tennessee and South Carolina are considering similar reforms.[26] Employers that opt out, however, are still liable for workplace injuries under the common law's negligence standard. In five states—North Dakota, Ohio, Washington, West Virginia, and Wyoming—employers are obligated to either buy insurance coverage from a state-owned fund or obtain approval from the state agency to self-insure.

In a number of other jurisdictions, state or residual (assigned risk) funds provide insurance as a last resort to employers who are unable to obtain insurance from private carriers. Such risk pools are necessary because when employers are required to have coverage, the state must make an alternative available.

Problem: Inflexibility and Perverse Incentives in Public Systems. In general, the current system gives rise to six underlying problems: (1) imperfect incentives to create safer workplaces, (2) inability to choose more efficient health coverage, (3) inability to choose more efficient disability coverage, (4) inefficient markets for workers' compensation insurance, (5) lack of portability of insurance coverage, and (6) inability to modify strict employer liability.[27] These problems result from state laws that prohibit employers and employees from choosing workers' compensation arrangements other than those mandated by the state and free from state controls over the insurance markets.

As a result, workplaces are less safe and treatment costs for similar injuries are higher when paid for by workers' compensation insurance than by group health plans. A study comparing medical costs in workers' compensation with employers' group health insurance in Florida, Illinois, Oregon, and Pennsylvania found that the average cost of treating the same injuries or conditions was twice as much under workers' compensation than under group health plans.[28] The study found, for example, that back injury cases received treatments over an average of 241 days under workers' compensation, compared to sixty-eight days under group health plans, and average payments for treatment were 2.25 times greater ($2,629 versus $1,166) under workers' compensation.[29] The higher costs were explained entirely by more service use and a different (more expensive) mix of services in workers' compensation. The researchers attributed the higher costs largely to perverse incentives to maximize the use of medical benefits (see figures 7.3 and 7.4).

Figure 7.3 Cost of Treatment for Back Injury by Type of Payer

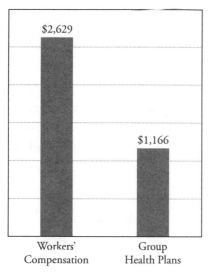

Source: David Durbin, D. Corro and N. Helvacian, "Workers' Compensation Medical Expenditures: Price vs. Quantity," *The Journal of Risk and Insurance,* Vol. 63, No. 1, March 1996, 13–23.

Figure 7.4 Number of Treatment Days for Back Injury by Type of Payer

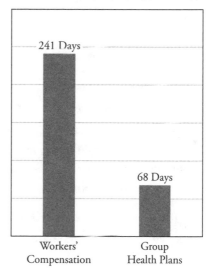

Source: David Durbin, D. Corro and N. Helvacian, "Workers' Compensation Medical Expenditures: Price vs. Quantity," *The Journal of Risk and Insurance,* Vol. 63, No. 1, March 1996, 13–23.

Additionally, wide variation exists in medical claim costs for treating similar injuries in different areas within a typical state. For similar claims and diagnoses in Texas, for example, workers' compensation medical claim costs were 58 percent higher in Houston than in Austin, with excessive use of services accounting for 76 percent of the difference.[30]

Long disability periods also impose substantial financial costs on the workers who make claims because statutory benefits do not replace all wage losses—because of statutory waiting periods before employees can start receiving benefits and because a smaller percentage of higher-wage workers' wages are replaced. As a result, benefits typically replace only about half of a worker's lost wages. Additionally, research indicates that employees who are absent from work for long periods have lower future wages than others in their cohort.[31]

Finally, like employer-sponsored group health insurance, workers' compensation coverage is not portable. The incentive of workers under both systems is to consume as much medical care as possible—since medical care is a use-it-or-lose-it benefit.

Disability Benefits for Veterans

Given the sacrifices they have made in wars they probably should never have been fighting, veterans who file for disability benefits will not be begrudged by most Americans. That's understandable. But veterans themselves are blowing the whistle on a system that appears to be wasting a lot of money that could be better spent. Writing in the *New York Times*, Ken Harbaugh, a former navy pilot and mission commander, acknowledges that:

> Today, it is taboo to question the honor of a veteran seeking compensation, and those who dare challenge the benefits system are deemed insufficiently patriotic.[32]

Yet he goes on to say:

> [W]hile most vets who receive disability checks deserve them, one of the worst-kept secrets among those seeking a disability rating is that the system can be beaten. Claim the right combination of symptoms, whether you are suffering or not, and there is a decent chance you can get a monthly disability check, tax free, for the rest of your life. There are even blogs out there to walk you through the process of claiming an injury that cannot be disproved.[33]

Harbaugh argues that some of the $60 billion a year we are spending on veterans' disability payments could help veterans more if it were spent in other ways. These sentiments are echoed by Stanford University professor Mark Duggan, who suggests that disability payments risk becoming a means of paying people not to work. Duggan writes:

> A large body of research has investigated the effect of federal disability programs on the labor market. US-based studies have focused almost exclusively on the Social Security Disability Insurance program.... [T]hese studies have tended to find that the program substantially reduces labor force participation.[34]

Duggan then goes on to say that studies of veterans are producing similar results, including his own study of Vietnam veterans—following the liberalization of disability benefits in 2001:

> Our estimates suggest that for every one hundred veterans made newly eligible for [disability] benefits as a result of the 2001 policy change, approximately eighteen dropped out of the labor force by 2017. This estimated average effect is similar to the results from recent research regarding the corresponding effect of the SSDI program on labor force participation.[35]

Individual Purchase of Disability Insurance

Prior to the Affordable Care Act, the tax law favored employer provision of health insurance over individual purchase, and that is still the case for upper-income families. Unless you qualify for one of the Obamacare tax subsidies or unless you qualify for the tax breaks available for the self-employed, if you are purchasing health insurance on your own, you basically have to do it with after-tax dollars. At work, by contrast, employers can purchase it for you (rather than pay taxable wages) with pretax dollars. If you are in the 50 percent tax bracket, for example, these differences add up to a lot of money.

The same rules apply to disability insurance. If you purchase it yourself, you must do it with after-tax dollars. Your employer can purchase it for you with pretax dollars. There is, however, this difference: If you have an employer-purchased plan, the disability income you receive is taxable. If you purchased your own policy, the income is nontaxable.

These provisions of the tax law make no sense. If there is a public policy reason to encourage disability insurance (and we assume there is), that reason doesn't vanish when people are forced to buy the insurance on their own accounts.

In general, private disability plans replace about two-thirds of your income if you are unable to work. The premium is typically 1 to 3 percent of your annual income—although that could be more after you are subject to a medical test and after you answer questions about risky activities in which you typically engage. As in the pre-Obamacare health insurance marketplace, there is "underwriting."

Large employers have traditionally offered disability insurance as a fringe benefit. But just as other benefits are becoming individualized (401[k] plans instead of defined benefit pensions, defined contribution health insurance instead of defined benefit, etc.), disability insurance is following the same course. Writing in the *New York Times*, Ron Lieber notes that:

> Many large employers still provide it gratis, but an increasing number are lowering the payouts and giving employees the option of purchasing more. Other employers may pay nothing toward the premium and simply give workers the opportunity to buy it with their own money via payroll deduction.[36]

8

The Risk of Facing a Major Health Event and Being Unable to Afford Needed Medical Care

Health Care

IN THE FIRST quarter of 2020 a revolution occurred in the way medical care was delivered in the United States. It occurred almost overnight.

People stopped going to hospital emergency rooms. They stopped going to doctors' offices. Most of the nation was self-isolating, as protection against the coronavirus. Doctors and patients were no exception.

They communicated by means of phone, email, Skype, Zoom, and other devices or services. In December 2019, Zoom was the host of ten million video conferences a day. Within three months, the company was hosting two hundred million video conferences a day.[1] Many of those were patient/doctor communications.

If you are like a great many people, you are probably wondering why it took so long. Think of the other professionals you deal with: lawyers, accountants, architects, engineers, etc. It's normal and natural to communicate with these folks by phone, email, or even video conferencing when face-to-face meetings are unnecessary. Why did it take so long for medicine to step into the twenty-first century?

Answer: government.

Before the coronavirus hit, it was basically illegal for doctors to treat Medicare patients by means of telemedicine. That was by law of Congress. State laws also interfered. You might be inclined to think that as long as you are going to video-conference, the doctor could be anywhere. State laws said otherwise. At the beginning of 2020, if you were a patient in Texas, the doctor on your video screen had to be licensed to practice in Texas. Doctors in Illinois, or even in neighboring Arkansas, were off limits.

It gets worse. I don't need to tell you that the coronavirus doesn't just strike during working hours. You are at risk on nights and weekends as well. What happens then? Direct primary care (what we used to call concierge medicine) has become increasingly popular, and it's cheap. Under one national model, the monthly cost is fifty dollars for a mother and ten dollars for a child.[2] For that, the family has 24/7 access to all primary care—including access by means of phone, email, etc. But until recently, this was illegal for Medicare patients. It was also illegal for employers to put money into a personal account so that employees could pay these monthly fees to the doctor of their choice.

It's almost sacrilegious to suggest that anything good can come from a lethal virus. But there was this totally unplanned and surprising blessing: the coronavirus forced politicians to deregulate the delivery of medical care. Although much of the deregulation was intended to be temporary, it's hard to imagine that voters will be willing to allow their newfound freedoms to be taken away.

We will have more to say about the coronavirus and the government's response in Chapter 10.

The Strange History of U.S. Health Reform

There has been strong interest in reforming U.S. health care for at least one hundred years. For most of that time it was the progressive left pushing for national health insurance. Yet at times the reform effort came from the right. President Nixon proposed national health insurance at a time when most Democrats were showing little interest. In the 2008 election, John McCain's health plan was a lot more radical than Barack Obama's.[3]

But what exactly do the reformers have in mind?

To me, an ideal health system would look a lot like the market for cell phone repairs. In the city where I live, I can pop into any one of a dozen or so repair facilities, without an appointment, and get high-quality, low-cost service. There are even firms that will send someone to my home and repair my iPhone in my condo.

If something happens to my body, on the other hand, the wait to see a new doctor in the United States is three weeks.[4] In Boston, where we were told there was "universal coverage" even before there was Obamacare, there is an extra month of waiting.[5] Before the coronavirus crisis, the average wait in a California hospital emergency room was five-and-a-half hours. At one hospital, almost one in ten patients left without ever seeing a doctor or completing their care—presumably because they got tired of waiting.[6]

If the reformers told me they want to make the market for medical care look a lot like the market for cell phone repair, they would get my attention in a heartbeat. They don't come close to saying that, however.

What I want to know is: how is a real patient going to interact with a real doctor under the reform? I can almost never find out.

Let's consider a handful of reform ideas: Obamacare itself, the Republican (Paul Ryan) plan to replace it, the Bernie Sanders plan to provide Medicare for all, and the half dozen other Democratic proposals to expand Medicare that came up during the 2020 election season.

What do any of these plans have to say about my being able to talk to my doctor by phone? Not a word. What about being able to email my doctor day or night? Zilch.

How about video conferencing? Nada. How about reducing the time patients spend waiting in ERs? Zero. How about reducing the time it takes to actually see a doctor? Nope, not at all.

I hope this short trek through the reformers' jungle convinces you that health reform in all its guises has almost nothing to do with real patients, real doctors, and how people are going to get medical care.

So what is health reform typically about? It's usually about blurry, unfocused, ill-formed, ill-thought-out ideas—usually just emotions—that are rarely explained, properly examined, or even acknowledged. I'll briefly go over the most important ideas below.

But first, let's give our health care system its due.

The last time you were anywhere near a hospital, did you see any patients dumped out on the sidewalk because they could not pay their bill? I haven't seen that either.

Our doctors and hospitals are willing to spend more than a million dollars to save a premature baby that other countries would allow to die—even if the parents pay nothing. We are willing to pay astronomical fees for lifesaving medicines that other countries refuse to purchase.

In the United Kingdom, the National Health Service actually puts a price on life, deciding how much it will spend on care for patients in critical condition. The cutoff: if the cost of care is judged to be more than $37,000 for each "quality" year of a patient's life, the care is not provided.[7] In the United States, the sky's the limit.

The most common complaint about U.S. health care is that it discriminates against people based on their ability to pay. Yet take a look at figure 8.1. People at the top of the income ladder pay substantially more than others to support our health care system. In fact, the more you earn, the more you pay. The receipt of care is the other way around. The less you earn, the more care you get. People in the bottom fifth of the income distribution get $12,130 in health care spending per person every year—50 percent more than people in the top fifth of the income distribution.

Overall, I would guess that the U.S. health care system is more progressive than the U.K. system. It may even be more progressive than the Canadian system. The idea that U.S. health care systematically discriminates against

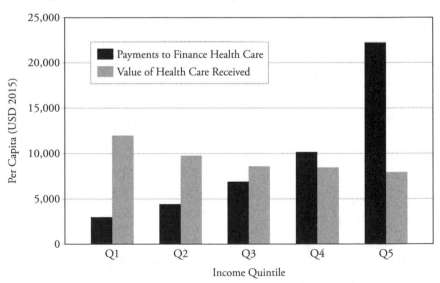

Figure 8.1 US Health Care Financing and Value Received, by Income

Source: Katherine Grace Carman, Jodi Liu, and Chapin White. "Accounting for the Burden and Redistribution of Health Care Costs: Who Uses Care and Who Pays for It." *Health Services Research.* April 2020.

people based on their income—at least in comparison to other countries—is one of a whole slew of myths perpetrated by people who argue that ours is the worst health care system in the developed world.[8]

In this chapter we are going to take a critical look at the U.S. health care system. We will find much that needs to be changed. But our most important problems do not arise because we are different from other countries. They arise because we are so very much alike.

Time and Money

Most Americans probably believe there is a significant difference between the U.S. health care system and the system north of our border. After all, this was a continuing theme of Bernie Sanders's stump speeches.

In fact, the two systems are about 80 percent the same. In Canada when you see a doctor, it's free. In the United States, it's almost free. Every time we spend a dollar at a doctor's office, less than ten cents comes out of our own pocket. The other ninety cents come from a third party—an employer, an insurance company, or the government.

In both countries the primary way we pay for care is not with money. It's with time. A recurring theme of critics on the left is that no one should ever have to choose between health care and other uses of money. Yet most of the time we never have to.

The reason the market for cell phone repair works so well is that entrepreneurs know that they can make millions of dollars if they meet our needs. In health care, by contrast, we have so completely suppressed the market that none of us ever sees a real price for anything—no patient, no doctor, no employer, no employee.

People pay for almost every good or service they buy in two ways—with time and with money. In health care, the left is obsessed with the idea of eliminating money prices. Yet when you suppress the price system, you invariably elevate the importance of nonprice barriers to care.

What are nonprice barriers? Think of how long it takes you on the phone to make an appointment with a doctor. How many days, weeks, or months must you wait until you see the doctor? How long does it take to get to the doctor's office and back again? How long do you have to wait once you are there?

Those are nonprice barriers. Even for low-income people, they are generally more important obstacles to obtaining care than the fees that doctors charge.[9]

In Dallas, where I live, there is a free clinic. Patients can go there and get primary care without any out-of-pocket charge. The clinic opens at 8:00 a.m. The other morning a young man arrived at 4:00 a.m. in order to be one of the first patients treated. If he earned fifteen dollars an hour at a job, that wait cost him sixty dollars of time. I assume if he showed up later in the day, the wait would have been much longer.

People on the left do not advocate long waits. But they believe that almost any amount of waiting—even people dying while they are on the waiting list—is an acceptable burden to bear if that is what it takes to abolish money prices from the health care system. And they have largely succeeded in shaping the way medical care is delivered in this country.

In what follows we will briefly review some additional problems with U.S. health care, with special attention to why this market doesn't work as well as the market for cell phone repair, or just about any other market in which you are a consumer.

How Federal and State Policies Affect Private Health Insurance

The most important problems in health care are not natural or inevitable. They are instead the artificial byproduct of the systematic suppression of normal market forces over the course of the twentieth century.[10] Today, federal and state policies have six pernicious effects on the medical marketplace. They (1) encourage millions of people to choose not to acquire health insurance, (2) encourage people who have insurance to overinsure, (3) encourage people to choose public insurance at taxpayer expense rather than private insurance at their own expense, (4) encourage job-specific insurance over portable insurance, (5) encourage third-party payment of medical bills rather than individual self-insurance, and (6) effectively outlaw the type of real insurance common in other markets.

Problem: Discouraging Health Insurance for People Who Don't Have It.
Federal and state laws increasingly have made it easy for people to obtain

insurance after they get sick. Beyond a brief waiting period, for example, employers cannot exclude an employee from a health plan nor charge a higher premium because of a health condition. Prior to the Affordable Care Act, in five states, the same regulation applied to private health insurance. Today, the ACA makes it illegal to deny coverage or charge a higher premium to anyone because of a health condition.

This makes it tempting for people to stay uninsured while they are healthy and obtain insurance only after they get sick and need medical care.

For several years, Obamacare tried to discourage this practice by imposing a tax penalty on people who were uninsured. However, the penalty was small, it apparently was weakly enforced, and the exemptions were so numerous and so liberal that the Congressional Budget Office predicted that 90 percent of the uninsured in 2016 would be exempt from the individual mandate. Even so, in 2016, 6.5 million people paid a tax penalty rather than purchase private insurance and roughly twenty-eight million people remained uninsured.[11]

In 2017, a Republican Congress abolished the penalty for being uninsured, but left in place the requirement that virtually all employers and all health insurers accept all applicants on the same terms and conditions, regardless of health status. This, of course, strengthens the incentive for people to remain uninsured until they get sick. That may explain why there has been very little increase in the number of people with private insurance over the past decade.[12]

Problem: Encouraging Too Much Insurance for People Who Have It. More than 90 percent of people with private health insurance receive it as a fringe benefit from an employer. Because employer-paid health insurance premiums are not included in the employee's taxable income, many workers effectively avoid a 25 percent income tax, a 15.3 percent Social Security (FICA) tax, and a 2 to 9 percent state and local income tax. Furthermore, by taking advantage of a special provision in the tax law, employees can pay their share of the premium with pretax dollars as well.

Although the FICA tax nominally is divided between the employer and the employee, economic studies show the full burden falls on the employee. Thus, the ability of employers and employees to obtain a nontaxed benefit as an alternative to taxable wages is the ability to avoid giving up as much as half the amount spent to the government. Put another way, the government (i.e., taxpayers) effectively pays as much as fifty cents of every dollar spent on health insurance provided by employers to average-wage employees.

The federal tax subsidy for employer-provided health insurance is an open-ended subsidy. The more health insurance that employers and employees buy, the less is available for taxable wages. Overall, 155 million Americans who get health insurance at work can always lower their taxes by obtaining more insurance.

Problem: Encouraging Public Rather than Private Coverage. Prior to the Affordable Care Act, most of America's uninsured had no opportunity to obtain tax-favored health insurance. If they bought private insurance at all, they had to pay with after-tax dollars. The Affordable Care Act provides federal funding to expand Medicaid, covering everyone who earns up to 138 percent of the federal poverty level, provided that the state in which they live accepts the expansion. Further, if people qualify for Medicaid, the ACA makes them ineligible for subsidized private insurance in the (Obamacare) health insurance exchanges.

In general, the expansion of free, public insurance crowds out private insurance. MIT professor Jonathan Gruber, who is often credited with being the intellectual designer of Obamacare, and Harvard University health economist David Cutler estimate that every extra dollar of Medicaid spending causes the private sector to contract by as much as seventy-five cents. For CHIP (children's health insurance), the crowd-out is as high as sixty cents. In other words, people stop paying private premiums when government insurance is offered to them for free.

A more recent study by Steven Pizer and colleagues estimates even larger crowding-out rates among people between 100 and 133 percent of the poverty line, the very people who have become newly eligible for Medicaid under the ACA in many states. The authors write:

> We find that Medicaid eligibility expansion will have relatively small effects on the number of uninsured, with about four-fifths of the public expansion crowding out private coverage.[13]

The Congressional Budget Office also predicted crowd-out in the CHIP program—as much as 50 percent.[14] Why are these estimates important? Because they suggest a large burden is being shifted to taxpayers with a small gain in return.

In general, moving from private insurance to Medicaid or CHIP makes access worse, not better, because Medicaid's reimbursements to doctors are well below what private insurance pays. Moreover, almost no state allows Medicaid funds to be used to enroll beneficiaries in an employer's health plan, and Medicaid eligibility makes people ineligible for subsidized private insurance in the exchanges.

Are the findings that public insurance crowds out private insurance consistent with our experience under Obamacare? It's too soon to tell. The economic studies focused on one-time expansions of public programs, other things being equal. Obamacare brought with it an on-again, off-again individual health insurance mandate, an employer mandate, and enactment during an economic expansion in which more people have jobs and access to employer-provided coverage. Future studies will have to sort all these changes out.

A study posted at the National Bureau of Economic Research working paper site compared nine states that expanded their Medicaid programs (in response to the incentives created under Obamacare) with twelve states that didn't expand. Under the law, states are able to expand eligibility to families up to 138 percent of the poverty level, nearly $36,000 for a family of four. However, the economists discovered that, in the expansion states, the income limits were apparently not enforced. It appears that people were able to enroll in Medicaid regardless of income![15]

As for crowd-out, writing in the *Wall Street Journal*, Brian Blase and Aaron Yelowitz report that "employer-sponsored coverage has steadily grown in non-expansion states with virtually no growth in expansion states."[16]

Problem: Outlawing Portable Insurance. As noted, prior to the Affordable Care Act, most people who did not have the opportunity to get insurance from an employer received no tax advantage when they purchased health insurance.[17] If they bought private insurance at all, they had to pay with after-tax dollars. They first paid taxes on their income and then purchased the insurance with what was left over. Under Obamacare, this is still the case for middle- and upper-middle-income families. About 40 percent of people in the individual market are not eligible for Obamacare subsidies because their income is too high. As a result, millions of people are encouraged to have group insurance rather than individually owned insurance.

One disadvantage of employer-based insurance is that employees must switch health plans whenever they switch employers. Before there were insurance company networks, this defect imposed less of a hardship because employees generally were free to see any doctor under any plan. Today, however, changing jobs often means changing doctors as well. For an employee or family member with a health problem, that means no continuity of care. Individually owned insurance that travels with employees as they move from job to job would allow employees to establish long-term relations both with insurers and with doctors. Yet portable health insurance largely was impossible under federal tax and employee benefit laws, even prior to Obamacare. The reason: employers were not allowed to buy individually owned insurance for their employees with pretax dollars.

Despite these barriers, some employers got away with the practice anyway. Although insurance brokers were not supposed to take premium checks if they suspected that the employer was putting up the money, many states allowed the brokers to cash the checks anyway under a policy of "don't ask, don't tell." The Obama administration brought this activity to a grinding halt, however, by threatening employers who engaged in the practice with draconian fines.

Interestingly, the Trump administration has completely reversed course. As of January 1, 2020, employers are now allowed to fund the employee purchase of individually owned, portable health insurance with pretax dollars. The administration estimates that eleven million people will eventually take advantage of this opportunity. But if state governments can clean up the problems in the individual health insurance market (described below), the number could be one hundred million.

Problem: Encouraging Third-Party Insurance Rather than Individual Self-Insurance. The most common source of problems in our health care system is the fact that most of the time people do not bear the full cost of their bad decisions or realize the full benefits of their good ones. On the buyer side of the medical marketplace, this means that patients who wastefully overuse health care resources usually pay only a small fraction of the cost of that waste.[18] Conversely, patients who economize and avoid waste usually reap only a small fraction of the savings from their frugality.

How the Trump Administration Has Changed Obamacare Regulations

In an ideal world, most people would own their own health insurance and take it with them as they travel from job to job and in and out of the labor market. Some employers may offer better insurance than people can find in the open market. But most employers would prefer to make a cash contribution to help employees pay their own premiums rather than provide insurance directly.

Before there was Obamacare, this is what some employers were actually doing.

They used an account called a Health Reimbursement Arrangement (HRA), providing funds employees could use to buy their own health insurance. These funds were not taxed as income to the employee, just as employer-provided insurance isn't taxed.

There was always legal uncertainty about this practice, however. Many insurance agents were fearful that if they knew the policies they sold were being purchased with employer money, they could be penalized. So, it was common practice for everyone to act on the principle of "don't ask, don't tell."

Then came Obamacare.

The Obama administration didn't just dislike the practice of employers helping employees obtain their own insurance. They hated the idea. An Obama regulation stipulated that employers caught giving their employees pretax dollars to purchase their own coverage could be fined as much as $100 per day for each employee, or $36,500 a year. This was the highest penalty in all of the Obamacare regulations.

Thankfully, the Trump administration has eliminated this penalty and much more. As of January 1, 2020, employers are able to use HRAs to help employees obtain their own coverage with the federal government's blessing.[19]

This regulatory change is coming at the right time. Readers may be surprised to learn that the extent of private insurance coverage has barely changed under Obamacare, despite huge federal subsidies in the

(Sidebar continued on the next page)

individual market and a government mandate requiring most employers to offer coverage. In fact, employer coverage has actually contracted.[20]

The biggest losses are among small businesses. Among firms that employ three to twenty-four workers, the percentage of employees covered by employer health benefits fell from 44 percent in 2010 to 30 percent in 2018. Among firms that employ twenty-four to twenty-nine workers, the percentage fell from 59 percent in 2010 to 44 percent in 2018.

Moreover, 27 percent of employees of small- and medium-sized firms (3 to 199 workers) turn down their employer's offer of health insurance. This is probably because Obamacare mandates have made all insurance more expensive and less attractive.

Will employees be able to find better coverage in today's individual market? That may depend on where they live. An acquaintance of mine in New York City has seen her individual market premium jump five-fold in the past four years. She now pays more than $25,000 for a family coverage with a high deductible and an increasingly narrow network of providers. Not many employees will envy her experience. Some states, however, have obtained Obamacare waivers. By using dedicated funds for high-cost enrollees, they are allowing premiums to fall for everyone else.

Employees may also benefit because of another Trump administration change. Employers are allowed to deposit up to $1,800 a year in an "excepted benefit HRA," and these funds can be used to purchase short-term, limited-duration insurance. This insurance does not have to comply with Obamacare regulations, including their prohibition on basing premiums on the health condition of the applicant. Traditionally, such plans only lasted up to one year, and they were purchased by people who were transitioning between jobs or from school to work.

To discourage their use, the Obama administration limited these plans to three months' duration. However, the Trump administration reversed that regulation and extended the duration to three years. It also allows people to buy a second kind of insurance that I call "health-status insurance." This second plan protects people from any extra premium they might be charged in a second three-year period, should their health condition deteriorate during the first three-year period.

(Sidebar continued on the next page)

By stringing together these two types of insurance, people will be able to purchase insurance that meets family needs, rather than the needs of bureaucrats and regulators—indefinitely, into the future. People will be able to purchase, say, a Blue Cross plan similar in benefits and price to what they could obtain before there was Obamacare.

Note, however, that state governments can sharply curtail these plans and even regulate them out of existence. Several blue states have already done so.

In promoting these reforms, President Trump has exercised a very aggressive use of executive authority. He is also providing needed leadership to a party that has lost its way when it comes to health policy.

In the last several years, the only Republican plan to reform Obamacare that included personal and portable insurance and health-status insurance was a bill sponsored by House Rules Committee Chairman Pete Sessions and Sen. Bill Cassidy. (Fair disclosure: I helped write it.) The other proposals, including ones preferred by the Republican leadership, did little more than help Obamacare work better.[21]

The reforms discussed here were well known (because regulatory changes invite public comments) before the last election. Can you think of a single Republican candidate in the 2018 election who campaigned on these reforms? I can't. Nor was there even a single congressional hearing designed to showcase the need for the reforms.

Trump has also taken on the special interests. Almost all the major players in health policy—especially the large insurance companies—oppose these changes. But just as he took on the pharmaceutical companies on drug prices and the hospitals on price transparency (and is being sued by both industries), the president doesn't seem to hesitate when Big Insurance objects.

Executive action can only go so far, however. Obamacare is still law. To fully realize the Trump vision of health reform, Congress needs to act. That means that Republicans and Democrats must ignore all the special interests and support reforms that work for ordinary citizens.

The culprit, again, is the tax law. Although employer-paid premiums are generously subsidized, deposits to an account from which individuals can pay medical bills directly receive no such subsidy. The exceptions are Health Savings Accounts (HSAs) and Health Reimbursement Arrangements (HRAs). Even though HSA and HRA plans are the fastest-growing products in the health insurance marketplace, many workers still do not have access to these accounts, and the complexities of federal tax law and employee benefits law are restricting their use as a way of empowering patients and curtailing costs. HRAs are only available to employees. People with individually owned insurance can have an HSA. But most plans sold on the (Obamacare) exchanges do not have an HSA option.

Another exception is the Flexible Savings Account (FSA). But these accounts are use-it-or-lose-it accounts. Any money left in the account at year-end must be forfeited. As a result, employers rarely contribute to these accounts or make them an integrated part of an employer health plan.[22]

One consequence of these policies is that third parties—employers, insurance companies, or government—pay almost all the medical bills:

- For every dollar spent on hospital care, the patient pays only about three cents out of pocket, on the average; ninety-seven cents are paid by a third party.
- For every dollar spent on physician services, the patient pays less than ten cents out of pocket, on the average.
- For the health care system as a whole, every time patients consume one dollar in services, they pay only twelve cents out of pocket.[23]

Thus, patients have an incentive to consume hospital services until they are worth only three cents on the dollar, on the average. The incentive is to consume physicians' services until they are worth only ten cents on the dollar. And for the health care system as a whole, patients have an incentive to utilize everything modern medicine offers until the value to them is only twelve cents out of the last dollar spent.[24]

On the provider side of the market, incentives likewise are distorted. Health care providers rarely reap the benefits of eliminating waste or being better at what they do. Consider:

- In a normal market, producers compete vigorously to meet consumer needs; in fact, the more unmet needs that exist, the greater are producers' opportunities.

- In a normal market, firms compete based on price and quality; in fact, price reductions and quality enhancements are the principal ways to attract customers and boost profits.

In health care, by contrast, these normal market processes are subverted:

- Providers have a financial incentive to avoid the sickest patients with the hardest cases, rather than compete to attract them.

- Doctors, hospitals, and other providers rarely vie for patients based on price or quality; in fact, they rarely compete at all, in any meaningful sense.

Problem: Outlawing Real Insurance. Well-developed insurance markets exist for a wide variety of unforeseen, risky events: life insurance (for an unforeseen death), automobile liability insurance (for an unforeseen automobile accident), fire and casualty insurance (for unforeseen damage to property), and disability insurance (for unforeseen physical injuries).[25] Indeed, virtually every risk is, in principle, insurable. The amount to be reimbursed is based on the damage the risky event produces. Once the event has occurred and the damage has been assessed, the insurer writes a check to the policyholder for the agreed-upon amount. Policyholders usually are free to do whatever they prefer with the money they receive.

In the market for health insurance, however, things are very different. Often, there need not be any unexpected event to trigger insurance payments. Once it is determined that a health insurer owes something, the amount to be paid is not a predetermined sum but instead varies with the consumption decisions of the policyholder. Finally, payment is made not to the insured but to medical providers, based on the treatment decisions that are made. These differences shape the way the health insurance market functions. In fact, in many respects, health insurance is not insurance at all. In many respects, it is instead prepayment for the consumption of medical care.

Consider a typical television or magazine advertisement by casualty insurers. Invariably, they try to sell insurance based on the viewer's expected need for their product.[26] Health insurance advertisements, on the other hand, almost never even talk about why you might actually need their product—unless by need you mean services that healthy people want (wellness checkups, preventive care, exercise facilities, etc.).

The difference? The casualty insurance market is a real market for risk in which real insurance is bought and sold. The health insurance market, by contrast, is an artificial market in which the price paid rarely ever reflects an individual's anticipated health care costs.

The fact that prices are artificially suppressed in the market for health care risks has two bad consequences. On the buyer side, people who are undercharged for coverage will overinsure. Relative to their needs, health insurance will appear relatively cheap. On the other hand, people who are overcharged for coverage will underinsure. Relative to their needs, insurance will appear very expensive.

On the seller side, insurers will recognize that they are making profits on the relatively healthy and losses on the relatively unhealthy. In marketing their products, they will try to attract the healthy and avoid the sick. After enrollment, their incentive will be to overprovide to the healthy (to keep the ones they have and attract more just like them) and underprovide to the sick (to encourage their exit from the plan and discourage enrollment by those just like them).

These are terrible incentives for institutions empowered to make decisions with life or death consequences.

The Affordable Care Act

Unfortunately, the Affordable Care Act, or "Obamacare," is making most of these problems worse in a number of ways. Even though the law has succeeded in insuring additional people, it is encouraging public insurance over private insurance; it is trying to force employers to provide more nonportable insurance; it is restricting the availability of self-insurance; and it is creating even more perverse incentives in the market for health insurance.

As I explained in *A Better Choice: Healthcare Solutions for America*, major changes in the law are needed urgently. These are changes that will require

Why Employers Pay Too Much for Health Care

Did you know that employers are paying hospitals more than twice as much as what Medicare pays?[27] At some hospitals they are paying four times as much. Those are the findings from a study by the RAND Corporation.[28]

It wasn't always so. In fact, as recently as 2000, private payers were paying only 10 percent more than Medicare. Since then, the gap has been growing by leaps and bounds.[29]

What makes this especially surprising is that it has happened at a time when employers have been getting increasingly aggressive about controlling health care costs.

So, what's going wrong? And who's to blame? In my opinion, employers are to blame.

A few employers are smart buyers of care. Rosen Hotels & Resorts in Orlando, for example, is spending from one-half to two-thirds of what other employers typically spend. By contrast, most employers are making four big mistakes.[30]

Before getting to that, let's dispense with a misconception that is popular both on the political left and in the business community. That's the idea that, because the federal government is such a large buyer of care, it can force hospitals to cough up large discounts that an ordinary employer has no hope of negotiating.

If that notion sounds sensible to you, consider that thousands of Canadians come to the United States every year for medical care—often because they are tired of waiting for care in their home country. For such big-ticket items as hip and knee replacements, these individuals (foreigners no less, without any government or employer bargaining for them) manage to pay prices similar to what Medicare pays.

Canadians use agencies to help them connect with providers. But these agencies don't discriminate. Whatever the Canadians are doing, you and I can do as well.

(Sidebar continued on the next page)

MediBid is another service available to everyone. It facilitates transactions between doctors and patients online. Last year the firm facilitated 7,575 transactions resulting in almost $75 million in billed charges. In almost all cases, the fees patients pay are equal to Medicare rates—or even less.[31]

Is this something employers can do? Indeed, it is. Empowering employees with money and letting them negotiate on their own may be far more effective than anything the employer is likely to achieve.

Several years ago, the health insurer Anthem discovered that the charges for hip and knee replacements in California were all over the map, ranging from $15,000 to $110,000. Yet there were forty-six hospitals that routinely averaged $30,000 or less. So, Anthem entered an agreement with CalPERS (the health plan for California state employees, retirees, and their families) to pay for these procedures in a different way.[32] Patients were encouraged to go to one of the forty-six hospitals. They were free to go elsewhere, but they were told in advance that Anthem would pay no more than $30,000 for a joint replacement.

The result: although 30 percent of the enrollees went to "out-of-network" hospitals, the cost of care at these hospitals was cut by one-third in the first year and quickly fell below the $30,000 benchmark.

Think about that. The insurer made no phone calls. Sent no letters. There was no bargaining. No discussions whatever. Employees were sent into the medical marketplace knowing they only had so much money to spend. And voilà! Prices came down.

So, what is the typical employer doing wrong? Ignoring four principles. One of them I learned from the president. The other three I learned from people I have worked with.

The Donald Trump Principle: "Be prepared to walk away from the table."

Before there was Obamacare, executives of Blue Cross of Texas told me their basic employer plan included every single hospital in the Dallas/

(Sidebar continued on the next page)

Fort Worth area—no matter how poor the quality or how high the cost. (At last count there were eighty-three of them.)

When Blue Cross entered the Obamacare exchange, it offered similar plans, and the result was disastrous. By some estimates, the insurer lost more than a billion dollars before it changed course.

The most successful Obamacare insurer in the country is Centene— which has captured one-fifth of the entire market nationwide. Centene started out as a Medicaid contractor. The private plans it offers in the individual market look like Medicaid with a high deductible. (In most places, Medicaid rates are about 10 percent less than Medicare.)[33]

If a doctor or hospital refuses to accept Centene's low fees, they are excluded from the Centene network.

Any health insurer that is still surviving in the individual market is likely following Centene's example. That means you cannot buy individual insurance in Dallas that includes UT Southwestern, probably the best medical research facility in the world. You can't buy individual insurance in Texas that includes MD Anderson in Houston, one of the top cancer treatment facilities in the country.

But employers need not follow in Centene's footsteps, and they don't have to live with the perverse incentives Obamacare has created for individual insurance. Ideally, they should aim for a network of providers that are both low cost and high quality.

The individual market shows conclusively that private buyers can lower their costs a lot if they are willing to say "no" to some providers.

The John Von Kannon Principle: "Have airline ticket, will travel."

Which hospitals are giving Canadians and MediBid patients 50 percent off? One could easily be a hospital right next door to you. Hospitals are willing to give traveling patients deals that they won't give those of us who live nearby. The reason? Hospitals believe that if you live in their neighborhood, they're going to get your business, regardless.

(Sidebar continued on the next page)

The "medical tourism market," as it's sometimes called, has three requirements: (1) you have to be willing to travel, (2) you have to pay up front, and (3) there can be no insurance company interference after the fact.[34]

John Von Kannon was for many years treasurer of the Heritage Foundation and probably the best fundraiser for right-of-center causes in the country. His theory of successful fundraising: you must travel to see the donors.

Eventually, hospital competition will come to your neighborhood. For the time being, the Von Kannon principle applies to health care as well as to fundraising.

The Gerald Musgrave Principle: "Economizing must benefit the economizers."

Health City Cayman Islands hospital attracts patients from all over the Caribbean, from Central and South America, and from the United States.[35] The cost is similar to what Medicare pays. The quality appears to be better than what is typical in the United States. So why aren't more employers taking advantage of it?

Some employers have tried medical travel by offering to waive the deductible for the employee. That means the employee saves, say, $1,000 so that the employer can save $15,000. They wonder why the employees don't jump at the opportunity.

Dr. Musgrave was my coauthor for *Patient Power,* and he helped develop the idea of Health Savings Accounts. Years ago, he recognized that people don't economize on spending in order to save money for someone else—especially their employer.[36]

Employers should consider giving all the savings of medical travel to the employees. Every study that has ever been done on the matter has concluded that employee benefits eventually substitute dollar-for-dollar

(Sidebar continued on the next page)

for wages. That means the reason to lower health care costs is not to save the employer money. It's to increase employee take-home pay.

It appears that some employers are learning. In July 2019, the wife of an employee of the Mississippi firm Ashley Furniture Industries traveled to Cancún for a total knee replacement at Galenia Hospital. Although the hospital is highly rated in its own right, she was joined by a highly rated American surgeon who flew in from Milwaukee and performed the operation. The entire procedure cost the employer $12,000 instead of the $30,000 it would have cost back in the United States.[37]

This arrangement solved several problems. To overcome the natural concern of patients that out-of-the-country care may not be of acceptable quality, a doctor trained at the Mayo Clinic performed the surgery. All out-of-pocket costs to the patient were waived, and the employer paid travel and hotel costs as well. The company cut its costs in half. And when the patient got home, she was given a check for $5,000.

The Thomas Smith Principle: "I was never conned by someone I didn't like."

There is very little difference today between a garden-variety, nonprofit hospital and one that is for profit. They do the same things. They operate the same way. Yet all too often, nonprofit hospitals pose as charities. Employers are encouraged to believe that supporting these institutions is a civic duty.[38]

Tom Smith was for many years the chairman of a think tank I started, and I learned much from his leadership. If you're wondering if this particular principle applies in your community, check out how many executives of the nonprofit hospital next door are making seven-figure salaries.

To employers who want to stop wasting money on health care, I urge you to pay attention to all four principles.

bipartisan cooperation—something that is rare in health policy. The changes are needed because at least six major problems aren't going away.[39]

Impossible mandates. Obamacare was introduced with two mandates: a mandate for most individuals to obtain health insurance and a mandate for most employers to provide health insurance.[40] Each mandate was enforced by a tax penalty for those who failed to comply.

In 2017, a Republican Congress repealed the tax penalty for individuals who fail to insure, thereby eliminating the practice of coercing individuals into buying insurance. But the act did nothing to change insurance regulations. So, although individuals do not have to buy Obamacare insurance, the only thing insurers are allowed to sell is Obamacare insurance. Put differently, although the individual mandate has been effectively repealed on the buyer side of the market, it still remains in force on the supplier side. And, of course, the employer mandate is still in force.

What difference does this make?

The slowdown in the rate of increase in health care spending over the past decade is welcome news, but no one is predicting that health care spending will not exceed the growth of income in future years. In fact, for the past forty years, real per capita health care spending has been growing at twice the rate of growth of real per capita income. That's not only true in this country; it is about the average for the entire developed world.

You don't need to be an accountant or a mathematician to know that, if the price of something you are buying is growing faster than your income, it will crowd out everything else you are consuming. Health care spending will take more and more of the family budget. It will take an ever-larger share of workers' gross pay. The Affordable Care Act did not create this problem. But that law limits our ability to manage it by restricting our ability to choose a smaller, more sensible package of benefits, more cost sharing, etc. In short, the ACA is trying to force us to remain on an unsustainable path.

Further, the ACA contains three "global budgets," and (ironically) they are likely to make matters worse for ordinary citizens. The law restricts the growth of total Medicare spending, the growth of Medicaid hospital spending, and (after 2018) the growth of federal tax subsidies in the health insurance exchanges to no more than the rate of growth of real GDP per capita plus about one-half of a percent. This means that as health care costs become more and more of a burden for the average family, they will get less and less help from government through time.

The traditional idea of a global budget is to restrict overall spending. The global budgets in the ACA limit only the government's outlays.

Think about this for a moment. The law is trying to force all of us to purchase health insurance whose cost is likely to grow faster than our incomes. But government's share of the burden is capped—ensuring that more and more of the cost is shifted over time to ordinary citizens.

An obvious solution is to jettison the whole idea of a defined health insurance benefit. Instead, make a defined (tax subsidy) contribution to each family and let competition determine what benefits the market can provide for that sum of money.[41]

Bizarre Subsidies. A family of four at 138 percent of the federal poverty line is able to enroll in Medicaid in about half the states and obtain insurance that let's say costs about $16,000 per year.[42] Since the coverage is completely free, that's a $16,000 annual gift. If they earn one dollar more, they will be entitled to go into a health insurance exchange and obtain a private plan that costs, say, $14,000—but with substantial out-of-pocket exposure (deductibles and copayments). Most of that cost will be offset by a generous government subsidy, leaving the family with little more than $500 of out-of-pocket premium cost. That's a gift of about $13,500 per year. At the same time, a hotel employing people earning pretty much the same wage is legally required to offer an expensive family plan, and the hotel and its employees are getting no new help from the government (beyond the tax advantages that preceded Obamacare). Assuming that all employee benefits are dollar-for-dollar substitutes for wages, and after calculating the value of employers' ability to pay premiums with pretax dollars, let's call that a newly created $10,000 burden. This example illustrates only one of scores of ways in which ACA's treatment of people is arbitrary and unfair.

But the biggest problem is not unfairness. It is the real impact the law's differential subsidies are having on our economy. For low-income families, the subsidy in the Obamacare exchange is much higher than the tax advantage of employer purchase. For middle- and higher-income families, the reverse is true: the tax subsidy at work is quite generous, and there is no subsidy in the exchange.

As businesses discover that almost everyone who earns less than the average wage gets a better deal from the federal government in the exchanges or from Medicaid, and most people who earn more than the average wage get a better deal if insurance is provided at work, they have an incentive to change their employee benefit packages radically and maybe even restructure the organization of entire firms.

Since the employer mandate doesn't apply to firms with fewer than fifty employees, small businesses have an incentive to stay small. Since the mandate doesn't apply to part-time workers or contract labor, employers have an incentive to prefer part-time workers and independent contractors over full-time employees.

These changes may be well underway in Silicon Valley, where janitors, bus drivers, food service workers, and security guards who staffed corporate campuses in times past might have been employed directly by the businesses for which they cooked lunches, cleaned floors, etc. Today those workers are much more likely to be independent contractors. One study, extrapolating from the size of the tech industry in Silicon Valley's two counties, estimated that between nineteen thousand and thirty-nine thousand people are contracted to work for tech companies, along with potentially seventy-eight thousand workers in contracted jobs more broadly. Although this trend was well underway before the passage of the Affordable Care Act, Obamacare no doubt is encouraging its acceleration.

All of these perversions have a common source: treating people at the same income level very differently depending on where they get their insurance, how many hours they work, how many other employees they work with, etc.

A straightforward solution is available: make the tax subsidy for health insurance the same regardless of where people get it. It would be even better if we let people on Medicaid leave the program and claim a tax credit to buy private insurance instead. At a minimum, this would liberate the job market from the arbitrary burdens of health insurance reform.

Perverse Incentives for Health Plans. Before the ACA went fully into effect, insurers in most states were allowed to charge individuals premiums that reflected their expected health care costs.[43] This practice is no different from what it is in life insurance, casualty insurance, or almost any other kind of insurance. However, since these other forms of insurance are not usually obtained through employers, people don't lose coverage when they switch jobs. By encouraging everyone to have group health insurance, federal tax law virtually created the problem of preexisting conditions. Before Obamacare, people with health problems could face higher premiums, exclusions, and even outright denials of coverage after they leave their group and try to obtain insurance on their own. This didn't happen very often. But it happened enough to cause people to worry.

The ACA solved this problem in the worse possible way. Insurers are now required to practice community rating, under which the healthy and the sick are charged the same rate. (The ACA permits insurers to consider only four factors in setting premiums: individual versus family enrollment, geographic area, age, and tobacco use.[44])

You don't have to be in the health insurance business to understand what kind of incentives the ACA's rating restrictions create for insurers. With few exceptions, it is in the self-interest of every insurer to attract the healthy and avoid the sick. How might they do that? One way is to design plans that on the surface are more appealing to the healthy than to the sick.

Traditional insurance theory holds that patients should pay out of pocket for expenses that are small and over which they have a great deal of discretion. Insurance, on the other hand, should pay for expenses that are large and over which patients don't have much discretion. The insurance offered in the ACA exchanges turns that theory on its head, however.

Under a typical California plan, for example, patients make only nominal copayments when they see a doctor, get a blood test, or take an X-ray exam—measures that are often discretionary and the source of a great deal of unnecessary care. But if they go into a hospital, where patients have almost no control over what is done and no prior knowledge of what anything costs, they will be charged from 10 to 20 percent of the total bill. For an individual earning only a few thousand dollars above the poverty level, a hospital visit will cost $2,500. For a lower-to-middle-income patient, the charge will be $6,350. A moderate-income family can end up paying hospital expenses of $12,500—every year. Clearly, this plan will be attractive to people who don't plan to enter a hospital and unattractive to people for whom a hospital stay is likely.

Think of an insurance plan as having three main components: (1) a premium, (2) a list of covered benefits, and (3) a network of doctors, hospitals, and other providers. Under the ACA, benefits that insurers must offer are regulated strictly—right down to free contraceptives, questionable mammograms, and non–cost-effective preventive care procedures. At the same time, health plans have been given enormous freedom to set their own (community-rated) premiums and choose their own provider networks. They are using that freedom in yet another way to attract the healthy and avoid the sick.

In the ACA exchanges, the insurers apparently believe that only sick people (who plan to spend a lot of health care dollars) pay close attention to networks. Healthy people tend to buy on price. Thus, by keeping fees so low that only a minority of physicians will agree to treat the patients, some insurers are banking on attracting the healthy; and they may even have the good luck to scare away the sick.

Consider the incentives on the buyer side. In the ACA exchanges, if I were healthy, why wouldn't I buy on price? If I later develop cancer, I'll move to a plan that has the best cancer care. If I develop heart disease, I'll enter a plan with the best heart doctors. And these new plans will be prohibited from charging me more than the premium paid by a healthy enrollee.[45]

As a result, we are getting a race to the bottom on access—with private plans in the exchanges looking increasingly like Medicaid, just as they do in Massachusetts.[46] How is this affecting patients? According to a report in *USA Today*:

- Shawn Smith of Seymour, Indiana, spent about five months trying to find a primary care doctor on the network offered by a subsidized silver-level insurance plan.

- Jon Fougner, a recent Yale Law School graduate, sued Empire Blue Cross because he couldn't find a primary care doctor who would see him after calling thirty doctors' offices.[47]

These just are two examples of a much wider problem. A report from Avalere finds that the average provider networks for plans offered on the

(Obamacare) health insurance exchanges contract with 34 percent fewer providers than the average commercial plan offered outside the exchange. Specifically, the analysis finds that exchange plan networks embrace 42 percent fewer oncology and cardiology specialists; 32 percent fewer mental health and primary care providers; and 24 percent fewer hospitals.

Researchers at the Leonard David Institute of Health Economics approached the same issue in a different way. They categorized network sizes into five groups: extra small (fewer than 10 percent of the providers are participating), small (10 to 25 percent are participating), medium (25 to 40 percent), large (40 to 60 percent), and extra large (more than 60 percent). Given those categories, the researchers found that more than 40 percent of networks can be considered small or extra small, including 55 percent of networks in HMOs and 25 percent of PPO networks.

Since those studies were done, things have gotten worse. There has been a race to the bottom in terms of provider networks. Prior to Obamacare, patients who were uninsurable could often get risk-pool insurance that looked like a regular Blue Cross employer plan. Under Obamacare, they too often find themselves in networks that pay Medicaid rates and exclude the best doctors and the best hospitals.

The most successful Obamacare insurer, for example, is Centene—a company that had previously specialized in contracting with state governments to provide insurance to Medicaid patients. Centene has captured about one-fifth of the entire (Obamacare) individual insurance market. The product it offers is essentially Medicaid with a high deductible.

All too often insurers on the Obamacare exchanges are trying to attract the healthy and avoid the sick. In Dallas, for example, no individual insurance plan includes Southwestern Medical Center, which may be the best medical research center in the world. In Texas, generally, cancer patients with Obamacare insurance don't have access to MD Anderson Cancer Center in Houston. This pattern is repeated all over the country.[48]

The most successful Obamacare insurers are Medicaid contractors. The plans that have survived in the exchanges look like Medicaid managed care with a high deductible. The networks include only those doctors who will accept Medicaid fees coupled with all the hassle of managed-care bureaucracy.

Furthermore, if a doctor or facility is "out of network," the patient is responsible for 100 percent of the bill. Take the case of Robert Martin, an eighteen-year-old Los Angeles resident who hurt his ankle playing football. Before taking him to the emergency room, his mother was careful to make sure that the hospital was in her insurance plan's network. But after paying the required copayment, she received an additional $1,400 bill from the doctor. Even though the hospital was in-network, the doctor wasn't! Similar stories can be told about pharmacies and medical laboratories.

Think how different this is from what was promised. During the 2008 election, every serious candidate for the Democratic presidential nomination parroted the "universal coverage" mantra over and over again—and on the left "universal coverage" means universal access to care. No candidate even hinted that access to providers might not be any better than under Medicaid.

Incidentally, the problem here is not merely one of narrow networks and large deductibles—defects that you might suppose are fixable. The more general problem is that, in any system of managed competition, insurers have an incentive to underprovide to the sick.

There is a better way. Entities such as Cancer Treatment Centers of America need to be able to enter the individual market, restrict enrollment to patients who have cancer, and receive a premium that covers their expected costs.

Instead of expecting every health plan to be all things to all patients, we should encourage specialization. We need focused facilities for such chronic conditions as cancer care, diabetic care, and heart disease.[49] To make the market work better, medical records need to travel with the patient from plan to plan, and insurers need to be able to design risk-adjustment mechanisms under which plans compensate each other when high-cost patients move from one plan to another.[50]

Incentives for Health Insurance Buyers. The great fear of the Obama administration (and indeed the entire health insurance industry) was that millions of healthy people would avoid enrolling in the insurance exchanges during the first open-enrollment period.[51] That possibility was made more likely by a long, complicated enrollment form and an arduous enrollment procedure. Unless you were really sick and needed health insurance immediately, the temptation was to wait to enroll until you had a health care problem. To make matters worse, the healthy were being overcharged from the beginning.

In Massachusetts, people who game the system are called "jumpers" and "dumpers." They wait until they are sick to enroll and "jump in." Then, after they get the care they need and get their medical bills paid, they drop their coverage. Of course, if the only people who have health insurance are people who are sick, the cost of insurance will go right through the roof.

To combat this possibility, the Obama administration launched a desperate offensive prior to the exchanges' initial open-enrollment period, enlisting professional athletes, Hollywood actors, rock stars, librarians, and anybody else who could help persuade the healthy, especially the young and healthy, to join up.

Without a sufficient percentage of healthy enrollees, a state exchange could become vulnerable to a death spiral. This occurs when pricing in an insurance market spins out of control. If an insurance pool turns out to be more expensive than originally thought, the insurers must raise their premiums. As the premiums rise, some healthy people drop their coverage. With a sicker group of enrollees, the average cost per enrollee will be higher, and premiums must be raised again. That leads more healthy people to drop out—leading to more premium increases. This cycle continues until the only people left in the pool are very sick and very expensive to insure. They must be charged a premium that roughly equals the expected cost of their care. But that is a premium they can't afford, of course, and so it is a premium the insurer cannot collect. The ultimate end of a death spiral is the insurance pool equivalent of bankruptcy.[52]

The reasons for a death spiral are community rating and guaranteed issue (everyone is charged the same premium and the insurer must take all comers). Healthy people leave the pool because they are being overcharged. Sick people remain because they are being undercharged. This would not occur if each enrollee were charged a premium that reflects his/her actuarial risk.

The threat of a death spiral in the exchanges is made worse by five developments.

First, state risk pools and the federal (ACA) risk pools have closed and dumped their high-cost enrollees on the health insurance exchanges. On January 1, 2014, for example, the state of Texas formally ended its risk pool, and the twenty-three thousand people who were enrolled presumably sought coverage in the Texas exchange.[53] It was a good deal for the state, which had been spending more than $12,000 per enrollee operating the pool.[54] Other states followed suit. So did the ACA's risk pools—some run by state governments and some run by the federal government—which collectively were insuring about 107,000 people.[55]

Second, public and private employers are dumping their retirees onto the exchanges. City governments across the country have promised postretirement health care benefits to retirees who are not yet eligible for Medicare. This is the age group that is the most expensive to cover. Under the ACA, the exchanges receive federal subsidies, and the law limits premiums to no more than three times the premium charged to enrollees in their twenties (although the actual cost of coverage is more on the order of six to one). Detroit, for example, sent eight thousand city retirees to the Michigan exchange.[56]

The private sector is following suit. According to a Towers Watson survey, more than half of employers that offer health care benefits to pre–sixty-five-year-old and post–sixty-five-year-old retirees plan to discontinue them.[57]

Third, workers are no longer trapped in jobs they might otherwise have left because their health conditions would have caused them to pay much higher premiums in the individual market or to be denied insurance coverage altogether. Millions of people can now leave their employers' plans and enroll in an exchange, paying premiums well below the expected cost of their care.

Fourth, people can game the system from within the exchange. That is, they can buy a cheaper silver or bronze plan while they are healthy and then upgrade to platinum or gold if they develop a serious illness.

Finally, employers who self-insure (covering more than half of all insured workers) have options not available to other employers. They have more freedom to configure their plans in ways that are unattractive to the chronically ill, thereby encouraging them to quit work and seek coverage in the exchange.

Is there evidence that a death spiral is underway? Yes, among those people who buy individual insurance and do not receive a subsidy. No, among the part of the market that is subsidized. Obamacare subsidies phase out at close to $50,000 for single individuals and about $100,000 for a family of four. A report by the Centers for Medicare and Medicaid Services (CMS) finds that

Figure 8.2 Subsidized and Unsubsidized
Individual Market Average Monthly Enrollment

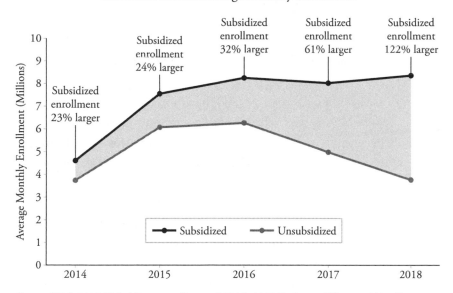

Source: 2014–2018 Risk Adjustment Data and 2014–2018 Exchange Effectuated Enrollment and Payment Data, https://www.cms.gov/CCIIO/Resources/Forms-Reports-and-Other-Resources/Downloads/Trends-Subsidized-Unsubsidized-Enrollment-BY17-18.pdf.

between 2016 and 2018 enrollment in unsubsidized individual plans dropped by 40 percent—or 2.5 million people (see figure 8.2).[58]

These people are apparently being priced out of the market by premium increases that nationwide jumped by 21 percent in 2017 and 26 percent in 2018.[59]

In some states, the drop-off was even more pronounced—91 percent in Iowa, 79 percent in Arizona, 78 percent in Nebraska, 76 percent in Tennessee, and 71 percent in Georgia and Oklahoma.[60]

In the subsidized part of the market, however, premium payments by buyers are capped as a percentage of income, and the cap is made possible by increased subsidy amounts to the insurers. So, if a person's income doesn't change, his out-of-pocket premium doesn't change either. As the total premium rises, the subsidy rises in lockstep. The government's unlimited ability to subsidize keeps the death spiral from ever happening.

That said, lots of people who are eligible for subsidies seem to be gaming the system. It appears that for every person who has subsidized individual insurance, two other eligible people are uninsured.[61]

Before leaving this section, let's go back to first principles: why did Obamacare impose a mandate in the first place? Clearly we don't want people to game the system. If they can wait until they get sick to insure, then pay the same premium as a healthy person would, and then drop their insurance after they get care and the bills are paid—the whole insurance system will be financially unsound. Even with a mandate in place, we were getting this kind of gaming. The people buying insurance in the exchanges were older and sicker, while a lot of healthy people were sitting on the sidelines. Without the mandate, the incentives to game the system are worse.

Yet here's something a lot of people have been ignoring. We have already found effective ways to deal with this problem without mandates. Medicare Part B, Medicare Part D, and Medigap insurance are all guaranteed issue and community rated. But if people don't enroll when they first become eligible, they are penalized. In Medicare, the premiums are higher the longer they wait. In Medigap, in most places, the applicant can be underwritten and charged a higher premium because of ill health.

Impossible Expectations: Increasing Demand with No Change in Supply. One interesting finding from the first year's experience with the ACA is that there was no surge in doctor visits and no real increase in hospitalizations.[62]

This was surprising. The ACA not only increased the number of people with health insurance, it also increased the number of services people with insurance were supposed to get for free. The elderly, for example, were given the opportunity to receive an annual wellness exam. The nonelderly with private insurance were entitled to a long list of free preventive services that previously would have required out-of-pocket payments in most cases.

If the economic studies are correct, the newly insured should try to consume twice as much health care as a result of their insurance coverage. And those who are being forced to obtain more generous insurance than they had previously should be likely to seek more care. Yet, while Obamacare potentially expanded the demand for care considerably, it did virtually nothing about supply.

To see the problem, let's look at free preventive care. In a 2003 study, researchers at Duke University Medical Center estimated that it would take 1,773 hours a year—or 7.4 hours every working day—for the average doctor to counsel and facilitate patient care for every procedure recommended by the US Preventive Services Task Force.[63] These are essentially the free preventive services that Obamacare tries to make available to everyone. And remember, every so often a screening test turns up something that requires more testing and more doctor time.

So if doctors tried to deliver the services that Obamacare promised, there would be no time to do anything else. Moreover, the current supply of medical personnel cannot come anywhere close to providing what has been promised, at least for the next ten to fifteen years.[64]

What we are describing is a huge potential increase in the demand for care, with no increase in supply.

So what happened? Nothing much happened.

We are now ten years into Obamacare and there has been no obvious increase in the amount of care patients are receiving.

Take hospitalization. The number of hospital discharges per 100 people per year actually went down—falling from 12.8 per 100 in the six years prior to Obamacare to 12.7 per 100 in the two years following its enactment. There was some redistribution of hospital services—with fewer days by higher-income patients and more days by lower-income patients—but no overall increase in hospital care.[65]

Interestingly, the same thing happened after the introduction of Medicare and Medicaid, according to the same study. While there was a small increase in hospital stays by the elderly and the poor, it was offset by a small decrease by the nonelderly and the nonpoor.

So, how do we explain the disconnect between what economic studies would lead us to expect and the reality we are observing? It could be that the demand really is higher, but providers are imposing "rationing by waiting" on their patients.

A study by Merritt Hawkins found that the average time to see a doctor rose by 30 percent in the fifteen metropolitan areas studied in the first two years of Obamacare. The number of days of waiting rose from 18.5 days to 24 days. The longest waiting time was in Boston, which has had Obamacare-like insurance longer than the rest of the country. Residents of Boston wait fifty-two days to see a new doctor.[66]

No doubt the waits would be much longer were it not for another discovery. It appears that most people don't like going to the doctor's office if they don't perceive they have a problem. And that's probably a good thing. Screening tests and similar services are rarely cost-effective. They add to health care costs, rather than reduce them.[67]

Casual observers are probably aware that waiting for care has been a large problem in the Veterans Administration health care system. But there have been very few studies of how rationing-by-waiting actually works. Obviously, it raises the time cost of care. Less obviously, almost anything patients and doctors do to circumvent the cost of waiting will also add to the money cost of care.

As waiting times grow longer, those who can afford it will turn to concierge practices.[68] But every time a doctor elects to become a concierge provider, he gives better access to about five hundred traditional office patients while leaving two thousand to fend for themselves. Add to this the growing pressure by third-party payers to keep fees down and a doctor's response is predictable. Those patients who are in plans that pay below market fees will be the last ones the doctors see. And unfortunately these are the most vulnerable populations: the elderly and the disabled on Medicare, the poor on Medicaid, and low-income families with private insurance purchased on the insurance exchanges.[69]

To make matters worse, about ten million people have been enrolled in Medicaid because of Obamacare. A recent study of Oregon's experience affirms what previous research had already shown: Medicaid enrollees use the emergency room about 40 percent more than the uninsured. So traffic to our safety-net institutions has been increasing at the very same time Obamacare has been reducing federal subsidies to these facilities for uncompensated care.

Also, provisions of the ACA that mandate preventive care without any deductible or copayment make it impossible to give enrollees financial incentives to use nonphysician health care services (say at a MinuteClinic), which could expand the supply of care while maintaining quality.

Many things need to be done to correct all of this. But, for starters, we should make it as easy as possible for people to manage their own primary care dollars in a Health Savings Account that they own and control. Let people do their own cost-benefit analysis, and let them keep the money they save by avoiding wasteful spending.

In addition, we need a more rational way of funding the health care safety net. Under the ACA, the federal government is offering millions of people tax credits for purchasing health insurance, and a great many of them are turning those offers down. Under current law, unclaimed tax credits simply fatten the Treasury's bank account. Instead, these unclaimed subsidies should be sent to safety-net institutions in the communities where the uninsured live.[70]

An Impossible Burden for the Elderly and the Disabled. About half the cost of the ACA is paid for by cuts in Medicare spending, and the only practical way those cuts can be made is by reducing fees to providers.[71] As we have seen, Medicare's actuaries have noted with alarm that fees to doctors will drop below current levels in the near future, and the combined effect of lower Medicare and Medicaid hospital spending will drive one in seven hospitals from the market in the next five years.

Although the Obama administration talked about making Medicare more efficient, three separate reports by the Congressional Budget Office (CBO) have concluded that the pilot programs and demonstration projects that are supposed to find these efficiencies are not working. In fact the only Medicare innovations that show any promise at all are in the Medicare Advantage (MA) program. But although the Obama administration delayed the ACA's cuts in MA subsides, it appeared to pay no attention whatever to the efficiencies that MA's entrepreneurs are discovering. More on that below.

Because no serious budget analyst believes that the scheduled Medicare spending cuts can withstand the inevitable political backlash and because they don't believe the pilot programs will work either, both the CBO and Medicare's trustees are publishing "alternative forecasts" every year in an effort to predict when and how Congress will cave. But if Congress does cave and restores the previous Medicare spending path, that means that the ACA isn't paid for. That, in turn, means additional, large unfunded liabilities stretching out indefinitely into the future.

There is no simple way out of this financial bind. But at a minimum it is time to consider some fairly radical changes to Medicare. We consider those changes in the next section.

If the Court Strikes Down Obamacare, How Bad Would That Be?

Some state governments have decided to challenge the constitutionality of the Affordable Care Act (Obamacare) in court, and the Trump administration has joined them.[72] Some Republicans in Congress and even some in the administration resisted this decision. Critics assume that if there were no Obamacare, we would revert to the pre-Obamacare health system. If so, how bad would that be?[73]

Let's take a look.

More private insurance. The most important goal of Obamacare was to increase the number of people with private health insurance, primarily through individual and employer mandates and generous subsidies in health insurance exchanges.

Yet, the day Barack Obama left office, the percentage of people with private coverage was only slightly higher than the day he was elected (67.5 percent in 2016 versus 67.2 percent in 2008). The economy was coming out of a deep recession during those years, and ordinarily the number of people with private coverage would have risen in lockstep with the growth of the civilian labor force.

We have been spending more than $100 billion a year on private insurance subsidies, with little to show for it.[74]

Better insurance. Although the Obamacare individual mandate is gone, people who are sick still need health insurance. Under Obamacare, people who must purchase their own insurance have seen (1) their premiums double, (2) their deductibles double and triple, and (3) their access to care increasingly restricted to an ever-narrower network of providers.

All three problems arise for the same reason: under current law, insurance plans have perverse incentives to attract the healthy and avoid the sick. The way insurance companies hold down costs is by paying

(Sidebar continued on the next page)

rock-bottom fees for medical services and engaging only those providers who will accept those low fees.

The race to the bottom in the individual insurance market is producing plans that are little better—perhaps even worse—than Medicaid with a high deductible.[75]

Portable insurance. Prior to Obamacare, some employers used Health Reimbursement Arrangements (HRAs) to give employees tax-free funds with which they could buy their own insurance. Individually owned insurance has the virtue of traveling with the worker from job to job and in and out of the labor market.

Under the Obama administration, however, employers who did this could be fined as much as $100 per employee per day, or $36,500 per employee per year—the largest fine in all of Obamacare.[76]

The Trump administration has ended those fines and is encouraging the purchase of individually owned insurance with employer funds. Achieving portable insurance would be easier if there were no Obamacare from the get-go.[77]

Insurance tailored to family needs. Suppose you have a choice between a plan with a $10,000 deductible and $1 million of coverage and a plan with no deductible but only $25,000 of coverage. Suppose the premium for the two plans was the same. Which would you prefer?

For people with high incomes and high net worth, the former option is a no-brainer. Yet young, healthy, low-income families living paycheck to paycheck often prefer the latter option. How do we know that? Because that's the kind of insurance they and their employers chose to buy before there was Obamacare.[78]

Limited-benefit insurance won't pay every medical bill. But it will get people into the health care system, where early treatment may avert the need for expensive, catastrophic care. Obamacare's high deductibles, by contrast, are inducing people to wait until it may be too late.

(Sidebar continued on the next page)

Less waste in Medicaid. As a result of Obamacare, roughly ten million additional people are now enrolled in Medicaid. How much difference does that make?

The most thorough study of the matter was the Oregon Health Insurance Experiment, in which researchers found no difference in the physical health of new Medicaid enrollees versus a similar group of people who did not enroll.[79] This doesn't mean the insurance was worthless. It provided families with additional financial security, for example. But research showed the value the enrollees placed on Medicaid coverage was as little as 20 percent of its actual cost.[80]

Surely there are a lot better uses for the $50 billion a year we are spending on Medicaid expansion, including investments in public health.

Relief for the victims of Medicaid expansion. Obamacare has been paying 95 percent of the cost of expanding Medicaid to mostly healthy people, while traditional Medicaid has been paying only 50 or 60 percent. This has given the states an incentive to take from the care of the low-income sick to serve the low-income healthy.

Nationwide, more than 650,000 people are on Medicaid waiting lists. About two-thirds of these are patients with severe intellectual disabilities, severe developmental disabilities, or traumatic brain and spinal cord injuries. To live outside an institution with their families, they need a variety of services, including home health aides, adult day care, respite care for family caregivers, and homemaker services.[81]

The Foundation for Government Accountability estimates that 21,904 people have died while waiting.[82]

A more reliable safety net. Prior to Obamacare, very few people were ever denied health insurance because of a preexisting condition. The short-lived Obamacare risk pool only attracted 107,000 enrollees. Most states had their own risk pools. These were not always fully funded,

(Sidebar continued on the next page)

and some states had waiting lists. But with $150 billion a year of Obamacare money freed for other uses, states should easily be able to find better ways to take care of preexisting conditions as well as a host of other problems.[83]

Under Obamacare almost twenty-eight million people are uninsured. Another ten million have deductibles so high many regard their insurance as almost worthless.[84]

An additional seventy million are trapped in a Medicaid system that rations-by-waiting.[85] For example, it's not unusual for a patient to spend all day going back and forth with bus transfers to get a simple blood test that could have been done by the MinuteClinic in the shopping center next door.

Surely we can do better than that.

9

The Risk of Becoming Unemployed and Finding No Market for One's Skills

IN FEBRUARY 2020, the U.S. unemployment rate stood at 3.5 percent. That was the lowest it had been in fifty years.

Less than two months later, seventeen million Americans had filed for unemployment compensation; economists estimated the unemployment rate was 13 percent; and a headline in the *Washington Post* read, "America is in a Depression."[1]

The difference of course was the coronavirus crisis.

In response, Congress increased the generosity of unemployment benefits and made them easier to get—as we describe below. It is easy to understand why government would step in to provide relief in the face of a sudden health/economic crisis. But is unemployment insurance something we really need in normal times?

Unemployment is an expected characteristic of a dynamic, productive labor market. In normal times, millions of jobs are created and millions are destroyed every month in the United States. For example, the Bureau of Labor Statistics (BLS) reported that 273,000 new jobs were created on net in January 2020.[2] But the BLS also reported 5.6 million total separations and 5.8 million new hires.[3]

In some European countries, it is almost impossible to lay off workers. As a result, employees have job security protected by government regulations and employer agreements with unions. However, few new private sector jobs are created and unemployment is high. US labor regulations also can be inflexible, and programs designed to help the unemployed have perverse consequences.

Much of the remainder of this section is based on a study by my colleague, William Conerly.[4]

Unemployment Insurance

In 1935, the federal government set up the unemployment insurance (UI) system to pay benefits to laid-off workers. The system we have today has changed little since then. State governments administer the system by collecting their own payroll taxes, maintaining a trust fund, and paying cash benefits to the unemployed. The federal government collects an additional unemployment insurance tax (the Federal Unemployment Tax Act) from employers and makes loans to states when their trust funds run low.

Benefits are paid for a limited time. The standard is twenty-six weeks. But Congress acts to extend that limit during periods of high unemployment, up to as long as ninety-nine weeks in recent years. Benefits for low-wage workers typically replace 50 to 70 percent of their previous wage. A ceiling is placed on the maximum benefit, so middle- and higher-income workers receive smaller portions of their lost pay than those at the bottom end of the income ladder.

The nation's unemployment insurance system changes behavior in harmful ways: It encourages employers to lay off workers and discourages unemployed workers from looking for new jobs. Furthermore, it treats some workers unfairly. Unfortunately, the states have no incentive to improve the system's efficiency.

Problem: Encouraging Layoffs. The unemployment insurance system increases unemployment by creating perverse incentives for employers to lay off workers. It does so by shielding employers and their workers from the true cost of layoffs. Under the current system, an individual firm's (UI) tax rate is adjusted according to how many of the firm's laid-off workers file claims for benefits. This experience rating varies from state to state, however, and all states impose floors and ceilings on the tax rates. As a result, if a company already paying the maximum tax rate lays off one more worker, no penalty is assessed. Also, the tax schedules in some states are not actuarially linked to the costs that different employers impose on the system. Thus, the system itself insulates many companies from the full economic impact of their own layoff decisions.

Numerous economic studies on the subject have concluded that the unemployment insurance system in the United States induces layoffs. Figure 9.1,

Figure 9.1 Increase in Temporary Layoffs
Due to Imperfect Experience Rating

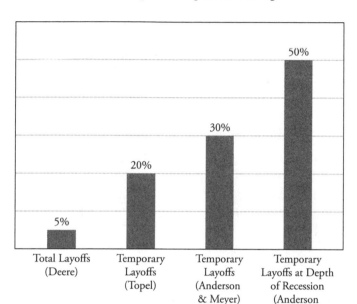

Source: Donald R. Deere, "Unemployment Insurance and Employment," *Journal of Labor Economics,* October 1991; Robert H. Topel, "On Layoffs and Unemployment Insurance," *American Economic Review,* September 1983; Patricia Anderson and Bruce D. Meyer, "The Effects of Unemployment Insurance Taxes and Benefits on Layoffs Using Firm and Individual Data," NBER Working Paper No. 4960, January 1996; and David Card and Phillip B. Levine, "Unemployment Insurance Taxes and the Cyclical and Seasonal Properties of Unemployment," *Journal of Public Economics,* January 1994.

which summarizes several studies, shows that during the depths of recession, the system itself may cause as much as half of all temporary layoffs.[5]

Problem: Discouraging Job Search. Unemployment insurance benefits discourage unemployed workers from actively seeking new jobs.[6] For example, if a low-wage worker is receiving benefits equal to 50 percent of his normal wage, the loss of benefits upon reemployment acts like a 50 percent tax, in addition to all other taxes. Since leisure itself is valued, an individual may prefer not to work while benefits are available rather than receiving twice as

Figure 9.2 Duration of Unemployment

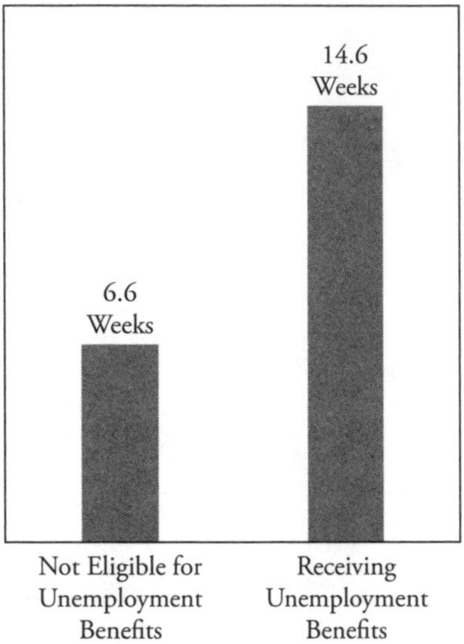

Source: Mark Gritz and Thomas MaCurdy,
"Measuring the Influence of Unemployment
Insurance on Unemployment Experiences,"
Journal of Business and Economic Statistics,
April 1997.

much pretax income from a job. Research supports the idea that the unemployed respond to these economic incentives:

- Workers eligible for unemployment insurance benefits are unemployed longer than those who are ineligible.[7] (See figure 9.2.)

- Workers who are offered bonuses for rapid reemployment find work faster than typical workers receiving unemployment benefits, and their new wages are slightly higher (disproving the claim that longer job searches produce better-paying jobs).

- The probability of an unemployed worker finding a job rises dramatically the week before the end of the person's eligibility for unemployment insurance.[8] (See figure 9.3.)

Studies of other developed countries, including Canada, Spain, and Sweden, and of Europe in general, have reached similar conclusions.[9]

Figure 9.3 Likelihood of Reemployment

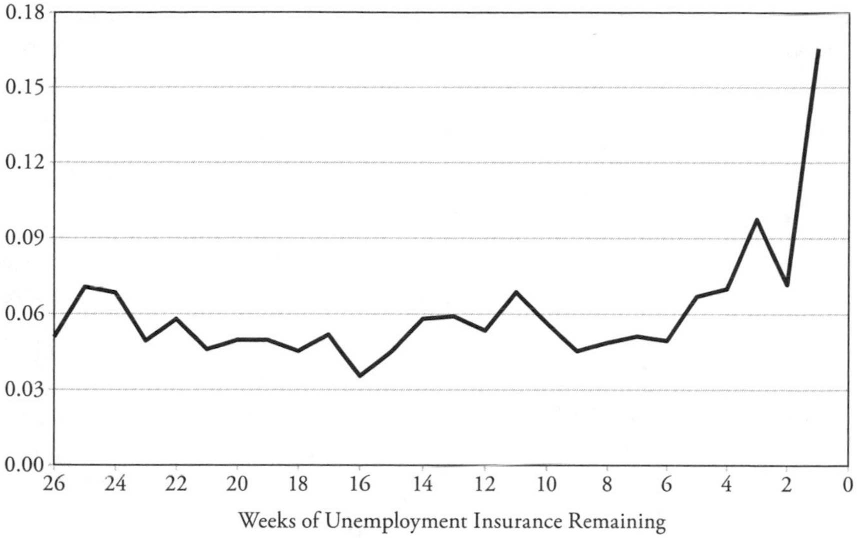

Weeks of Unemployment Insurance Remaining

Source: Bruce Meyer, *Econometrica,* "Unemployment Insurance and Unemployment Spells," July 1990.

The disincentive effect of unemployment benefits probably has the greatest impact on individuals at the margin of an employment decision.[10] For example, many mothers have mixed feelings about working while their children are young. They may enjoy the extra income and the adult contact that jobs provide, but their lives as working mothers tend to be stressful; they incur extra expenses for child care; and progressive tax rates leave them with reduced take-home pay. Imagine a mother who is nearly indifferent between working and not working, and who is laid off from her job at the beginning of her children's summer break. It is not surprising that she would decide that she is better off collecting unemployment insurance benefits in the summer rather than returning to work.

Many students hold part-time jobs. They are not fully self-supporting, but they earn extra spending money. The laid-off student who collects unemployment insurance benefits has spending money plus leisure. (Some states do not provide unemployment insurance benefits for a person who is looking only for part-time work, but such regulations are seldom enforced.)

Consider a retiree who wants the extra income that part-time work could provide to afford a few luxuries. Walmart is famous for its senior-citizen greeters, and McDonald's has expanded its hiring of older workers for day shifts. When laid off, these individuals may find the unemployment insurance benefit fully adequate as a supplement to their pensions. People who are at the margin of the employment choice in this way will exhibit substantial disincentive effects from unemployment insurance.

Harvard University Economics professor Lawrence Summers estimates that if unemployment insurance were eliminated, the unemployment rate would drop by more than half a percentage point, a reduction in the number of unemployed people by roughly 750,000. This estimate is all the more significant in light of the fact that less than half of the unemployed receive insurance benefits, largely because many have not worked enough to qualify.[11]

An even more dramatic finding comes from fellow Harvard economist Robert Barro. During the Great Recession, Barro estimates that more generous unemployment insurance benefits raised the unemployment rate by 2.7 percentage points.[12]

Problem: Perverse Effects on Family Finances. One way that families appear to respond to unemployment benefits is by reducing other income. Economists Julie Cullen and Jonathan Gruber find that wives' earnings fall between thirty-six and seventy-three cents for each dollar of UI benefits received by their husbands.[13] Another effect is the reduction in incentives to save for an unexpected drop in income. Eric Engen and Gruber find that raising a fraction of wages replaced by unemployment insurance by 10 percentage points lowers financial asset holdings by 1.4 to 5.6 percent. This implies that unemployment insurance crowds out up to one-half of private savings for the typical unemployment spell.[14]

Problem: Increasing Long-Term Unemployment. A small subset of the millions of workers who file unemployment claims each year will remain unemployed for a year or more.[15] Long-term unemployment is a growing problem in the United States; in fact, in July 2015, the civilian labor force participation rate was 62.6 percent.[16] That is the lowest it has been since October 1977.[17] The

Figure 9.4 Average Unemployment Duration
in Select OECD Countries (2010, in Months)

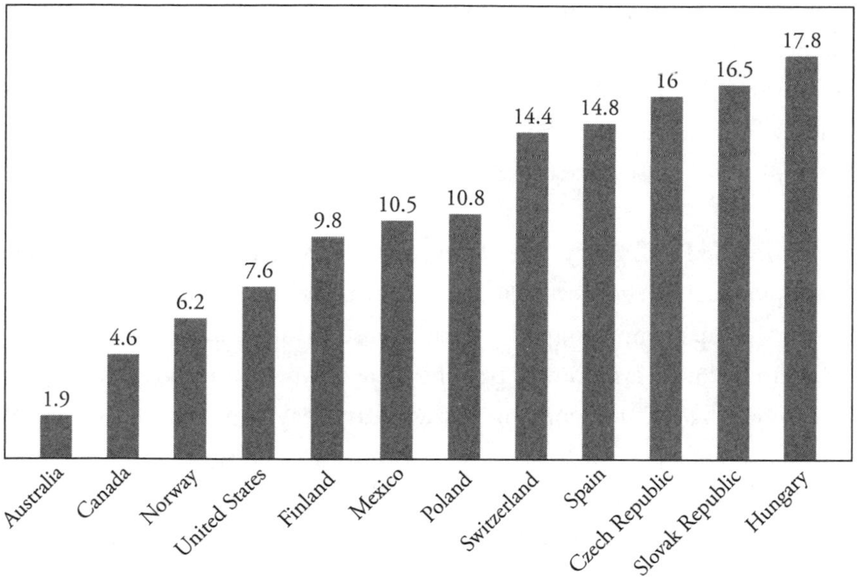

Source: Organization for Economic Cooperation and Development.

labor force participation rate for men in July 2015 was 72.1 percent, which was the lowest on record going back to at least 1950, and probably ever in US history.[18] The longer a person is unemployed, the more difficult it is to become reemployed—owing to the loss of work habits, outdated skills, or growing gaps in the work history. Some job seekers mistakenly think a longer search will lead to a higher-paying job. Yet empirical research shows that it does not.[19]

On occasion, Congress has extended unemployment benefits in regions or states where unemployment rates are higher than the national average. Such extended benefits, however, contribute to the problem of long-term unemployment. In countries that provide more generous benefits than the United States, and do so for two or more years, the average unemployment spell is much longer (see figure 9.4).[20]

Problem: Treating Workers Unfairly. Workers who are ineligible for benefits nonetheless must pay taxes to support the benefits they cannot themselves receive.[21] Moreover, consistently employed people are realizing no monetary benefit in exchange for the taxes they pay. Ironically, the current system often does not provide benefits to some low-wage workers because in order to qualify for benefits they must have a minimum employment history. Thus, workers who are employed seasonally, in cyclical industries or only part-time, may not qualify for benefits, even though they (through their employers) are paying unemployment insurance taxes.

Encouraging Inefficiency. The current system provides no incentives to state unemployment agencies to reduce administrative costs or fraudulent claims, or to speed up reemployment.[22] Potential cost savings are available in each of these areas. States lose about 9 percent of their funds on the average because of erroneous or fraudulent benefit claims and payments, with some states losing nearly 20 percent.[23]

Case Study: North Carolina. In most states, unemployment benefits are paid for a maximum of twenty-six weeks.[24] However, in 2008, as the country was sliding into a deep recession, Congress passed a measure designed to extend benefits by at least seven weeks in every state, and by thirteen weeks in states with unemployment rates of at least 6 percent.

In 2013, however, North Carolina did something very unusual. The state reduced its unemployment insurance benefits and quit the federal extended-benefits unemployment program. It was the only state in the nation to do so. Although critics claimed that the state was waging a "war on the unemployed," North Carolina saw one of the biggest labor market improvements of all fifty states:

- In the first six months following the reduction in unemployment benefits, North Carolina's labor market improvement, as well as its economic growth, was among the best in the country.

- Payroll jobs rose 0.8 percent across the country but increased by 1.5 percent in North Carolina.

- North Carolina's unemployment rate fell from 8.3 percent in June 2013 to 6.9 percent in December 2013, a 17 percent decline. Nationwide, the unemployment rate fell by only eight-tenths of a percentage point.[25]

Some critics of the reform say that the drop in unemployment was explained by North Carolinians exiting the labor force. However, the decline in labor force participation has been a nationwide phenomenon. Moreover, North Carolina's labor force has contracted by only 0.04 percent since June 2013, compared to a drop of 0.1 percent in the United States overall.[26]

Case Study: Federal Extension of Unemployment Benefits. In most states, unemployment benefits last for twenty-six weeks. However, when unemployment levels are high, such as during and shortly after a recession, the federal government usually steps in and provides additional benefits.

As noted, after the 2007–2009 recession, Congress repeatedly authorized emergency extended benefits, lasting as long as ninety-nine weeks. When the extended benefits finally were allowed to expire in December 2013, they had been in effect twenty months longer than following any previous recession.[27]

As University of Georgia economist Jeffrey Dorman points out, state unemployment benefits are funded by payroll taxes, so they are essentially a prepaid insurance policy. However, extended benefits are paid from general tax revenues, so they are essentially welfare payments.

Early in 2014, *New York Times* columnist Paul Krugman suggested that the sudden end of the extended unemployment benefits could provide a test of whether they were discouraging job creation. Krugman, as well as many Democrats in Congress, predicted that the end of extended benefits would result in nothing but harm. In fact, payroll employment rose by over three million in 2014, more than seven hundred thousand more than in 2013, an already pretty good year.

The CARES Act. As the coronavirus began to create economic and health care chaos in March 2020, Congress scrambled to pass the third phase of a stimulus package, ostensibly designed to keep the economy from falling into a Great Depression. A key component of the act was a boost in unemployment insurance benefits for private- and public-sector workers.

One provision of the act (extending for four months) was a weekly unemployment benefit of $600 to be added to the unemployment benefits the recipient was already receiving. Since the average unemployment benefit was $400, this amounted to a $1,000 weekly payment to the average person receiving UI benefits.

One problem with this was explained by University of Chicago economist Casey Mulligan and health policy analyst Brian Blase, writing in the *Wall Street Journal* at the time:

> A thousand dollars a week is more than what the majority of full-time workers were getting paid before the virus arrived.... [N]ever before in American history could a majority of the workforce get a raise merely by receiving a pink slip.[28]

Moreover, this bonus was twenty-four times the size of the bonus Congress legislated in response to the Great Recession.[29] So if Barro's estimate of the unemployment effects of the previous boost in UI benefits is anywhere near correct, the effects of the CARES Act, if extended for any length of time, could be many times worse.

10

The Risk of Plagues, Pandemics, and Other Threats to Public Health

FOR THE FIVE risks that we have discussed so far, the principal means of insurance throughout most of human history consisted of families and extended families. But there is a sixth kind of risk for which families don't offer much protection. This is the risk that people will transmit communicable diseases to each other. As long as people take advantage of the economic and social benefits of living in communities, they are at risk of infecting, sickening, and maybe even inadvertently killing each other.[1]

There isn't much an individual family can do in these circumstances, acting unilaterally. Almost by definition, any successful response to a killer virus has to be community-wide.

So in the past, what did the typical community do in response to a serious communicable disease? No matter where they were or what kind of social organization they had, historically the pattern has always been the same. People have always been completely unprepared for plagues. And when one hits, they invariably turn to isolation or quarantine.

There have probably been many plagues throughout human history, but one of the earliest that we have much detailed knowledge about was the plague of Athens, thanks to the record left by the historian Thucydides.[2]

The plague arrived in ancient Greece during the second year of the Peloponnesian War (430 BC). It killed 25 percent of the Athenian population, estimated at between seventy-five thousand and one hundred thousand. The devastation was probably made worse by the decision of Pericles to pursue a policy of retreat within the city walls of Athens. This caused a massive migration from the countryside into an already highly populated city.[3] Due to the close quarters and poor hygiene at that time, Athens became a breeding ground for disease.[4]

The effects of the plague were very one-sided—affecting the Athenians much more than their Spartan enemies. However, the sight of the burning funeral pyres of Athens caused the Spartans to withdraw their troops, being unwilling to risk contact with their diseased opponents.[5]

In the years that followed there were many more episodes of devastation by disease. One of the most memorable was called the Black Death, which swept across Europe in the mid-fourteenth century.[6] It killed as many as fifty million people—more than half the population of Europe. As in all previous pandemics, people learned to survive by avoiding the sick and those who were already dead.

The worst pandemic to hit the United States was the 1918 pandemic, often called the Spanish flu. The flu infected an estimated five hundred million people, about a quarter of the world's population.[7] It killed an estimated fifty million people worldwide, including an estimated 675,000 in the United States.[8] The reason it was called the Spanish flu is because World War I censors (on both sides) suppressed news about it in the combatant countries. But since Spain was neutral, the media was free to report on that country—leading people to falsely assume that the flu was worse in Spain or even that it originated there.

By the way, social distancing (which you can think of as a moderate form of quarantine and which is being urged in the face of the coronavirus) worked. St. Louis, which practiced it rigorously, did much better than Philadelphia, which did not.[9]

Even though they occur only periodically, plagues and epidemics have been a recurrent theme in art, literature, poetry, and modern film. They appear in Homer's *Iliad* and in the Bible. One of Edgar Allan Poe's more memorable stories is the *Masque of the Red Death*, in which one hundred nobles party at a ball while the peasants outside are dying a horrible death. (Spoiler alert: the isolation didn't work.) My favorite movie on the subject is *Andromeda Strain*.

The Dawn of Public Health

It wasn't until the middle of the nineteenth century that serious thought was given to whether there was something government might do to combat communicable diseases and perhaps prevent them from arising in the first place. It came in the form of the *Sanitary Report*, a British document authored by Sir Edwin Chadwick.[10]

As it turns out, Chadwick didn't know very much about fever, consumption, cholera, or any other disease. But his instincts were right. He believed that a filthy, unsanitary living environment was conducive to the spread of disease, just as Thucydides thought.[11]

In Chadwick's day, cities in the Western world were immensely more polluted than they are today. It was not unusual, for example, for people to dump human waste from their windows onto the street below. The streets were typically not paved and there usually was no drainage system to wash away the filth. Wood-burning stoves polluted the air. A principal form of transportation (the horse) left its droppings wherever it went. People dumped whatever they wanted to get rid of into rivers and streams—even the dead bodies of humans and animals.

In concluding his report, Chadwick argued that he had shown that "various forms of epidemic, endemic, and other disease [are] caused, or aggravated, or propagated chiefly...by atmospheric impurities produced by decomposing animal and vegetable substances, by damp and filth and close and overcrowded dwellings."[12]

In fact he had shown none of these things. But Chadwick's report was not mainly concerned with medicine. He was concerned with engineering. On the goals of public health, he wrote:

> The great preventive—drainage, street, and house cleaning by means of sullies of water and improved sewerage, and especially the introduction of cheaper and more efficient modes of removing all noxious refuse from the towns—are operations for which aid must be sought from the science of the civil engineer, not from the physician.[13]

No matter how well founded or how weakly reasoned, Chadwick's view of the world won the day. Long before people sought to eliminate pollution for "environmental" reasons, cities and towns enacted measures to create a cleaner environment for health reasons.

The Little-Known Dark Side of the Public Health Movement

The health problems that Chadwick wrote about are what economists call "externalities." They arise when people who are pursuing their own interests create costs for their neighbors. When there are externalities, people are not paying the full cost of their actions. Part of the cost is imposed on others.

Economists generally agree that when externalities are significant, there is a role for government. Or, if not government, some other mechanism for collective action.

In the early part of the twentieth century, however, the Progressive movement extended this idea into areas that many readers might find surprising. They argued that the decision of parents to have children has external effects on other people. An individual's sex life might affect other people. The decision to get vaccinated might affect other people. The history of this Progressive approach to public health is not a pretty one.

Forced sterilization of patients was one of the most popular reforms among political progressives in the early part of the twentieth century. They believed that in order to protect the gene pool, it was necessary to sterilize all manner of patients—including the feeble-minded, epileptics, others with mental and physical disabilities, and even people with proclivities toward alcoholism, drug abuse, crime, and prostitution.[14]

Although this was primarily a Progressive movement reform, such conservative politicians as Winston Churchill also advocated it.

One case, *Buck v. Bell*, went all the way to the Supreme Court. In ruling in favor of sterilization, Justice Oliver Wendall Holmes made the memorable statement that "three generations of imbeciles are enough." Only one justice dissented.[15]

In all, an estimated seventy thousand Americans were forcibly sterilized. *The Lynchburg Story* is a heartbreaking video with patient interviews that describe the human side of the tragedy.[16] Many Americans associate the eugenics movement with Nazi Germany. If anything, the Nazi eugenics program was imported to Germany from the United States.

In an ironic twist of fate, government today intervenes in the opposite way. In general, Down syndrome children are not capable of making rational decisions about sex and procreation. So, to prevent unwanted pregnancies, their parents often turn to sterilization. Yet in doing so, they face legal obstacles, and many procedures are performed illegally.

But why must government be involved at all?

It wasn't until 1972 that the American news media discovered that for forty years the United States Public Health Service had been conducting a medical experiment in Tuskegee, Alabama, involving several hundred black males with syphilis. The experiment? It consisted of observation without treatment, including withholding penicillin.[17]

Although the general public didn't know about the exercise for four decades, the medical community as a whole was well aware of it. Through the years, the Tuskegee experiment led to numerous articles in medical journals. After public exposure, many doctors throughout the country came to the experiment's defense.

Note: This was a federal government experiment, funded with our tax dollars.

The swine flu fiasco in the mid-1970s is another program some people would probably like to forget. Haunted by the specter of the 1918 flu pandemic, public health officials rushed into a mass vaccination program for an outbreak that never occurred. Gerald Ford even weighed in—getting his vaccination in front of the national news media.[18]

Unfortunately, there were dangerous side effects of the vaccine. They included the widespread occurrence of the Guillain-Barré syndrome, whose progressive paralysis leads to death in 5 percent of cases.[19]

To get the drug companies to produce the vaccine, the government had to assume liability for all the risks associated with inadequate warnings. But even with that, the swine flu episode led to a major change in liability law. The result: sharp increases in the price of all vaccines and a reduction in their availability.[20]

The legal scholar Richard Epstein writes that the idea of trying to regulate behavior under the guise of public health is still very much with us. The goal of traditional public health, says Epstein, was to "contain epidemics, contagion, and nuisances" by means of "inspection, quarantine, and vaccination."

Today, politicians acting under the banner of public health are combatting such "non-communicable epidemics" as obesity and diabetes. Thus, regulating the size of soda that can be sold and mandating calorie counts on menus are justified as public health measures.[21]

Attack of the Coronavirus

There is a general consensus among almost all public health experts: in all previous plagues and pandemics, government didn't do enough. From Edwin Chadwick right down to the present day, the conventional wisdom is that government needs to do more to promote sanitation, even if there is no killer virus threat. In the face of past pandemics, the conventional wisdom is that government should have done more to ensure isolation and social distancing and to make sure the health care system was prepared to meet the challenge of a surge in medical need.

Yet the coronavirus pandemic may be the first time when public policy experts began to conclude that government was more often the problem rather than the solution.

Think about all of the medical supplies that are needed to care for coronavirus patients: testing kits, masks, gloves, gowns, respirators, ventilators, hospital beds, etc. In the first few months of 2020, all of these were in critically short supply.

Ordinarily you would think that the private sector would step up to meet the surging demand. Industrial-use masks can be retrofitted to meet medical needs. The same is true of ventilators and respirators. One U.S. company quickly developed a product that could test for the virus almost anywhere—in homes, schools, offices, airports, etc.—and produce results in ten minutes.

The problem: they were producing these items for customers overseas. In the United States, none of this could be done without permission from government agencies, including the Centers for Disease Control and Prevention (CDC), the federal Food and Drug Administration (FDA), the Department of Health and Human Resources (HHS), etc. The approval process in the United States was so long, laborious, and bureaucratic that many companies meeting the demand elsewhere in the world didn't even try to get their products approved in this country.

Even the *New York Times* (no friend of the Trump administration) concluded that the most important barrier to COVID-19 testing was government regulation.[22]

With a lockdown occurring in city after city, many hotels became completely empty. Ideally, this could have been an opportunity to use some of them as intermediate care facilities, where nurses could care for and monitor patients who didn't need hospitalization. Yet federal law didn't allow this either. Not only may the private sector not create patient beds without government permission, Medicare even tells hospitals how many beds they can have.

The Trump administration's approach to the COVID-19 challenge is by now well known. Ideally, patients should stay in their homes and communicate with doctors by means of phone and Skype and similar devices. The private sector should be encouraged and incentivized to produce the medical supplies that caregivers need.

Yet Donald Trump frequently complained that the entire government apparatus was completely unprepared to meet a twenty-first-century challenge with twenty-first-century technical and scientific know-how. He was right. Consider that:

- When Donald Trump took office, Medicare was not allowed to pay for doctor consultations by phone, email, or Skype, except in rural areas, and even then patients couldn't be in their own homes.

- The virus didn't just hit during working hours, and there were services willing to provide round-the-clock access to a doctor (including telemedicine) for a little as fifty dollars a month for a mother and ten dollars for her child. The cost for a senior was one hundred dollars.

- But when Trump took office, Medicare was not allowed to pay for this type of care. Employers were not allowed to put money into an account so that employees could select a "direct primary care" doctor of their own choosing.

- When the first coronavirus patient was diagnosed in the United States, the Centers for Disease Control and Prevention (CDC) in Atlanta was the only facility in the entire country that could legally test for the virus, and the test results took days.

- Both the president and the Congress were adamant that patients should not be burdened with deductibles and copayments when they sought relief from the coronavirus.

- Yet, when Donald Trump took office, if employers and insurers had waived deductibles and copayments for coronavirus detection and treatment, patients would have lost access to their Health Savings Accounts under federal law.

- When millions of people were losing their jobs, the most valuable kind of health coverage they could have was a health plan they could take with them.

- Yet when Donald Trump took office, it was illegal for employers to purchase individually owned health insurance for their employees.

- When Donald Trump took office, terminally ill patients did not have the "right to try" drugs that might save their lives. That same principle applied to COVID-19. On national TV, President Trump suggested more than once that there were perfectly safe drugs that appeared to work with the coronavirus, and he encouraged doctors to try using these drugs "off label."

- If an executive of a pharmaceutical firm that produced one of these drugs went on TV to say the same thing, he could wind up in prison.

One of the few positive government programs in place when the coronavirus struck was a program started under President George W. Bush to stockpile masks in case of a pandemic. Yet the number of masks in stockpile appears to be about 1 percent of the estimated need.[23]

In the next section, we will see how the president and Congress surmounted these regulatory barriers to meet the challenge of the worst pandemic in our lifetime.

Taking a Closer Look at Some Solutions

HOW CAN WE give individuals the opportunity to insure against risks with assets that they own and control, rather than being hostages to the promises of politicians? How can we create real markets for social insurance risks instead of institutions in which everyone faces perverse incentives? How can they save, invest, and provide for their own future instead of depending on the willingness of taxpayers to bear future burdens? In this section we will search for answers.

11

Addressing the Risks of Old Age

WE HAVE IDENTIFIED numerous ways in which Social Security, Medicare, and other entitlement programs for the elderly could be improved with win/win changes. But what about the entire programs themselves? Can they be fundamentally reformed in ways that better meet the needs of the beneficiaries and reduce the taxpayers' burden at the same time?

Opting Out of Social Security

Our Social Security system generates a stream of taxes and benefits, now and in the future. Looking forward, individuals can expect to pay payroll taxes for as long as they earn wages. What if a taxpayer made a lump-sum payment today in order to avoid all future payroll taxes? Would that be good for the taxpayer? Would that be good for the rest of us? On the benefit side, what if we could offer the individual a lump-sum amount today in return for his forgoing any future Social Security benefits?

Just as parties to a lawsuit may find it in their self-interest to enter a settlement agreement today in order to avoid an uncertain future outcome at trial, everyone who has a stake in our elderly entitlement systems may come to a similar conclusion. Most individuals will not be in a position to make a once-and-for-all agreement, however. What they can do is take small steps to opt out partially—with the degree of independence growing over time.

Personal Retirement Accounts: The 4 Percent Solution. In order to eliminate Social Security's long-run unfunded liabilities in perpetuity, without reductions in future benefits under current law, an immediate and permanent payroll tax hike of 3.6 percentage points would be required, assuming that the funds are invested at the government's borrowing rate until they are spent. As an alternative to paying this tax, employees could make private provision for retirement income over the course of their working lives. For older workers, this would involve opting out partially. For most younger workers, this would involve opting out fully.

Under this proposal, private savings equal to 4 percent of wages would be invested in a diversified portfolio that reflects the capital market as a whole. Researchers at Texas A&M University modeled reforms that would allow all workers to prefund a portion of their retirement benefits by creating personal retirement accounts.[1] They estimate that for about 4 percent of wages, saved and invested over a working lifetime, an average-wage worker could replace Social Security benefits with an annuity funded from a personal retirement account. For the purposes of this simulation, the basic structure of benefits was subjected to "progressive indexing"—which reduces the benefits for higher-income retirees. The simulations assume that Social Security benefits would be offset at retirement dollar for dollar by income from the personal account. At retirement, a worker's account balance would be used to purchase an inflation-protected lifetime annuity—providing monthly retirement income. The government would guarantee each retiree a pension income no less than what would have been promised by Social Security alone. For most retirees, the combined payments from the personal accounts and the reformed defined benefits would be comparable to currently scheduled Social Security benefits. Those with lower lifetime earnings would actually receive higher total benefits.

How would the accounts be funded? One way is to have workers and their employers deposit the funds as an alternative to paying a higher payroll tax. This particular simulation, however, assumes that workers who open a personal account (along with their employers) receive a 4 percent reduction in payroll taxes. That implies that government must borrow to make up for the revenue shortfall. The reformed Social Security retirement benefit would equal previously promised benefits minus the amount of a monthly annuity that could be purchased with the account balance if it were invested in the capital market over the course of the individual's remaining work life. The benefit offset allows the reformed program to repay taxpayers for the costs of the transition to a new system. The combination of the new current debt and the ultimate offset would repay all the borrowing with interest and lead to no net change in the government's total debt position.

Personal Retirement Accounts in Chile. In 1981, Chile replaced its pay-as-you-go system with one in which workers contribute to accounts they individually own. The analysis of the transition from the old system to the new one described below is based on the work of my colleague, former World Bank economist Estelle James.

The old system was essentially bankrupt. It had promised more benefits than the taxes of workers and employers could finance. Retirees received their benefits under the old system, but workers had a choice between staying under the old system or switching to the new funded system. Those who switched received "recognition bonds" for past contributions. The bonds have been paid off gradually from general government revenues.[2] (See the discussion on "Financing the Transition to Personal Accounts" below.)

Under the reformed system, money is invested by a pension fund chosen by each worker from among a number of competing, privately owned firms. The retirement benefits of workers are prefunded by their own savings, rather than by taxes paid by others.[3]

How does this system work? Workers in Chile must make mandatory contributions to accounts they own. The contribution totals 12.4 percent of wages, of which 10 percent goes to a personal retirement account and an additional 2.4 percent covers disability and survivors insurance. Funds are invested according to strict regulations. Like the US Social Security system, but unlike our 401(k) plans, workers cannot borrow money from these accounts or withdraw money for the purchase of a home, education, or medical expenses.[4]

Although the "normal" retirement age is sixty for women, and sixty-five for men, people may choose to "retire" earlier if they have enough money in their personal accounts to fund at least 70 percent of the average wage they earned over the past ten years. Upon retirement, people can choose a lifetime annuity payment, a programmed withdrawal, or a combination of both. About two-thirds of workers choose the annuity. Retirement, however, does not mean that an individual stops working. In Chile, individuals can receive retirement benefits and continue to work—without having to make additional contributions to their personal account.

If workers have contributed to their accounts for at least twenty years, the government will guarantee a minimum retirement income. Under the original law, the minimum monthly benefit was to be price indexed, but in actuality it has been wage indexed because of political pressure.[5] The minimum benefit also applies to survivors and disability benefits. Widows receive 60 percent of the minimum pension guarantee based on their husbands' savings, and with special adjustments, they may receive 100 percent of the guarantee.

Reforms to the Chilean System. Chilean personal accounts have worked well for individuals who contributed on a regular basis.[6] However, the system provided meager benefits for those who didn't earn wages, were self-employed, or worked outside the formal labor market. Moreover, once the twenty-year requirement was met in order to qualify for the minimum-benefit government subsidy, contributions based on additional earnings replaced the government guarantee dollar for dollar. This was, effectively, a 100 percent implicit tax on incremental contributions. For this reason, workers would cease contributing to their accounts before normal retirement age even if they continued to work.

In 2008, a council appointed by Chile's new government introduced some important reforms:[7]

- Some two hundred thousand self-employed workers, including doctors and other self-employed professionals were required to participate.

- Individuals who had modest personal accounts are entitled to a government subsidy regardless of the number of years they contribute to the account.

- New regulations made it less likely that those who take programmed withdrawals will exhaust their funds and fall back on public benefits.

- Those who receive a supplemental pension are no longer penalized for making their own contributions. They no longer lose a dollar of the minimum benefit for each additional dollar their savings and investments can finance.

- The minimum benefit phases out slowly for higher-income retirees.

- Finally, the government-guaranteed minimum benefit does not begin until the normal retirement age, which incentivizes workers to continue contributing to their accounts until the age of retirement.

- Overall, practically everyone is eligible for some benefit, and two-thirds of all pension income will continue to come from prefunded retirement accounts, compared with 77 percent previously.[8]

Personal Account Investment Options. A reformed American system could be similar to the Chilean system.[9] Workers' contributions would be invested by competing funds managed by Fidelity, Schwab, etc. Workers would have a limited number of funds to choose from, such funds reflecting slightly varying degrees of risk. For instance, an equity fund could be included, provided that it is a low-cost index fund. In Chile, workers currently can choose from five portfolios, including equities and international investments. But for each portfolio, the funds essentially are offering the same mix of assets.

Owing to the restrictions on fund selection, fund managers could not compete by offering high-risk, high-return funds. Instead, they would compete on the basis of lower administrative fees and by serving the other needs of the account holders.

Financing the Transition to Personal Accounts. When a country with a pay-as-you-go pension system switches to a system that includes a funded component, some of the workers' contributions usually are shifted to the funded component.[10] This "carve-out" approach creates a temporary funding gap between the remaining pay-as-you-go revenues and the remaining obligations of the old system. Some other revenue source must be found to cover this short-run gap, in addition to the long-run, preexisting funding gap of the old system. This short-run gap is known as the transition cost problem.

Countries that finance their funded systems by requiring an extra contribution do not face this problem. For example, most developed countries with reformed systems take this "add-on" approach by mandating additional worker contributions. An add-on also has the advantage of helping to increase national saving. The downside to this strategy is that workers who participate have less take-home pay.

Chilean Annuities Market

Relative to the size of its economy, Chile has the largest annuities market in the world.[11] It is the only country that has a large life insurance industry with annuities as its major product. In 1980, the Chilean life insurance industry was in its infancy, and the annuity portion was virtually nonexistent. However, the new social security system, which forced people to save for their retirement and greatly constrained their choices during the payout stage, changed this situation dramatically. The industry grew rapidly, and the annuity part grew fastest of all—measured by premiums, reserves, and payouts.

- In 1985, life insurance premiums in Chile totaled only $145 million; by 2000 they had reached $2 billion.

- Two-thirds of premium income in Chile is for immediate-payout life annuities—in contrast to the United States, where less than 2 percent of total life insurance premiums are for individual payout annuities—and most of these are for fixed payout periods, not for life.

Under annuitization, workers turn their entire accumulated pensions over to an insurance company that provides the annuity, subject to detailed rules set by the insurance regulator. The retiree forgoes future control over investments and gives up the right to leave bequests (except for that embodied in a joint annuity for a spouse or children, or for a guaranteed period annuity) in exchange for a stable income stream that is guaranteed for life.

Regulations originally required annuities to be fixed rate and price indexed for inflation. Chile has since changed the rules to allow for variable-rate annuities as well as those issued in foreign currencies. If the amount of the guaranteed minimum benefit is larger than the annuity, the government tops up the payout. Above the minimum, the government insures 75 percent of the worker's annuity, in case the insurance company becomes insolvent. To prevent insolvencies, the government

(Sidebar continued on the next page)

sets stringent reserve, equity, and asset-liability-matching requirements. So far it has never had to pay a claim. Subject to meeting regulatory requirements, insurance companies determine annuity payouts and bear the longevity and interest rate risk. They are not permitted to charge fees or to require annuitants to cover sales commissions explicitly.[12]

Under programmed withdrawals, workers keep their money in a managed account, and the annual permissible withdrawal depends on a formula that is based on assumed mortality and interest rates that are set by law. Workers retain control and bequest rights over the remainder of their accumulations, subject to regulatory constraints. Their investments may lose money, but even if they don't, the pension is likely to decline dramatically through time because of the way the formula works. If the payout falls to the minimum pension guarantee level, payouts stay at that level until the account is used up, at which point the government pays the guaranteed amount.

As with annuities, programmed withdrawals must be joint for married men and for women with dependents. The same companies that manage investments during the accumulation stage manage them during the payout stage, subject to rules established by the regulator. Fund administrators have no control over the formula that determines payouts, nor do they bear the mortality and interest rate risks. (These risks are borne by retirees and, ultimately, by the government as guarantor.) In contrast to insurance companies, fund administrators are required to make all fees explicit, and all investment earnings must be passed on to pensioners.

Over a twenty-five-year period, Chile's private accounts generated an average annual return of 10 percent. Even at a lower 5 percent rate, however, an individual who works most of his life will have an average wage replacement of 57 percent.[13] Furthermore, in order to protect older workers who might soon retire from market volatility, as workers age they become ineligible for funds that are heavily invested in instruments with variable returns.[14]

All Latin American and Eastern European countries have used the carve-out approach and therefore have faced the transition cost problem. How did they finance the transition? Because money is fungible, it is difficult to answer that question precisely. If government debt and taxes both rise, it is difficult to know how much of the larger debt, versus higher taxes, was used to finance the pension transition. Knowing that would require knowing the counterfactual—what would have happened otherwise.

While we cannot give precise numbers, we can describe more generally the five strategies countries have used:

- Making the carve-out relatively small and keeping some workers in the old system so that most of the payroll tax contribution continues to flow into the pay-as-you-go pot;

- Downsizing the benefit obligations of the pay-as-you-go system, particularly for young workers, expecting the growth of the funded system to restore those benefits;

- Using state-owned assets or budgetary surpluses to offset the pension debt;

- Borrowing temporarily to spread the burden of transition costs across generations; and

- Using general revenues (higher taxes, lower government expenditures) to repay the loan over time.

Transition costs arise from the need to meet obligations that exist already. These costs diminish as the old obligations are paid off. In the long run, the drop in new pay-as-you-go obligations exceeds the drop in pay-as-you-go revenues. At that point, "transition costs" become "transition gains." Moreover, if the new system enhances economic growth by increasing long-term saving, labor supply, and productivity, this will generate additional revenue for the treasury that can be used to finance the transition.

One underexplored avenue for generating revenue is the liquidation of federal assets. A 2020 report by the Congressional Research Service counted 615 million acres of federal land.[15] A 2017 Independent Institute analysis by William F. Shughart II and Carl P. Close finds that selling off federal assets could pay down much of the national debt without raising taxes or printing money. Unproductive and unused federal assets in the form of buildings, infrastructure, and land, including mineral and energy deposits, could generate, conservatively, $25 trillion in revenue and perhaps as much as $11 trillion more.[16]

Moreover, they show that reforms in this direction are already feasible:[17]

Politics is about building effective coalitions. Can a coalition form to successfully campaign for federal asset liquidation? Grounds for optimism come from an existing federal asset program. Title V of the McKinney-Vento Homeless Assistance Act, signed into law by President Ronald Reagan in 1987, gave homeless-assistance organizations the right of first refusal to acquire federal properties. By giving them a stake in the sale of federal assets, Title V encouraged advocates for the homeless to support passage of the Federal Asset Sale and Transfer Act nearly 30 years later.

The law, signed by President Barack Obama in December 2016, is expected to raise at least $8 billion, exclusively for debt reduction, through the sale of unneeded, underutilized surplus federal buildings and associated real estate. Although this sum would barely put a dent in a $20 trillion national debt, it takes an essential step: it provides proof of concept. Just as homeless groups had material reasons to support the 2016 asset liquidation law, a broader coalition of interest groups could be formed and incentivized to support a bold initiative to sell a much larger portfolio of federal assets, including the rights to most oil, natural gas, and coal deposits on federal lands.

Most reforming countries have made the new system mandatory for young workers but allow current workers to stay in the old system if they wish. Workers over age forty-five usually choose to stay in the old system, while younger workers usually switch. The former group continues contributing to the pay-as-you-go system, while the latter group partially withdraws with the expectation that the individual accounts will build up by the time they retire.

One advantage of a voluntary switch is that it mitigates opposition to reform from groups most anxious to stay in the old system and permits a lower value to be placed on past service credits for those who switch. By choosing the minimum terms that are needed to convince the desired number of workers to switch, a government can substantially reduce its recognized debt and transition costs (e.g., Hungary). Obviously, the higher the expected rate of return on the individual accounts, the lower the compensation needed to induce workers to switch. In effect, the transition can be partially self-financed through capital market investments.

Expected Returns for Low-Wage Workers in the United States. In 2001, President George W. Bush appointed a 16-member commission to study the reform of the Social Security system, with special emphasis on the creation of individual retirement accounts.[18] To assist the commission in its deliberations, scholars at Texas A&M University simulated the retirement savings of workers at various income levels, investing in various portfolios. They compared the returns from these savings to the wage replacement rate of Social Security. For male earners at the tenth percentile (in the bottom 10 percent of the earnings distribution):

- Social Security replaced about 120 percent of earnings for men who retired in 1984, declining to about 100 percent for those who retired in 2003.

- Social Security replaced more of retirees' incomes than an account invested solely in bonds.

- However, the 100 percent equity account outperformed Social Security for workers who retired in 1992 and subsequent years.

- A life-cycle account, which gradually shifts from equities to bonds to reduce risk as the worker ages, outperformed Social Security for workers who retired in 1999 and thereafter.

Expected Returns for Median-Wage Workers in the United States. Moving up the earnings distribution, the Social Security replacement rate drops and the retirement year when market investments exhibit superior performance occurs sooner than for low-wage workers. For median-wage workers:

- The 100 percent equity investment outperformed Social Security beginning with 1986 retirees, and the life-cycle account outperformed Social Security for retirees in 1989 through 2003.

- For workers retiring in 1998 and subsequent years, Social Security's replacement rate was comparable to the return on government bonds.

Expected Returns for High-Wage Workers in the United States. For workers at the threshold of the top 10 percent of lifetime wages (the ninetieth percentile):

- The market outperformed Social Security because the latter's benefit formula replaced a smaller percentage of high-income workers' earnings.
- The 100 percent equity portfolio outperformed Social Security for workers who retired in 1986 and later.
- The life-cycle account did better than Social Security beginning in 1987; beginning in 1990, the all-bond account did better.

For workers born later than those considered here, the performance of Social Security will likely decline further relative to the market alternatives, owing to the increase in taxes necessary to support Social Security. The comparable market account contributions will also rise, and the larger account balances will produce larger annuities. Additionally, the rising full retirement age for Social Security will reduce the program's replacement rates at all retirement ages.

Protecting Account Funds from Market Volatility. We envision that the government can afford to guarantee that no one will be worse off as a result of opting out, provided that their funds are invested in diversified portfolios. Even so, some people worry about the effects of a fall in stock prices right before the time of retirement. To analyze this possibility, researchers considered people retiring at different wages up to 2003. The analysis therefore includes the 2002–2003 stock market drop. The researchers found that:

- For median-income earners, the wage replacement rate from the all-equity portfolio peaked for retirees in 2000 at 246 percent of their average earnings but dropped to 129 percent for individuals who retired in 2003.
- This drop is equal to more than 100 percent of average earnings, but the replacement rate is still well above Social Security's promised benefit.

- The life-cycle account was less volatile but would have provided a lower replacement rate—107 percent in 2000 and 85 percent for new retirees in 2003.
- The all-bond portfolio performed more poorly than the alternatives.

Other ways to protect against volatility are available. Chile's practice of allowing workers to annuitize up to ten years prior to the normal retirement age gives them the opportunity to take advantage of a wide window rather than being forced to buy an annuity on their first day of retirement. (See sidebar, "Chilean Annuities Market.")

Opting Out of Medicare

As in the case of Social Security, Medicare is a program with potential substitutes. Nine million veterans, for example, are enrolled in the Veterans Health Administration system, and since there are almost twenty million veterans overall, the number using the VA could be much higher.[19] As we noted at the outset of this book, much could be done to improve the efficiency of VA medical care, including significant privatization. Were that done, the VA system has the potential to substitute for a very large share of the Medicare population.

The methods of opting out would be similar to those discussed in connection with Social Security. For veterans willing to use VA health care rather than Medicare, payroll taxes could be reduced and promised benefits could be transformed into an annuity or paid in a lump sum. Going forward, young people could have the option of paying a reduced payroll tax provided they agree to provide for their own postretirement health care—using, for example, the methods described below.

The VA system could also be used as an alternative to Medicare for the spouses of veterans and perhaps for people who have no connection with military service at all. In that way the Veterans Health Administration and Medicare could compete against each other. Postretirement health care programs established by employers could also be competitors.

In what follows, we will consider a particular type of reform that is similar to the 4 percent solution for Social Security.

As we have seen, the Affordable Care Act commits Medicare to steep cuts in spending relative to its historical growth path. No one knows what these spending caps will mean or even if they will actually be implemented. Yet for someone turning sixty-five today, the reduction in spending is roughly equal to three years of average Medicare benefits. For fifty-five-year-olds, the loss expected is the rough equivalent of five years of benefits. For forty-five-year-olds, it's almost nine years.

Clearly, the future is uncertain.

In this section we assume that Medicare returns to its original underlying growth path. In fact, we assume that the government guarantees that growth path along with reforms that, in the long run, will keep the taxpayer burden as a percentage of national income no higher than it is today.

Five fundamental reforms would improve Medicare immediately, empowering today's seniors by giving them the same private insurance options available to nonseniors and allowing younger workers to opt out of Medicare altogether:[20]

- Using a special type of Health Savings Account, beneficiaries would be able to manage at least one-fifth of their health care dollars—thus keeping each dollar of wasteful spending they avoid and bearing the full cost of each dollar of waste they generate.

- Physicians would be free to repackage and reprice their services, thus profiting from innovations that lower the costs and raise the quality of care.

- Medicare beneficiaries would have immediate access to walk-in clinics and a raft of other services, where prices are being set in a medical marketplace rather than by bureaucratic fiat.

- Insurers would have complete freedom to provide seniors with the full range of products available to nonseniors.

- Workers (along with their employers) would save and invest 4 percent of payroll—eventually reaching the point at which each generation of retirees pays for the bulk of its own postretirement medical care.

Economists at Texas A&M University estimate that for the average worker, an annual deposit of 4 percent of wages over a full work life should be sufficient to fully opt out of traditional Medicare by the time of retirement.[21] In terms of the impact of Medicare on the economy as a whole, with no reform, the size of the Medicare program will more than triple (relative to national income) over the next seventy-five years. With reform, funding Medicare will take no more of the national income than it does today.

Under reasonable assumptions, we can reach the mid-twenty-first century with seniors paying no more (as a share of the cost of the program) than the premiums they pay today and with a taxpayer burden (relative to national income) no greater than it is now.[22] Along the way, the structure of Medicare financing will be totally transformed:

- Whereas today, 86 percent of all Medicare spending is funded through taxes, by 2080, taxes will be needed for only one out of every four dollars of spending.

- Whereas Medicare is not prefunded today, 60 percent of all Medicare spending eventually will be financed by savings generated by beneficiaries during their working years.

- Tax-financed health expenditures would be directed mainly toward the poor, disabled, and chronically ill, and to fund safety-net institutions.

These reforms are expected to moderate the growth of Medicare spending and reduce the burden on taxpayers over time. Moreover, this is accomplished without any reduction in currently scheduled benefits. Of the future reduction in taxes and premiums, 10 percent will come from supply-side reforms, 20 percent from demand-side reforms, and 70 percent from the effects of prefunding. Furthermore, all of these changes are accomplished while preserving the progressivity of the current system. (See figure 11.1.)

New Opportunities for Patients. Under the current structure, seniors pay as many as three premiums to three plans (Medicare Part B premium, Medigap premium, and Medicare Part D premium) and often still do not have the coverage nonseniors typically have. What follows is a description of how to replace this complex structure with a new, simplified system that mimics the health insurance benefits the rest of Americans enjoy.[23]

Figure 11.1 Closing the Gap in Medicare

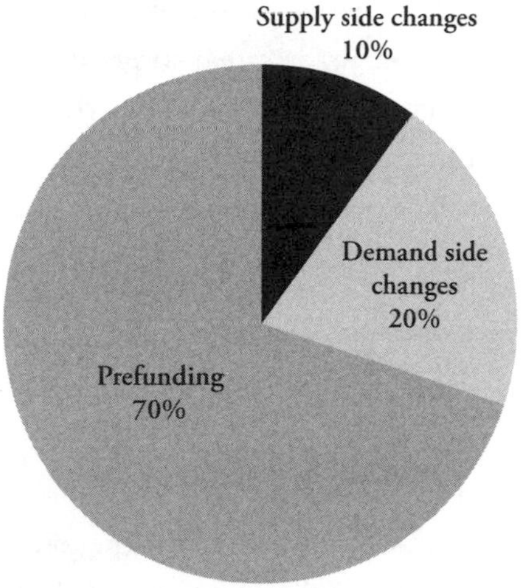

Source: John C. Goodman, "A Framework for Medicare Reform," National Center for Policy Analysis, Policy Report No. 315, September 2008. Available at http://www.ncpathinktank.org/pdfs/st315.pdf.

Standard Comprehensive Plan. The Standard Comprehensive Plan (SCP) would have an across-the-board $2,500 deductible and comprehensive coverage above the deductible. Only one premium would be needed to enroll in this plan, equal to about 15 percent of Medicare's total cost. All current Medicare beneficiaries would have the opportunity to enroll in an SCP as an alternative to traditional Medicare. For all future Medicare enrollees, the SCP would be the only government plan offered.

Roth Health Savings Accounts. All seniors enrolled in an SCP could deposit up to $2,500 in a Roth HSA. These deposits would be after-tax dollars, grow tax free, and could be withdrawn for any purpose tax free. It is expected that most seniors who enroll in SCPs would be able to fund their HSA deposits with money that would otherwise be spent out of pocket, plus the savings on premium expenses. Those who elect some of the options described below may be able to have larger accounts, funded by third-party insurer contributions or out-of-pocket contributions. In all cases, seniors would use their HSAs to pay for expenses not paid by third-party insurance.

Private Administration. Under the current system, Blue Cross and other private insurers, acting as no-risk claims processors, generally administer Medicare. Under the new system, private insurers also would administer the government's SCP plan; however, the private carriers may also offer plans, much as they do under the current Medicare Advantage Program (Part C). The government would pay these plans a risk-adjusted premium, and they would be at risk, with incentives to eliminate waste and inefficiency. (See the sidebar.)

Risk-Adjusted Premiums. People who are already enrolled in Medicare would continue to pay a premium equal to about 15 percent of Medicare's average costs.[32] For those who enroll in private plans, the government would add to this amount, producing an overall premium, adjusted for health risks the senior poses. The government's goal is to ensure that the total premium would always be actuarially fair—making all applicants equally desirable to the health plans, regardless of health status. (The current method of making risk-rated premium payments could serve as a guide; however, Congress, in response to special-interest pressures, imposes too many constraints.) People yet to retire would face additional costs, as described below.

Other Insurance Options. Seniors would have other insurance options. Following the method described above, it would be possible to reduce the taxpayers' liability. Once the government (taxpayer) contribution has been set, insurers would be able to offer different benefit packages, with higher or lower overall premiums. These options would include health maintenance organizations, preferred provider organizations, HSA plans with larger deductibles, and Special Needs Plans within HSAs. Also, retirees could remain in their previous employer's plan (if the employer is willing) by directing the government's contribution to that plan.

New Health Savings Account Design. Private insurers would be able to offer Roth Health Savings Accounts. Beneficiaries would be able to add their own after-tax contributions to these accounts, and withdrawals for nonmedical purposes would be tax free and penalty free. HSA plans would not be required to have an across-the-board deductible. They would instead be allowed to reduce the deductible to zero for services they want to encourage (such as medications for schizophrenia) and maintain high deductibles for services for which patient

Is Public Better than Private?

A large segment of the health policy community evinces an almost knee-jerk, negative reaction to the idea of private, for-profit firms rivaling each other in a competitive medical marketplace.[24] More generally, a belief is strongly held that the economic model and even the language of economics have no place in health care. This point of view is not just confined to the hard left. For most of its history, the American Medical Association pushed for nonprofit rather than for-profit firms and the systematic suppression of competition in the hospital and health insurance industries.

One writer who consistently reflects the antieconomics viewpoint is *New York Times* columnist Paul Krugman, even though he won a Nobel Prize in economic science. Krugman makes three assertions over and over again in his columns, namely: (1) Government health care in general is more efficient than private health care, (2) Medicare and Medicaid in particular are more efficient than private insurance, and (3) the health care systems of other countries are more efficient than our own.[25] What's wrong with all that?

One source of the error is the mistaken idea that Medicare and Medicaid actually are run by the government. They aren't. Medicare in the United States is managed almost everywhere by Blue Cross, Humana, WellPoint, and other private contractors. These, of course, are the same entities that manage private health insurance. Much of Medicaid is privately managed as well. Furthermore, one out of every three Medicare enrollees and two of every three Medicaid enrollees are enrolled in private health plans, even though government is paying the bill.[26]

A second source of error is the belief that the private and the public sector behave in fundamentally different ways. In other markets that might be true. However, in health care we have so completely suppressed the market that the distinction between private and public has become irrelevant. For the most part, private insurers pay providers the same way Medicare pays. They use the same billing codes and pay for the same services in the same way.[27]

(Sidebar continued on the next page)

A third source of error is the failure to understand what has really been happening in Medicare:

- There is not one Medicare program but two: conventional Medicare and Medicare Advantage (MA); under the latter, one-third of all Medicare beneficiaries have chosen to enroll in private health insurance plans.

- In the opinion of health economists who have looked at the subject seriously, the most innovative and successful attempts to lower cost, raise quality, and improve access in the entire country are found in Medicare Advantage plans—particularly those run by independent doctor associations, managed by entrepreneurs.[28]

- Probably the worst-run insurance plan in the entire country is conventional Medicare, which on any given day is setting about six billion prices—without any regard to supply-and-demand conditions and (for the most part) without any regard to how its administered prices affect quality of care or access to care.

- The results of the Affordable Care Act's pilot programs and demonstration projects have been almost uniformly mediocre—although some of these very same techniques are actually working and working quite well in the best-run Medicare Advantage plans.

- The Obama administration's attempt to encourage medicine to be practiced in Accountable Care Organizations is largely a failed experiment to duplicate what the Medicare Advantage plans already are doing. For example, of thirty-two "pioneer" ACOs participating in a demonstration project, the nineteen that remained in the program performed no better that the thirteen that dropped out.[29]

It appears that the only real hope for the ACOs is deregulation—allowing them to copy what the MA plans are doing. Far from being a threat to Medicare, privatization appears to be the only way it can work well.

(Sidebar continued on the next page)

The final mistake is made at both ends of the political spectrum: the belief that other health care systems are radically different from our own. They aren't.[30]

Take the United States and Canada. I would say that the health care systems of these two countries are 80 percent the same. In both countries, third parties pay the vast majority of medical expenses. In both countries, the third parties pay by task (fee-for-service). In Canada, when patients see a physician, it's free. In the United States, it's almost free. In both countries, people pay for care mainly with time and not with money. In both countries, normal market forces have been suppressed completely. Health care in both countries is bureaucratic, cumbersome, wasteful, inefficient, and unresponsive to consumer needs.

One reason so many people get misled is that in Canada, government is the third-party payer, whereas in the United States, about half of all spending is private. True enough, our public insurance looks just like the socialized insurance we find in Canada. But so does our private insurance.

People on the left and right who are prone to stress the differences between US health care and the health care of other countries invariably ignore the 80 percent commonality and focus on the remaining 20 percent. On the left, the focus is usually on the ways we appear to be worse; on the right, the focus is usually on the ways we appear to be better. But even here the differences are narrowing, and I expect that trend will continue.

Doctors who object to managed-care interference with the practice of medicine in this country will not be pleased to learn that everything that is happening here is finding its way to other countries as well. Indeed, US insurance companies are contracting with governments in other countries to export what they do here to other places. If you are concerned about rationing-by-waiting in other countries, brace yourself. Waiting times are growing in the United States as well.[31]

discretion is appropriate and desirable (for example, choices of drugs for arthritis or allergies). Additionally, plans would be able to carve out whole categories of care (such as primary care or diagnostic tests), which patients would pay entirely from their HSAs without any deductible or copayment.[33]

Insurers would also be able to create special HSA accounts for the chronically ill, allowing them to manage more of their own health care dollars. The "cash and counseling" experiments—pilot projects in more than half the states—have provided one possible model to follow. In these programs, disabled Medicaid patients manage their own health care budgets and can hire and fire those who provide them with custodial care and even medical services. Incredibly, the satisfaction rate in these programs is 90 percent.[34] The insurer's incentives to improve plan design would be enhanced by long-term contracts. (See the discussion under *Life Under a Reformed System*.)

New Opportunities for Providers. Physicians participating in Medicare today must practice medicine under an outmoded, wasteful payment system.[35] Until 2020, they received no financial reward for talking to patients by telephone, email, Zoom or Skype. They typically receive no financial reward for teaching patients how to manage their own care, or helping them be better consumers in the market for drugs. Indeed, doctors are not even paid by Medicare to treat comorbidities. As physician Richard Young points out, physicians face perverse incentives when they treat a patient with, say, five or more conditions (diabetes, heart disease, high blood pressure, obesity, etc.). These are the patients who spend the most Medicare dollars—typically costing taxpayers $60,000 a year. The ideal way to treat such patients is to treat all five problems during one visit. This economizes on the patient's time and ensures that the treatment regimens are integrated and consistent. Yet if a specialist does this, he gets a full fee only for the first morbidity and receives half the normal fee for the remaining four problems. Family doctors typically get no fee for treating the four additional problems.

As a result, the normal practice is for doctors to treat only one problem per visit. For the additional problems, the patient is referred to another specialist or scheduled for future visits. A better solution is to let doctors bid to provide full-service treatment for the patient with multiple chronic problems. Let the market determine how much Medicare must pay for efficient integrated care.[36]

Take diabetic care. Suppose a doctor made this proposal: take the money Medicare has been spending on diabetic care for a group of patients and give part of it as a lump sum to the physician on a monthly basis and put the remainder in a Health Savings Account for each patient. The payment to the physician would fund infrastructure (home monitoring devices, etc.) and cover the physician's cost of electronic records. The patient would use HSA funds to pay other out-of-pocket expenses, including, perhaps, the cost of telephone and email consultations.[37] If Medicare's cost is reduced and the quality of care rises, Medicare should not hesitate at the chance to accept such arrangements.

This example shows how we can produce high-quality care for a cost well below what we are paying today. An enormous amount of money—by some estimates, 75 percent of all health care dollars—is spent on the care of the chronically ill.[38] In general, "any provider should be able to propose and obtain a different payment arrangement, provided that (1) the total cost to government does not increase, (2) patient quality of care does not decline, and (3) the provider proposes a method of measuring and ensuring that (1) and (2) have been satisfied."[39]

Liberating the Marketplace. The way Medicare attempts to set prices is a nearly impossible task.[40] Instead, we should begin the process of allowing medical fees to be determined in the marketplace. Former Medicare trustee Thomas Saving and I have proposed eight important policy changes that can help us achieve this goal:[41]

- *Retail outlets*: Walk-in clinics, doc-in-the-box clinics, and freestanding emergency care clinics post prices and usually deliver high-quality care. Since these fees are way below what Medicare would have paid at a physician's office or hospital emergency room, we should allow patients to add to Medicare's low fee structure and pay the market price for this type of care. This reform would lower Medicare's costs, even as it makes primary care more accessible.

- *Phone and email services*: Medicare should allow enrollees to take advantage of commercial phone and email consultations, paying out-of-pocket when necessary.[42] (See the sidebar, "Standing between You and All the Benefits of Telemedicine: Medicare and the AMA.")

- *Concierge doctors*: Medicare should encourage—rather than discourage—the emergence of concierge doctor arrangements (often called direct primary care arrangements), perhaps by paying some or all of the entire annual fee.[43]

- *Billing by time, rather than task*: We should allow doctors to change the mix of services they offer and pay them for their time. If the change in practice is substantial enough, we should allow patient copayments and let the hourly fee be determined in the marketplace.

- *Paramedical personnel*: The supply of low-cost medical care could be expanded through greater use of nurses and physician assistants to perform tasks that do not require a physician's level of expertise.

- *Bundling*: Providers should be encouraged to offer package prices for bundled services, and Medicare should be willing to pay the package price wherever it is expected to be less than what taxpayers would otherwise have paid. Patients should share in the savings as well—in order to encourage them to patronize lower-cost, higher-quality provision.

- *International medical tourism*: The international medical tourism market is real. Providers routinely compete for patients based on price and quality, and Medicare should take advantage of it. If a patient saves money for Medicare by traveling, the patient should share in the savings.

- *Domestic medical tourism*: As a rule, US hospitals only step outside the system and charge package prices to people who travel to another city because such patients would likely not use that hospital if it did not compete on price.[44] Seniors too could be in this market, and they would be if Medicare allowed the senior to share in the savings created by traveling to a higher-quality, lower-cost facility.

In addition, selective relaxation of Medicare's price controls should be used to determine whether Medicare patients under the current system are being denied convenience, amenities, and perhaps quality that they are willing to pay for in the market.

Standing between You and All the Benefits of Telemedicine: Medicare and the AMA

Experts believe that telemedicine has great promise— to reduce the cost of health care, improve the quality, and give patients prompt access to the medical help they need from some of the best doctors in the country.[45]

For example, suppose you are a patient in an intensive care ward in an area including southern Minnesota and parts of Iowa and Wisconsin. There is a chance that your vital signs are not being monitored by the staff of the hospital you are in. The clinical staff of the Mayo Clinic— miles away—could be monitoring them. The Mayo Clinic's eICU, or electronic intensive care unit, currently monitors seventy-three ICU beds in remote locations.[46]

Jim Spencer, writing in the *Minneapolis Star Tribune*, explains how the Mayo staff works:

> They zoom in remote video cameras to get detailed focus on individuals. They watch blood pressure numbers and respiration. They talk to patients. If they need to insert a breathing tube or reinflate a collapsed lung, they contact technicians at the hospitals where the patients are located and tell them what to do. They also listen to those technicians' feedback on how patients are progressing.[47]

Mayo is able to provide expertise that generally is not available in local community hospitals—especially for complicated stroke victims. Odds are that the cost of this kind of care is lower than the alternative. The quality is certainly better. Patients get access to the best that Mayo has to offer without ever having to go there. There is even international interest in what Mayo is doing. Several Middle Eastern countries have approached the clinic about supplying these same services abroad.

So, who could be against this? Until recently, the American Medical Association was for one. The federal government was another. The of-

(Sidebar continued on the next page)

ficial position of the AMA was that doctors must be present physically with a patient in order to deliver appropriate care. And this is not a small issue with organized medicine. The Texas Medical Association (TMA) waged an extended court battle to outlaw the activities of Dallas-based Teladoc—a firm that provides medical consultation by phone to nearly eleven million patients every year.

Suppose you are traveling, and you need to have a prescription refilled. A call to Teladoc puts you in touch with a doctor (usually within thirty minutes) who has access to your electronic medical records and can meet your request. The TMA claimed that in opposing this practice it is only concerned with the welfare of the patient. But this is pure hypocrisy.

The same organization that thinks you shouldn't be able to get a prescription from a Teladoc doctor you have never met thinks it's perfectly okay for you to get a prescription from an "on-call" doctor you also have never met, who is subbing for your regular doctor and who probably isn't looking at your medical records when he orders the prescription.

As I wrote at Forbes:

> Why is one okay and not the other? The only difference I can see is economic. On-call doctors add to total health care spending. They increase revenue for doctors as a whole. Teladoc, on the other hand, is challenging orthodoxy. It threatens to lower the cost of care and reduce overall doctor incomes.[48]

Today, as in the past, organized medicine acts as a cartel agent for the doctors.

Another traditional opponent of telemedicine was Medicare. In general, the federal government wouldn't pay for telemedicine except under special circumstances. As Spencer explains:

> Medicare currently reimburses only for a limited number of telehealth services and then only when patients receiving it live in an officially defined "Health Professional Shortage Area" or a county outside of a Metropolitan Statistical Area. The treatment

(Sidebar continued on the next page)

also has to take place in a medical facility. Medicare will not pay if it takes place in a patient's home.[49]

But telemedicine in the home can be just as important as in a medical facility. Take the case of Jessica Todd, an eighty-year-old who suffers from mini strokes:

> She wears a monitor that records her health information and ships it to a company that immediately passes any suspicious readings on to Mayo for near-instant analysis by technicians sitting in a room full of computer monitors. The technicians measure what's happening to Todd against a protocol that tells them whether to refer the situation up a medical chain of command that can lead to immediate intervention when necessary.[50]

Meanwhile, one market is really poised to take off. Writing in the *Dallas Morning News*, Jim Landers says:

> Tractica, a market analysis firm, last week predicted video health visits would soon be the prevailing virtual medicine technology. Tractica predicted video consultation sessions would increase from 19.7 million in 2014 to 158.4 million per year by 2020.
>
> At the moment, there are 1.25 billion ambulatory care visits every year to physician offices, emergency rooms, and outpatient clinics, according to the Centers for Disease Control and Prevention. Teladoc expects virtual medicine could handle 417 million of those.[51]

In other words, one-third of all doctor visits don't really require a physical visit.

What Does Uber Medicine Look Like?

Uber is completely revolutionizing the market for urban ground transportation.[52] Could a similar revolution occur in other fields, including the market for medical care?

(Sidebar continued on the next page)

A number of firms will bring a doctor to your doorstep at the flick of a cell phone app, including Doctors Making Housecalls (North Carolina), Pager (New York), and Heal (California).

Insurance rarely pays for the service. Like so many other innovations in meeting the medical needs of patients (walk-in clinics, telephone consultations, etc.), these firms cater to patients who pay with their own money.

Take Sarah Sheehan, a Brooklyn resident who was reeling from a painful earache one weekend. Her conventional choices were to endure the hassles and long waits at a hospital emergency room or to delay treatment until Monday morning and take a forty-five-minute subway ride to reach a doctor's office. Pager offered her a better option: let the doctor come to her.

Here is how Pager works. Customers pay a $50 fee for their first visit and $200 for subsequent visits from one of the company's forty health practitioners, including doctors, nurses, and physician assistants. Assuming that the first-visit charge is a loss leader, Pager's service costs a lot more than a typical doctor's office visit. But it's a lot less than the national median emergency room charge of $505.

Heal, which launched in the Los Angeles area and has now expanded to San Francisco, promises a doctor within an hour, between the hours of 8 a.m. and 8 p.m., seven days a week. The charge is $99 a visit.

One reason why the market for these kinds of services is likely to be large is that they address a big problem with the American health care system. Although the rest of the world often views our system as "capitalistic" medicine, the fact is that patients in this country pay for care the same way patients pay in most other developed countries—we primarily pay with time and not with money. Almost all the interesting (free-market) innovations in meeting patient needs address this problem. They give patients the opportunity to pay money to avoid waiting and inconvenience.

For example, the Doctors Making Housecalls (DMH) website advertises its services with this pitch:

(Sidebar continued on the next page)

Next time you find yourself waiting interminably for an appointment or languishing in a doctor's office, urgent care clinic, or emergency room, worrying about exposure to other sick people not to mention the bill you're going to receive for care that is not a true emergency, please remember—there is a better way! DMH offers prompt appointments in the comfort of your own home or business, for any medical condition except life-threatening emergencies. We come to you when and where you need us, seven days a week, so you'll get the right care, in the right place, at the right time—and never have to wait in a doctor's office again.[53]

Right now, the house call services are not "hyperlocalized." That is, you can't see where the doctor is in relation to you by looking at the app on your cell phone. Also, unlike Uber, they don't automatically connect the closest doctor with the closest patient. And unlike Teladoc, which provides telephone consultations and other telemedicine services, the house call doctors don't have access to your electronic medical history.

But I suppose all that will be coming next.

Expected Changes in Consumer Behavior. Almost three decades ago, a RAND study found that when people pay a substantial share of their health care bills out of pocket, they reduce their health care spending significantly, with no apparent harmful effects on their health.[54] In that study:

- People with a deductible of about $2,500 (in today's prices) cut back on spending by about 30 percent relative to people who faced *no out-of-pocket costs.*

- Aside from some minor quibbling, there was *no negative impact on health* from the higher deductible.

- But people with high deductibles were as likely to cut back on useful health services as they were to cut back on unnecessary care.

The third point above was seized upon by latter-day critics to argue that patient choices appear to be random, and therefore the experiment in consumer-directed care showed it to be a failure. In fact, the patients' behavior is exactly what you would expect from a rational consumer of any product. When something is free, the temptation is to take everything that is offered. The incentive to distinguish between what is "necessary" or "useful" and "unnecessary" or "unuseful" is largely nonexistent. When consumers pay market prices, however, they have an incentive to pay more attention—figuring out what is "unnecessary" and dropping that as well as those "necessary" items whose value is less than their price.

In the thirty-year period since the RAND experiment was conducted, virtually every serious study of consumer-directed health care has reached similar conclusions. Indeed, since that time, a number of experiments have been conducted—both within this country and abroad—exploring ways to create greater patient cost sharing without encouraging people to forgo needed care. These include Medisave Accounts in Singapore (dating from 1984) and Medical Savings Accounts (MSAs) in South Africa (dating from 1993), and in the United States an MSA pilot program (dating from 1996), the current HSA program (dating from 2004), Health Reimbursement Arrangements (dating from 2002), and even cash accounts in Medicaid.[55] Many of these experiments have been subjected to considerable academic scrutiny.[56]

In a 2006 follow-up study, RAND researchers paid special attention to the plight of "vulnerable families" (low income and/or high risk).[57] The finding: these patients are not disadvantaged by the spending reductions. The researchers report:

> There are no statistically significant differences between nonvulnerable families and low-income or high-risk families in terms of dollar reductions in total spending that result from benefit designs and few differences in the components of spending. However, since high-risk families have higher levels of spending, the proportional reductions in total annual spending are generally smaller for those at high risk.[58]

RAND researchers were particularly concerned about whether vulnerable families would fail to receive recommended preventive care services. They found:

As with spending, there are few significant differences between low-income and nonvulnerable families regarding the effect of plan design on receipt of the cancer screening. However, there are significant differences for those at high risk. For them, a high deductible is not associated with reductions in receipt of two of the three recommended procedures and the reduction for the third is significantly less than for the nonvulnerable population, though this latter is not significant when we adjust for multiple comparisons.[59]

In other words, people at high risk are not deterred by the plan design from getting needed screening.

When patients are managing their own health care funds, they make prudent decisions—for example, substituting generic drugs for brand-name drugs, reducing unnecessary trips to physicians' offices and hospital emergency rooms, engaging in comparison shopping, seeking second opinions on surgery, questioning the necessity of certain diagnostic tests, and so forth.[60]

New Opportunities for Workers. For current workers who will become future generations of seniors, health care expenses in retirement can be prefunded through the creation of Health Insurance Retirement Accounts (HIRAs), based on contributions of about 4 percent of an average individual's wages over his working life.[61] Eventually, each generation would pay its own way. By saving enough during their working years and paying additional amounts from their retirement incomes, individuals would be able to cover the cost of care completely during the years of retirement.

Investment of HIRA Funds. All HIRA funds would be invested in diversified, conservative, international portfolios consisting of stocks, bonds, real estate, and other assets.

Management. The investment of HIRA funds would be managed by private security agencies. As is the case with Chile's social security system, these companies would compete not so much on portfolio selection (about which they would have little choice), but on reporting, accounting, and other services.

Contingent Ownership. Individuals would be the nominal owners of their HIRAs, but their rights to these funds would be contingent on several factors. First, they must survive to the age of eligibility for Medicare. In case of an early death, a worker's HIRA funds would be distributed to the accounts of all remaining workers. In this sense, an individual's property rights in a HIRA would be like contractual rights under an annuity insurance contract. Second, the Standard Comprehensive Plans would receive risk-rated premiums for all their enrollees. In the early years, the risk rating could be accomplished fully by adjusting the government's contribution. Over time, however, HIRA balances in overfunded accounts could be "taxed" to make risk-rated premium payments on behalf of individuals with underfunded accounts. At that point, HIRA owners would be entitled to a risk-rated annual withdrawal.

HIRA Retirement Health Insurance Options. Owners of HIRA accounts would be given three options: (1) They could cede their HIRA funds to the government and enroll in a conventional Medicare Standard Comprehensive Plan (discussed previously); (2) they could purchase an annuity—a stream of cash for their remaining years to be used to pay private health insurance premiums and to purchase health care directly; or (3) they could keep the account and withdraw an amount each year for the payment of premiums, with the withdrawal percentage determined by the government.

Opting Out of Medicaid Long-Term Care

Few people self-insure or purchase private insurance for long-term care, most likely because of Medicaid's backstop. However, instead of viewing entitlement and public programs as the most viable solution to eldercare issues, we should view Medicaid as an unattractive last resort compared to privately funded solutions.

Moreover, win/win opportunities exist to substitute private responsibility for long-term care for government responsibility. The following reforms have been proposed by my colleague Pam Villarreal.

Private Long-Term Care Insurance. The purchase of private long-term care policies by individuals is growing, but only 14 percent of individuals over age sixty have them.[62] Long-term care policies have some advantages over Medicaid:

- The most obvious advantage of long-term care insurance is that private policies protect individuals' assets without requiring "spending down" to qualify.

- Long-term care policies offer various waiting periods before coverage kicks in, from thirty days up to a year; a longer waiting period means lower monthly premiums.

- The vast majority of them cover institutional, assisted living, *or* at-home health and custodial care—whereas not all states allow Medicaid to cover long-term, at-home custodial care.[63]

- Individuals are not limited to nursing homes that accept Medicaid.

Long-term care insurance has some disadvantages, owing partly to regulatory restrictions. For instance:

- Some private policies are not adjusted for inflation and may have a rather low maximum daily reimbursement amount; this could be problematic, particularly if a policy were purchased, say, ten years before an individual enters a nursing home.

- Private long-term care policies can be expensive, even for those who purchase insurance when they are younger. For example, annual premiums for a fifty-five-year-old average $2,050 for a single male or $2,700 for a single female—for $164,000 in initial benefits—reaching a value of $386,500 by the time the individual is eighty-five.

- In general, the tax deductibility of long-term care premiums is limited. Since they are considered a medical expense, they are deductible only if a household's total out-of-pocket medical expenses exceed 10 percent of their adjusted gross income. Moreover, the amount of premium that can be deducted depends on the individual's age.

The tax law is more generous with respect to these exceptions, however:

- Long-term care premiums can be paid for with untaxed funds in a Health Savings Account; although premiums cannot be paid from untaxed funds in a Flexible Spending Account (FSA).

- Employer-provided Health Reimbursement Accounts can also be used for long-term care premium expenses.

- Also, employer-provided long-term care insurance is an untaxed employee benefit.

Public-Private Partnership Programs. A majority of states now have public-private partnerships, which allow individuals to shield a certain amount of their assets from Medicaid's asset-eligibility test in return for purchasing private long-term care insurance. Some states provide dollar-for-dollar coverage (for each dollar coverage of long-term care insurance purchased, a dollar of assets is protected). Some states allow complete asset protection for purchasing a minimum amount of coverage. Others do a combination of both.[64]

However, these policies have not been very popular, even among the elderly. One reason is that the most valuable asset most individuals and couples own is their home. Medicaid exempts the value of a house owned by a couple completely and exempts more than $500,000 in home value for an individual. As a result, people who protect their home from fire and other calamities, or purchase life insurance in order to pay the mortgage if the principal earner dies, have no incentive to protect their home against the risk that they might need nursing home care.

Needed Change: Access Home Equity. The most important change that could be made to Medicaid long-term care eligibility is for the program to recognize the income-producing value of a home. Consider reverse mortgages. Although fairly new, they should be integrated into Medicaid eligibility and long-term care financing. Reverse mortgages allow individuals age sixty-two and older to receive a lump sum or monthly income stream from the equity in their homes. This is a way for people to turn their homes into an income flow from which to pay for long-term care without having to go through the hassle of selling their home and waiting for months or even years to collect on the sale. Importantly, with a reverse mortgage, as long as a spouse or other dependent lives in the house, or if the nursing home resident returns, the house cannot be sold to satisfy the mortgage.

Medicaid generally does not count this money as income for the purpose of its income-eligibility test, provided that it is spent in the same month it is received. But if the money is put into an account and not spent immediately, it is considered income that must be spent down before the individual is eligible for Medicaid.

Needed Change: Reduce the Amount of Home Value Exempted from the Medicaid Eligibility Test. Medicaid could encourage the utilization of the home as a liquid asset by doing the following:

- Lower the home exemption for both singles (which is more than $500,000) and couples (which is unlimited) to an amount closer to the median home value.[65]

- For individuals or couples who are older and likelier to spend the last few years of their lives in a nursing home, require them to return any equity above the exempt amount through a reverse mortgage to Medicaid and/or to a long-term care facility.[66]

- In exchange for accessing home equity, Medicaid programs should waive the requirement that individuals must spend down their incomes in order to qualify for Medicaid.

Ideally, the home value exemption should be reduced and combined with other asset value limits, so that people have the same incentive to purchase long-term care insurance whether or not they own a house. Furthermore, lowering the home value exemption for Medicaid eligibility would give middle- and high-income individuals an incentive to purchase long-term care insurance, limiting Medicaid to the truly poor.

Needed Change: Include Spousal Income in Determining Eligibility. Married Medicaid applicants are required to count only income received in their own name, not that of their spouses. This means, for example, that a healthy working spouse earning $5,000 a month and also receiving a spousal allowance from the Medicaid applicant could be living quite well while the long-term care spouse is living at the expense of the taxpayers. This policy should be changed.

Needed Change: Create Incentives to Purchase Long-Term Care Insurance.
Changes in the tax treatment of long-term care insurance would encourage
more people to buy the policies:

- At the federal level, individuals should be allowed to deduct the long-term care insurance premiums from their federal taxes and exempt any share of the premium paid by the employer from taxable compensation.[67]
- An individual with an HRA, FSA, or HSA should be allowed to pay premiums with funds from these tax-advantaged accounts.

Such changes would save federal and state Medicaid dollars in the long run
and increase the attractiveness of private alternatives to Medicaid.

Needed Change: Allow Seniors to Control More of Their Own Health Care.
Critics of consumer-directed health care often argue that patients are not
knowledgeable enough and the market is not transparent enough for consum-
erism to work in health care. But a study by the Commonwealth Fund notes
there is an international trend toward self-directed care and that it is focused
on a most unlikely group of patients: the frail, the old, the disabled, and even
the mentally ill.[68]

- In the United States, Medicaid "cash and counseling" programs—underway for over a decade—allow homebound, disabled patients to manage their own budgets and choose services that meet their needs.[69]
- In Germany and Austria, a cash payment is made to people eligible for long-term care with few strings attached and little oversight on how the money is used.
- In England and the Netherlands, the disabled and the elderly manage budgets in a manner similar to cash and counseling in the United States.
- Florida and Texas offer self-directed care programs for patients with serious mental illness, and the Veterans Administration operates a program in twenty states for long-term care and mental illness.

Moreover, it appears that we have barely scratched the surface in taking
advantage of patient power opportunities.

The greatest potential in this area is in the treatment of chronic illness. Studies show that chronically ill patients can often manage their own care with results as good as or better than under traditional care. If patients are going to manage their own care, it makes sense to allow them to manage the money that pays for that care.

Long-Term Care and Personal Accounts. Most home care and most institutional care needs could be met by the private sector for about 1 percent of earnings over the career of an average-wage worker. While they are in the workforce, individuals could purchase a minimum amount of long-term care insurance (similar to the minimum coverage required for auto insurance). Coverage for three years' worth of care would provide for the needs of more than 75 percent of individuals who will need long-term care.[70] The cost of such policies could be reduced in the following ways:

- First, patients would draw on their long-term care insurance; any cost sharing involved would be paid out of the patient's annuitized pension account (just as Medicaid currently requires cost sharing from an institutionalized individual's Social Security benefits).
- Second, in the event that long-term care insurance expires, patients could then draw on their assets—spending down other savings, selling a home, obtaining a reverse mortgage, and so forth.
- Third, Medicaid would provide remaining coverage only after all other options are exhausted.

Workers would have the option of purchasing more insurance to protect their assets by making an additional payment. The chances are that Medicaid safety-net coverage would not be common, except in the event that an individual is in a nursing home for many years.

How the Trump Administration Is Reforming Medicare

The Trump administration is making fundamental changes to the Medicare program.[71] These reforms are every bit as radical as the changes we have seen in federal policy governing employer-provided coverage and the market for individual insurance.[72] (Further, it seems likely that the changes initiated so far are only the beginning of a continuing shift in the role of government in health care.

The vision behind these reforms can be found in "Reforming America's Healthcare System through Choice and Competition." This 124-page, HHS document challenges a premise behind fifty years of thinking in health policy circles: the idea that our most serious problems in health care arise because of flaws in the private sector. Most problems arise because of government failure, not market failure, the document declares, and it goes into great detail on how to correct the policy errors.[73]

Trump policy toward health care is based on the idea of promoting choice, competition, and the role of market prices. In Medicare, so far, that means liberating telemedicine, liberating Accountable Care Organizations, ending payment incentives that are driving doctors to become hospital employees, promoting hospital price transparency, paperwork deregulation, and creating more transparency in the market for prescription drugs.

Liberating "Virtual Medicine." The ability to deliver medical care remotely is growing by leaps and bounds. It promises to lower costs, increase quality, and lower the time and travel cost of patient care. For example:[74]

- After hip and knee replacements at Tallahassee Memorial HealthCare, patients are transported to rehab facilities, nursing homes, and even to their own homes—where follow-up observations are made with video cameras.[75]

- A nurse at Mercy Virtual Hospital in St. Louis can use a camera in a hospital room in North Carolina to see that an IV bag is almost empty. She can then call and instruct a nurse on the floor to refill it. The telemedicine cameras are powerful enough to detect a patient's skin color. Microphones can pick up patient coughs, gasps, and groans.[76]

The problem? On the day Donald Trump became president, Medicare didn't pay for any of this. And since private insurers and employers tended to pay the way Medicare paid, the entire country was missing out on incredible advances in telemedical technology.[77]

This was not an accident. Federal law (the Social Security Act) allowed Medicare to pay for telemedicine only under strictly limited circumstances. For the most part, doctors could examine, consult with, and treat patients remotely only in rural areas, and even there, they couldn't be treated in their own homes.

Readers may be surprised to learn that even Medicare Advantage (MA) plans faced the same legal constraints. An MA plan could contract with a separate vendor, like LiveHealth or Teladoc, that had met the many onerous regulations required by CMS for telehealth vendors. But MA plans could not pay their own doctors to conduct remote consultations with their patients.

From early on, the Centers for Medicare and Medicaid Services (which oversees Medicare and Medicaid) acted aggressively to change that. Doctors in MA plans and Accountable Care Organizations (ACOs) were allowed to bill Medicare if they used the phone, email, Skype, and other technologies to consult with patients remotely to determine if they needed an in-office visit. These were called "virtual check-ins." Patients could be anywhere, including their own homes. Doctors were also allowed to bill Medicare to review and analyze medical images that patients send them. And, they could bill for telemedical consultations with other doctors.[78]

So, how did Seema Verma (administrator of CMS) and her colleagues overcome the legal barriers? By classifying these activities as "virtual medicine" or "communications technology" instead of "telemedicine."

The new changes didn't go as far as people in the industry would have liked. But a CMS white paper makes clear that the administration intended to do more. For example, CMS aggressively used its authority to sponsor federal telemedicine demonstration projects. As of 2020, Medicare Advantage plans and next-generation ACOs (see below) were allowed to seek and obtain waivers to use telemedicine for the monitoring and treatment of diabetes, heart disease, and other chronic conditions.[79]

Then came the coronavirus. As noted earlier, that sparked an immediate revolution in the way doctors and patients interacted.

Congress acted first, by allowing Medicare doctors and patients to use the phone, email, Skype, Zoom, and other technologies to communicate with each other. There were three restrictions: the communication had to be between a doctor and a patient who had seen each other face to face within the previous three years; the consultation had to relate to the coronavirus; and the relaxation of federal law was temporary, lasting only for the duration of the coronavirus threat.

The first restriction meant that every telemedicine company in the country and every hospital that was using online screening would be ineligible. The second restriction was probably impossible to enforce, since in every consultation the virus would undoubtedly be mentioned. The third restriction meant that the newfound freedom to employ twenty-first-century technology would go away when the threat from the virus went away.

Fortunately, the Trump administration asserted "emergency authority" to ignore the three-year restriction and gave broad discretion to doctors in deciding whether a consultation had any relationship to the virus. Within days, Congress, in yet another bill, put its stamp of approval on these moves—but, again, only as temporary measures.

Seniors who were members of Medicare Advantage (MA) plans were probably the first to realize the benefits of these changes. That's because of the deregulation that had already been underway. In one MA plan, the number of doctors using telemedicine jumped from 40 to 90 percent in one week!

Still, all of these changes were taking place in a sort of legal limbo. Who knew what would happen when the virus went away?

We will have more to say on these changes below.

Liberating ACOs. The idea behind Accountable Care Organizations and Medicare Advantage plans is similar. In both cases, the federal government is encouraging the private sector to find innovative ways to reduce costs and improve quality—generally through integrated, coordinated, managed care. If the plan successfully reduces costs, it gets to keep some or all of the savings. If it improves quality, it receives a bonus payment. Beyond that, the two models diverge.

In general, almost anything an ACO can do, an MA plan can do better. The reason? ACOs are structured differently and they are shackled with all manner of limitations, rules, and restrictions that do not encumber a garden-variety MA plan.

On the buyer side, enrollees in MA plans pay one premium to one plan, covering all Medicare Part A, B, and D benefits. The premium is usually no more than the Part B premium in ordinary Medicare. Not only are out-of-pocket expenses significantly reduced, compared to traditional Medicare, most beneficiaries also typically receive such additional benefits as free transportation, dental, eye care, and hearing aid benefits, a possible health club membership, and an allowance for health-related, over-the-counter products.

Seniors in an ACO plan, by contrast, are usually paying three premiums to three plans: Part B, Part D, and a Medigap policy that becomes more expensive as the enrollee ages.

On the provider side, MA doctors are dealing with a relatively stable population that can be monitored, tracked, and serviced over a multiyear period. This is what makes integrated care possible. Enrollees know that they must generally stick to a network of providers as a condition of receiving the full set of benefits from their MA plan.

By contrast, seniors in ACO plans are not actually enrolled. They are assigned by CMS to a primary care physician, and they usually don't know they are assigned. Further, until recently ACO plans were muzzled. Under the Obama administration, any communication to patients required CMS approval. Also, when ACO beneficiaries go to an "out-of-network" provider, they (without their knowledge) might be assigned to another ACO. This type of churning, along with physician turnover, apparently happens so frequently that it's amazing ACOs have had any success at all.[80]

The MA market is better designed to meet four social goals: lower cost, higher quality, better information, and the ability to adjust to changes in market conditions.

CMS pays MA plans a global capitation rate each month, based on beneficiary demographics, chronic conditions, patient satisfaction, and quality scores. Given a fixed payment, when an MA plan saves a dollar, it gets to keep the whole dollar. The plan reaps the entire benefit of its cost-reducing successes and bears the entire cost of its failures. If the MA market as a whole succeeds in lowering the social cost of care, Medicare can reduce its payment across the board to all plans (thus capturing the gain for the taxpayers) without changing these incentives.

By contrast, ACOs are not paid anything beyond Medicare's standard fees unless they achieve cost savings greater than 2 to 3 percent (depending on size) and an acceptable quality score. Even then, they are entitled to receive only a portion of the savings they generate. Some plans get to keep as little as twenty-five cents of every dollar they save, for example.

As plans become successful, Medicare raises the bar—changing the measurement of what constitutes a dollar saved, with a different standard for each plan. Thus, the more successful the ACO, the less it can expect to keep of each dollar actually saved—compared to other plans.

Also, ACOs do not receive their shared savings payment from CMS until at least September or October of the following year. This means that ACOs must use their own capital to fund integrated and coordinated care for up to almost two years before they receive a CMS payment.

For all these reasons, the incentives to reduce costs are much weaker for ACO plans than for MA plans. Notably, only one-third of ACOs were paid anything by CMS in 2017.

MA plans are rewarded on a star system for meeting access, patient satisfaction, quality, and outcome measures. Although the measurement of quality is imperfect—sometimes highly imperfect—the more stars, the more money the plan gets. Although Medicare may make the quality standard stricter over time, all plans are treated the same.

ACOs are also rewarded for meeting quality measures. The more successful the plan, the higher the percentage of monetary savings it gets to keep. However, since CMS continually raises the bar on what constitutes savings (plan by plan), ACOs that are more successful in reducing cost receive less of the quality reward than other plans with the same quality scores. And, as noted, there is a delay in payment. For these reasons, incentives for quality improvement are much weaker in the ACO system.

All systems for rewarding cost-reducing/quality-improving changes work only so well as the ability to adjust plan populations for case severity. Without this ability, we have no idea what we are paying for.

The Medicare Advantage program is the only place in all of Medicare where supplemental information can be abstracted from patient medical records and sent to CMS in order to make Medicare's risk adjustment more accurate. This practice probably results in higher average patient risk scores than otherwise. But higher risk scores are not a problem as long as the risk adjustment system is uniform across all doctors. Medicare can always lower the capitated fees it pays across the board.

Risk adjustment coding is a problem when it differs from doctor to doctor—as it undoubtedly does in traditional Medicare and in the ACO program. The Medicare Advantage risk adjustment process helps Medicare by making its information more accurate.

As previously noted, Medicare is trying to set hundreds of millions of physician fees every day. When it gets these prices wrong (as is inevitable), we get shortages and surpluses in the various specialties.[81]

In Dallas and other cities, for example, there are many family practitioners and internists who are refusing to take new Medicare patients. Unlike ACO plans and traditional Medicare, where paying standard Medicare rates is mandatory, MA plans are free to pay higher rates to PCPs and other providers in order to attract the services their patients need. MA plans can adjust to changes in market conditions. No other provider in Medicare can do that.

So why do ACOs even exist? The reason appears to be political. Although prominent Democrats have supported premium assistance for private Medicare plans in the past, by 2008 it was hard to find any Democrat who would support "privatization" in general, let alone privatization of Medicare. Also, Barack Obama ran for president that year criticizing Medicare Advantage plans. So, when Obamacare was created, the administration turned to stealth privatization. Seniors were led to believe they were paying doctors fee-for-service as they always had, while (unbeknownst to them) the doctors who treated them gained financially if they reduced the volume of care.

Attachment to ACOs exploded, almost overnight. At last count, there were 32.7 million patients enrolled in ACOs, including 10.4 million Medicare beneficiaries.[82] Yet, unlike MA plans, which generally have lower costs and higher quality ratings than traditional Medicare, the ACO experiment has been largely disappointing.[83] Without the tools routinely used by Medicare Advantage plans, ACOs are neither saving money in the aggregate nor improving the quality of care.[84]

That said, the top plans in both systems appear to be doctor-run. In fact, most MA insurers now contract with independent physician associations (IPAs) to run their plans. By contrast, the low-performing plans tend to be hospital-run.[85]

Also, fee-for-service payment is not the important factor. IntegraNet Health has some of the top-performing MA plans in the country and one of the best ACOs as well. Yet IntegraNet doctors are paid fee-for-service. They do not order medical tests willy-nilly—depending on how the spirit moves them, however. IntegraNet doctors know that if they lower costs and improve quality, they will earn a financial bonus at the end of each period.[86]

The original plan for ACOs was one of progression—evolving from shared savings to more savings for plans that take more risks with progression to full capitation. At the end of the line, ACOs will look more and more like Medicare Advantage HMOs. For the Trump administration, we can't seem to get there quickly enough.

The administration is allowing next-generation ACOs to (a) have greater freedom to communicate with patients, (b) reward patients for meeting compliance measures, (c) offer additional benefits that patients must forgo if they go "out of network," (d) have broad freedom to utilize telemedicine, and in some cases (e) opt for full capitation.[87]

Equalizing Physician Fees. The CMS vision paper expresses alarm over increasing concentration in medical markets—especially in the hospital and physician sectors. It cites studies that conclude that increasing concentration means less competition and higher consumer prices. One reason for concentration in physician services appears to be the acquisition of doctors by hospitals. In 2010, 27.7 percent of primary care physicians worked for hospitals. By 2016, that number had climbed to 43.5 percent.[88]

One reason for such consolidation appears to be that Medicare pays higher fees for the same service when the doctor is employed by a hospital. According to the Ambulatory Surgery Center Association, Medicare pays almost twice as much for hospital-based outpatient services as it pays for the same services provided by a freestanding facility. For example, Medicare pays hospitals $1,745 for performing an outpatient cataract surgery while paying surgery centers only $976.[89]

Under a new CMS rule, Medicare will be moving toward parity over the next two years for billing codes covering about 50 percent of outpatient services. According to the CMS, current Medicare payment for a typical hospital-based clinic visit is approximately $116, with an average beneficiary copayment of $23. After two years, the payment rate for the clinic visit will fall to $46 and the beneficiary copayment will fall to $9, thus saving beneficiaries an average of $14 each time they visit the clinic.[90]

The American Hospital Association is suing to block the rule change. But this illustrates something important about the powers of the executive branch. Many of the reforms described here would have been done by Congress—but for the influence of powerful special interests.[91]

When Congress tries to reform health care institutions, special interests stop the reforms in committee. Under the Trump administration, they must turn increasingly to the courts.

Price Transparency. When customers pay for goods and services out of their own pockets, price transparency is never a problem. This is just as true in health care as it is in any other market. For cosmetic surgery or LASIK surgery, for example, patients are never unsure what the cost will be.[92] Similarly, in the market for medical tourism, patients are almost always given an up-front package price, or a reasonably good estimate.[93] When Canadians come to the United States for joint replacements, for example, they not only know the price, they usually pay in advance.

For ordinary Americans, however, the US hospital sector is completely dominated by third-party payment. As a result, hospitals don't complete for patients on price. And when providers don't compete on price, they don't compete on quality either.[94] Hospital competition is mainly competition on amenities.[95]

The Trump administration would like to change that. Under the new rules, every hospital in the United States is required to post its standard price for the procedures it performs. Unfortunately, that may not help patients as much as might be hoped. It appears that many hospitals are meeting this CMS requirement by posting their charge master numbers.[96] These are like list prices that no one actually pays. Also, some hospitals are posting services in technical language that most patients won't understand. For example, Vanderbilt University Medical Center lists a charge of $42,569 for a cardiology procedure described as "HC PTC CLOS PAT DUCT ART."[97]

But this doesn't mean the exercise is not worth doing. Hospitals are fearful that patients will be deterred when they see the charge master amount, unaware that the price patients and their insurers are actually paying is much lower. They may ameliorate that fear by posting additional information— such as the real price patients can expect.

If hospitals start doing that, patients will soon discover something health policy analysts already know: what people are paying for the same service varies widely, even for facilities that are within a few blocks of each other.[98]

The first response of providers to the CMS rule may not be all that helpful. But the secondary and tertiary responses may be increasingly valuable. Indeed, the CMS transparency rule may ultimately coax providers into real price competition. That, in turn, might lead to quality competition and a genuinely competitive hospital marketplace.

Paperwork Deregulation. CMS has launched a major initiative to do something most doctors probably think is long overdue. Based on input from thousands of practitioners, the agency has made changes it estimates will eliminate fifty-three million hours of burden, costing as estimated $5.2 billion, over the first five years. Despite some complaints, these changes have been generally well received.[99]

Ending Rebates and Gag Clauses for Drugs. At the risk of oversimplification, the market for prescription drugs can best be understood as two separate markets. About 85 percent of all prescriptions in the United States are for generic drugs, and Americans pay some of the lowest prices in the world for most of them—lower than in Europe or in Canada, for example.

That outcome has been recently helped along by the Food and Drug Administration approval of a record number of generic drugs last year, saving consumers an estimated $26 billion.[100] Pharmacy benefits managers (PBMs) do a very good job negotiating price discounts for these drugs, and consumers gain as a result.[101]

The other market is the market for more expensive, brand-name drugs. It is in this market that Americans pay the highest drug prices in the world. Consumers often don't benefit from PBM discounts.[102] All too often they pay more than they should at the local pharmacy.

According to a University of Southern California study, in almost one-fourth of all prescription transactions, patients are likely paying more in health insurance copays than the cash price of the drug they are buying.[103] Gag clauses often prohibit pharmacists from telling patients about more affordable options.

Under PBM contracts for these drugs, most of the discounts go to the PBM itself in the form of a rebate. In return, the PBM is induced to position an expensive drug on its formulary so that patients are induced to choose it over a less expensive drug.

In general, all parties have perverse incentives in this system. The pharmaceutical companies have an incentive to raise prices, because the higher the price, the larger the rebate for the PBMs. High rebates give the PBMs an incentive to structure their formularies in a way that induces patients to choose the more expensive drugs.

Under the legislation that created the Part D Medicare drug benefit, the PBMs get a safe harbor from federal anti-kickback laws that would otherwise prohibit such arrangements.

To promote needed reforms, the president has signed two pieces of legislation to ban pharmacy gag clauses, and a new HHS rule will classify PBM rebates as illegal kickbacks unless the benefits are passed on to the consumer.[104] A study by Milliman estimates that this policy change could reduce federal spending on government programs by between $78 and $98 billion over the next ten years and reduce costs to seniors in the Part D program by as much as 18 percent.[105]

The administration admits uncertainty over these effects, but it seems reasonably clear that the out-of-pocket costs to patients who use expensive drugs will be lowered and the system will be more transparent.[106] Transparency, in turn, is a prerequisite for more competitive market.

Although these changes affect Medicare and Medicaid patients only, UnitedHealthcare has already announced a new policy under which it will pass along rebates to the patients in its private-sector plans—perhaps in anticipation of the administration's new initiative.[107] Many private employer plans are also beginning to share the rebates with their employees.[108]

Conclusion. The Trump administration is clearly pushing the envelope—in many cases acting to fill a void left by Congress. These changes will result in a very different health care system. It will be one that is shaped more by individual choice and market forces than by rules and regulations.

I2

Opting Out of Survivor Insurance

ONE ASPECT OF the Social Security system that has been over-looked often in reform discussions is survivors' benefits. As Estelle James has shown, Chile offers us solutions for the financial risks of lost income owing to the death of a worker with a dependent spouse or children. The Chilean system also includes protection against income loss for retirees whose spouse dies.[1]

Survivors Benefits for Younger Workers in Chile. In Chile's prefunded retire-ment system, younger workers do not have accounts large enough to provide many years of benefits for minor dependent children or a spouse. To supple-ment funds from the retirement account, "survivors' benefits for the spouse and minor children of a deceased worker are covered by a group disability and survivors' (D&S) insurance contract" purchased by a pension fund for its clients.[2] Workers pay an annual fee for disability and survivors' insurance of only 1 percent of wages, of which about two-thirds is for disability and one-third is for survivors. In other Latin American countries that have adopted the Chilean model—such as Argentina and Colombia—D&S fees are 0.9 to 1.7 percent of wages.[3]

If a worker accumulates a pension account balance sufficient to pay survi-vors benefits for the rest of a spouse's life and until any minor children reach adulthood, he no longer has to pay the fee for survivors' insurance.

Survivors Benefits for Retirees in Chile. "In Chile's pension system, benefits for widows are financed by their husbands' account contributions rather than by the public treasury. As noted, at retirement, most workers annuitize the balance in their accounts, providing a stream of inflation-protected income.

Married men who annuitize must buy joint annuities, which provide the surviving widow at least 60 percent of the husband's annuity. If dependent children are among the survivors, the annuity provides 50 percent to the widow plus 15 percent to each child. The formula for programmed withdrawals also includes these provisions for widows and survivors."[4]

Importantly, spouses in Chile do not give up benefits funded from their own accounts in order to receive spousal benefits or survivors' benefits. Since each individual funds his own retirement benefits, a surviving spouse is able to receive both benefits.

Adapting the Chilean Model for the United States. The Chilean system is built on some assumptions that would not be made in a US system. For example, in Chile the primary breadwinner usually is male, and many women are not in the labor force. Additionally, the "normal" retirement age for women (sixty) is lower than the age for men (sixty-five).

In the United States, we would likely consider the earnings of both spouses in determining the amount of survivors' insurance required. This would reduce the cost of survivors' insurance further. A small percentage of workers' accounts (about 1 percent) would be used to purchase group life insurance through a pension fund provider. Workers would be required to purchase life insurance only until their pension accounts are funded enough to cover 70 percent of their wages at retirement. After that, life insurance purchases would be optional. For spouses who die before retirement age, the life insurance component of the account would provide immediate income to the surviving spouse and children; upon retirement, the surviving spouse would then be entitled to what is accumulated in the account (which would not be paid out until his or her retirement), in addition to what the surviving spouse has accumulated in his/her own account.

Opting Out of Disability Insurance

AS ESTELLE JAMES writes, "Disability is the fastest-rising component of US Social Security, growing at nearly twice the rate of retirement benefit spending. Chile, however, reversed this trend when it implemented a new retirement and disability benefits system in 1981."[1] Chile's experience could be used as a model for disability reform in this country.

I will summarize James's descriptions of the system established in 1981, followed by a brief description of the 2008 reforms. Then, we will turn to opportunities to create an alternative to our workers' compensation system.

Opting Out of Social Security Disability Insurance. The disability insurance system in Chile is less well known than its pioneering pension system, but it is equally innovative.[2] It differs from traditional public disability insurance in four important ways: (1) it is largely prefunded; (2) the disability assessment procedure includes participation by private pension funds and insurance companies, which have a direct pecuniary interest in controlling costs; (3) disability benefits are determined in a way that does not give beneficiaries incentives not to work; and (4) disability insurance has been integrated successfully into its retirement system.

"If workers become disabled before retiring, they receive a defined benefit (equal to 70 percent of their average wage if totally disabled or 50 percent if partially disabled). Part of this benefit is covered by their own retirement accounts. The remainder is covered by an insurance policy purchased by each pension fund, which provides the top-up needed for disability and survivors' benefits. This is accomplished through the private insurance market, with government imposing detailed regulations and providing backup guarantees."[3]

Private Disability Insurance in Chile. Like the pension system, Chile's disability system is prefunded—so each generation covers its own disability costs. Workers make additional contributions to their retirement accounts to cover the contingency of disability, and they pay fees for group disability policies for any portion of their wages that can't be replaced from their own accounts.[4] "In the long run, workers' savings are projected to cover about 50 percent of their disability benefits. Widows and children of covered workers also receive a defined benefit."[5]

"Since workers fund their own disability benefits partially from their accounts, they have less incentive than American workers to claim disability. The private pension funds that handle their investment accounts and the insurance companies that provide group coverage participate in the process of assessing workers' disabilities, and they benefit financially from controlling costs. Workers also benefit from this private-sector participation through lower premiums for the disability insurance. This has led to lower disability rates and lower total costs than in other countries. For example, the disability rate among middle-aged workers in Chile is less than half that of US workers and less than one-third that of Western Europeans.[6] Insurance costs for disability in Chile would be four times greater without the investment accounts."[7]

Financing Disability Insurance in Chile. Workers who qualify for disability insurance are guaranteed a defined benefit for the balances of their lives.[8] During an initial three-year period, a disabled worker receives a temporary defined benefit directly from his pension provider. If a worker is certified as permanently disabled after the three-year provisional period, he has a choice of a lifetime annuity or a gradual withdrawal of money from his account.[9] The programmed withdrawal gives the worker the right to bequeath any money left in the account if he should die.

If the worker doesn't have enough money in his account to purchase an annuity that covers the defined benefit, the pension fund is responsible for "topping up" the account to the required level. To cover the cost of this top-up and the three-year provisional benefit, each pension fund is required to purchase a group term life insurance policy.[10] Survivors' benefits are covered in the same way, by the same insurance policy.

The group disability insurance policy is funded by the general administrative charge each worker pays the pension fund. Each fund sets its own fees and, apart from a small flat component, charges all its affiliated workers the same percentage of their wages—regardless of age, gender, occupation, or size of the account. These fees currently average about 2.4 percent of a workers' wages. This includes the combined cost of the group disability and survivors' insurance, which is about 1 percentage point of wages (of which the disability portion is two-thirds), and general administrative charges, which account for the other 1.4 percent.[11]

Thus, the total future income of the disabled individual is prefunded—partly out of his own retirement savings and partly by the group insurance policy purchased by the pension fund and financed by the group insurance fee paid by the workers.

Eligibility for Disability Insurance. While certification of a disability is made purely on medical grounds, eligibility for the insured defined benefit depends on recent work history. Workers qualify for disability insurance benefits if they were working and contributing at the time of the claim, or meet certain other requirements.[12] In addition, the worker must not be receiving a retirement pension or be above the normal retirement age. Individuals who postpone drawing pensions past the normal retirement age, or who continue working while retired, are no longer covered by disability and survivors' insurance and do not have to pay the insurance fee. These eligibility conditions are less stringent than those of other countries.[13] Workers who are certified as permanently disabled but are not eligible for insurance can withdraw money from their accounts as a life annuity or programmed withdrawal, but do not get the top-up that ensures the defined benefit.

The Minimum Pension Guarantee. Whether or not they are eligible for the private insurance, disabled workers may qualify for the publicly funded minimum pension guarantee. This requires ten years of contributions (and sometimes even less) over their lifetimes. Disabled pensioners with large account balances tend to annuitize in order to have protection against the risk of outliving their savings. Those with small accumulations tend to take programmed withdrawals and rely on the minimum guaranteed pension.[14]

Wage Replacement Rates in Chile versus Other Countries. Chile's 70 percent wage replacement rate is larger than that of many other countries. In fact, Chile's replacement rate is nearly three times larger than the rate in the United States or in the United Kingdom.[15]

- In the United States and United Kingdom, the average wage replacement rate for disability is 24 percent; Japan, Australia, and Canada also have rates below 30 percent.

- Sweden, Italy, the Netherlands, and Spain have the highest average replacement rates for the disabled, exceeding 70 percent.

However, many disabled Chilean workers get less than 70 percent because they haven't worked regularly for the last ten years, and in the Anglo-Saxon countries, public disability benefits are sometimes supplemented by private disability insurance.

Benefits of the Chilean System. Because each pension fund pays for the disability and survivors' insurance of its affiliated workers, it has a financial incentive to choose a low-cost insurance company and contest questionable claims. Medical boards appointed by a public agency make decisions on claims, but pension funds participate by providing information, asking questions, filing appeals, and helping establish objective medical criteria for determining a disability. This weeds out weak cases and discourages workers from making dubious claims. Indeed, after the system was reformed in 1981, disability recipients tended to have more serious medical conditions (measured by their subsequent mortality rates) than was the case before the reform. In this sense, the new system targets the medically disabled more accurately. In the United States, by contrast, disability determinations are made by government agencies with no direct financial interest in the outcome.[16]

As a result of this process and other factors, the disability rate among Chilean workers has fallen significantly since 1981 and is now less than half that in the United States, after controlling for age:

- Workers in the new Chilean system are only 21 to 35 percent as likely to start a disability pension as they were in the old system, after controlling for age and gender.

Figure 13.1 Newly Classified Disabled in 1999 (per 1,000 Insured)

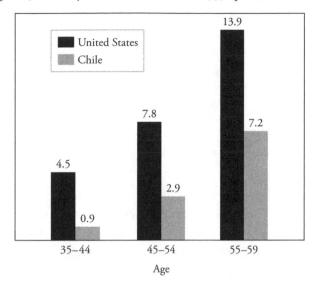

Source: U.S. data from the Organization for Economic Coopera-
tion and Development, *Transforming Disability into Ability* (Paris:
OECD Press, 2003). Chilean data from Estelle James and Augusto
Iglesias, "Integrated Disability and Retirement Systems in Chile,"
September 2007. Available at http://www.ncpathinktank.org/
pdfs/st302.pdf. Also see Estelle James, Alejandra Cox Edwards
and Augusto Iglesias, "The Impact of Private Participation and
Countervailing Information on Disability Costs: Evidence from
Chile," *Journal of Pension Economics and Finance,* 2009.

- In 1999, among forty-five-to-fifty-four-year-olds, 2.9 per thousand covered members of Chile's new system were accepted into newly disabled
  status, compared to 7.8 per thousand in the United States.

- For fifty-five-to-fifty-nine-year-olds, these numbers were 7.2 per thousand in Chile, compared to 13.9 per thousand in the United States.[17]
  (See figure 13.1.)

Problems with the Chilean System. The system adopted in 1981 posed some
troublesome equity questions, at least in the minds of some Chileans. For
example, it gave pension companies a financial incentive to try to attract
workers with lower disability risks and discourage high-risk workers from af-
filiating with them. Since insurance costs ultimately were passed on to workers

through fees, two workers with the same risk profile might pay different implicit premiums depending on their pension company. Furthermore, women were required to pay the same insurance rates as men but got smaller expected benefits because they were less likely to die young or become disabled.

Note: A solution to both problems is to allow actuarially fair premiums.

Changes to the Disability System. In 2008, Chile introduced significant reforms to its disability system.[18] Payments continue largely to be prefunded, but the pension companies now are required collectively to purchase disability coverage through a single public auction at which private insurance companies bid to cover all workers. Therefore, all pension companies pay the same premiums regardless of their separate claims experiences. This creates scale economies in bargaining with insurance companies and eliminates the incentive for pension companies to attract low-risk workers. However, it also eliminates the incentive to dispute questionable claims, which could add to costs.

In addition, employers, rather than workers, now pay the insurance fee. Shifting insurance payments will, in the short run, increase labor costs and may reduce employment. In the long run, the cost will likely be passed to workers in the form of lower wages. The cost, and negative impact on wages, will grow as the workforce ages.

In the future, women will get larger benefits. Insurance fees will be based on the experiences of men, but women will get a rebate deposited into their retirement accounts equal to the difference between actual male and female disability rates, thereby increasing their pensions. Additionally, women who work between ages sixty and sixty-five will continue to be covered by disability insurance. Previously, benefits for women stopped at age sixty.

At the first public auction in 2009:

- The Ministry of Finance estimated that insurance costs would rise from 1 to 1.2 percent of wages because of the increased benefits to women.

- Yet, actual costs as determined by the public auction are now 1.88 percent of wages—57 percent higher than projected and 88 percent higher than in the past.

- A rebate of 0.2 percent of wages will be deposited into women's accounts, but the net charge to women and men will rise.

Much of these higher fees appear to be attributable to the new process, which reduces incentives for pension companies to control disability rates and costs.

Disability in a Personal Account System. The transition of disability insurance from the current government program to a private system is relatively simple. In the United States, many firms already offer free or low-priced short-term disability (six months or less), and many workers have the option of purchasing employer-provided long-term disability at a reasonable price. The personal account system would be similar except for the fact that disability insurance would be mandatory (costing about 1 percent of payroll) and would not have the rigid work prohibitions of the Social Security system.

Opting Out of Workers' Compensation

Why have workers' compensation at all?[19] If on-the-job injuries created no negative externalities—costs imposed on society as a whole—employers and employees could exercise freedom of contract. Presumably, the willingness to trade higher wages for a greater risk of injury differs from worker to worker and occupation to occupation. People pursuing their own interests in the private sector made these trade-offs prior to the enactment of workers' compensation laws, and they could do so again. They also make these trade-offs now between wages and other types of benefits. However, workers' compensation arrangements may have external effects on the rest of society. Injured workers without health insurance and disability coverage potentially will rely on Medicaid, welfare, and other government programs. When they do so, taxpayers will have to pay the costs of decisions to which they were not a party.

However, we can protect employees' and employers' rights to choose the arrangements that best meet their needs, and society's interest in avoiding additional costs for social programs, without imposing perverse incentives on an inefficient system. The system can be improved greatly if employees and employers have the flexibility to make efficiency-improving changes in workers' compensation coverage, just as they routinely make trade-offs between wages and other benefits in the labor market.[20]

Texas (and for a while Oklahoma) adopted a unique approach, allowing employers essentially to opt out of the system. See the sidebar, "Opting Out of Workers' Compensation in Texas."

In what follows we will briefly review reforms suggested by Michael Helvacian.

Needed Reform: Integrating Health Insurance and Workers' Compensation. For reasons discussed in section 2, it makes no sense to have two separate health plans for workers—paying different fees to providers. Integrated health care plans would provide both group health and workers' compensation medical benefits to employees. They would have the following advantages:

- Employees could use the same provider networks for job-related injuries they use for regular health coverage, and in most cases they would have the option to change doctors or (for an additional fee) go out of network if not satisfied with the services provided.

- Employers and insurers could use the same negotiated fee schedules for work-related injuries and illnesses as under regular health plans—fees that generally are lower than those paid by workers' compensation.

- Since employees would pay the same deductibles and copayments as in their regular health plans, no longer would any incentive exist to claim that a nonwork injury or illness is work related or vice versa."[21]

- Where workers are given a choice of health plans, they would be able to choose a single plan to cover both types of health needs.

Savings from integrating the two health plans would be passed on to workers as higher wages or other types of job-related benefits. Some employers allow employees to choose less expensive plans and "bank" the premium savings in Health Savings Accounts (HSAs), from which they can pay small medical bills. Employees could be given a similar choice for their workers' compensation coverage. Alternatively, employees could use the workers' compensation premium savings to purchase other benefits or make deposits into a disability account.[22]

Needed Reform: Integrating Disability Insurance and Workers' Compensation. Under the current system, employers are also prevented from integrating workers' compensation wage replacement benefits with their regular disability insurance. This is unfortunate. Compared to private disability policies, workers' compensation generally has a shorter waiting period before a claim can be filed and often has a lower wage replacement rate. Workers' compensation disability benefits typically replace only about half of a worker's lost wages, and employees who miss work for long periods earn lower wages afterward.[23]

How Opting Out Works. The idea behind the workers' compensation system is that companies become strictly liable for on-the-job injuries and pay benefits to workers based on a schedule set by the state. In return, the employer avoids the costs of litigation that otherwise would be incurred under the common-law tort system. Texas always has allowed employers to opt out of the system, but until the last several decades, few employers had an interest in doing so. The benefits of avoiding tort law litigation seemed far superior to the costs of workers' comp. But as the cost of workers' comp began to soar, interest in an alternative began to rise as well.

A legal solution appears to have been discovered by Dallas lawyer Bill Minick, whose consulting firm PartnerSource is a one-stop shop for employers who want to opt out. Minick discovered that the Employee Retirement Income Security Act (ERISA), passed by Congress in the early 1970s, appeared to allow self-insured companies to set up their own workers' compensation system—fully shielded from state regulations in the same way that their health and pension plans are exempt from state law.[29]

This isn't the only approach, though. Oklahoma (with Minick's help) rewrote its entire workers' comp law to accommodate opting out, and it applied to all employers, not just companies large enough to self-insure. The state has since reverted to the traditional system, however.

Benefits of Opting Out of Workers' Compensation. As Paul O'Donnell writes in the *Dallas Morning News*, Minick has no difficulty rattling off the problems with conventional workers' comp:

Companies dig in their heels at the first sign of a claim and turn workers into adversaries. Insurers don't communicate about benefits, causing workers to hire lawyers. Doctors are often picked based on discounts rather than quality.

As a result, injured workers no longer have any accountability. They can report claims late, skip doctors' appointments, and appeal every perceived wrong to workers' comp court rather than trying to work it out with their employers.[30]

And he has no problem explaining the benefits of opting out:

Under opt-out plans, companies must be engaged in the process, educating new workers about their benefit plans and managing their medical care if they get hurt. This control allows employers to better monitor workers' progress and ensure they return to work as soon as possible.[31]

An analysis by PartnerSource shows that opt-out plans save companies between 40 and 90 percent because they have lower costs per claim, get injured employees back to work faster, and handle fewer disputes.[32]

Complaints about Opting Out. One source of complaints in Texas is the fact that different companies have different benefits. For example, Texas workers' comp law requires the payment of $97,524 for the loss of a hand. By contrast, Albertsons, Baylor, Scott & White, and Walmart pay $125,000 and J.B. Hunt and Macy's pay only $50,000, but Home Depot pays as much as $1 million.

Another complaint is that opted-out companies may be less tolerant. For example, workers' comp gives employees thirty days to report an injury in Texas. Under opt-out plans, employees typically must report by the end of the work shift or within twenty-four hours or lose all benefits. Several companies, including Home Depot, Pilot Travel Centers, and McDonald's, exclude injuries caused by safety violations or the failure to obtain assistance with a particular task. And some companies do not cover cumulative trauma such as carpal tunnel syndrome.[33]

Solutions. Oklahoma's short-lived experience with opting out appears to have avoided many of these problems with a more standardized approach. For

Opting Out of Workers' Compensation in Texas

Texas is the only state that allows employers freely to opt out of the workers' compensation system.[24] Employers in the system must purchase a workers' compensation policy from a licensed insurance company, or be certified to self-insure by the Texas Department of Insurance, or be a member of an approved self-insurance group.[25] Firms that do not participate in the system, called "nonsubscribers," can make a variety of alternative arrangements, including integrating treatment of injured workers with their regular health plans and wage replacement benefits with their disability plans.

Nonsubscribing firms can also "go bare." That is, they make no alternative arrangements and take the chance that they will not be held liable in court for a worker's injury. The liability of nonsubscribers is unlimited under the traditional tort liability system, if an injured employee can prove in court that the employer was negligent. On the other hand, firms that participate in workers' compensation are held strictly liable for injured workers' medical expenses and lost wages, regardless of fault, but limits are placed on the compensation workers receive.

Whereas the workers' compensation system pays the cost of legal representation for participating employees, attorneys for workers who sue nonsubscribing employers receive compensation only if their litigation is successful. Thus, the workers' compensation system encourages attorney involvement, while the tort liability system discourages the pursuit of weak cases. Only 3 percent of nonsubscribers report being sued over a work-related injury in a five-year period.

Although Texas always has allowed employers to opt out, the trend began accelerating in the first decade of the twenty-first century in response to the rising cost of workers' compensation insurance. According to the most recent data from the Texas Department of Insurance:

- About 37 percent of Texas businesses, employing 23 percent of Texas workers, opted out of the workers' compensation system in 2006.

(Sidebar continued on the next page)

- In the past, nonsubscribing employers were smaller-size firms for the most part, but in more recent years, the largest employers—firms with more than five hundred employees—increasingly are opting out, rising from 14 percent in 2001 to 26 percent in 2006.

What difference does nonsubscription make? One study found that the nonsubscriber option helps Texas employers control workers' compensation costs.[26]

- Accident frequency was slightly greater among nonsubscribing firms than subscribing firms.

- However, subscribing firms had 10 to 50 percent more lost days from work (per occurrence) than nonsubscribing firms.

- "In about half of industries examined in the study, payments for lost time (indemnity costs) were less for nonsubscribing firms than subscribing firms, ranging from 0.5 percent lower in the personal services industry to 169 percent less in food stores."[27]

Finally, the study concluded that litigation costs per employee (combined employer and claimant legal expenses) were similar, though slightly higher for nonsubscribing firms than subscribing firms ($9.20 and $9.02, respectively).[28] Thus, although the workers' compensation system is supposed to be an alternative to the tort liability system for subscribing firms, employers and employees still incurred significant legal expenses.

example, opted-out Oklahoma companies had to match the state's workers' compensation benefits.

Another problem is federal tax law. Benefits under opt-out plans are subject to income and payroll taxes. Under workers' comp, they're not. There seems to be no good reason for this quirk in the tax law.

Improving Workers' Compensation. Reform of the workers' compensation system would lead to greater efficiency and enhance workers' welfare. Efficiency is promoted when public policy allows employers and employees to write simple and enforceable contracts for workers' compensation benefits, as they currently do for wages and other employee benefits. Begun in an era when employee benefits were a rarity, current workers' compensation laws and regulations impede such contractual arrangements. We should also deregulate insurance rates and products so that employers and employees can realize full gains from promoting efficiency. Efficiency gains would accrue to employers as lower insurance costs, and to employees as higher wages and a better choice of benefits that they value most.

Although Chile currently uses a different system for workers' compensation, the same principles of prefunding and individual savings used in the Chilean disability insurance system could be applied. Wage replacement benefits under workers' compensation, disability, unemployment, and early retirement are close substitutes. If workers fund their own benefits, they have stronger incentives to stay in the workforce and do not have perverse incentives to claim benefits unnecessarily.[34]

14

Addressing the Risk of Ill Health

HEALTH POLICY IN general and Obamacare in particular gives us ample opportunities for win/win changes. Let's begin with some fundamental mistakes we have been making for over half a century. Then we will turn to the Affordable Care Act.

Reforming Our Private Health Care System

In health care, as we have seen, people make five major choices.[1] In each case, unwise public policies perversely encourage all of us to make socially undesirable decisions. Ideally, government would encourage us to make good decisions. But in what follows I want to set a more modest goal: neutrality. If people must choose between a socially desirable alternative and an undesirable one, government policy is "neutral" if it gives the same encouragement to both alternatives. Under a set of neutral policies, government is not solving any problems. On the other hand, it also is not creating them. As long as government policy is neutral, we can seek solutions to problems, confident that government is not standing in the way. This is the "first, do no harm" principle, familiar to those in the medical profession who are guided by the Hippocratic oath. If government health policy followed that same principle, what would our health care system look like?

Choice: To Insure or Not to Insure. Why do we care whether other people have health insurance? One reason we care is that uninsured people may incur medical bills they cannot pay from their own resources. When that happens, the cost is often borne by other people, either by shifting costs to insured (paying) patients or through free-care programs subsidized by tax-payers. The choice to insure or remain uninsured often means, as a practical matter, the choice to insure or to rely implicitly on the social safety net. How do government policies affect our incentives with respect to this choice?

As we have seen, generous tax subsidies encourage people who might otherwise be uninsured to obtain employer-provided insurance. There are two problems with the way these subsidies are structured, however: the largest subsidies are given to people who need them least and the subsidies often are not available to the uninsured.

What happens to people who are uninsured? They often obtain free care, obtained through a local social safety net. The existence of a safety net encourages people to be uninsured. Why pay for expensive private health insurance when free care provided through public programs is de facto insurance?

Society should not be indifferent about this choice. For one thing, the choice to rely on safety-net care is a choice to be a "free rider" at the taxpayers' expense. For another thing, the two types of care are not equivalent. The privately insured patient has more choices of physicians and hospital facilities and more often than not gets better care.

Further, safety-net care is generally much less efficient care. For instance, uninsured patients often use emergency rooms to provide care that is more economically provided in a doctor's office or at a freestanding clinic. Per dollar spent, the privately insured patient typically gets more care and better care. For that reason alone, it is in society's interest not to encourage people to be in the public sector rather than the private sector.[2]

Suppose the government offered every individual a uniform, fixed-dollar subsidy. If the individual obtained private insurance, the subsidy would be realized in the form of lower taxes by way of a tax credit. The credit would be refundable, so that it would be available even to those with no tax liability. (See sidebar, "The Case for a Fixed-Sum Tax Credit.")

How large should the tax credit be? Let's assume that we want to establish a floor and that, roughly speaking, the floor is equivalent to the kind of health care we make available to people who are enrolled in Medicaid. In 2015, I recommended a tax credit of $2,500 for an adult and $1,500 for a child. I showed that a credit of those amounts, combined with the average state's share of Medicaid spending, would allow someone living below the poverty level to purchase a plan similar to a well-managed, privately administered Medicaid plan. If an additional premium was required, it would have been no more than a few dollars a month. For higher-income people, who did not get a subsidy from Medicaid, the cost of such a plan would have been about $100 a month when added to the tax credit.[3]

(If we were to implement a tax credit system in 2022, say, the amount of the credit might be twice this size. But I will continue with the example for easy reference to the explanatory information in the footnoted documents.)

This credit would be offered to everyone and it would be a dollar-for-dollar credit up to the maximum amount. For example, adults would get one dollar for every one dollar they spend on health insurance premiums and deposits into Health Savings Accounts up to $2,500. The value of the credit would grow through time in line with increases in the cost of Medicaid.

Offered such a credit, no one would have a reason to be uninsured. Yet, undoubtedly many people would turn down that offer, just as millions have turned down the offer of an Obamacare tax credit. In that case, the credit amount should be made available to safety-net institutions in the communities where the uninsured live—and that would be the only federal funding for safety-net care.

Under this proposal, money would follow people.

For example, suppose everyone in Dallas County chose to obtain private insurance, relying on a refundable federal income tax credit to pay the premiums. In that case, Dallas safety-net institutions would receive no federal money.

On the other hand, if everyone in Dallas County opted to be uninsured, the $2,500 per person in unclaimed credits would be available to institutions that provide health care services to the uninsured.

To implement the program, all the federal government needs to know is how many people live in each community. In principle, it will be offering each of them an annual tax credit. Some will claim the full credit. Some will claim a partial credit (because they will be insured only for part of a year). Others will claim no credit. What the government pledges to each community will be $2,500 times the number of adults and $1,500 times the number of children.

The portion of this sum that is not claimed on tax returns should be available as block grants to be spent on indigent health care at the local level.

Where would the federal government get the money to fund the private insurance tax credits? We could begin with nearly $300 billion in tax subsidies the federal government already "spends" to subsidize private insurance. Add to that the money the federal, state, and local governments already spend on indigent care. For the remainder, the federal government could make certain tax benefits conditional on proof of insurance. For example, the $2,000 child tax credit could be made conditional on proof of insurance for each child.[4] For middle-income families, a portion of the standard deduction could be made conditional on proof of insurance for adults. For lower-income families, part of the Earned Income Tax Credit refund could be made conditional.

How would the federal government manage to reduce safety-net spending when uninsured people elect to obtain private insurance? Because much of the safety-net expenditure already consists of federal funds, the federal government could use its share to fund private insurance tax credits instead. For the remainder, the federal government does not have direct control over the budgets of state and local governments. However, the federal government could reduce block grants to the states for Medicaid and other programs instead.

Choice: Private or Public Coverage? Many poor and near-poor families have a choice of public or private insurance. Because of their low incomes, they can either qualify for Medicaid or the state-run Children's Health Insurance Program (CHIP) or obtain private insurance (typically through an employer). Clearly, we should not be indifferent about this choice. Private insurance means people are paying their own way. Further, as noted, private insurance often means better health care.

Public policy, however, overwhelmingly encourages people to drop private insurance and enroll in public programs. Tax subsidies for employer-provided, private insurance are quite meager for those with near-poverty incomes (basically consisting of the avoidance of the 15.3 percent FICA tax), whereas public programs are free to the enrollee. And (surprisingly) families below the federal poverty line get no subsidy in the health insurance exchanges.

One might be tempted to assume that Medicaid insures people who otherwise would not have access to private insurance. However, Medicaid induces

The Case for a Fixed-Sum Tax Credit

The most important question in health reform is this: how should the government encourage the purchase of private health insurance? I believe that the encouragement should come in the form of a fixed-sum tax credit. The issue warrants special discussion.

Consider the traditional way of encouraging health insurance. For employer-provided insurance, the inducement is in the form of a tax exemption. Unlike wages, an employer's premium payments are not included in the employee's taxable income. (They are a deductible business expense for the employer.) For the self-employed, the inducement is in the form of a tax deduction. And for other individuals, health insurance premiums and medical expenses can be deducted to the extent that they exceed a certain percentage of adjusted gross income (currently 10 percent).

In all three cases, people face the following perverse incentive:

- If they purchase more insurance, their taxes will go down, and if they purchase less health insurance, their taxes will go up. In this way, the tax system encourages all of us to choose more generous coverage than we would otherwise select.

- If we combine a 15 percent (FICA) payroll tax with a 25 percent federal income tax and a 5 percent state and local income tax, a middle-income family is facing a 45 percent marginal tax rate. In high-tax states, the rate can exceed 50 percent—even though the family is far from wealthy.

- At a 50 percent marginal tax rate, government at all levels is paying for half the cost of any additional insurance the family chooses to buy. Insurance that costs one dollar will be viewed as worthwhile, even if the buyer values it at only fifty-one cents.

In other words, insurance can be extremely wasteful and still be attractive to tax-subsidized purchasers. Alternatively, if the buyer saves a dollar by choosing less generous coverage, that dollar will become

(Sidebar continued on the next page)

taxable income. The government will seize one-half of it. This tax treatment helps explain a great deal of waste in our health care system.

But those incentives change significantly under a fixed-sum tax credit. Here is how it works in the ACA exchange:

$$\text{Subsidy} = \text{Premium} \times (1 - hY)$$

where the Premium is the second-lowest premium charged for silver plans, Y is the buyer's income, and h is the maximum fraction of income people have to pay for such a plan. Notice that this sets the subsidy at a fixed-dollar amount.

The tax subsidy is refundable: buyers get the credit even if they don't owe any income taxes. It is also advanceable: within the exchange, the subsidy goes directly to the insurer, bypassing the buyer altogether. But what is most important, the subsidy is the same whether the individual chooses another silver plan or a bronze, gold, or platinum plan. That means buyers who choose more expensive plans pay 100 percent of the extra premium out of their own pockets. Alternatively, buyers who choose a less expensive bronze plan get to keep 100 percent of the savings.

Any extra expense is paid with after-tax dollars. Any reduction in expense increases the buyer's after-tax resources. Since most other consumption spending is also financed with after-tax dollars, this puts health insurance premiums and other goods and services on a level playing field.

With a fixed-sum tax credit, buyers are not encouraged to overinsure or underinsure. Every costly feature of health insurance (lower deductibles and copayments, wider networks, more generous benefits) will be at the expense of all other ways of spending the consumer's dollars.

---

some people to turn down or drop private coverage to take advantage of free health insurance offered by the state. As a result of such crowding out, the cost of expanding public insurance programs has been high relative to the gain. For example, if for each new enrollee in a public program at least one person loses private insurance, there will be no net reduction in the number of the uninsured, despite the heavier taxpayer burden.

Economists David Cutler and Jonathan Gruber found that Medicaid expansions in the early 1990s were substantially offset by reductions in private coverage. For every additional dollar spent on Medicaid, private-sector health care spending was reduced by 50 to 75 cents, on the average.[5] Thus taxpayers incurred a considerable burden, but at least half, and perhaps as much as three-fourths, of the expenditures replaced private-sector spending rather than buying more or better medical services.

A similar principle applies to CHIP. Take a low-income working family covered by an employer-sponsored health plan. The employer might have covered some or all of the cost of insurance premiums for the employee and family with pretax dollars. However, paying wages is more attractive to actual and potential employees if coverage is provided by the state. Thus, CHIP offers some employers the opportunity to increase wages and reduce their health insurance costs at the same time.

The solution here is very similar to the solution to the previous problem. If the federal government is spending $2,500 a year per adult enrolled in Medicaid, it ought to be willing to spend an identical sum on private insurance instead.

On paper, Medicaid coverage often looks more generous than private insurance—covering almost all physicians, facilities, and procedures at no out-of-pocket cost to the patient. In practice, many physicians refuse to see Medicaid patients, and because of the low rates of reimbursement, rationing-by-waiting often emerges. As a result, a policy that is financially neutral would be one that encourages private insurance.

Choice: Individual or Group Insurance? Individual insurance has the virtue of portability. People can take their coverage with them as they move from job to job. Further, in the individual market, people have a better opportunity to purchase insurance tailored to individual and family needs (or at least that was the case before the Obamacare-mandated benefits kicked in). On the downside, individual insurance tends to have higher administrative costs and (under Obamacare) it has become increasingly expensive—some unsubsidized exchange plans cost two or three times what they cost prior to Obamacare. But why not let employers buy individual insurance for their employees the way they currently buy group insurance?[6] Most small employers and their employees would probably jump at the chance.

Under Obamacare, most people who earn below-average wages get larger subsides in the Obamacare exchange than they do at work. That is, the tax subsidies for health insurance premiums and the reimbursement of out-of-pocket expenses far exceeds the tax advantage associated with the ability to purchase health insurance with pretax dollars at work. For above-average-wage workers, the incentives are reversed. They get little or no subsidy in the exchanges, and they get generous tax relief at work.

We are encouraging roughly half the population to gravitate to the individual market and the other half to be in the group market—for no other reason than a bizarre system of tax subsides, none of which were devised with this end result in mind.

By contrast, neutral policy is easy to envision and implement. A neutral government would give the same tax subsidy to every form of insurance. Accordingly, individual and group coverage would compete on a level playing field. In such a world, employers would not offer insurance at all unless they had a comparative advantage in doing so in their competition for labor. Undoubtedly, many large companies do have an advantage. They can do things for their employees that the employees cannot do for themselves. Many small firms, however, have no such advantage and probably would be better off paying higher wages instead of paying for health insurance.[7]

Choice: Self-Insurance or Third-Party Insurance? In every insurance field, people must decide how much risk to transfer to an insurer and how much to retain.[8] Often, the decision focuses on the size of the deductible. There are other ways, though, to divide up responsibilities for risks. In general, risk is transferred to an insurer in return for third-party insurance. When risk is retained, the individual is said to self-insure. In a competitive market, individuals would decide how much risk to transfer to third parties based on their own attitudes toward risk and willingness to pay insurance premiums. Unfortunately, government policies intervene.

As noted, every dollar an employer pays in health insurance premiums avoids income and payroll taxes. For a middle-income employee, this generous tax subsidy means that government is effectively paying for almost half the cost of the health insurance. On the other hand, government will tax away almost half of every dollar the employer puts into a savings account for the employee to pay medical expenses directly, with exceptions below. The result is a tax law that lavishly subsidizes third-party insurance and severely penalizes individual self-insurance. This encourages people to use third-party bureaucracies to pay every medical bill, even though it often makes more sense for patients to manage discretionary expenses themselves.

A number of vehicles are available to make it easier for individuals to self-insure for medical expenses. These include tax-free Health Savings Accounts (HSAs), Health Reimbursement Arrangements (HRAs), and Flexible Spending Accounts (FSAs).[9] All of these are steps in the right direction, but the restrictions on these accounts are too onerous. For example, employees cannot even have an HSA unless the employer has a qualified plan, and the restrictions that burden such plans prevent many sensible arrangements. Moreover, unlike the Medicaid (cash and counseling) program, employers are not allowed to put different amounts in the accounts of the chronically ill to match the severities of their illnesses. Also, the law requires the same across-the-board deductible for inpatient and outpatient expenses, as if patient discretion were equally appropriate in all cases.

A neutral policy is one that treats third-party insurance and individual self-insurance the same. For example, if government allows third-party insurance premiums to be paid with pretax dollars, then deposits to an HSA account should also be made with pretax dollars.

In the case of a lump-sum tax credit, neutrality can be created in another way. Remember, with such a credit, the incremental premium is paid with after-tax dollars. In this case, deposits to HSA accounts also should be made with after-tax dollars; the balance would grow tax free, and withdrawals would be tax free. This would be a Roth HSA.[10]

Choices in the Market for Health Insurance. In 1980, Census Bureau statistics showed that fewer than 1 percent of the population had been denied health insurance because of a health condition. Moreover, that was a time when few legislative remedies were available. Even so, this 1 percent was a politically vocal group, and, in many cases, they evoked understandable sympathy. However, rather than deal with this group directly (for instance, by creating risk pools or offering direct subsidies), politicians through the years have imposed unwise restrictions on the other 99 percent of the people.[11]

Even before Obamacare, a proliferation of state laws made it easy for people to obtain insurance after they get sick. Guaranteed-issue regulations (requiring insurers to take all applicants, regardless of health status) and community-rating regulations (requiring insurers to charge the same premium to all enrollees, regardless of health status) are a free rider's heaven.

They encourage everyone to remain uninsured while healthy, confident they will always be able to obtain insurance once they get sick. Moreover, as healthy people respond to these incentives by electing to be uninsured, the premium that must be charged to cover costs for those who remain in insurance pools rises. These higher premiums, in turn, encourage even more healthy people to drop their coverages. And on the vicious cycle goes.

Federal legislation has also increasingly made it easy to obtain insurance after one gets sick. The Health Insurance Portability and Accountability Act (HIPAA) of 1996 had a noble intent: to guarantee that people who have been paying premiums into the private insurance system do not lose coverage simply because they change jobs. However, a side effect of pursuing this desirable goal is a provision that allows any small business to obtain insurance regardless of the health status of its employees. This means that a small mom-and-pop operation can save money by remaining uninsured until a family member gets sick.

Individuals can also opt out of an employer's plan and reenroll after they get sick. They are entitled to full coverage for a preexisting condition after an eighteen-month waiting period. A group health plan can apply preexisting condition exclusions for no more than twelve months, except in the case of late enrollees, to whom exclusions can apply for eighteen months.

Under Obamacare, the perverse incentives to remain uninsured until you get sick are intensified. Basically, anyone who is uninsured is able to obtain insurance for the same premium as a healthy individual in the exchanges, regardless of how long or why the person is uninsured. For a few years, a mandate to buy insurance was backed up by a tax penalty for being uninsured. However, the tax penalty was small compared to the cost of insurance in the exchanges, and it appears to have been enforced weakly.

By far, the worst consequence of government regulation of the market for risk is the unintended harm done to the very people the laws were intended to help. Precisely because the premium attached to high-risk individuals is much lower than their expected health care costs, insurers seek to avoid enrolling them in the first place. Precisely because payments to providers likewise do not reflect expected costs, they too have an incentive to avoid attracting the hard cases, especially among the chronically ill.

If health care markets worked the way normal markets do, health insurers and providers would compete vigorously for the business of the sick. A market for sick people would literally emerge. In normal markets, entrepreneurs make profits by figuring out how to better solve other people's problems. In health care, by contrast, entrepreneurs run from other people's problems.[12]

Current policy toward risk encourages all of us to remain uninsured while we are healthy. The consequences are unfortunate. People cannot make rational choices about risk if risk avoidance is not available at market prices.

A neutral policy would allow risk to be freely priced in the marketplace, with government intervening to help specific individuals only in special cases.

It might seem that the genie is out of the bottle and that there is no way to restore normal market prices—especially now that the individual market has been replaced with the (Obamacare) exchanges. Yet all is not lost. (See the sidebar.)

Turning the Exchanges into Real Markets

The Obamacare exchanges are tightly regulated markets in which every buyer and every seller faces the wrong price.[13] As a result, every buyer and every seller faces perverse incentives.

On the seller side, an obvious race to the bottom has materialized, as insurers try to attract the healthy and avoid the sick. After enrollment, the insurers have a perverse incentive to overprovide to the healthy (to keep the ones they have and attract more of them) and to underprovide to the sick (to encourage the exodus of the ones they have and discourage enrollment by any more of them). It appears that the health plans actively are trying to dump their most costly enrollees on other plans.

On the buyer side, individuals face perverse incentives to wait until they get sick to buy insurance and then to drop their coverage once the

---

(Sidebar continued on the next page)

medical bills are paid. When they do obtain insurance, their incentive is to choose low-cost plans with skimpy benefits and skimpy networks while they are healthy and then switch to very generous plans after they get sick. Every time an individual games the system in this way, he pushes up costs for everyone else.

A better way fortunately is at hand. The health insurance exchanges should be deregulated and denationalized and turned into genuinely free markets. Here is what that would look like.

Exchanges without mandates. The first things that need to go are the individual and employer mandates. As far as getting people insured, the employer mandate appears to have a negligible effect anyway, and it's very bad for the job market. Although the individual mandate has been repealed on the buyer side of the market, the only insurance that insurers are allowed to sell in the individual market has to conform to all of Obamacare's mandated benefits.

This means people who buy insurance are forced to buy a product designed by politicians, rather than ones that meet individual and family needs. What woman would willingly choose to buy health insurance that offers free mammograms while she is healthy but makes her pay full price if there is a symptom of something wrong? That's only one of the many needlessly wasteful and expensive consequences of letting health insurance benefits be determined by the political system.

But don't we need mandates in order to keep people from gaming the system? We have found better ways in Medicare Part B, Medicare Part D, and Medigap. In those markets, if you don't buy when you are eligible, you can face penalties. In most places, if you don't sign up for Medigap insurance when you are first eligible, you can be underwritten and charged a premium that reflects your expected health care costs.

Does getting rid of the mandates mean we have to give up on the idea of universal coverage? Not necessarily. We have seen already that when people are offered a tax credit to purchase health insurance, millions of people will turn down the offer. What should we do with the

(Sidebar continued on the next page)

unclaimed tax credits? As noted, we should send them to safety-net institutions in the communities where the uninsured live.[14] That way, money would follow people. If everyone in a community opted to be insured, the tax credits would help pay for private insurance. If everyone elected to be uninsured, the money would go to a local safety-net institution as a backstop in case patients cannot pay their medical bills.

That's probably as close to universal coverage as we are ever going to get.

Exchanges without artificial prices. Obamacare regulations are inducing insurers to choose narrow networks in order to keep costs down and premiums low. They are doing that on the theory that only sick people pay attention to networks, while the healthy buy on price. In that way they are trying to attract the healthy and avoid the sick. The perverse incentives that are causing these perverse results have one and only one cause: when individuals enter a health plan, the premium the insurer receives is different from the enrollee's expected medical costs.

Precisely the opposite happens in the Medicare Advantage program, where Medicare makes a significant effort to pay insurers actuarially fair premiums. The enrollees themselves all pay the same premium, but Medicare adds an additional sum, depending on the enrollee's expected costs. For example, some special-needs plans are paid as much as $60,000 or more per enrollee. Under this system, all enrollees are financially attractive to insurers, regardless of health status.

Exchanges without government risk adjustment. What we call "health status risk adjustment" would begin with the Medicare Advantage risk adjustment formulas. However, the extra premium adjustments would be paid by insurers to each other—not by Medicare. Furthermore, the insurers would be able to improve on Medicare's formulas as they learn of better methods of adjustment. They would also be able to use "look-back" techniques to adjust the payments through time, when they discover that the initially estimated expense was too high or too low.

(Sidebar continued on the next page)

The risk adjustment we are describing here is adjustment produced by the marketplace, not by a bureaucracy.

Exchanges without limited enrollment periods. Outside of the open enrollment period, no one in the United States can buy individual or family coverage, unless he experiences a qualifying event (divorce, loss of a job, and so on). The next opportunity will be next November, and even then you will only be able to buy insurance that becomes effective next January. These limited enrollment periods exist in order to keep people from switching plans as their health conditions change. And the reason that is viewed as undesirable is that people would take advantage of the system—paying low premiums for skimpy coverage when they are healthy and then choosing a generous plan after they need serious medical care.

But it is actually good for people to switch plans after they get sick. Don't we want to fit the right plan to the right patient when health conditions change? The only reason plan switching is viewed as a problem is that none of the premiums are actuarially fair. In a rational insurance market, people would be able to buy insurance at any time, night or day. And they would be able to move continually from plan to plan.

Exchanges without perverse incentives. In the reformed marketplace described here, the healthy and the sick would be equally attractive to the insurers. That's because every insurer would receive an actuarially fair premium for any new enrollee. Obamacare's promise to end discrimination against those with preexisting conditions was an example of "bait and switch." Insurers cannot exclude the chronically ill or charge them higher premiums, but they are free to discriminate in other ways—by excluding the best doctors and the best facilities from their networks and by charging exorbitant out-of-pocket fees for lifesaving specialty drugs.

In the reformed market we envision, health plans would compete to enroll the sick—just as special-needs plans do in the Medicare Advantage program. In all likelihood, health plans would specialize in expensive-to-treat conditions. Cancer Treatment Centers of America,

(Sidebar continued on the next page)

for example, might recruit cancer patients actively from other health plans.[15]

On the buyer side, individuals would no longer be able to game the system by waiting to insure until they get sick. Individuals would be free to switch health plans all year round, 24/7. But they would have to pay the full actuarially fair price of any upgrade, and they would receive the full actuarially fair discount for any downgrade.

Consequences of a Policy of "Do No Harm." Under a policy of neutrality, government no longer would be a cause of the problems about which so many people complain.[16] Furthermore, if government were removed as a source of problems, the resulting system would have some remarkably attractive features. The following is a summary.

A Form of Universal Coverage. Under the neutrality reforms envisioned here, government would promise every citizen a fixed sum of money. Those who choose private insurance would get a tax credit against premiums. For those who are uninsured, the sum would be used to fund a healthcare safety-net in their locality. Moreover, because money follows people, a minimum amount of funding would always be available regardless of how many people are uninsured.

A Level Playing Field for Public and Private Insurance. Low-income families would no longer be trapped in public systems for which the quality of care frequently is suspect, and care is often rationed, especially by waiting. Instead, people would be able to apply funds spent on their behalf to enroll in an employer's plan or purchase health insurance directly.

A Level Playing Field for Individual and Group Insurance. No longer would tax policy be biased in favor of an employer-based system in which people lose their insurance whenever they leave or change jobs. Instead, tax law would grant the same subsidy to all forms of insurance, regardless of how it is purchased. Furthermore, employers would be able to purchase individually owned, portable insurance for their employees in the same way they purchase group insurance today.

A Level Playing Field for Third-Party Insurance and Individual Self-Insurance. No longer would the tax law encourage the health maintenance organization (HMO) form of insurance by subsidizing third-party insurance while penalizing self-insurance. Instead, all forms of insurance would compete against each other on a level playing field. The expected outcome would be an evolving system under which people manage more of their own health care dollars, especially for those expenditures for which patients can exercise discretion and where it is appropriate for them to do so.

A Genuine Market for Risk. If healthcare markets worked the way normal markets do, health insurers and providers would compete vigorously for the business of the sick. In normal markets, entrepreneurs make profits by figuring out how to better solve other people's problems. In health care, by contrast, entrepreneurs run from sick people's problems.

People cannot make rational choices about risk if the market is not free to price risk avoidance. For that reason, risk should be priced freely in the marketplace, with government intervening to help specific individuals only in special cases.

The risk-adjusted premiums in the Medicare Advantage program are a step in the right direction. When seniors enroll in private Medicare plans, the plans receive a premium payment based on the senior's expected health care costs. In the early years, these adjustments were limited and inadequate. However, the federal government now has a payment system that reflects sixty or seventy different variables. Similar risk-adjusted payments are being used in Florida's Medicaid program.

We have described in the sidebar how to transition from the (Obamacare) insurance exchanges to such a market. Here is what is most important: No longer would government require insurers to charge prices for risk that are totally unrelated to an individual's actual health costs. Instead, healthy people would be able to buy into the system at prices that reflect their lower expected costs. The insurance they buy would most likely be portable, making possible long-term relationships with their insurer and their physicians. In case of a serious illness, people would be able to transfer to other health plans at market prices (not artificially low prices) paid mainly by their current insurer. As a result, insurers would actively compete for sick people, including the chronically ill, and providers would compete to deliver that care.

The system described above would not be perfect. Far from it. It would, though, be a considerable improvement over the system we have today. The bottom line is that much good can come from undoing the harm that unwise governmental policies routinely inflict on the nation's healthcare system.[17]

Alternatives to Obamacare

According to Gallup, the number of people who are uninsured rose by seven million during 2017 and 2018.[18] Although this conclusion is disputed by government estimates, it's very possible that no one is measuring the phenomenon correctly.[19]

The reason? Large numbers of Americans are turning to alternatives to Obamacare—including alternatives that are not called "insurance" by government regulators or even by the plans themselves.

The four top "sharing" organizations, for example, are now insuring more than one million people—up fivefold since the passage of the Affordable Care Act.[20] To put that in perspective, only about ten million people are currently enrolled in the Obamacare exchanges, and the vast majority of those are receiving subsidies.

Among people who don't get subsidies, there may now be more who have an alternative (non ACA compliant) plan than the number with an unsubsidized Obamacare plan.

In what follows I will briefly review three popular alternatives to Obamacare: health sharing plans, indemnity insurance, and short-term plans.

Health Sharing Plans. These plans originally had a religious motive for their existence and some still do. To become a member of Medi-Share, for example, applicants must agree to a detailed statement of faith and "attest to a personal relationship with the Lord Jesus Christ." Samaritan Ministries even requires verification of regular church attendance.[21]

(Sidebar continued on the next page)

Although there are nonreligious plans (discussed below), almost all sharing plans tend to avoid paying for health expenses related to "non-Biblical lifestyles and choices." The two most attractive features of these plans are the price and the lack of a restrictive provider network. According to Jake Thorkildsen—a financial advisor whose post I am relying on for most of the material in this section, premiums are well below what others are paying in the private sector for comparable coverage.[22] Christian Healthcare Ministries (CHM), for example, offers a family of three unlimited coverage per health care incident for a monthly premium of $478.[23] That's less than one-third the cost of a typical employer plan and less than half the cost of insurance on the Obamacare exchanges.[24]

Although some plans have networks with negotiated fees, members can see almost any doctor or enter almost any hospital. The only requirement is that patients must aggressively bargain for the "cash price" of care, typically about 60 percent or less of usual and customary fees. Liberty HealthShare considers hospital bills fair and reasonable if they are from 150 to 170 percent of Medicare rates. If the patient needs help negotiating a rate, the plan supplies it.[25]

A typical plan has a deductible associated with a health incident, rather than an annual deductible. If a member has a heart attack, for example, the deductible applies to all the expenses related to the episode, regardless of the time period. Also the typical plan has a monetary limit on benefits, which may be $125,000 or even $1 million. This is not an annual limit, however; it is a limit applied to each health incident.

Under a conventional arrangement, members send their monthly premium to a central hub, which then pays medical claims. However, some plans have members send money directly to other members who have medical bills instead. Say a member of Samaritan Ministries has a monthly premium of $400. He might send $250 to Jeff in Montana and $150 to Mary in Virginia. These checks are often accompanied with get-well cards or notes with kind words and well-wishes.

(Sidebar continued on the next page)

Health sharing organizations were grandfathered under the Affordable Care Act. As a result, they can exclude people with preexisting conditions, although, in most plans, coverage for preexisting conditions is phased in over a period of three years. Also, these plans are not regulated as insurance companies in any state. In fact, the plans typically go out of their way to avoid insurance terminology. Premium payments are often called a monthly "share" and the deductible is called the "unshared amount."

Even so, members of these plans were specifically excluded from the Obamacare mandate penalty assessed against those who lack health insurance.

Because they are unregulated, the plans are not required to have reserves. Also, their agreements are not insurance contracts. In fact, they are not contracts at all. Members, therefore, must *trust* the organization to keep its word and pay medical bills. But trust is a two-way street. The plans must *trust* the members to pay the doctor after they are reimbursed for a medical expense.

If you Google "Christian health sharing ministries," you will find some complaints. Nonetheless, according to Thorkildsen, the arrangement seems to be working well. CHM, for example, has paid out over $3.5 billion in claims, has never failed to pay a claim for lack of funds in thirty-seven years, and has had no increase in premiums for its basic product in a decade.

One downside of health sharing plans is that they typically don't pay for health maintenance. If a diabetic goes to the emergency room, for example, the plans pay for the treatment. But they don't pay for insulin or other maintenance drugs beyond, say, 120 days.

However, a nonreligious plan offered by MPowering Benefits Association assists patients with drug costs by connecting them with foreign pharmacies that sell drugs at prices paid by patients in other countries. This practice is perfectly legal so long as the patient is buying for personal use and not to resell in the US market.[26]

(Sidebar continued on the next page)

Unlike other plans described here, MPowering Benefits typically sells to employer groups. It helps employers meet their Obamacare mandate to provide minimum essential benefits by providing enrollees with sixty-three preventive services at no charge, the ability to consult with physicians 24/7 by phone, and access to a "concierge desk" that helps patients connect with specialists and obtain lower prices for medical tests. This package also has a Health Savings Account component that can be used in conjunction with a health sharing plan—to pay for deductibles, maintenance drugs, and other out-of-pocket costs.

Limited Benefit Indemnity Insurance. This is another type of insurance product that is becoming increasingly popular. These plans pay a fixed amount of money for each medical incident, regardless of the actual cost of care. There is generally no annual deductible.

Although limited benefit plans are offered by Blue Cross, United-Healthcare, Cigna, and other insurers, they are not considered major medical insurance. They are regulated as insurance, but they are not subject to Obamacare regulations.[27]

An especially popular form of limited-benefit insurance pays for primary care but provides much less coverage for inpatient care.

Since my name is often associated with high-deductible insurance, this is probably a good place to stop and explain why noncatastrophic plans appeal to so many buyers.

Suppose you have a choice between a plan with a $10,000 deductible and $1 million of coverage and a plan with no deductible but only $25,000 of coverage. Suppose the premium for the two plans is the same. Which would you prefer?

For people with high incomes and high net worth, this is a no-brainer. They would choose the former option in a heartbeat. By the way, these are the types of people who designed Obamacare.

But young, healthy, low-income families living paycheck to paycheck invariably prefer the latter option. How do we know that? Because that's the kind of insurance they and their employers chose to buy before there was Obamacare.

(Sidebar continued on the next page)

The biggest fear these people have is that someone in the family will have an accident (the source of 66 percent of all ER visits under the age of forty-five) and they won't be able to afford the urgent care visit. In today's marketplace, these families are rejecting Obamacare and choosing limited-benefit insurance instead.

Hooray Health is a Dallas-area firm catering to that very market. For $99 a month ($229 for a family) the company offers individuals and employees access to more than three thousand retail clinics and urgent care clinics in forty-six states.[28] All that is required is a $25 copay for each visit.

The basic plan does not cover preventive care. However, for $139 a month ($329 for a family), an employer can add minimum essential coverage (MEC) for the full panoply of preventive services required by Obamacare (immunizations, flu shots, colonoscopies, mammograms, etc.), and there is zero copay for these.

Basically, anything that can be done under the roof of a primary care doctor's office or urgent care facility is covered by the plan. That may come as a surprise to people who think these types of plans are "skimpy. (Note, however: since the number of visits is limited to five per year, per person, this plan is not likely to appeal to patients with a continuing chronic condition.)

Hooray Health includes other benefits that are also not skimpy. Enrollees have 24/7 free access to doctor consultations by phone, through MyTelemedicine.[29] The wait for a response is typically two or three minutes, and the doctors responding have immediate access to the patient's medical records. They also have 24/7 access to a medical concierge— where they can get advice on finding doctors, scheduling medical tests, and purchasing drugs.

Short-Term Insurance. This type of insurance has existed for a long time. It is usually purchased by people who need to fill a gap in coverage—say, on the way from school to a job or on the way from one job to another. It appears these plans are now becoming an alternative to Obamacare.

(Sidebar continued on the next page)

The reason? They are exempt from Obamacare regulations, including mandated benefits and a prohibition against pricing based on expected health expenses. Also, unlike Obamacare's narrow enrollment window, these plans can be purchased at any time of the year.

Although they typically last up to twelve months, the Obama administration restricted them to three months and outlawed renewal guarantees, which protect people who develop a costly health condition from facing a big premium hike on their next purchase.

The Trump administration has now reversed those decisions, allowing short-term plans to last up to twelve months and allowing guaranteed renewals up to three years.[30] The ruling also allows the sale of a separate plan, which I call "health-status insurance," which protects people from premium increases due to a change in health condition should they want to buy short-term insurance for another three years.[31]

By stringing together short-term and health-status insurance, people potentially could be able to remain insured indefinitely, with the kind of coverage that was readily available before Obamacare.

Like indemnity insurance, these plans are often referred to as skimpy. Yet Beverly Gossage, president of the Kansas Association of Health Underwriters, says short-term insurance may be as good as or better than Obamacare plans for some people. And if you are healthy, they cost a lot less money. She gives the following example from Overland Park, the second largest city in her state:

> A twenty-five-year-old could pay $397 a month for an unsubsidized (Obamacare) silver plan with a $6,000 deductible and maximum out-of-pocket payment of $7,900. Yet a comparable short-term plan that has all the benefits a young person would likely want has a $2,500 deductible and no additional out-of-pocket costs and runs only $98 a month.[32]

So for one-fourth the premium, the buyer can have a much lower out-of-pocket cost should an emergency strike.

(Sidebar continued on the next page)

To take full advantage of the new Trump regulations for these plans, states must act, however.[33] They must allow three years of guaranteed renewability and allow health-status insurance to fill the gap between three-year periods. In some cases that may require legislation. In other states, the insurance commissioner alone may have the power to pave the way.

But even without further state action, short-term insurance appears to be a popular alternative to Obamacare.

Moving from Obamacare to a Market-Based Health Care System

The ACA is 2,700 pages long. Regulations written to implement it now run to some 20,000 pages—and counting. Despite Nancy Pelosi's promise ("We have to pass the bill to find out what's in it."), there still is a lot of uncertainty about what can and cannot be done. (See the sidebar, "Alternatives to Obamacare.")

How can something like that possibly be fixed?

It's easier than you might suppose. Here are five simple reforms that would solve many of the problems caused by the ACA:

- Replace all ACA mandates and subsidies with a universal tax credit that is the same for everyone.

- Allow young, healthy, low-income families to buy limited-benefit insurance covering their likely health care expenses and protect their income and assets against medical debts up to the limits of these polices.

- Replace all of the different types of medical savings accounts with a Roth Health Savings Account (after-tax deposits and tax-free withdrawals).

- Allow Medicaid to compete with private insurance, with everyone having the right to buy in or get out.

- Denationalize and deregulate the exchanges and require them to institute health-status insurance instead.

Clearly much more needs to be done. But you could keep an awful lot of the ACA and still have a workable health care system by making these changes and these changes alone.[34]

Technical Problems with the Online Exchanges Would Be Gone. Virtually every problem with the online exchanges has one and only one cause: people at different income levels and in different insurance pools get different subsidies from the federal government. If the system were working ideally, when you apply for insurance on an exchange the exchange would check with the IRS to verify your income; it would check with Social Security to see how many different employers you work for; it would check with the Department of Labor to see if those employers are offering affordable, qualified insurance; and it would check with your state Medicaid program to see if you are eligible for that.[35]

Here is the problem: no one has ever designed a program that can link all the different computer systems used by different departments of the federal government. For example, after trying for more than a decade and spending more than a billion dollars, the VA's computers still can't talk to the Department of Defense's computers about service personnel medical records.[36]

All of this may help explain why the state exchanges have been such a disaster. Take the state of Oregon. Grace-Marie Turner writes:

> Oregon, under then-Gov. John Kitzhaber, aspired to create a shining model for other Obamacare exchanges, but instead, it became its poster child of dysfunction. After spending more than $300 million in federal taxpayer dollars, Oregon pulled the plug last year and decided to default to the federal exchange.[37]

The state became involved in lawsuits with Oracle, the primary vendor, and the federal government could actually ask for its $300 million back. Like the federal exchange (healthcare.gov), the Oregon exchange seems to have been designed by people who knew a lot about health care, but nothing about technology.

Even the federal exchange still isn't working the way it is supposed to. All of the emergency repairs have been focused on the front end of the system—where enrollees (voters) were having so much trouble and enduring so much frustration. But the back end, which is supposed to reconcile payment, subsidy, and eligibility data, still isn't complete at the time of this writing. The exchanges for small businesses were delayed. It's hard to know the precise extent of the problems because the Obama administration forced the health insurance companies to keep quiet about them.

To make matters worse, the subsidy you get this year is almost certain to be the wrong amount. Whether people use last year's income or guess what this year's will be, they are almost certain to err. If they underestimate what they will earn, their subsidy will be too large, and they will have to give money back to the IRS next April 15. If they overestimate, their subsidy will be too small, and they will be entitled to a refund. All of this will be annoying. It may also cause financial hardship. Consider that after the first year of operation:

- About half of the people eligible for a subsidy owed higher taxes, and about 45 percent were entitled to a refund because almost everyone failed to accurately predict their income when they obtained their insurance.[38]

- The average repayment was estimated at $794, and the average refund was $773, with the amount reaching several thousand dollars for some people.[39]

- The tax treatment of Obamacare subsidies was so complicated that even the IRS has trouble getting things right. In 2015, the agency admitted that it sent the wrong forms to eight hundred thousand taxpayers.[40]

One reason for these problems is that the way the subsidy is calculated is inconsistent with the way low- and moderate-income people manage their family budgets. People who are living paycheck to paycheck don't have a couple of thousand dollars to give back to Uncle Sam, because they didn't accurately predict their income last year. With a universal tax credit, no one would have needed to guess their income—because the subsidy would have been the same, regardless of income.

A second reason for these problems is that the Obamacare law represents a Rube Goldberg set of compromises, designed to meet the needs of special interests rather than the needs of ordinary people. With a universal tax credit, it would not matter where you work or what your employer offers you. It would not matter what your income is. It would not matter if you qualify for

Medicaid. You would get the same subsidy regardless of any of those things. That means that we could turn all of the exchanges over to a private firm like eHealth, which has been operating an online private exchange for a decade and has insured more than four million people.

All Perverse Outcomes in the Labor Market Would Be Gone. To avoid the costs imposed by the ACA, employers have perverse incentives to keep the number of employees small, reduce their hours of work, use independent contractors and temp labor instead of full-time employees, end insurance for below-average-wage employees, self-insure while the workforce is healthy, and pay fines instead of providing full insurance if their employees become unhealthy.

With a universal tax credit and no mandate, all of these perversions would evaporate. The subsidy for private health insurance would be the same for all: whether they work on the assembly line or they are CEOs; whether they work less or more than thirty hours a week; whether their workplace has fewer or more than fifty employees; whether they are in a union or not; and whether their employer provides the insurance or they obtain it on their own.

The "Race to the Bottom" in the Health Insurance Exchanges Would End. Insurance has three main features: a benefit package, a network of providers, and a premium. The ACA's regulations fix the benefit package and leave insurers free to compete on networks and premiums. Insurers are responding by choosing narrow networks to keep costs down and premiums low. They are doing that on the theory that only sick people pay attention to networks and the healthy buy on price; and they are clearly trying to attract the healthy and avoid the sick.

The perverse incentives that are causing these counterproductive results have one and only one cause: when individuals enter a health plan, the premium the insurer receives is different from the enrollee's expected medical costs.

Precisely the opposite happens in the Medicare Advantage program, where Medicare undertakes a significant effort to pay insurers an actuarially fair premium. The enrollees themselves all pay the same premium, but Medicare tops that up, depending on the enrollee's expected costs. For example, some special-needs plans are paid as much as $60,000 per enrollee. Under this system, all enrollees are financially attractive to insurers, regardless of health status.

What we are calling health-status insurance would accomplish the same result. The only difference is that one insurer would pay the extra premium adjustments to another, and the amount paid would be determined in the marketplace—not by Medicare.[41]

Perverse Incentives to Overinsure and Overconsume Health Care Would Be Gone. As we have seen, the current system of subsidizing employer-provided health insurance is open ended. The more employees (through their employers) spend on health insurance, the lower their taxes. The same perverse incentive applies to the self-employed, who can deduct insurance premiums as a cost of doing business.

If we replaced the current system with a fixed-sum tax credit, some people would gain (mainly lower-income employees and those with limited insurance benefits) and some would lose (mainly high-income employees and those with very generous benefits), provided no one's behavior changes. But almost certainly people would change their behavior. The reason: with a fixed-sum credit, the tax benefits are moved up front. The government would be subsidizing the core insurance that we want everyone to have, leaving them free to add bells and whistles with their own, after-tax dollars.

Consider an employee getting $20,000 of family coverage from an employer. Since the benefit is tax free, if this employee is in the 30 percent tax bracket (payroll and income tax combined), the tax subsidy is $6,000. But to get the entire subsidy, the employee has to obtain $20,000 of insurance. Now suppose we let employees have the tax subsidy in a different way: they can have a dollar-for-dollar subsidy for the first $6,000 of insurance, but all remaining insurance must be purchased with after-tax dollars.

Why is this a good deal for employers and employees? Because they can have the same tax relief they had before without having to buy expensive health insurance. When the last $14,000 of insurance is completely unsubsidized (all paid with after-tax dollars), the alternative is more take-home pay. Any newly discovered efficiencies or economies or even a less generous package of benefits could be turned into more income for the employee without any adverse tax consequences. With this new and better way to subsidize health insurance, people at work can get 100 percent of the benefit of eliminating waste and eliminating insurance benefits that have marginal value.

People Would No Longer Be Forced to Buy Inappropriate Insurance That Doesn't Meet Their Family Needs. One of the strangest things about Obamacare is that it is forcing millions of families to obtain the wrong kind of insurance.[42] In fact, 7.5 million people faced higher taxes in 2016 (Obamacare's individual mandate penalty) because they decided the insurance offered to them was not worth the price, even after government subsidies.[43]

Consider employees of fast-food restaurants. They typically have low incomes and few assets. In most urban areas you need to earn almost the median family income to be able to buy a house. If these families have a car, it probably has very little resale value. Most likely, they are living paycheck to paycheck.

Say one of these families has the misfortune of having a premature baby with very high medical expenses. Whether those expenses are $100,000 or $1 million doesn't really matter very much. The family will not be able to pay even a small fraction of the bill. If they obtain Obamacare's mandated health insurance with no annual or lifetime maximum, health insurance will pay the bill (beyond their out-of-pocket exposure). That may be great for the hospital that provides the care. But how does that help the family?

The typical Bronze plan offered to employees of fast-food restaurants has a deductible of $7,000 or more and it's double that for family coverage. With this type of plan the family will still have to pay almost all its expected medical bills out of pocket. And doctors and hospitals know that collecting amounts below the deductible for families like this is no easier than if they were uninsured. The Obamacare exchanges provide some additional protection for the lowest-income families, but the deductibles still are outrageously high.

What kind of health insurance would these employees want in the absence of government interference? We have some idea already. Pre-Obamacare employers of low-income workers often provided "mini-med" plans in lieu of taxable wages. These plans paid for expenses the employees were most likely to incur, with a cap, say, of $25,000. If the law had allowed it, they no doubt would have included generous deposits to Health Savings Accounts—a more efficient way of paying small medical bills.

Still, what happens as the family earns more income, accumulates some assets, and becomes vulnerable to some of the health problems that accompany aging? Does it have to be sky's-the-limit insurance or mini-med? Or could we have something in between?

I propose allowing people to have a partial tax credit in return for obtaining limited-benefit insurance.[44] Such insurance would cover medical bills up to $25,000 or $50,000 or even $100,000—depending on the policy. Individuals who buy this insurance would have complete protection of income and assets up to the limits of their policies. The remainder of the tax credit would go to local safety-net institutions to cover the rare cases for which a medical bill exceeds these limits.

Suppose a family buys $100,000 of coverage. Insurance would pay not only for the first $100,000 of care. The family's income and assets would be protected from claims arising from unpaid medical bills up to that amount. Creditors could garnish wages and seize assets above that amount. But as families get wealthier, they could increase the limits of their coverage.

It's becoming increasingly obvious to everyone in health policy that the Affordable Care Act was designed by above-average-income people to meet the needs of other people who are just like them. Of course, they want coverage without annual limits. If they have a premature baby, do you think they want creditors to seize their million-dollar house or their new foreign sports car? And if they face a $6,000 deductible, so what? In the worst case, they can cancel their next vacation.

Obamacare takes care of the needs of the upper-income, special-interest-group representatives who designed it. Now it's time to create an insurance plan than meets the needs of the bottom half of the income ladder.[45]

People Would No Longer Be Trapped in One Insurance System Rather Than Another. Under the ACA, if an employer offers you affordable coverage, you are not allowed into the exchange.[46] If you are a dependent of an employee who is offered affordable individual coverage, you are not allowed into the exchange, even if the coverage offered to you is not affordable. If you are eligible for Medicaid, you are not allowed into the exchange. If your income is 100 percent of the federal poverty level, you are not allowed into the exchange, even if you aren't eligible for Medicaid.

To make matters worse, eligibility for one system versus another will change frequently for millions of people because of fluctuations in their incomes. Here is how a study published in *Health Affairs* characterizes the situation:

> Nearly 40 percent of adults experienced a disruption in Medicaid eligibility within the first six months. After a year, 38 percent were no longer eligible, and an additional 16 percent had lost eligibility but then regained it (churning). By three years, 47 percent of adults had incomes above the 133 percent cutoff, and an additional 30 percent of adults were below the cutoff but had experienced at least one episode of churning. By the end of the study period, at four years, only 19 percent of adults would have been continuously eligible for Medicaid.[47]

All of these problems have one and only one source: the federal government is giving markedly different subsidies to people at the same income level, depending on where they get insurance. With a universal tax credit that is independent of income, it would not matter where people get their insurance. If everyone could be in Medicaid, regardless of income, Medicaid enrollees could stay there if they like. If everyone in Medicaid could claim the tax credit and buy private insurance, they could keep their insurance regardless of fluctuations in income.

This change would work best if the universal tax credit were set at a level aligned with the cost of well-managed Medicaid in the manner described above.

The Financial Burden of High Deductibles Would Be Reduced. The out-of-pocket exposure under many plans in the health insurance exchanges is quite high—more than $7,000 per person in some cases. And this is only for in-network expenses. If a patient has to go out of network to get needed care or a lifesaving drug, the insurer may pay nothing.

To reduce this burden and the horror stories it has produced, we should spend fewer taxpayer dollars subsidizing benefits people may not want or need and use the savings to match contributions to Roth Health Saving Accounts.[48] For example, we might match the first $1,000 contributed for an adult and the first $500 for a child. The enrollee, the insurer, or an employer could make the deposit. With this opportunity in place, insurers would almost certainly offer plans with $1,000 HSA deposits because they could use the government's $1,000 match to make the total package more attractive.

There Would Be Real Protection for Preexisting Conditions. Just like the Medicare Advantage program, insurers in a well-run exchange should always receive premiums that are actuarially fair.[49] That is, the insurer's premium should equal the enrollee's expected medical costs. The enrollees themselves will pay a community-rated premium. If there is an additional cost, it should be paid by the enrollee's previous insurer. Put differently, no insurance pool (whether inside or outside the exchange) should ever be able to dump its high-cost, sickest enrollees on an exchange plan. This ensures that health plans have ideal incentives to compete for all potential enrollees, regardless of health status. It also encourages health plans to become high-quality, low-cost providers of specialized care, say, for heart disease or cancer.

At the same time, individuals should not be allowed to game the system. For example, no one should be allowed to upgrade to a richer plan (with more benefits), paying a community-rated premium, after they develop a costly illness. After a one-time enrollment, people who wish to upgrade to a richer plan should be charged the full actuarial cost of the upgrade. If they downgrade, they should realize the full actuarial savings.

Similarly, no one should be allowed to remain uninsured until sickness arrives and then buy insurance for the same premium everyone else is paying. As in the Medicare Parts B and D programs and in the Medigap market, people should be penalized if they do not insure at the first opportunity. The ideal penalty is medical underwriting, where the premium charged equals the expected cost of care.

In a well-run insurance marketplace, people will pay the full cost and reap the full benefits of every change they make. That leaves them with an undistorted economic incentive to buy insurance and to choose the insurance that best meets their individual and family needs.[50]

The Results. With these five changes, we will have converted a health system in which incentives are perverse in every direction into one in which everyone's economic incentives are ideal.

APPENDIX TO CHAPTER 14

How the Trump Administration Is Reforming the Health Care System

The Trump administration has been pushing the limits of executive authority to make fundamental changes in our health care system.[51] If Congress would do its part, the system would be radically different from what it was the day Donald Trump was elected president.

So why do so few people seem to know about this?

It's not for lack of trying on the part of the administration. The vision behind the Trump reforms can be found in "Reforming America's Healthcare System through Choice and Competition."[52] This 124-page Health and Human Services document argues that the most serious problems in health care arise because of government failure, not market failure. It goes into great detail on how to correct the policy errors.

Moreover, for each of its major policy changes, the administration has put out press releases and background documents for all to read. Unfortunately, most of this has gone unreported in the mainstream media. More often than not, it has been ignored by the health care media as well.

What follows is a brief summary of some of the most interesting changes. For additional explanation, readers should consult an article by Marie Fishpaw (Heritage Foundation) and me at National Review Online.[53]

Personal and Portable Health Insurance. This is by far the most impactful change. As of January 2020. employers are able to use an account called a Health Reimbursement Arrangement (HRA) to provide tax-free funds employees can use to buy their own health insurance. This is health insurance that employees can take with them as they travel from job to job and in and out of the labor market.[54]

This is an abrupt change from the Obama regulations, which threatened to fine employers as much as $100 per employee per day—or $36,500 per year—for giving their employees the opportunity to own their own insurance.

The Council of Economic Advisers estimates this change will affect eleven million workers. But it could affect one hundred million if states cleaned up their individual markets to make individual insurance a more attractive option.

Round-the-Clock Medical Care. Concierge doctors used to be available only to the rich. Today, "direct primary care" is far more affordable. AtlasMD in Wichita, for example, provides all primary care along with 24/7 phone and email access and generic drugs for less than what Medicaid pays. They help patients gain access to specialist care and diagnostic tests, with minimal waiting. The cost: fifty dollars a month for a middle-aged adult and ten dollars a month for a child.[55]

A number of employers are creating access to direct primary care as an employee benefit. Under current law they cannot put tax-free dollars into an account and let employees use the money to select a direct-pay doctor of their choosing. However, the Trump administration has issued an executive order that will allow Health Reimbursement Accounts (HRAs) to be used as vehicles to overcome the current regulatory obstacles.[56]

In addition, the administration hopes to make Medicare open to direct primary care.[57] Under the arrangement, Medicare would pay a fixed monthly fee to a physician or physician group instead of the traditional fee-for-service payments. In return, the physicians would provide virtually all primary care. The fees would range from $90 to $120 a month, depending on the patient's age and medical complexity.[58]

Access to Telemedicine. The ability to deliver medical care remotely is growing by leaps and bounds.[59] It promises to lower medical costs, increase quality, and reduce the time and travel cost of patient care. For example, most people in hospital emergency rooms don't really need to be there. With an iPhone and an app or two, most of them could be examined in the comfort of their own homes.

The problem? Until the coronavirus hit, Medicare didn't pay for any of this.[60] And since private insurers and employers tended to pay the way Medicare pays, the entire country is missing out on incredible advances in telemedical technology.

As noted, the Centers for Medicare and Medicaid Services (CMS) was acting aggressively to change this.[61] Under the new rules, doctors in Medicare Advantage plans and Accountable Care Organizations were allowed to have "virtual check-ins" and experiment with telemedicine in other ways.

With the advent of COVID-19, both Congress and the administration acted quickly to remove essentially all barriers to telemedicine in a series of actions described above. These changes are only temporary, however. To make them a permanent feature of our health care system, Congress will have to legislate again.

Access to Centers of Excellence. On the Obamacare exchanges, there has been a race to the bottom as health plans try to attract the healthy and avoid the sick.[62] Increasingly, enrollees have been denied access to the best doctors and the best facilities.

Instead of expecting every health plan to be all things to all patients, we should encourage specialization. We need focused facilities for such chronic conditions as cancer, diabetes, and heart disease.[63] To make the market work better, medical records need to travel with the patient from plan to plan, and insurers need to be able to design better risk-adjustment mechanisms rather than being forced into federal government-designed systems.

President Trump has taken aggressive steps in this direction, giving states new authority to experiment.[64] This has already led to lower costs in seven states.[65]

Patient Power. There is mounting evidence that patients suffering from diabetes, heart disease, cancer, and other chronic illnesses can (with training) manage a lot of their own care as well as—or better than—traditional doctor therapy can.[66] If they are going to manage their own care, they will do an even better job if they are also managing the money that pays for that care.[67]

The Trump administration recently made a major announcement that is a step in the right direction. Going forward, employees with HSAs will be exempt from the high-deductible requirement for the treatment of chronic disease.[68] This means that the employer or insurer will be able to provide first-dollar coverage for some services without running afoul of HSA regulations.

Going Forward. These reforms don't solve every problem. But they constitute a remarkable improvement over where we started.

I think of these as phase 1 reforms. They need to be done before we do anything else. In phase 2, I would tackle universal coverage. In phase 3, I would reform government subsidies for health insurance—to make them more efficient and more fair.

15

Opting Out of Unemployment Insurance

IF THE UNITED STATES implemented a system of individual accounts, it would eliminate employer incentives to lay off workers. The cost of benefits would no longer be shifted from workers with unstable employment to workers with stable employment. Workers would demand a wage premium for unstable employment to make up for the smaller account balance expected at retirement. The safety net for workers who are new to the labor force or are frequently unemployed could be funded by experience-adjusted tax rates. Workers would have an incentive to find new jobs quickly, so that they will have more money in their accounts at retirement. Private administration of unemployment insurance also offers the potential for improved performance through appropriate encouragement, as well as sanctions for failure to engage in active work search. We know that unless it is reformed, the current system will cause higher unemployment rates and waste human resources.

The solutions discussed here come from William Conerly, an expert in labor economics and a student of the Chilean unemployment insurance system.

Individual Unemployment Accounts. Like Social Security, unemployment insurance is funded by payroll taxes. People who are working pay the benefits of people who are not. As with Social Security, unemployment insurance is managed by a federal trust fund. In this case, the fund reimburses state governments for administration costs, while benefits are paid from state trust funds. Like proposals to reform Social Security with personal accounts, a second personal account could be established that sets aside a portion of payroll taxes to pay unemployment benefits. During periods of unemployment, workers could draw on their unemployment funds, together with investment returns. If they do not use the funds during periods of unemployment, they could access them when they retire.

Chile's Experience. Chile, which led the world in establishing individual social security accounts for retirees, also has led in the creation of individual accounts for unemployment insurance. Economists Martin Feldstein and Daniel Altman proposed the idea in 1998. Chile began implementing the system in 2002. It works like this:

- Workers pay 0.6 percent of their wages into individual accounts, while employers pay a 2.4 percent payroll tax, divided between individual accounts and a "joint account," that pays benefits to new or low-wage workers when their accounts are exhausted.

- The accounts are administered by the same private pension funds that manage Chilean workers' retirement accounts and are invested conservatively in a variety of securities.

- The individual account is held in the worker's name and is paid out when the worker becomes unemployed or retires. (See figure 15.1.)

- After a worker's account is funded sufficiently to support five months of benefits, taxes are refunded to the employee, not to the unemployment account.

Figure 15.1 Unemployments Benefits Funding in Chile

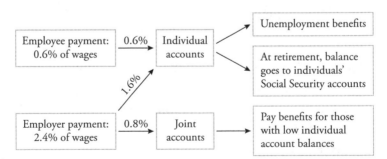

Source: William B. Conerly, "Chile Leads the Way with Unemployment Accounts," National Center for Policy Analysis, Brief Analysis No. 424, November 12, 2002. Available at http://www.ncpathinktank.org/pdfs/ba424.pdf.

- Unemployed individuals with fully funded accounts are able to draw 30 to 50 percent of their previous wages for up to five months at a time.

The US system of personal accounts need not duplicate the Chilean system. However, some elements in the Chilean system are critical for the success of a US program:

- Each worker in the personal account system has his own account, funded like the current system—by payroll taxes.

- A backup system, also funded by payroll taxes, covers those who have not built up a large enough individual account balance to cover their unemployment benefits for five months.

- Another option would be to allow loans from the joint account to the individual accounts of unemployed workers whose balances are too small to meet their living expenses, to be paid back out of the workers' future earnings.[1]

- Unused balances in individual accounts could be withdrawn in cash or rolled into a personal retirement account when the worker retires.

Employment Benefits of Individual Accounts. The biggest problem with the current US unemployment insurance system is that it discourages rapid reemployment. Individual accounts help solve this problem. Workers with individual accounts will feel urgency about finding a job, because finding one will allow them to add to their retirement incomes. In Chile, the unemployment insurance administrator trains the worker to understand the connection between unused unemployment funds and retirement income by mailing the employee's annual unemployment insurance account statement in the same envelope containing quarterly individual social security account statements.[2]

Unlike the US unemployment system, Chileans can draw upon their funds even if they quit or are fired from their last jobs. This allows workers more flexibility in changing employment and reduces the need for costly adjudication of claims.

Unemployment Account Implementation Issues. A personal account system in the United States would be easy for states to administer. Current state-run systems raise issues when people move from one state to another. If people are nervous about changing to a new system, it need not be mandatory. States could offer traditional unemployment insurance in exchange for employer contributions. With good experience rating of employer taxes, the system could pay for itself. However, workers should not be allowed to change back and forth between the two systems, since this could make both systems financially unstable. Over time, the system would be self-funded through existing employment taxes.

16

Combatting the Coronavirus

CRITICS OF PRESIDENT Trump's response to the coronavirus crisis characterize it as knee-jerk, spur of the moment, and grasping at any straw within reach.[1] In fact, many of the executive actions taken in the first three months of 2020 reflect a new approach to health policy. Some had been underway almost since the day Donald Trump was sworn into office.

These include the ability to be diagnosed and treated without ever leaving your own home; the ability to talk to doctors 24/7 by means of phone, email, and video conferencing; and the ability of the chronically ill to have access to free diagnoses and treatments without losing their access to Health Savings Accounts.

In each of these areas, the Trump administration had already pushed the limits of executive authority. The "emergency" created by the coronavirus gave the administration the freedom to do much more.

The Ideal Response. Have you ever wondered how a free market for health care would handle the COVID-19 crisis?

Most patients would have a health kit in their home, with a temperature gauge, blood pressure cuffs, and an O2 sensor. Patients would have these devices because doctors, hospitals, and health plans would encourage their usage. Patients with older models would call in the readings to their doctors. Newer models would send the doctor an automatic, electronic alert if there was reason to be concerned.

The initial doctor/patient contact would probably take place by phone. If warranted, a virtual face-to-face examination by Skype or a similar service would take place. If the services of a specialist were required, that connection would be made—again, remotely and electronically. Also, a variety of smartphone apps would help doctors more easily diagnose and connect with their patients remotely.

If the patient was suffering from a cold or a mild case of the flu (which would be the case more than 90 percent of the time), the doctor would order a prescription, which would be filled and delivered by a local pharmacy.

In the face of coronavirus indications, a doctor or nurse would arrive at the patient's home (within an hour), take a swab sample, and perform a COVID-19 test—with results in, say, ten minutes.

In serious cases, patients would go to the emergency room. But hospitals would know in advance which patients had the virus. A special team would be there to greet these patients. They would be escorted to isolated rooms with appropriate equipment and safeguards to protect other patients and hospital personnel.

The demand for special masks (with better protection than the masks you see surgeons wearing on TV), ventilators, and other equipment would rise dramatically. But it would be a targeted demand, informed by real data. You wouldn't see hoarding and oversubscribing by providers that scramble to get more supplies than they need "just in case." The demand would be met by suppliers that would work nights and weekends to step up production because—well—because they expect to get paid extra, just as in any other market.

So why weren't these things being done when the coronavirus hit? They were being done. But not nearly as often as they should have been. The reason: government.

Getting Diagnosed in Your Own Home. If you go to a doctor's office or a hospital emergency room, you risk infecting other patients or being infected yourself. So why not stay home? Telemedicine was used extensively in China to diagnose the coronavirus.[2] In March 2020, Vice President Michael Pence and major health insurance companies said telemedicine is "the first line of defense" against the virus.[3] Yet federal and state laws were still standing in the way.

In the private sector, the ability to deliver medical care remotely, say by means of phone, email, Skype, and Zoom, had been growing by leaps and bounds.[4] Telemedicine promised to lower costs, increase quality, and lower the time and travel cost of patient care. As we entered 2020, however, Medicare rarely paid for any of this. Congress was the culprit.[5]

Federal law (the Social Security Act) allowed Medicare to pay for telemedicine only under strictly limited circumstances. For the most part, the law allowed doctors to examine, consult with, and treat patients remotely only in rural areas, and, even there, the patients couldn't be treated in their own homes.

The Centers for Medicare and Medicare Services had been acting aggressively since 2018 to expand telemedicine.[6] Under one rule change, Medicare Advantage plans and Accountable Care Organizations (ACOs) were allowed to bill Medicare if they consult with patients remotely to determine if they need an in-office visit. Patients could have remote consultations from anywhere, including their own homes.

How did Seema Verma (who administered Medicare and Medicaid) get away with these changes? By reclassifying these remote services as "virtual medicine" instead of "telemedicine." The communications are labeled "virtual check-ins."

Still, these were baby steps. The coronavirus created an opportunity for bolder action under the rubric of emergency authority.

After the coronavirus struck, Verma used the president's executive authority to give Medicare Advantage plans broad discretion with respect to remote diagnosis and treatment. Congress also chipped in with legislation that allowed Medicare to pay for telemedicine in connection with the coronavirus. But it imposed an onerous restriction: the doctor must have had a prior relationship with the patient within the previous three years.

Congress's requirement was a disastrous barrier to remote medical care. It would have made ineligible virtually every telemedicine company in the country and every hospital online screening service. Fortunately, the administration used its emergency powers to override the restriction.

Medicare doctors were then allowed to use telemedical devices to diagnose and treat anyone even suspected of having the virus, regardless of where they lived and any previous doctor/patient relationship.

Also, the Trump administration in June 2019 suspended federal licensing regulations so that doctors licensed in any one state could provide services to patients who resided in some other state.[7] For the reform to be fully operational, however, governors needed to use their emergency powers to suspend state-level restrictions as well. In March 2020, Texas and Massachusetts became early states that lifted the licensing barriers.[8]

Having 24/7 Access to Your Doctor. Coronavirus symptoms didn't occur just during working hours. But the ability to talk to a doctor by phone at any time—including nights and weekends—was once a privilege available only to the very rich. Fortunately, what is now commonly called "direct primary care" was becoming widely available.[9]

A model first developed in 2010 by AtlasMD in Wichita, Kansas, made round-the-clock care available to almost everyone. In 2020 a mother, for example, can have full access to all primary care 24/7 for only $50 a month. A child costs an additional $10. A senior costs $100. With the spread of the coronavirus, demand for this kind of service soared.[10]

The Trump administration made two regulatory changes to facilitate the opportunity. First, enrollees were allowed to get direct primary care services under Medicare.[11] Second, employees were allowed to use their Health Reimbursement Accounts to pay the monthly fee for direct primary care.[12] Neither option was allowed under the Obama administration.

Getting Tested in Your Own Home. In both Korea and in the United States the first person known to have the COVID-19 virus was discovered at about the same times. South Korea engaged in a massive testing campaign (including drive-through testing) to determine who had the virus and who didn't. By mid-March 2020, that country had tested more than 5,000 people for every one million residents. By contrast, the number tested in the United States was 125 for every one million residents.[13] In fact, the U.S. testing rate at that point was about the lowest in the developed world!

U.S. officials claim that the tests used in other countries are not as accurate as those approved by our government. Even so, the proof was in the pudding. As Alec Stapp wrote in *The Dispatch*:

> South Korea has effectively contained the coronavirus without shutting down its economy or quarantining tens of millions of people. . . .

Hong Kong, Singapore, and Taiwan have also managed to contain the virus via a combination of travel restrictions, social distancing, and heightened hygiene.[14]

Until early February 2020, all testing for COVID-19 in the United States had to be done at the Centers for Disease Control and Prevention (CDC) in Atlanta. Once the CDC recognized it was ill prepared to handle a pandemic, it sent out testing kits to about a hundred public health centers around the country. Unfortunately, about half of the kits were defective.

President Trump on numerous occasions made clear his desire to wipe away regulatory obstacles. Following suit, Alex Azar, the Secretary of Health and Human Services, declared a public health emergency on February 4, thereby enabling any lab that wanted to conduct its own tests for the new coronavirus to get testing authority under the FDA's Emergency Use Authorization (EUA) program.[15]

Although this move was supposed to usher in deregulation, the EUA process brought with it a new set of bureaucratic obstacles. The entire process, which was described in great detail by Robert Baird in *The New Yorker,* read like an episode of the Keystone Kops.[16]

Within weeks the Trump administration responded to this regulatory morass by successively relaxing the rules on EUA approval. In response, Roche, Eli Lilly, and other drug companies stepped forward.[17] But the process was still too slow.

For example, Biomerica developed a test that involved little more than a finger prick, with results available in ten minutes.[18] It could be performed by trained professionals almost anywhere—airports, schools, offices, homes, etc. The test, which sells for ten dollars per patient, has been approved in Europe and was being used in other countries, even though it was not approved for use in the United States.

It was not until the end of March that Abbott Laboratories finally got approval for a test that could deliver results in as little as five minutes.

Here is a reasonable rule that should guide the government in a public health crisis: if a test is approved in Europe, it should be available to patients in the United States.

Getting Treated in Your Own Home. In principle, most patients who have a cold, the flu, or even the coronavirus can be monitored and treated in their own homes. A smartphone is a powerful computer connected to a communications device. Smartphones are already being used by physicians to monitor patients and by patients to send data to their doctors for a variety of conditions. Due to the bureaucratic nature of American medicine, we have only begun to scratch the surface of the possibilities. There are apps to monitor cardiac health and perform EKGs and devices to perform ultrasound scans and allow endoscope exams of the throat.[19] If needed, a nurse practitioner could visit the home and help with the procedure.

Other alternatives to hospitalization exist that could meet the needs of many patients, absent oppressive regulation. Intermediate care centers, for example, could isolate and care for patients. Such a center could be a medical hotel near a hospital with a small on-call nursing staff. Patients who need to be monitored or who run the risk of infecting family could convalesce in a setting that costs a few hundred dollars per day rather than thousands or tens of thousands for a hospital stay.

But in the first three months of 2020, not a single hotel in the entire country had the government's permission to do that.

Getting Care without Excessive Out-of-Pocket Spending. In the Obamacare exchanges there appears to be a race to the bottom, as insurers try to attract the healthy and avoid the sick. They attract the healthy by keeping their premiums as low as possible. They repel the sick with high deductibles and very narrow provider networks. (Employers face these same perverse incentives, but the response has not been quite as bad.)

President Trump persuaded the major insurance company executives to verbally agree to waive deductibles and copayments to encourage potential coronavirus victims to get tested and treated.[20] The administration also stretched its regulatory authority by defining coronavirus treatment as an "essential health benefit," whose coverage is required by law.[21]

A related development concerns Health Savings Account (HSA) regulations. As of March 2020, more than twenty-eight million people have an HSA, and these accounts contain almost $68 billion in assets.[22] Employees and their employers can make tax-free deposits to them and the balances grow tax-free. However, these tax advantages arc only possible if the account is combined with a catastrophic health insurance plan that has an across-the-board deductible ($1,400 for individuals and $2,800 for families in 2020).

Say an employer with a diabetic employee encourages compliance with needed treatment by making certain drugs and monitoring devices free without charge. This makes good medical sense and good economic sense. But it would disqualify the HSA plan, since patients must spend up to their deductibles before getting services for free.

To deal with this problem, the administration relaxed the HSA rules to allow some chronic care to be provided without violating the high deductible requirement in 2019. Then, in March 2020, an IRS ruling solved the same problem for coronavirus detection and treatment. Considering that HSAs were created by an act of Congress, these executive actions were very aggressive.[23]

Getting Health Insurance That Is Personal and Portable. In a dynamic economy, people change jobs frequently, and that is generally not a bad thing. But job changes typically mean changing your health insurance, and that often means changing your doctor as well. For the chronically ill, continuity of care achieved by a continuing relationship with doctors is usually better care.

Insurance owned by the workers—coverage that travels with them from job to job and in and out of the labor market—would have been precisely the type of insurance most valuable to employees who lost their jobs because of the coronavirus.

Under the Obama administration, employers who provided pretax dollars to the employees to purchase individually owned health insurance could be fined as much as $100 per employee per day, or $36,500 a year. This was equal to the highest fine in all of Obamacare. And it brought the practice to a grinding halt.

The Trump administration abolished the fine and encouraged the practice that the Obama White House wanted to outlaw. As of January 2020, employers have been allowed to provide pretax dollars to employees who can buy their own health insurance.

Getting Health Care Providers the Equipment They Need. The health care industry is the most regulated industry in our economy. Virtually everything that is used to treat a coronavirus patient is regulated by the federal government—masks, gloves, gowns, respirators, ventilators—you name it. A normal business can't produce and sell any of these items without the government's permission. And getting permission can be a long and laborious process. The federal government even tells hospitals how many beds they can have!

Small wonder, then, that when the COVID-19 crisis hit, there was a shortage of everything—and everyone predicted that the shortage would only get worse as the virus made its way through the population. Since 2005, there had been federal stockpile of protective medical gear—to guard against a pandemic. But in early 2020, the number of masks on hand equaled about 1 percent of what some predicted the national need would be.[24] Several attempts were made to stockpile ventilators, under the well-founded belief that they would be in short supply in any future epidemic. The efforts were complete failures, however.[25]

If we had followed the rules, thousands, perhaps millions, of patients would have been unable to get the medical care they need. Fortunately, the Trump administration was willing to bend the rules. Deregulation of industry was a major goal of the administration since day one. And there was no sector of the economy where it was more needed than the health care industry, faced with the COVID-19 pandemic.

Private industry stepped up to meet the need because relaxation of burdensome regulations allowed it to do so:

- 3M was able to convert industrial-use masks to health care purposes and, after Congress gave it protection against lawsuits, began producing thirty-five million N95 masks a month.[26]
- Ventilators made for industrial use can be retrofitted for health purposes. General Motors partnered with Ventec Life Systems. Ford partnered with 3M and General Electric. General Motors and Ford are in talks with Tesla to do the same.[27]
- Before the coronavirus hit, Ventec was producing 150 ventilators a month; it was soon able to ramp up to 1,000.[28]

Hundreds of other companies followed suit.

Both on the right and the left there were calls for a command-and-control approach. For example, some in Congress called on the president to invoke the Defense Production Act—a Korean War–era authority—to compel private industry to step up production of masks, ventilators, and other items.[29] Apparently, FEMA came close to invoking the act to get increased production of masks.[30] New York governor Andrew Cuomo even suggested that the relevant companies be nationalized, if needed.[31]

President Trump wisely resisted this approach in most instances, noting that Venezuela shows the futility of command-and-control economies.

As in the case of medical tests, more could have been done. Given the current state of emergency, we should approve any medical device that has already been approved in Europe. And as Hoover Institution economist John Cochrane has suggested, if you want people to work nights and weekends to step up their output, government should be willing to chip in and make it worth their while.[32]

Exercising the Right to Try. Another reform championed by President Trump was allowing patients to try drugs that have not been approved by the FDA if the patient is terminally ill. In March 2020 the president said the same principle should apply even if the patient was not terminally ill. Hydroxychloroquine, for example, is an existing drug used to treat rheumatoid arthritis and systemic lupus and appears to be effective with COVID-19.[33] Chloroquine is an eighty-five-year-old drug that is safe for use to prevent malaria and it appears to be effective as well. (It had worked for other SARS viruses.) Of course, the true effectiveness of these and other drug treatments for COVID-19 requires clinical trials to determine, but for those most vulnerable who have the virus, time is of the essence. The president asks, "What have you got to lose?"[34]

The president was criticized for mentioning these drugs at White House briefings. What the critics rarely mentioned was that one in five of all drugs prescribed in the United States are "off label"—prescribed for a use that has never undergone a controlled clinical trial.[35] The president was encouraging doctors to approach the coronavirus the way they typically approach other health problems.[36] Also, doctors themselves apparently believed these drugs were worth a try. They were hoarding the drugs for possible personal use.[37]

Although off-label uses of drugs are quite common, it is illegal for a drug company to advertise the off-label uses of a drug it manufactures and sells. Drug companies can't even send out medical journal articles to physicians that report on the success of off-label uses. If an executive of a company that makes a malaria drug went on TV and made the same statements President Trump made, the executive could wind up in prison.

Things took a radical turn for the better, however, on March 29, 2020. That's when the FDA took the highly unusual step of issuing an emergency use authorization, allowing the malaria drugs to be used by doctors to treat coronavirus.[38] The Department of Health and Human Services issued a statement announcing that Sandoz had donated thirty million doses of hydroxychloroquine, and Bayer had donated one million doses of chloroquine to a federal stockpile to be distributed to physicians.[39]

More generally, the White House encouraged the medical community to ignore the red tape and try to find out what works.[40]

Making Health Reforms Permanent. One reason the country was doing as well as it was in defending against COVID-19 was that President Trump began deregulating the health care market early in his presidency.[41] Those efforts laid the groundwork for further deregulation that freed patients, doctors, and other providers to meet the health care challenge unrestrained by unwise, counterproductive legal restrictions. A second reason has been the willingness of Congress to enact additional deregulation by law.

However, almost every good reform passed by Congress is limited to the duration of the coronavirus crisis. If the crisis goes away, the freedom of doctors to efficiently meet patient needs also goes away. Additionally, reforms created by the president's executive orders could easily be reversed by the next president's counter-executive orders.

What is needed is to make these reforms permanent—by securing them in law.

Conclusion
Life under a Reformed System

PEOPLE OF ANY age should have the choice to opt out of social insurance in favor of alternatives that better meet their individual and family needs. They should be able to substitute assets and arrangements they have chosen voluntarily, and that they own and control, for the government systems to which they are now forced to belong. In particular:

- People should be able to substitute private savings, private pensions and annuities, and private insurance for participation in Social Security.
- They should be able to substitute private insurance and private health savings for participation in Medicare and in the federalized health care system sometimes called Obamacare.
- They should be able to substitute private disability insurance for participation in the federal disability program.
- They should be able to substitute private savings, private pensions and annuities, and private insurance for participation in Medicaid's long-term care insurance.
- At their places of work, employees and their employers should be free to choose private unemployment insurance arrangements, private disability insurance, and private alternatives to workers' compensation.[1]

Furthermore, the choice does not have to be all or nothing. People should also be free to opt out partially and to opt out progressively over time.

Terms and Conditions. Only one general condition must govern these choices: they must not increase the expected burden for other taxpayers. This means that a reasonable expectation should exist that (1) the direct tax burden for others will not rise as a result of an individual's opting out and (2) the individual will not try to return to the government program (thus creating an additional burden for everyone else) if the private option turns out to be disappointing.[2]

This condition implies that opting out must be a win/win proposition. It must be good for the individual who exercises choice as well as for everyone else.

What does all this mean for everyday workers? We have seen what will happen if we stay on the current course:

- The implicit unfunded liabilities in Social Security and Medicare total more than $119 trillion—roughly six times the size of the economy.
- When the implicit unfunded promises in Medicaid, Obamacare, and other programs are added, the total is almost $165 trillion—and growing.

That means each new generation of workers will be progressively worse off:

- Closing the gap through tax hikes alone will require an immediate and permanent increase in this worker's federal taxes of 64 percent, including income taxes, payroll taxes, excise taxes, and other taxes and fees.
- Alternatively, benefits, including Social Security and Medicare benefits, at retirement could be cut by 40 percent.

Effects of a Reformed Social Security System. Over time, a Social Security reform that applies progressive indexing and creates personal retirement accounts equal to 4 percent of wages will allow our representative worker to retire with a benefit equal to what he is scheduled to receive from the current system.

Individuals who are unable to fund their own benefits would still depend on contributions from the taxpayers. But tax rates would fall overall as existing obligations are paid off, and future generations would not be born into a world in which they are saddled at birth with a mountain of debt.

Effects of a Reformed Medicare System. The effects of prefunding combined with better incentives have a dramatic impact on the future financial health of Medicare.[3] Eventually, the taxes and premiums needed to pay benefits comparable to what Medicare promises today will be only a fraction of what they will need in the absence of reform. Consider:

- Under the current system, the taxes and premiums needed to support Medicare spending will more than triple, growing from 3.2 percent of GDP today to 11.3 percent by 2080.

- By contrast, under a reformed model, estimates show that the taxes and premiums needed to support Medicare spending will fall to 2.9 percent of GDP by 2080.

Reforms include (1) allowing providers to repackage and reprice their services in ways that improve quality and reduce price, (2) allowing beneficiaries to manage more of their own Medicare dollars through Roth Health Savings Accounts, and (3) requiring the working-age population (along with their employers) to prefund much of their postretirement health care benefits by saving a portion of their wages from now until the time of retirement.[4]

For the average worker, an annual deposit of 4 percent of wages over a full working life should be sufficient to fully opt out of Medicare by the time of retirement. Without reform, the size of the Medicare program will more than triple (relative to national income) over the next seventy-five years. With reform, Medicare will take no more of the national income than it does today.

Integrating Medicare Solutions with Social Security Retirement, Disability, and Medicaid Reforms. A major trend in postretirement living is the assisted living facility.[5] These entities typically offer room and board—in some cases quite luxurious—plus nonacute health care services. In theory, an initially healthy senior could progress through Alzheimer's disease and then death without ever leaving the facility.

The emergence and growth of assisted living facilities causes us to focus on an often-ignored reality: it is becoming increasingly difficult to separate living needs from health care needs—especially for senior citizens. That being the case, why do we need three separate programs: Social Security for living expenses, Medicare for health care, and Medicaid as a fallback insurance for long-term care? Why can't all three programs be rolled into one? They could.

In a reformed Social Security system, each generation would save through private accounts to pay its own retirement living expenses. In a reformed Medicare system, each generation would save through private accounts for its own postretirement health care. But why have two accounts? Why have separate investment strategies? Wouldn't a single account be more efficient and make more sense? Additionally, there is no reason why the same account could not also be used for long-term care insurance—thereby replacing the largest, fastest-growing part of Medicaid.

It might work like this: At the time of retirement, an annuity would be purchased that generates two separate cash flow streams. One would be for living expenses (like a pension), and the other would be for health insurance. However, the two income streams could be combined and redivided in different ways. For example, one stream of payments could cover the cost of living, outpatient care, and long-term care at an assisted living facility, while the remaining stream pays for insurance for catastrophic inpatient care.

> For an additional 2 percent of wages, young workers would be able to securely replace the promises made by (Social Security's) disability insurance and by (Medicaid's) long-term care insurance.

Integrating Unemployment and Workers' Comp Insurance with the Other Reforms. In addition to other government programs, unemployment insurance and workers' compensation could be integrated into this system, based on additional contributions. A variety of arrangements is possible. For instance, in lieu of paying a percentage of their payroll into state unemployment and workers' compensation funds, employers and employees could opt out and deposit some of their savings into individual accounts owned by employees. The accounts would provide portable benefits that a worker could draw on as needed (with appropriate safeguards) or save for use in retirement.

A Better Way: Choice, Ownership, and Responsibility. The reforms proposed in this study will allow each individual, family and generation to pay its own way. Whereas the current system inevitably creates conflicts between individuals, groups, and generations as each seeks to reap benefits paid for by someone else, these reforms provide opportunities for win/win solutions.

The transition to the new system will not be painless. However, implementing these reforms is not costly compared to the alternative of doing nothing: every year that we do not make these needed changes, the burden of the current system we are handing to future generations will increase.

In exchange for choices that allow individuals to opt out of dysfunctional public programs and exert greater control over the money that funds those systems, people will have to take more responsibility. A social safety net will still be there for the most unfortunate in society, but everyone will also have opportunities for greater security from life's risks and less dependence on government. People will live under a neutral system that never penalizes choices such as the decision to work or to stay out of the workforce to raise one's children or care for an elderly relative, and that never penalizes the decision to save for the future and invest in the economy. In the long run, future generations will enjoy higher rates of economic growth, leading to higher incomes and lower tax rates.

Appendix 1

Ten Things You Need to Know
about Medicare for All

QUITE A FEW Democratic candidates for office in 2020 cam-
paigned on the idea of enrolling everyone in Medicare.[1] It's not just the left.
A significant number of doctors in the American Medical Association are
for it.[2] Public opinion polls show that 70 percent of Americans like the idea.[3]

Here are ten things you need to know.

1. Medicare is not really government insurance. Almost everybody on the
political left thinks that Medicare is a government plan—one that is completely different from private insurance. Yet that view is wrong.

Although Medicare is largely funded with tax dollars, it has never been
a strictly government program. Medicare's original benefit package copied a
standard Blue Cross plan that was common back in 1965. And Medicare
has always been privately administered—in many places by Blue Cross itself. That's the same Blue Cross that administers private insurance sold to
nonseniors.

Moreover, in recent years, more than one-third of all seniors are enrolled in
plans offered by Humana, Cigna, UnitedHealthcare and other private insurers under the Medicare Advantage program. These private plans are virtually
indistinguishable from the private insurance nonseniors have.

2. The most successful part of Medicare is run by private insurers. A study
published in *Health Affairs* finds that the Medicare Advantage program costs
less and delivers higher-quality care than traditional Medicare.[4] Moreover,
within the Medicare Advantage program, the most successful plans are
the ones administered by independent doctors' associations.[5] These plans

are showing that integrated care, coordinated care, medical homes, and sharing of electronic information actually work—to keep patients healthier and improve medical outcomes.

But there is nothing special about Medicare in this regard. These are private-sector innovations that are also available to nonseniors under contract with private insurers.

3. Medicare is often the last insurer to adopt innovations that work. In 2003, the benefit structure of Medicare looked pretty much the same as it did forty years earlier. But in 1965, drugs were relatively inexpensive and their impact on care relatively modest. Through time, they became more expensive. They also became the most cost-effective medical therapy. When Medicare began covering drugs (through Part D) in 2004, it started providing coverage that virtually all private insurers and all employers had already offered years earlier.

Medicare has also been slow to adopt technologies that are becoming more common in the private sector.[6] Until the coronavirus hit, it wouldn't pay for doctor consultations by phone, email, or Skype in most cases; and unless there is new legislation, the ability of doctors and patients to use telemedicine will go away when the virus goes away. It won't pay for Uber-type house calls at night and on weekends, although the cost and the wait times are far below those of emergency room visits.[7] And in most cases it will not pay for concierge doctor services, now available to seniors for as little as one hundred dollars a month—despite the potential to improve access and reduce costs.[8]

4. Medicare has wasted enormous sums on innovations that don't work. Although Medicare tends to be the last insurer to adopt innovations that work, it has shown no reluctance to experiment with innovations that don't work. Medicare has spent billions of dollars on pilot programs and demonstration projects, trying to find ways of lowering costs and raising the quality of care. Many of these efforts have focused on integrated care and coordinated care. Yet instead of finding places in the health care system where these techniques seem to work (e.g., private Medicare Advantage plans), Medicare set out instead to reinvent the wheel. Three separate Congressional Budget Office reports concluded that these efforts would be unsuccessful, and those predictions seem to be vindi-cated by the test of time.[9] Other efforts to change hospital behavior appear to have raised costs rather than lower them.[10]

5. Most seniors in conventional Medicare are participating in stealth priva-tization, even though they are unaware of it. By far the biggest recent change in Medicare has been the Obama administration's stealth program to privatize conventional Medicare and enroll seniors in managed care programs called Accountable Care Organizations. At last count, there were 32.7 million pa-tients enrolled in an ACO. About one-third of them think they are participat-ing in traditional fee-for-service Medicare.[11]

The reason for the word "stealth" is that President Obama never used the words "privatization" or "managed care," even though ACOs are mainly pri-vate entities with essentially the same economic incentives as the hated HMOs of the 1980s and 1990s. Not only did the Obama administration never tell seniors they were participating in a grand experiment, they made it illegal for an ACO to tell a senior he is actually enrolled!

This experiment has largely been a failure. Without the tools routinely used by Medicare Advantage plans (including the right to transparent com-munication with patients), ACOs are neither saving money in the aggregate, nor are they improving the quality of care.[12]

Democratic candidates for office often rail against the idea of privatizing Medicare. AARP frequently parrots the same message. Yet eleven million seniors who think they are in traditional Medicare are actually in a private-sector ACO. It was Democrats who put them there with legislation that AARP supported!

6. There is nothing Medicare can do that employers and private insurers can't do. For many years, the Physicians for a National Health Program argued that a single-payer health insurer would be a monopsonist (a single buyer) in the market for physicians' services. It could therefore use this power to bargain down the fees it pays to physicians. Putting aside the puzzle about why a doc-tors' organization would advocate putting the financial squeeze on themselves and their colleagues, the whole idea turns out to be wrong.

Medicare doesn't bargain with anyone. It simply puts out a price and doctors can take it or leave it. But private insurers can do that too. In fact, they can put out a take-it-or-leave-it price lower than what Medicare pays. That's what has been happening in the (Obamacare) health insurance exchanges, where the only profitable insurers have tended to be Medicaid contractors that pay Medicaid rates to providers.

Unfortunately, that means that enrollees are often denied access to the best doctors and the best facilities.[13]

Obamacare insurance, for example, excludes MD Anderson Cancer Center in Houston (cited by *U.S. News & World Report* as the best cancer care facility in the country), Southwestern Medical Center in Dallas (rated as the top medical research center in the world by the British journal *Nature*), and the Mayo Clinic in Rochester, Minnesota.[14]

Employers and private insurers could be far more aggressive in keeping prices down than they are today and far more aggressive than Medicare is. Canadians who come to the United States for knee and hip replacements (because they get tired of waiting in Canada) pay about half of what Americans typically pay. Employers and private insurers could offer the same service to patients who are willing to travel and pay up front.

MediBid is a service that offers patients a national exchange where providers submit competitive bids that are routinely less than what Medicare pays.[15]

7. Medicare for all would be costly. "Medicare for all" sounds attractive to some people because it suggests you are going to get something for nothing. But when pressed, even Bernie Sanders admits there is no such thing as a free lunch.

A study by Charles Blahous at the Mercatus Center estimates that Medicare for all would cost $32.6 trillion over the next ten years.[16] Other studies have put the cost even higher.[17] They imply that we would need at least a 25 percent payroll tax. And that assumes that doctors and hospitals provide the same amount of care they provide today, even though they would be paid Medicare rates, which are far below what private insurance has been paying. Without those cuts in provider payments, the needed payroll tax would be closer to 30 percent and maybe more.

Of course, there would be savings on the other side of the ledger. People would no longer have to pay private insurance premiums and out-of-pocket fees. In fact, for the country as a whole this would largely be a financial wash—a huge substitution of public payment for private payment.

But remember, in today's world, how much you and your employer spend on health care is up to you and your employer. If the cost is too high, you can choose to jettison benefits of marginal value and be choosier about the doctors and hospitals in your plan's network. You could also take advantage of medical tourism (traveling to other cities where the costs are lower and the quality is higher) and phone, email, and other telemedical innovations described above. The premiums you pay today are voluntary, and (absent Obamacare mandates) what you buy with those premiums is a choice you and your employer are free to make.

With Medicare for all, you would have virtually no say in how costs are controlled other than the fact that you would be one of several hundred million potential voters.

Remember also that there is a reason why Obamacare is such a mess. The Democrats in Congress convened special interests around a figurative table—the drug companies, the insurance companies, the doctors, the hospitals, the device manufacturers, big business, big labor, etc.—and gave each a piece of the Obamacare pie in order to buy their political support.[18]

As we show below, every single issue Obamacare had to contend with would be front and center in any plan to replace Obamacare with Medicare for all. So, the Democrats who gave us the last health care reform would be dealing with the same issues and the same special interests the second time around.

It takes a great deal of faith to believe there would be much improvement.

8. The real cost of Medicare includes hidden costs imposed on doctors and taxpayers. Blahous estimates that the administrative cost of private insurance is 13 percent, more than twice the 6 percent it costs to administer Medicare. Single-payer advocates often use this type of comparison to argue that universal Medicare would reduce health care costs. But this estimate ignores the hidden costs that Medicare shifts to the providers of care, including the enormous amount of paperwork that is required in order to get paid.

Medicare is the vehicle by which the federal government has been trying to force the entire health care system to adopt electronic medical records—a costly change that appears to have done nothing to increase quality or reduce costs, while making it easier for doctors to "up code" and bill the government for more money.[19]

There are also the social costs of collecting taxes to fund Medicare, including the costs of preparation and filing and the costs of avoiding and evading taxation. By some estimates, the social cost of collecting a dollar of taxes is estimated to be between twenty-five and forty-four cents.

A study by a Milliman (formerly Milliman & Robertson) estimates that, when all these costs are included, Medicare and Medicaid spend two-thirds *more* on administration than private insurance spends.[20]

Single-payer advocates are also fond of comparing the administrative costs of health care in the United States and Canada—again claiming there is a potential for large savings. But these comparisons invariably include the cost of private insurance premium collection (advertising, agents' fees, etc.), while ignoring the cost of tax collection to pay for public insurance. Using the most conservative estimate of the social cost of collecting taxes, economist Benjamin Zycher calculates that the excess burden of a universal Medicare program would be twice as high as the administrative costs of universal private coverage.[21]

Health economist Chris Conover has more recently estimated the hidden costs of Bernie Sander's plan for Medicare for all (endorsed by one hundred members of the House of Representatives) as follows:[22]

- The deadweight losses generated by collecting the income taxes needed to pay for the plan are between $625 billion and $1.1 trillion per year. (This is the economic cost of tax collection described above.)[23]

- The excess waste resulting from spending on services that are worth less to the patient than their actual costs—produced by first-dollar coverage—is between $453 and $626 billion per year.[24]

- The estimated burden for patients due to rationing-by-waiting would result in at least $152 to $914 billion in annual costs.[25]

- There would be from $23 to $152 billion in annual social losses stemming from reduced innovation.[26]

All told, the hidden burden of the Sanders plan is between $1.25 and $2.8 trillion. That implies that for every dollar we would be spending on health care, the nation would be burdened by thirty-four to seventy-seven cents in hidden costs.

In terms of family budgets, these hidden costs would be about $12,500 to $28,000 per household per year.

Conover also estimates that the plan would add $61 trillion to the nation's unfunded liabilities.

9. Not a single problem in Obamacare would go away under Medicare for all. If everyone could join Medicare, what premium would they have to pay? Would the premiums be actuarially fair, representing the expected cost of the enrollee's heath care? Or would there be subsidies and cross-subsidies as there are under Obamacare? Would the premium vary by age? By income? By health status? By healthy living choices?

What about the role of employers? Obamacare tried to force them to pay a large part of the cost of reform by imposing a mandate and requiring them to cover a liberal set of benefits. Economists tell us that employee benefits are substitutes for wages and are therefore "paid for" by the employees. But on paper, employers write checks for about 75 percent of the cost of insurance for about 95 percent of the people who have private insurance. Under Medicare for all, would they get off scot-free?

Then there is the exchange. Medicare has one. It's how roughly one-third of seniors get into Medicare Advantage plans. Like the Obamacare exchanges, the Medicare Advantage exchange has government subsidies for private insurance, mandated benefits, annual open enrollment, and no discrimination based on health status. And, it seems to work reasonably well.

The Obamacare exchanges, by contrast, have been a disaster—with spiraling premiums, unconscionably high deductibles, extra charges for chronic patients who need specialty drugs, and a race to the bottom in provider networks that exclude more and more of the best doctors and the best hospitals.

What will happen when the same politicians, catering to the same interest groups that gave us Obamacare, set out to design an exchange for their Medicare-for-all program? That's anyone's guess.[27]

But if Democrats know how to defy the special interests and create a workable exchange, wouldn't they have done that already in the market for individual insurance?

10. Medicare is already on a path to health care rationing. Medicare is already on an unsustainable path. It has made future promises that far exceed expected revenues, based on the Medicare payroll tax and Medicare's share of general federal revenues. Ironically, Democrats, rather than Republicans, were the first to formally acknowledge this fact. At the time Congress passed the Affordable Care Act (ACA) creating Obamacare, the Medicare trustees estimated the unfunded liability in the program at $89 trillion—stretching out indefinitely into the future. Yet, in the next trustees report, that figure had dropped to $37 trillion.[28]

When Barack Obama signed the ACA into law, he wiped away $52 trillion of federal government debt. How did that happen? By theoretically putting the government's health care spending on a budget.

For the past forty years, real per capita health care spending has been growing at twice the rate of growth of real per capita income.[29] That's not only true in this country; it is about the average for the whole developed world. You don't need to be an accountant or a mathematician to know that if an expenditure item is growing at twice the rate of growth of income, it will crowd out more and more of other spending—eventually taking up the entire pie.

To deal with this problem, Obamacare imposed three global budgets on government health care spending. These constraints promise to restrict three spending programs to a rate of growth no greater than the rate of real GDP growth per capita plus about one-half of a percent. These programs are total Medicare spending, Medicaid hospital spending, and (after 2018) federal tax subsidies in the health insurance exchanges.[30]

If these budgets are binding, the burden of excess growth in health care spending for the federal government will have been relieved—forever.

But here is the problem. The Obama administration only "solved" the problem with pen and ink. It didn't give the private sector any new tools to control costs. It didn't empower doctors or hospitals to practice medicine in a more efficient way.

There was an enforcement mechanism: an Independent Payment Advisory Board (IPAB), tasked with the job of keeping spending below the cap—mainly by recommending reductions in fees to doctors and hospitals. In a bipartisan budget deal in 2017, Republicans in Congress abolished the IPAB.[31] But in their latest report, the Medicare trustees imply that they believe future administrations will still have the power to enforce the spending cap. Department of Treasury budgets make the same assumption.[32]

That means that Medicare fees to providers will fall progressively behind private-sector fees through time. And that means one of two things must happen. Either providers will respond to lower fees by providing less care to seniors or they will shift costs to nonseniors in the form of higher fees, higher insurance premiums, and higher state and local taxes.

One way providers could cut costs is by providing fewer amenities. Hospital patients could be in wards with, say, four or six beds instead of single-room occupancy—the way hospitals used to be configured in this country and the way they still are in some other countries. Hospital food could be Meals, Ready-to-Eat (MRE, what combat soldiers take into the field) rather than the fancy cuisine some facilities serve up today.

Another way to cut costs is to deny seniors access to the most expensive care. Writing in *Health Affairs* soon after the passage of the ACA, Harvard health economist Joe Newhouse noted that many Medicaid enrollees are forced to seek care at community health centers and safety-net hospitals because Medicaid payment rates are so low. He speculated that senior citizens may eventually face the same plight under Obamacare.[33]

A third way to cut costs is rationing-by-waiting. It is already common practice for doctors to prioritize—seeing private-pay patients first, Medicare patients next and Medicaid patients last. As in other countries with rationing problems, those at the end of the line may never get seen.

But if everyone were in Medicare, would seniors be on equal footing with nonseniors? Since there would be no more cost shifting (no private patients to shift costs to), the entire burden of spending cuts would fall on Medicare patients themselves. Yet everyone in the medical world knows that older patients have more difficult problems and take more time. That observation wouldn't be lost on practitioners in a system in which time is money and the payment for time keeps getting smaller and smaller. Seniors would be less-favored patients—just because they are seniors.

Appendix 2
What Socialized Medicine Looks Like

LEFT-WING DEMOCRATS in Congress have decided on a new version of health reform.[1] Several versions of "Medicare for all," including one in the House of Representatives by Pramila Jayapal (D-WA) and one in the Senate by Bernie Sanders (I-VT), turn out to be nothing like the Medicare program seniors are used to. What they have in mind is something similar to what we see in Canada—and then some.

Everyone (except American Indians and veterans) will be in the same system. Health care will be nominally free. Access to it will be determined by bureaucratic decision-making.

Here's what to expect.

Overproviding to the Healthy, Underproviding to the Sick. The first thing politicians learn about health care is this: most people are healthy. In fact, they are very heathy—spending only a few dollars on medical care in any given year. By contrast, 50 percent of the health care dollars are spent on only 5 percent of the population in a typical year.

Politicians in charge of health care, however, can't afford to spend half their budget on only 5 percent of the voters, including those who may be too sick to vote at all. So, there is ever-present pressure to divert spending away from the sick toward the healthy.

In Canada and in Britain, patients see primary care physicians more often than people in the United States. In fact, the ease with which relatively healthy people can see doctors is probably what accounts for the popularity of these systems in both countries.

But once they get to the doctor's office, British and Canadian patients receive fewer services. For real medical problems, Canadians often go to hospital emergency rooms—where the average wait in Canada is four hours.[2] In Britain, one of every ten emergency room patients leave without ever seeing a doctor.[3]

The Canadian system is often described as a system that provides high quality care at a much lower cost than the US system. However, Harvard Business School Professor Regina Herzlinger has shown that after adjusting for population age, Canada's cost is actually high and its quality is inferior.[4] A study by former Congressional Budget Office director June O'Neill and her husband, Dave O'Neill, found that:

- The proportion of middle-aged Canadian women who have never had a mammogram is twice the US rate.

- Three times as many Canadian women have never had a pap smear.

- Fewer than 20 percent of Canadian men have ever been tested for prostate cancer, compared with about 50 percent of US men.

- Only 10 percent of adult Canadians have ever had a colonoscopy, compared with 30 percent of US adults.[5]

These differences in screening may partly explain why the mortality rate in Canada is 25 percent higher for breast cancer, 18 percent higher for prostate cancer and 13 percent higher for colorectal cancer.

A study by Brookings Institution scholar Henry Aaron and his colleagues found that:

- Britain has only one-fourth as many CT scanners as the United States and one-third as many MRI scanners.

- The rate at which the British provide coronary bypass surgery or angioplasty to heart patients is only one-fourth of the US rate, and hip replacements are only two-thirds of the US rate.

- The rate for treating kidney failure (dialysis or transplant) is five times higher in the United States for patients age forty-five to eighty-four and nine times higher for patients eighty-five years of age or older.[6]

We can see the political pressure to provide services to the healthy at the expense of the sick in our own country's Medicare program. Courtesy of Obamacare, every senior is entitled to a free wellness exam, which most doctors regard as virtually worthless.[7] Yet if elderly patients endure an extended hospital stay, they can face unlimited out-of-pocket costs.

Rationing by Waiting. Although Canada has no limits on how frequently a relatively healthy patient may see a doctor, it imposes strict limits on the purchase of medical technology and on the availability of specialists. Hospitals are subject to global budgets—which limit their spending, regardless of actual health needs.

In addition to having to wait many hours in emergency rooms, Canadians have some of the longest waits in the developed world for care that could cure diseases and save lives. The most recent study by the Fraser Institute finds that:

- In 2016, Canadians waited an average of 21.2 weeks between referral from a general practitioner to receipt of treatment by a specialist—the longest wait time in over a quarter of a century of such measurements.

- Patents waited 4.1 weeks for a CT scan, 10.8 weeks for an MRI scan, and 3.9 weeks for an ultrasound.[8]

Similarly, a survey of hospital administrators in 2003 found that:

- Twenty-one percent of Canadian hospital administrators, but less than 1 percent of American administrators, said that it would take over three weeks to do a biopsy for possible breast cancer on a fifty-year-old woman.

- Fifty percent of Canadian administrators versus none of their American counterparts said that it would take over six months for a sixty-five-year-old to undergo a routine hip replacement surgery.[9]

Jumping the Queue. Aneurin Bevan, father of the British National Health Service (NHS), declared, "The essence of a satisfactory health service is that rich and poor are treated alike, that poverty is not a disability and wealth is not advantaged."[10] Yet, more than thirty years after the NHS was founded, an official task force (*The Black Report*) found little evidence that the creation of the NHS had equalized health care access.[11] Another study (*The Acheson Report*), fifty years after the NHS founding, concluded that access had become *more* unequal in the years between the two studies.[12]

In Canada, studies find that the wealthy and powerful have significantly greater access to medical specialists than the less-well-connected poor.[13] High-profile patients enjoy more frequent services, shorter waiting times, and greater choice of specialists.[14] Moreover, among the nonelderly white population, low-income Canadians are 22 percent more likely to be in poor health than their US counterparts.[15]

These results should not be surprising. Rationing-by-waiting is as much an obstacle to care as rationing-by-price. It seems that the talents and skills that allow people to earn high incomes are similar to the talents and skills that are useful in successfully circumventing bureaucratic waiting lines.

No Exit. The worst features of the US health care system are the way in which impersonal bureaucracies interfere with the doctor-patient relationship. Those are also the worst features of Canadian medical care. In Canada, when patients see a doctor, the visit is free. In the United States, the visit is almost free—with patients paying only ten cents out of pocket for every dollar they spend, on the average. In both countries, people primarily pay for care with time, not with money. The two systems are far more similar than they are different.

In Britain, private sector medicine allows patients to obtain care they are supposed to get for free from government. Middle- and upper-middle-income employees frequently have private health insurance, obtained through an employer. A much larger number of Britons use private doctors from time to time. The rule seems to be, "If your condition is serious, go private."

Canada, by contrast, has basically outlawed private-sector medical services that are theoretically provided by the government. If doctors, patients, and entrepreneurs think of better ways of meeting patient needs, they have no way of acting on those thoughts.

This is where the US system is so much better—even though, as in the Canadian system, US Medicare pays doctors the same way it did in the last century, before there were iPhones and email messages, and many US employer plans are just as bad.

But because US employers are free to meet the needs of their employees rather than live under the dictates of a politically pressured bureaucracy, one of the fastest-growing employee benefits is concierge care. For as little as fifty dollars a month for a young adult, patients can have 24/7 access to a doctor by phone and email and all the normal services that primary care physicians provide.

Uber-type house calls, consultations by phone, email, and Skype, cell phone apps that allow people to manage their own care, and other innovations in telemedicine are taking some parts of the private sector by storm.[16]

These are the kinds of innovations that would be outlawed if the congressional Democrats have their way.[17]

Notes

Introduction: A New Approach to Public Policy

1. Previously published as John C. Goodman, "Why Are We Going Broke?," *Townhall*, March 10, 2012.

2. Nasser Gayed, "A Simple Way to Reduce VA Waiting Lists," *Wall Street Journal*, August 19, 2015. RP00fm

3. Business Dictionary, "Economic Inefficiency," accessed 2016, http://www.business dictionary.com/definition/economic-inefficiency.html.

4. Previously published in Goodman Institute, "How a Little Common Sense Could Save Billions in Government Health Care Spending," https://www.goodmaninstitute.org /how-a-little-common-sense-could-save-billions-in-government-health-care-spending/.

Chapter 1: The Case for Change

1. Congressional Budget Office, "Understanding the Long-Term Budget Outlook," last modified July 9, 2015, https://www.cbo.gov/publication/50316.

2. Laurence J. Kotlikoff, "Is Uncle Sam Bankrupt?," National Center for Policy Analysis, Brief Analysis No. 689 (January 29, 2010), http://www.ncpathinktank.org/pdfs/ba689.pdf.

3. Peter Orszag, "Financing Projected Spending in the Long Run," letter to Honorable Judd Gregg, Congressional Budget Office, July 9, 2007.

4. Except for the data in the first sentence, this paragraph was previously published in John C. Goodman, "Why Are We Going Broke?," *Townhall*, March 10, 2012.

5. National Center for Policy Analysis, "Measuring the Unfunded Obligations of European Countries," last modified January 2009, http://www.ncpathinktank.org/pdfs/st319.pdf.

6. The text in this bulleted list is previously published in John C. Goodman, "Why Are We Going Broke?," *Townhall*, March 10, 2012.

7. Laurence Kotlikoff, "Why We're Going Broke," Goodman Institute, February 19, 2020, http://www.goodmaninstitute.org/kotlikoff-why-were-going-broke/.

8. This estimate was made before the passage of health care reform, what some people call Obamacare. But even if reform succeeds in dramatically slowing the rate of growth of Medicare, the tax rates will still be 43 and 60 percent, respectively. See Peter Orszag, "Financing

Projected Spending in the Long Run," letter to Honorable Judd Gregg, Congressional Budget Office, July 9, 2007. The ACA also induced many states to expand Medicaid eligibility requirements, thereby adding to taxpayers' future tax burden.

9. Parts of this section were previously published as John Goodman and Thomas Saving, "What Health Reform Means for Medicare," *Health Affairs*, May 12, 2011, http://health affairs.org/blog/2011/05/12/what-health-reform-means-for-medicare/.

10. Note: If the provisions of the PACA are fully enacted, Medicare spending will be radically slowed by more than what is called for in the Bowles-Simpson deficit reform commission report or in the separate proposals made by Paul Ryan and Alice Rivlin and by Pete Domenici and Alice Rivlin. But it will still grow faster than what is called for in the original Ryan/House Republican budget.

11. John Goodman, "Is Public Policy Changing the Practice of Medicine?," *Health Affairs*, May 21, 2014, http://healthaffairs.org/blog/2014/05/21/is-public-policy-changing-the -practice-of-medicine/.

12. Richard S. Foster, "Estimated Financial Effects of the 'Patient Protection and Affordable Care Act' as Passed by the Senate on December 24, 2009," *Department of Health and Human Services*, December 24, 2009, https://www.cms.gov/Research-Statistics-Data-and -Systems/Research/ActuarialStudies/downloads/S_PPACA_2010-01-08.pdf.

13. In 2015, Congress finally agreed on a "doctor fix" that does not require annual legislative action. The measure will result in higher spending between now and 2030. Yet, ironically, beyond 2030 Medicare spending under the "doctor fix" will actually be lower than it otherwise would have been. See the 2015 Medicare Trustee Report, figure III.C4.

Chapter 2: Balancing Individual and Societal Interests

1. Parts of this section were previously published as John C. Goodman, "How We Can Keep from Going Bankrupt," *Health Policy*, National Center for Policy Analysis, April 4, 2012, http://healthblog.ncpathinktank.org/how-we-can-keep-from-going-broke-part-ii/#sthash .GKD3l3Qp.dpbs.

2. Portions of this section were previously published as John C. Goodman, "How We Can Keep from Going Broke," *Townhall*, March 17, 2012.

3. Department of Labor, "Private Pension Plan Bulletin Historical Tables and Graphs, 1975–2017," last modified September 2019, https://www.dol.gov/sites/dolgov/files/ebsa /researchers/statistics/retirement-bulletins/private-pension-plan-bulletin-historical-tables -and-graphs.pdf.

4. Karen Demasters, "How Much Do People Really Have In IRAs?," Financial Advisor, June 6, 2012, http://www.fa-mag.com/news/how-much-do-people-really-have-in-iras-10914 .html.

5. John C. Goodman, "A Framework for Medicare Reform," National Center for Policy Analysis, Policy Report No. 315, September 2008, http://www.ncpathinktank.org/pdfs/st315 .pdf.

6. Paragraph adapted from John C. Goodman, "How We Can Keep from Going Broke," *Townhall*, March 17, 2012.

7. Social Security is sometimes said to be "progressive" because it gives a larger benefit to lower-income retirees as a percentage of lifetime payroll taxes paid. This progressivity is somewhat offset, however, by the growing life expectancy gap between higher- and lower-income retirees.

8. Pension Benefit Guaranty Corporation, "PBGC Pension Insurance: We've Got You Covered," http://www.pbgc.gov/wr/find-an-insured-pension-plan/pbgc-protects-pensions .html.

9. Three paragraphs were previously published as John C. Goodman, "How We Can Keep from Going Broke," *Townhall*, March 17, 2012, http://townhall.com/columnists/john cgoodman/2012/03/17/how_we_can_keep_from_going_broke.

10. Andrew J. Rettenmaier and Thomas R. Saving, "Social Security and Progressive Indexing," National Center for Policy Analysis, Policy Report No. 520, http://www.ncpathink tank.org/pdfs/ba520.pdf. See also Andrew Rettenmaier and Thomas Saving, "Social Security without Illusion: the Five Percent Solution," National Center for Policy Analysis, NCPA Policy Report No. 272, December 17, 2004, http://www.ncpathinktank.org/pdfs/st272.pdf.

11. John C. Goodman, "A Framework for Medicare Reform," National Center for Policy Analysis, Policy Report No. 315, September 2008, http://www.ncpathinktank.org/pdfs/st315 .pdf.

12. Note: This does not necessarily mean that the average person's lifetime savings will go up. If people are required to save for retirement in one account, they can partially or fully offset that with lower savings in some other account. Indeed, economic evidence indicates that people tend to be "consumption smoothers." That is, they manage their affairs so as to even out their consumption over a lifetime.

Chapter 3: Alternatives That Offer Individual Choice

1. This section was previously published as John C. Goodman, "Why Was Social Security Designed Like a Ponzi Scheme?," *Forbes*, August 24, 2015.

2. Investopedia, "Provident Fund," http://www.investopedia.com/terms/p/provident -fund.asp?layout=infini&v=5B&adtest=5B&ato=3000.

3. The Boston Consulting Group, "Global Wealth 2012: The Battle to Regain Strength," https://www.bcg.com/documents/file106998.pdf.

4. See Michael Sherraden, "Provident Funds and Social Protection: The Case of Singapore," in *Alternatives to Social Security: An International Inquiry*, eds. James Midgley and Michael Sherraden (Westport, Connecticut, 1997); William A. Haseltine, *Affordable Excellence: The Singapore Health Care System* (Washington, D.C.: Brookings Institution, 2015); and John C. Goodman, "Singapore Has Found a Workable Alternative to the Welfare State," April 4, 2015, https://townhall.com/columnists/johncgoodman/2015/04/04/singapore-has -found-a-workable-alternative-to-the-welfare-state-n1980683.

5. Estelle James, "Private Pension Annuities in Chile," National Center for Policy Analysis, Policy Report No. 271, December 9, 2004, http://www.ncpathinktank.org/pdfs/st271.pdf.

6. Estelle James and Augusto Iglesias, "Integrated Disability and Retirement Systems in Chile," National Center for Policy Analysis, Policy Report No. 302, September 1, 2007,

http://www.ncpathinktank.org/pdfs/st302.pdf. See also William B. Conerly, "Chile Leads the Way with Individual Unemployment Accounts," National Center for Policy Analysis, Brief Analysis No. 424, November 12, 2002, http://www.ncpathinktank.org/pdfs/ba424.pdf.

7. Adapted from Ray Holbrook and Alcestis "Cooky" Oberg, "Galveston County: A Model for Social Security Reform," National Center for Policy Analysis, http://www.ncpathinktank.org/pdfs/ba514.pdf.

8. Ray Halbrook and Alcestis Oberg, "Galveston Country: A Model for Social Security Reform," National Center for Policy Analysis, April 26, 2005, http://www.ncpathinktank.org/pdfs/ba514.pdf.

9. Merrill Matthews, "How Three Texas Counties Created Personal Social Security Accounts and Prospered," *Forbes*, May 12, 2011, http://www.forbes.com/sites/merrillmatthews/2011/05/12/how-three-texas-counties-created-personal-social-security-accounts-and-prospered/#67e20cf4753c. Note, however, that when Galveston did the transition you could get the past taxes paid into Social Security placed in the new system. This is no longer possible.

10. Ray Holbrook and Alcestis Oberg, "Galveston County: A Model for Social Security Reform," NCPA, http://www.ncpathinktank.org/pdfs/ba514.pdf.

11. Teladoc, "How It Works," http://www.teladoc.com/how-does-it-work/.

12. Melinda Beck, "Startups Vie to Build an Uber for Health Care," *Wall Street Journal*, August 11, 2015, http://www.wsj.com/articles/startups-vie-to-build-an-uber-for-health-care-1439265847.

13. Minute Clinic, "Receive a text when you're next," http://www.cvs.com/minuteclinic/info/texting?WT.ac=MC-M-MCS-TEXT-MCBCC0022-33015-300X250-OP.

14. John C. Goodman, "Why Everything We Are Doing in Health Policy May Be Completely Wrong," National Center for Policy Analysis, July 25, 2011, http://www.ncpathinktank.org/commentaries/why-everything-we-are-doing-in-health-policy-may-be-completely-wrong.

15. John C. Goodman, "Will Texas Medicine Return to the Middle Ages?," *Forbes*, May 22, 2015, http://www.forbes.com/sites/johngoodman/2015/05/22/will-texas-medicine-return-to-the-middle-ages/.

16. Stephen T. Parente, "Obamacare's Prices Will Keep Surging," *Wall Street Journal*, July 16, 2015, http://www.wsj.com/articles/obamacares-prices-will-keep-surging-1437087242.

17. Atul Gawande, *Being Mortal: Medicine and What Happens in the End* (New York: Metropolitan Books, 2014).

18. Marina Gafanovich, "End of Life Care Constitutes Third Rail of U.S. Health Care Policy Debate," Dr. Marina Gafanovich (blog), September 17, 2015, http://www.mynycdoctor.com/end-of-life-care-constitutes-third-rail-of-u-s-health-care-policy-debate/.

19. Andy Puzder, "Shunning Obamacare," *Wall Street Journal*, January 13, 2015, http://www.wsj.com/articles/andy-puzder-shunning-obamacare-1421192654.

20. John C. Goodman and Linda Gorman, "Limited-Benefit Insurance," Goodman Institute, Brief Analysis No. 104, April 6, 2016, http://www.goodmaninstitute.org/wp-content/uploads/2016/04/BA-104.pdf.

21. John C. Goodman, John R. Graham, and Greg Scandlen, "The Economics of Health Insurance Exchanges," National Center for Policy Analysis, February 5, 2014.

22. "Turning the Exchanges into Real Markets,", Goodman Institute, Brief Analysis No. 106, April 6, 2016, http://www.goodmaninstitute.org/wp-content/uploads/2016/04/BA-106.pdf.

23. John H. Cochrane, "Health-Status Insurance: How Markets Can Provide Health Security," *Cato Institute*, Policy Analysis No. 633 (2009), http://www.cato.org/publications/policy-analysis/healthstatus-insurance-how-markets-can-provide-health-security.

Chapter 4: Choice, Ownership, Responsibility

1. Opening of the chapter previously published as John C. Goodman, "How We Can Keep from Going Bankrupt," *Health Policy*, National Center for Policy Analysis, April 4, 2012.

2. Previously published as John C. Goodman, "How We Can Keep from Going Bankrupt," *National Center for Policy Analysis Health Policy Blog*, April 4, 2012, http://healthblog.ncpathinktank.org/how-we-can-keep-from-going-broke-part-ii/.

3. The preceding text was previously published as John C. Goodman, "How We Can Keep from Going Bankrupt," *National Center for Policy Analysis Health Policy Blog*, April 4, 2012, http://healthblog.ncpathinktank.org/how-we-can-keep-from-going-broke-part-ii/.

4. Sean Ingham, "Pareto Optimality," *Britannica*, https://www.britannica.com/topic/Pareto-optimality.

5. The 1983 reforms cut benefits in three ways: they raised the retirement age, ended "double indexing," and instituted a tax on Social Security benefits.

6. Wikipedia, "National Commission on Fiscal Responsibility and Reform," last modified May 9, 2016, https://en.wikipedia.org/wiki/National_Commission_on_Fiscal_Responsibility_and_Reform.

7. This section is drawn from John C. Goodman, "Better Than Government: A New Way of Managing Life's Risks," Independent Institute, https://www.independent.org/pdf/policy_reports/2016-10-06-goodman.pdf.

8. Wikipedia, "Rational ignorance," last modified May 25, 2016, https://en.wikipedia.org/wiki/Rational_ignorance.

9. David Henderson, "Kevin Williamson on Social Security," *Library of Economics and Liberty*, August 15, 2015, http://econlog.econlib.org/archives/2015/08/kevin_williamso.html.

10. Estelle James, "Reforming Social Security: Lessons from Thirty Countries," National Center for Policy Analysis, Policy Report No. 277, 2005.

11. Washington's Blog, "France, Ireland, and Hungary Seize Pensions as Part of Move by Governments to Use Long-Term Assets to Fill Short-Term Deficits," last updated November 29, 2010; Liz Alderman and James Kanter, "Cyprus Makes Plan to Seize Portion of High-Level Deposits," *New York Times*, March 23, 2013; Andrey Oustroukh, "Russia to Grab Pension Money, Temporarily," *Wall Street Journal*, October 3, 2013.

12. Jan Iwanik, "European Nations Begin Seizing Private Pensions," *Christian Science Monitor*, January 2, 2011.

Chapter 5: The Risk of Growing Too Old and Outliving One's Assets

1. Laurence J. Kotlikoff, "Is Uncle Sam Bankrupt?," National Center for Policy Analysis, Brief Analysis No. 689, January 29, 2010, http://www.ncpathinktank.org/pdfs/ba689.pdf.

2. Moneywise 411, "Social Security: The $1.2 Million 'Asset' You May Not Know You Have," https://moneywise411.com/the-1-2-million-asset-you-may-not-know-you-have2/.

3. According to the Medicare News Group, Medicare has no official estimate of the amount of money lost to fraud each year, but the Federal Bureau of Investigation refers to estimates of 3 to 10 percent of all health care billings. For fiscal year 2019, Medicare spending is estimated at $630 billion. That would mean fraud of $19 to $63 billion a year. See also "Dollars Lost to Fraud," Senior Medicare Patrol, https://www.smpresource.org/Content/Medicare-Fraud/Dollars-Lost-to-Fraud.aspx, and Juliette Cubanski, Tricia Neuman, and Meredith Freed, "The Facts on Medicare Spending and Financing," Kaiser Family Foundation, August 20, 2019, https://www.kff.org/medicare/issue-brief/the-facts-on-medicare-spending-and-financing/#:~:text=Medicare%20Spending%20Projections&text=Looking%20ahead%2C%20CBO%20projects%20Medicare,in%202029%20(Figure%206). Medicare fraud can come through "phantom billing," which is when the medical provider bills Medicare for unnecessary procedures, or procedures that are never performed, or for unnecessary medical tests or tests never performed, or for unnecessary equipment, or equipment that is billed as new but is, in fact, used; "patient billing," which is when a patient who is in on the scam provides his Medicare number in exchange for kickbacks, and the provider bills Medicare for any reason and the patient is told to admit that he indeed received the medical treatment; and "upcoding schemes," which is inflating bills by using a billing code that indicates the patient needs expensive procedures. See also Tristram Korten, "Cracking Down on $70 Billion Worth of Medicare Fraud," *Fast Company*, accessed August 12, 2015, http://www.fastcompany.com/1793537/cracking-down-70-billion-worth-medicare-fraud.

4. Credit card fraud amounts to about 0.05 percent of credit card transactions. John Kiernan, "Credit Card & Debit Card Fraud Statistics," WalletHub, http://www.cardhub.com/edu/credit-debit-card-fraud-statistics/.

5. Steve Calfo, Jonathan Smith, and Mark Zezza, "Last Year of Life Study," Centers for Medicare and Medicaid Services, Office of the Actuary, 2002.

6. Andrew J. Rettenmaier and Thomas R. Saving, "Paying for Medicare Now and in the Future," Private Enterprise Research Center at Texas A&M University, March 2016.

7. Andrew J. Rettenmaier and Thomas R. Saving, "Thinking about Tomorrow," National Center for Policy Analysis, Policy Report No. 317, December 2008, http://www.ncpathinktank.org/pdfs/st317.pdf.

8. Pieces of this section were previously published as John C. Goodman, "How Much Do We Owe? $72 Trillion and Counting," *Forbes*, August 7, 2015.

9. Ibid.

10. Pieces of this section were previously published as John C. Goodman, "Why Are Some People Healthier Than Others?," *Forbes*, January 20, 2016.

11. See https://finance.zacks.com/there-minimum-monthly-social-security-payment-regardless-retirement-earnings-6330.html for an explanation of the minimum benefit.

12. Mark McClellan and Jonathan Skinner, "The Incidence of Medicare," *National Bureau of Research*, Working Paper No. 6013 (1997), http://www.nber.org/papers/w6013.

13. Adapted from http://www.goodmaninstitute.org/why-are-some-people-healthier-than-others/.

14. Victoria Turk, "The Difference in Life Expectancy Between the Rich and Poor Is Getting Worse," *Vice*, April 30, 2015, https://www.vice.com/en_us/article/3dkw4y/the-difference-in-life-expectancy-between-the-rich-and-poor-is-getting-worse.

15. Michael Grossman, "The human capital model," in the *Handbook of Health Economics*, edited by Anthony Culyer and Joseph Newhouse, 2000, vol. 1, pp 347-408, https://econpapers.repec.org/bookchap/eeeheachp/1-07.htm; Harold H. Gardner and B. Delworth Gardner, "Health as Human Capital: Theory and Implications. A New Management Paradigm," HCMS Group, January 16, 2012, https://www.hcmsgroup.com/wp-content/uploads/2012/05/WP01-HHC-Theory-and-Implications-2012-01-161.pdf; John C. Goodman, *Priceless: Curing the Healthcare Crisis* (Independent institute, 2012).

16. Lawrence J. Kotlikoff and Robert C. Pozen, "Let Older Americans Keep Working," *New York Times*, August 14, 2015, http://www.nytimes.com/2015/08/15/opinion/let-older-americans-keep-working.html?_r=0.

17. Steven J. Haider and David S. Loughran, "The Effect of the Social Security Earnings Test on Male Labor Supply," *Journal of Human Resources* 43, no. 1 (2008), https://msu.edu/~haider/Research/2008-jhr-published.pdf.

18. Lawrence J. Kotlikoff and Robert C. Pozen, "Let Older Americans Keep Working," *New York Times*, August 14, 2015, http://www.nytimes.com/2015/08/15/opinion/let-older-americans-keep-working.html?_r=0.

19. Laurence J. Kotlikoff, "Some Older Workers Face Astronomical Tax Rates," Goodman Institute, Brief Analysis No. 115, October 5, 2016, http://www.goodmaninstitute.org/wp-content/uploads/2016/10/BA-115.pdf.

20. Ibid.

21. Ibid.

22. This section previously published as Thomas Saving and John Goodman, "A Better Way to Approach Health Care's Impossible Task," *Health Affairs*, November 15, 2011, https://www.healthaffairs.org/do/10.1377/hblog20111115.015114/full/.

23. Brian Klepper and David Kibbe, "Rethinking the Value of Medical Services," *Health Affairs*, August 1, 2011, http://healthaffairs.org/blog/2011/08/01/rethinking-the-value-of-medical-services/.

24. John C. Goodman, "Will Texas Medicine Return to the Middle Ages?" *Forbes*, May 22, 2015, http://www.forbes.com/sites/johngoodman/2015/05/22/will-texas-medicine-return-to-the-middle-ages/.

25. John C. Goodman, "Standing between You and All the Benefits of Telemedicine: The AMA and the Federal Government," *Forbes*, July 9, 2015, http://www.forbes.com/sites/johngoodman/2015/07/09/standing-between-you-and-all-the-benefits-of-telemedicine-the-ama-and-the-federal-government/#6155aef74a3a.

26. John C. Goodman, "What Does Uber Medicine Look Like?," *Forbes*, July 24, 2015, http://www.forbes.com/sites/johngoodman/2015/07/24/what-does-uber-medicine-look-like/#6787336c1890.

27. Devon Herrick, "Retail Clinics: Convenient and Affordable Care," National Center for Policy Analysis, Brief Analysis No. 686 (2010), http://www.ncpathinktank.org/pdfs/ba686.pdf.

28. Bullet points previously published as John C. Goodman, "A Framework for Medicare Reform," National Center for Policy Analysis, Policy Report No. 315, September 2008, http://www.ncpathinktank.org/pdfs/st315.pdf.

29. Jordan Rau, "Why a Mammogram Can Cost Anywhere from $50 to $1,045 In Some States," *Washington Post*, October 12, 2015, https://www.washingtonpost.com/national/health-science/better-shop-around-for-mammograms-and-other-exams-because-cost-varies/2015/10/12/fcde8cce-6d06-11e5-9bfe-e59f5e244f92_story.html.

30. Fred Schulte and David Donald, "How Doctors and Hospitals Have Collected Billions in Questionable Medicare Fees," Center for Public Integrity, May 19, 20154 (updated), https://publicintegrity.org/health/how-doctors-and-hospitals-have-collected-billions-in-questionable-medicare-fees/.

31. This section previously published as John C. Goodman, "What Paul Krugman Doesn't Understand about Medicare," *Forbes*, July 28, 2015.

32. Christian Hagist and Laurence J. Kotlikoff, "Health Care Spending: What the Future Will Look Like," National Center for Policy Analysis, Policy Report No. 286, 2006, http://www.ncpa.org/pdfs/st286.pdf.

33. Amy Finkelstein and Robin McKnight, "What Did Medicare Do (And Was It Worth It)?," National Bureau of Economic Research, Working Paper No. 11609 (2005), http://www.nber.org/papers/w11609.

34. Avik Roy, "Why Medicaid Is a Humanitarian Catastrophe," *Forbes*, March 2, 2011.

35. Austin Frakt, "Medicaid Bashing," *The Incidental Economist*, January 20, 2011, https://theincidentaleconomist.com/wordpress/medicaid-bashing/.

36. Katherine Baicker et al., "The Oregon Experiment—Effects of Medicaid on Clinical Outcomes," *New England Journal of Medicine* 368 (2013), https://doi.org/10.1056/NEJMsa1212321.

37. Becky A. Briesacher et al., "Did Medicare D Affect General Trends in Health Outcomes or Hospitalizations?," *Annals of Internal Medicine* 162, no. 12 (2015), https://www.acpjournals.org/doi/10.7326/M14-0726.

38. John C. Goodman, "Are People Getting More Care or Better Care Under Obamacare? No," *Forbes*, April 2, 2015, http://www.forbes.com/sites/johngoodman/2015/04/02/are-people-getting-more-care-or-better-care-under-obamacare-no/#2eb1e15d1981.

39. June E. O'Neill and Dave M. O'Neill, "Who Are the Uninsured?," *Employment Policies Institute*, June 2009, https://www.epionline.org/studies/r122/.

40. Paul Krugman, "Zombies Against Medicare," *New York Times*, July 27, 2015, https://www.nytimes.com/2015/07/27/opinion/zombies-against-medicare.html.

41. John Goodman, "Health Policy Schizophrenia," Health Policy, August 17, 2011, http://healthblog.ncpathinktank.org/health-policy-schizophrenia/.

42. Thomas Saving and John Goodman, "A Better Way to Approach Medicare's Impossible Task," *Health Affairs*, November 15, 2011, https://www.healthaffairs.org/do/10.1377/hblog20111115.015114/full/.

43. John Goodman, "Why the Pilot Programs Failed," *The Health Care Blog*, February 1, 2012, http://thehealthcareblog.com/blog/2012/02/01/why-the-pilot-programs-failed/. John Goodman, "Health Policy Schizophrenia," *Health Policy*, August 17, 2011, http://healthblog .ncpathinktank.org/health-policy-schizophrenia/.

44. J. Michael McWilliams et al., "Performance Differences in Year 1 of Pioneer Accountable Care Organizations," *New England Journal of Medicine* 372 (2015), https://www.ncbi.nlm .nih.gov/pmc/articles/PMC4475634/.

45. John C. Goodman and Lawrence J. Wedekind, "How the Trump Administration Is Reforming Medicare," *Health Affairs*, May 3, 2019, https://www.healthaffairs.org/do/10.1377 /hblog20190501.529581/full/; John C. Goodman, "Is Public Policy Changing the Practice of Medicine?," *Health Affairs*, May 21, 2014, https://www.healthaffairs.org/do/10.1377/hblog 20140521.039122/full/.

46. Liqun Liu and Andrew J. Rettenmaier, "The Economic Cost of the Social Security Payroll Tax," National Center for Policy Analysis, Policy Report No. 252, 2002, http://www .ncpathinktank.org/pdfs/st252.pdf.

47. Ibid.

48. Ibid.

49. Laurence J. Kotlikoff, "Is Uncle Sam Bankrupt?," National Center for Policy Analysis, Brief Analysis No. 689 (2010), http://www.ncpathinktank.org/pdfs/ba689.pdf.

50. This section, "Problem: The Cost of Collecting Payroll Taxes," quoted from Liqun Liu and Andrew J. Rettenmaier, "The Economic Cost of the Social Security Payroll Tax," National Center for Policy Analysis, NCPA Policy Report No. 252, June 2002, http://www .ncpathinktank.org/pdfs/st252.pdf.

51. This section previously published as John C. Goodman, "What You Should Know about Social Security," *Forbes*, April 14, 2015.

52. Laurence J. Kotlikoff, Philip Moeller, and Paul Solman, *Get What's Yours: The Secrets to Maxing Out Your Social Security*, revised and updated (New York: Simon & Schuster, 2016).

53. Alicia H. Munnell et al., "Unusual Social Security Claiming Strategies: Costs and Distributional Effects," Center for Retirement Research at Boston College, CRR WP 2009-17, August 2009, https://crr.bc.edu/wp-content/uploads/2009/08/wp_2009-17-508.pdf

54. Laurence J. Kotlikoff, Philip Moeller, and Paul Solman, *Get What's Yours: The Secrets to Maxing Out Your Social Security*, revised and updated (New York: Simon & Schuster, 2016).

55. Ibid.

56. Ibid.

57. Laurence Kotlikoff, "Costly Surprises Are Hidden in Medicare's Rules," Goodman Institute, http://www.goodmaninstitute.org/costly-surprises-are-hidden-in-medicares-rules/.

58. Laurence Kotlikoff, "The Ultimate 13-Year Social Security Runaround — Commissioner Saul, Only You Can Fix This," *Forbes*, October 16, 2019, https://www.forbes.com/sites /kotlikoff/2019/10/16/the-ultimate-13-year-social-security-runaround--commissioner-saul -only-you-can-fix-this/#2e5d1cf23f75.

59. Laurence Kotlikoff, "Social Security Mix-up? Here's What You Should Do," PBS News Hour, August 26, 2015, https://www.pbs.org/newshour/economy/social-security-mix -heres.

60. Office of the Inspector General, "Higher Benefits for Dually Entitled Widow(er)s Had They Delayed Applying for Retirement Benefits," Social Security Administration, Audit Report A- 09-18-50559, February 2018, https://oig.ssa.gov/sites/default/files/audit/full/pdf /A-09-18-50559.pdf.

61. Laurence Kotlikoff, "Are You One of the 11,000 Widows Social Security Cheated Out of a Collective $130 Million? If So, Here's How to Sue at No Cost," *Forbes*, January 31, 2020, https://www.forbes.com/sites/kotlikoff/2020/01/31/are-you-one-of-the-11000-widows -social-security-cheated-out-of-a-collective-130-million-if-so-heres-how-to-sue-at-no-cost /#241742ab541e.

62. Laurence Kotlikoff, "A Social Security Application Mistake or a Malicious Policy with Frightening Consequences?," *Forbes*, April 1, 2020, https://www.forbes.com/sites/kotlikoff /2020/04/01/a-social-security-application-mistake-or-a-malicious-policy-with-frightening -consequences/#5b3264b45d76.

63. Peter J. Ferrara, *Power to the People: The New Road to Freedom and Prosperity for the Poor, Seniors, and Those Most in Need of the World's Best Health Care* (Chicago: The Heartland Institute, 2015), 14–15.

64. Social Security Administrations Website, https://www.ssa.gov.

65. Scott Burns, "Getting Our Social Security Money's Worth," *Dallas Morning News*, July 18, 2015, https://www.dallasnews.com/business/2015/07/19/burns-getting-our-social-security -moneys-worth/.

66. This section is from Thomas R. Saving, "Can Privatizing Social Security Be a Win/ Win for All Generations?," Brief Analysis No.108, Goodman Institute, March 1, 2016, http:// www.goodmaninstitute.org/wp-content/uploads/2016/04/BA_108.pdf.

67. Liqun Liu, Andrew J. Rettenmaier, and Thomas R. Saving, "Social Security's Individual Value and Aggregate Burden," *Journal of Retirement*, 3(1), 50-66, https://jor.pm-research .com/content/3/1/50/tab-article-info.

68. This section previously published as Thomas Saving and John Goodman, "What Health Reform Means for Medicare," *Health Affairs*, May 12, 2011, http://healthaffairs.org /blog/2011/05/12/what-health-reform-means-for-medicare/.

69. Ibid.

70. David Altig, Alan Auerbach, Elias Ilin, Laurence Kotlikoff, and Victor Ye, "Marginal Net Taxation of Americans' Labor Supply," National Bureau of Economic Research Working Paper, April 7, 2020.

71. Ibid.

72. Adapted from John C. Goodman, "Almost Everything You've Been Told about Inequality Is Wrong," *Forbes*, February 1, 2016, https://www.forbes.com/sites/johngoodman /2016/02/01/almost-everything-youve-been-told-about-inequality-is-wrong/#646f3f4113c3.

73. Alan J. Auerbach, Laurence J. Kotlikoff, and Darryl R. Koehler, "U.S. Inequality, Fiscal Progressivity, and Work Disincentives: An Intragenerational Accounting," National Bureau of Economic Research Working Paper, No. 22032. Rev. April 2016, https://www.nber.org /papers/w22032. See also Alan Auerbach and Laurence J. Kotlikoff, "We've Been Measuring Inequality Wrong—Here's the Real Story," Goodman Institute, Brief Analysis No. 101, March 14, 2016, http://www.goodmaninstitute.org/wp-content/uploads/2016/04/BA_101.pdf.

74. Loretti I. Dobrescu, Laurence J. Kotlikoff, and Alberto F. Motta, "Why Aren't Developed Countries Saving?," National Bureau of Economic Research, Working Paper No. 14580, December 2008, https://www.nber.org/papers/w14580.

75. Laurence J. Kotlikoff et al., "How Much Do Americans Depend on Social Security?," National Center for Policy Analysis, Policy Report No. 301, August 2007. www.ncpathink tank.org/pdfs/st301.pdf.

76. Bullet points taken from Laurence J. Kotlikoff, Ben Marx, and Pietro Rizza, "How Much Do Americans Spend on Social Security?" National Center for Policy Analysis, NCPA Policy Report No. 301, August 2007.

77. Andrew G. Biggs and Sylvester J. Schieber, "The Imaginary Retirement-Income Crisis," *Wall Street Journal*, September 29, 2014.

78. Cited in Andrew G. Biggs and Sylvester J. Schieber, "The Imaginary Retirement-Income Crisis," *Wall Street Journal*, September 29, 2014.

79. Andrew G. Biggs and Sylvester J. Schieber, "The Imaginary Retirement-Income Crisis," *Wall Street Journal*, September 29, 2014.

80. Martin Feldstein and Anthony Pellechio, "Social Security and Household Wealth Accumulation: New Microeconomic Evidence," *The Review of Economics and Statistics* vol. 41, no. 3, August 1979. See also R. J. M. Alessie, "Does Social Security Crowd Out Private Savings?," *Multidisciplinary Economics* (2005): 367–380, and Sudipto Banerjee, "Does Social Security Affect Household Saving?," Ohio State University, November 10, 2010.

81. https://www.medicaid.gov; www.cms.gov.

82. LTC Consulting Services, "Long-Term Care Statistics You Need to Know in 2018," https://www.ltccs.com/blog/long-term-care-statistics-2018/.

83. Kaiser Family Foundation, "Medicaid's Role in Behavioral Health," May 5, 2017, https://www.kff.org/infographic/medicaids-role-in-behavioral-health/.

84. National Association of Community Health Centers, "Community Health Center Chartbook," January 2019, http://www.nachc.org/wp-content/uploads/2019/01/Community -Health-Center-Chartbook-FINAL-1.28.19.pdf.

85. Robin Rudowitz et al., "10 Things to Know about Medicaid: Setting the Facts Straight," Kaiser Family Foundation, March 2019, https://www.kff.org/medicaid/issue-brief /10-things-to-know-about-medicaid-setting-the-facts-straight/.

86. Bullet points adapted from Patricia Gabow and Thomas Daschle, "Fifty Years Later: Why Medicaid Still Matters," *Health Affairs*, July 29, 2015, https://www.healthaffairs.org /do/10.1377/hblog20150729.049632/full/.

87. Patricia Gabow and Thomas Daschle, "Fifty Years Later: Why Medicaid Still Matters," *Health Affairs*, July 29, 2015, https://www.healthaffairs.org/do/10.1377/hblog20150729 .049632/full.

88. "Edem Hado and Harriett Komisar, "Long-Term Services and Supports," AARP Public Policy Institute, August 2019, https://www.aarp.org/content/dam/aarp/ppi/2019/08 /long-term-services-and-supports.doi.10.26419-2Fppi.00079.001.pdf.

89. Owing to the low reimbursement rate for Medicaid patients (relative to self-paying or private long-term care insurance patients), nursing homes will allocate only a certain percentage of their beds to Medicaid patients, while filling the remaining beds with higher-paying

private patients. However, if the desired ratio of Medicaid-funded patients to private patients increases because a large number of private payers exhaust their assets and turn to Medicaid, the nursing home cannot legally evict Medicaid patients to achieve a lower ratio.

90. "Who Pays for Long-Term Care in the U.S.?" The Scan Foundation, January 2013, http://www.thescanfoundation.org/sites/default/files/who_pays_for_ltc_us_jan_2013_fs .pdf; Julia Paradise, "Medicaid Moving Forward," Henry J. Kaiser Family Foundation, March 9, 2015, http://kff.org/health-reform/issue-brief/medicaid-moving-forward/.

91. Medicare has annual and lifetime maximum benefits for nursing home care, which it provides mainly for rehabilitation following injury, illness, or surgery.

92. When they retire, most Medicare enrollees do not meet Medicaid income and asset tests for long-term care coverage.

93. "Medicaid Rules," https://www.elderlawanswers.com/medicaid-rules.

94. Thomas Day, "About Medicaid Long-Term Care," National Care Planning Council.

95. "How Does Medicaid Treat Income?," ElderLawAnswers, https://www.elderlaw answers.com/how-does-medicaid-treat-income-12017. This is the federal maximum for qualifying for Medicaid long-term care.

96. Ibid.

97. Section previously published as John C. Goodman et al., "Opportunities for State Medicaid Reform," National Center for Policy Analysis, NCPA Policy Report No. 288, September 2006.

98. Kathryn G. Allen, "Medicaid: Transfers of Assets by Elderly Individuals to Obtain Long-Term Care Coverage," U.S. Government Accountability Office, GAO-05-968, September 2005.

99. See Ronald Lipman, "Trust Helps Person Qualify for Medicaid Nursing Care," *Houston Chronicle*, August 11, 2002.

100. A monthly amount may be paid to the nursing home from a qualified income trust. Elder Planning Alliance, "Income Trusts."

101. Long-term care premiums are not tax deductible unless an individual's total out-of-pocket health care expenses exceed 10 percent of adjusted gross income (AGI). For taxpayers sixty-five and older, this threshold drops to 7.5 percent.

Chapter 6: The Risk of Dying Too Young and Leaving Dependent Family Members without Resources

1. Adapted from Liqun Liu and Andrew J. Rettenmaier, "Social Security and Education," National Center for Policy Analysis, Policy Report No. 240, January 31, 2001, http:// www.ncpathinktank.org/pdfs/st240.pdf. See also Matt Moore, Anna Frederick, and Adrienne Aldridge, "Social Security, Women, and Working Families," National Center for Policy Analysis, Brief Analysis No. 466, February 19, 2004, http://www.ncpathinktank.org/pdfs /ba466.pdf.

2. Ibid.

Chapter 7: The Risk of Becoming Disabled and Facing Financial Ruin

1. Parts of this chapter were adapted from Pamela Villarreal and Alan Lin, "Giving No Credit Where It Is Due: Social Security Disability," National Center for Policy Analysis, Brief Analysis No. 612, March 17, 2008, http://www.ncpathinktank.org/pdfs/ba612.pdf.

2. 2019 Annual Report of the Board of Trustees of the Old-Age and Survivors Insurance and Disability Insurance Trust Funds, Table V.C5, 138; Bureau of Labor Statistics, The Employment Situation—June 2019, Summary Table A—Household Data.

3. Adam Hartung, "Is Disability the New Unemployment Insurance?," *Forbes,* August 22, 2012, https://www.forbes.com/sites/adamhartung/2012/08/22/is-disability-the-new -unemployment-insurance/#5e3fa51f64b0.

4. Social Security Administration, Annual Statistical Report on the Social Security Disability Insurance Program, 2017, table 25.

5. Social Security Administration, Annual Statistical Supplement: Table 7.C1—Number and percentage distribution of adult individuals and persons under age eighteen receiving federal SSI payments, by monthly payment and eligibility category, December 2017; Table 5. E1—Number and percentage distribution, by primary insurance amount and type of benefit, December 2017.

6. U.S. House of Representatives Committee on Oversight and Government Reform, *Systemic Waste and Abuse at the Social Security Administration: How Rubber-Stamping Disability Judges Cost Hundreds of Billions of Taxpayer Dollars,* Staff Report, U.S. House of Representatives, 113th Congress, June 10, 2014, https://republicans-oversight.house.gov/wp-content /uploads/2014/06/2014-06-10-Systemic-Waste-and-Abuse-at-the-SSA.ALJs_.pdf.

7. Pamela Villarreal, "Not All Disabilities Are Alike: Implementing a Rating System for SSDI," Policy Report No. 366, National Center for Policy Analysis, June 2015, http://www .ncpathinktank.org/pdfs/st366.pdf.

8. Ibid.

9. Quoted from Pamela Villarreal and Alan Lin, "Giving No Credit Where It Is Due: Social Security Disability," Brief Analysis No. 612, National Center for Policy Analysis, March 17, 2008, http://www.ncpathinktank.org/pdfs/ba612.pdf.

10. Pamela Villarreal, "Not All Disabilities Are Alike: Implementing a Rating System for SSDI," Policy Report No. 366, National Center for Policy Analysis, June 2015, http://www .ncpathinktank.org/pdfs/st366.pdf.

11. Ibid.

12. Damian Paletta and Dionne Searcey, "Jobless Tap Disability Fund," *Wall Street Journal,* December 28, 2011. Available at http://online.wsj.com/article/SB100014240529702042968 0457712139275046003.html; David H. Autor and Mark G. Duggan, "The Rise in the Disability Rolls and the Decline in Unemployment," *Quarterly Journal of Economics* 118, no. 1 (February 2003): 157–206; David H. Autor and Mark G. Duggan, "The Growth in the Social Security Disability Rolls: A Fiscal Crisis Unfolding," *Journal of Economic Perspectives* 20, no. 3 (Summer 2006): 71–96; Dan Black, Kermit Daniel, and Seth Saunders, "The Impact of Economic Conditions on Participation in Disability Programs: Evidence from the Coal Boom and Bust," *American Economic Review* 92 (2002): 27–50; Eric French and Jac Song, "The Effect of Disability Insurance Receipt on Labor Supply," *American Economic Journal:*

Economic Policy 6, no. 2 (May 2014), 291-337; Jon Gruber, "Disability Insurance Benefits and Labor Supply," *Journal of Political Economy* 108 (2000): 1162–1183.

13. Robert J. Samuelson, "Budget Quagmire Revealed by Social Security Disability Program," *Washington Post*, February 10, 2012. Available at http://www.washingtonpost.com/opinions /social-security-disability-program-reveals-budget-quagmire/2012/02/10/gIQA26iV9Q _story.html?wprss=rss_opinions.

14. Dave Altig and Ellyn Terry, "What Accounts for the Decrease in the Labor Force Participation Rate," Federal Reserve Bank of Atlanta, January 17, 2014, http://macroblog .typepad.com/macroblog/2014/01/what-accounts-for-the-decrease-in-the-labor-force -participation-rate.html; Dave Altig and Ellyn Terry, "How Has Disability Affected Labor Force Participation?," Federal Reserve Bank of Atlanta, May 9, 2014, http://macroblog.typepad .com/macroblog/2014/05/how-has-disability-affected-labor-force-participation.html.

15. John Merline, "The Sharp Rise in Disability Claims," *Region Focus*, Second/Third Quarter 2012, http://www.lexissecuritiesmosaic.com/gateway/FEDRES/SPEECHES/pdf _feature3.pdf.

16. "Grand Theft Disability," *Wall Street Journal*, January 9, 2014, https://www.wsj.com /articles/grand-theft-disability-1389313832.

17. Ibid.

18. Office of the Inspector General, Social Security Administration, "The Social Security Administration's Ability to Prevent and Detect Disability Fraud," September 2014, http:// oig.ssa.gov/sites/default/files/testimony/SSA's%20Ability%20to%20Prevent%20and%20 Detect%20Disability%20Fraud_0.pdf.

19. Adapted from N. Michael Helvacian, "Workers' Compensation: Rx for Policy Reform," National Center for Policy Analysis, Policy Report No. 287, September 2006, http:// www.ncpathinktank.org/pdfs/st287.pdf.

20. Quoted from N. Michael Helvacian, "Workers' Compensation: Rx for Policy Reform," National Center for Policy Analysis, Policy Report No. 287, September 2006, http:// www.ncpathinktank.org/pdfs/st287.pdf.

21. Ibid.

22. Adapted from N. Michael Helvacian, "Workers' Compensation: Rx for Policy Reform," National Center for Policy Analysis, NCPA Policy Report No. 287, September 2006, http://www.ncpathinktank.org/pdfs/st287.pdf; U.S. Department of Labor, "State Workers Compensation Laws: Table 6. Benefits for Temporary Total Disability Provided by Workers Compensation Statutes in the U.S." Available at
https://web.archive.org/web/20080725201751/http://www.workerscompresources.com /Statutes/DOL_Tables_Jan2006/Table6.pdf.

23. Social Security Administration, "How Workers' Compensation and Other Disability Payments May Affect Your Benefits," https://www.ssa.gov/pubs/EN-05-10018.pdf.

24. N. Michael Helvacian, "Workers' Compensation: Rx for Policy Reform," National Center for Policy Analysis, Policy Report No. 287, September 2006, http://www.ncpathink tank.org/pdfs/st287.pdf.

25. Quoted from N. Michael Helvacian, "Workers' Compensation: Rx for Policy Reform," National Center for Policy Analysis, NCPA Policy Report No. 287, September 2006, http://www.ncpathinktank.org/pdfs/st287.pdf.

26. Public Policy Research Institute at Texas A&M University and the Texas Department of Insurance Workers' Compensation Research Group, "Survey of Employer Participation in the Texas Workers' Compensation System." Available at https://web.archive.org /web/20051020224017/http://www.tdi.state.tx.us/wc/regulation/roc/wcresearchpres.html. In Texas, in 2004, a significant percentage of employers—38 percent, covering about 24 percent of the workforce—chose not to subscribe to the statutory system. See also http://www .dallasnews.com/business/headlines/20151021-dallas-lawyer-leads-push-that-lets-companies -put-values-on-body-parts.ece.

27. Quoted from N. Michael Helvacian, "Workers' Compensation: Rx for Policy Reform," National Center for Policy Analysis, NCPA Policy Report No. 287, September 2006, http://www.ncpathinktank.org/pdfs/st287.pdf.

28. David Durbin, Dan Corro, and N. Michael. Helvacian, "Workers' Compensation Medical Expenditures: Price vs. Quantity," Journal of Risk and Insurance 63, no. 1 (March 1996): 13–33.

29. David Durbin, Dan Corro, and N. Michael Helvacian, "Workers' Compensation Medical Expenditures: Price vs. Quantity," Journal of Risk and Insurance 63, no. 1 (March 1996): 17.

30. Richard Victor and N. Michael Helvacian, "Targeting More Costly Care: Area Variation in Texas Medical Costs and Utilization," Workers Compensation Research Institute, 2002.

31. A large body of recent economic literature published by researchers at the RAND Corporation and their associates explores the percentage of wage loss replaced by permanent partial disability (PPD) benefits over the PPD recipients' working lives. This research concludes that PPD benefits to employees who lose significant time from work replace about 50 percent of the employees' wage loss over a ten-year period. The analysis is based on a comparison of the income of employees who received PPD benefits with their cohorts who were not injured and lost no time from work. For a representative study, see Robert T. Reville et al., "An Evaluation of New Mexico Workers' Compensation Permanent Partial Disability and Return to Work," RAND Corporation, 2004.

32. Ken Harbaugh, "The Risk of Over-Thanking our Veterans," *New York Times*, June 1, 2015, https://www.nytimes.com/2015/06/01/opinion/the-risk-of-over-thanking-our-veterans .html.

33. Ibid.

34. David H. Autor, Mark Duggan, Kyle Greenberg, and David S. Lyle, "The Impact of Disability Benefits on Labor Supply: Evidence from the VA's Disability Compensation Program," Princeton University, February 2015, https://irs.princeton.edu/sites/irs/files/event /uploads/vdc-adgl-Feb17.pdf.

35. Ibid.

36. Ron Lieber, "Looking Out for Yourself with Disability Insurance," *New York Times*, September 12, 2014, https://www.nytimes.com/2014/09/13/your-money/life-and-disability -insurance/flat-on-your-back-not-a-good-time-to-consider-long-term-disability-insurance .html.

Chapter 8: The Risk of Facing a Major Health Event and Being Unable to Afford Needed Medical Care

1. Maggie Miller, "Zoom CEO Says Company Reached 200 Million Daily Users in March," *The Hill*, April 2, 2020, https://thehill.com/policy/cybersecurity/490794-zoom-ceo-says -company-reached-200-million-daily-users-in-march.

2. See AtlasMD, "Monthly membership fees," https://atlas.md/wichita/our-fees/.

3. John C. Goodman, "McCain Is the Radical on Health Reform," *Wall Street Journal*, July 30, 2008, https://www.wsj.com/articles/SB121737388416495023.

4. Pamela Ballou-Nelson, "How long are patients waiting for an appointment?," MGMA, https://www.mgma.com/data/data-stories/how-long-are-patients-waiting-for-an -appointment.

5. Megan Knowles, "Why Boston patients have longer appointment times," Becker's Hospital Review, October 30, 2018, https://www.beckershospitalreview.com/patient-experience /why-boston-patients-have-longer-appointment-wait-times.html.

6. Philip Reese, "As ER Wait Times Grow, More Patients Leave Against Medical Advice," Kaiser Family Foundation, May 17, 2019, https://khn.org/news/as-er-wait-times-grow -more-patients-leave-against-medical-advice/.

7. David D. Kirkpatrick and Benjamin Mueller, "U.K. Backs Off Medical Rationing Plan as Coronavirus Rages," *New York Times*, April 3, 2020, https://www.nytimes.com/2020 /04/03/world/europe/britain-coronavirus-triage.html.

8. John C. Goodman et al., "Health Care Reform: Do Other Countries Have the Answers?," National Center for Policy Analysis, March 10, 2009, http://www.ncpathinktank .org/pdfs/sp_Do_Other_Countries_Have_the_Answers.pdf.

9. John C. Goodman, "Why Everything We Are Doing in Health Policy May Be Completely Wrong," National Center for Policy Analysis, July 25, 2011, http://www.ncpathink tank.org/commentaries/why-everything-we-are-doing-in-health-policy-may-be-completely -wrong.

10. To understand how markets were systematically suppressed in the twentieth century, see John C. Goodman, *Regulation of Medical Care: Is the Price Too High* (San Francisco: Cato Institute, 1980), and the summary in John C. Goodman and Gerald L. Musgrave, *Patient Power: Solving America's Health Care Crisis* (Washington, D.C.: Cato Institute, 1992).

11. Dan Mangan, "Tax forms show fewer people paid Obamacare tax penalties, more received Obamacare aid," CNBC, January 11, 2017, https://www.cnbc.com/2017/01/11/fewer -people-paid-obamacare-tax-penalties-as-more-got-obamacare-aid.html.

12. Linda Gorman, "What Are We Getting for Our Obamacare Dollars?," Goodman Institute, Brief Analysis No. 126, August 6, 2018, http://www.goodmaninstitute.org/wp -content/uploads/2018/08/BA-126-What-Are-We-Getting-for-Our-Obamacare-Dollars.pdf.

13. Steven D. Pizer, Austin Frakt, and Lisa Lezzoni, "The Effect of Health Reform on Public and Private Insurance in the Long Run," SSRN, March 9, 2011, https://papers.ssrn .com/sol3/papers.cfm?abstract_id=1782210.

14. Congressional Budget Office (CBO), "The State Children's Health Insurance Program," Pub. 2970, May 1, 2007, https://www.cbo.gov/sites/default/files/110th-congress-2007 -2008/reports/05-10-schip.pdf.

15. Charles J. Courtemanche, James Marton, and Aaron Yelowitz, "Medicaid Coverage across the Income Distribution under the Affordable Care Act," National Bureau of Economic Research, Working Paper No. 26145, August 2019, https://www.nber.org/papers/w26145.

16. Brian Blase and Aaron Yelowitz, "Obamacare's Medicaid Deception," *Wall Street Journal*, August 14, 2019, https://www.wsj.com/articles/obamacares-medicaid-deception-11565822360.

17. This section quoted from John C. Goodman, "Health Insurance" in *The Concise Encyclopedia of Economics*, Library of Economics and Liberty, Second Edition, http://www.econlib.org/library/Enc/HealthInsurance.html.

18. Regina E. Herzlinger, the Nancy R. McPherson Professor of Business Administration at the Harvard Business School, was a forceful and early advocate of empowering consumers in the medical marketplace. Money has dubbed her the "Godmother" of consumer-driven healthcare. Her three books on the subject have all been best sellers. See *Market-Driven Health Care: Who Wins, Who Loses in the Transformation of America's Largest Service Industry* (Reading, MA: Basic Books, 1996); *Consumer-Driven Health Care: Implications for Providers, Payers, and Policymakers*, (San Francisco: Jossey-Bass, 2004); and *Who Killed Health Care? America's $2 Trillion Medical Problem-and the Consumer-Driven Cure*, (New York: McGraw-Hill, 2007).

19. An early advocate for allowing employees to use HRAs to purchase individually owned health insurance is Regina E. Herzlinger. See "The IRS Can Save American Health Care," Wall Street Journal, July 1, 2018, https://www.wsj.com/articles/the-irs-can-save-american-health-care-1530477705.

20. Linda Gorman, "What Are We Getting for Our Obamacare Dollars?," Goodman Institute, Brief Analysis No. 126, August 6, 2018. Available at http://www.goodmaninstitute.org/wp-content/uploads/2018/08/BA-126-What-Are-We-Getting-for-Our-Obamacare-Dollars.pdf.

21 See "The World's Greatest Health Care Plan," http://www.goodmaninstitute.org/topics/health-reform-bill/.

22. John C. Goodman, "Saving for Health Care: the Policy Pros and Cons of Different Vehicles," *Health Affairs* (blog), April 17, 2012, http://www.ncpathinktank.org/pdfs/041712-Saving-For-Health-Care-the-Pros-and-Cons.pdf.

23. Devon Herrick, "Why Health Costs Are Still Rising," *National Center for Policy Analysis*, Brief Analysis No. 731, November 18, 2010, http://www.ncpathinktank.org/pdfs/ba731.pdf.

24. Bullet points quoted from Devon M. Herrick, "Update 2006: Why Are Health Costs Rising?," Brief Analysis No. 572, National Center for Policy Analysis, September 21, 2006.

25. This section adapted from and previously published as John C. Goodman, "How Much Do You Trust Your Insurer?," *Psychology Today*, October 29, 2012, https://www.psychologytoday.com/us/blog/curing-the-healthcare-crisis/201210/how-much-do-you-trust-your-insurer; "Turning the Exchanges into Real Markets," Brief Analysis No. 106, Goodman Institute, April 6, 2016; John Goodman, "A Woman May Die Because of Obamacare," *Townhall*, November 9, 2013, https://townhall.com/columnists/johncgoodman/2013/11/09/a-woman-may-die-because-of-obamacare-n1743241.

26. One exception was a series of TV ads by UnitedHealthcare. The implicit message was: we know you don't think about insurance until something goes wrong, and that's when you are going to need us. However, UHC never was a major player in the individual health insurance market (where people make their own purchasing decisions) and at the time of this writing has indicated that it is exiting the health insurance exchanges altogether.

27. Originally published as https://www.forbes.com/sites/johngoodman/2019/05/17/why -employers-pay-too-much-for-health-care/#42699c033f29.

28. Chapin White and Christopher Whaley, "Prices Paid to Hospitals by Private Health Plans Are High Relative to Medicare and Vary Widely," RAND Corporation, Research Report RR-3033-RWJ, 2019, https://www.rand.org/pubs/research_reports/RR3033.html.

29. Austin Frakt, "Private vs. Public Prices," *Academy Health*, January 13, 2017, https:// www.academyhealth.org/blog/2017-01/private-vs-public-prices.

30. John C. Goodman, "Welcome to the World of Rosencare," Independent Institute, April 25, 2016, http://www.independent.org/news/article.asp?id=8747.

31. John C. Goodman, "Can the Market Really Work in Health Care?" *Forbes*, May 22, 2018, https://www.forbes.com/sites/johngoodman/2018/05/22/can-the-market-really-work -in-health-care/#6c0f005d787d.

32. John Goodman, "Stunning Results from California," *NCPA Health Policy Blog*, August 7, 2013, http://healthblog.ncpathinktank.org/stunning-results-from-california/#sthash .rHfzcOp6.q81qciBo.dpbs.

33. John C. Goodman, "Obamacare Can Be Worse than Medicaid," *Wall Street Journal*, June 26, 2018, https://www.wsj.com/articles/obamacare-can-be-worse-than-medicaid -1530052891.

34. Devon M. Herrick, "Medical Tourism: Global Competition in Health Care," National Center for Policy Analysis, NCPA Policy Report No. 304, November 1, 2007. Available at http://www.ncpathinktank.org/pub/st304?pg=7.

35. John C. Goodman, "Better Care at a Fraction of the Cost—Only a Plane Ride Away," *Forbes*, April 11, 2016, https://www.forbes.com/sites/johngoodman/2016/04/11/better-care -at-a-fraction-of-the-cost-only-a-plane-ride-away/#258596c447a2.

36. John C. Goodman and Gerald L. Musgrave, *Patient Power: Solving America's Health Care Crisis* (Washington, D.C.: Cato Institute, 1992).

37. Phil Galewitz, "A Mexican Hospital, an American Surgeon, and a $5,000 Check (Yes, a Check)," *New York Times*, August 9, 2019, https://www.nytimes.com/2019/08/09/business /medical-tourism-mexico.html.

38. Bradley Herring et al., "Comparing the Value of Nonprofit Hospitals' Tax Exemption to Their Community Benefits," *Inquiry*, February 13, 2018, https://www.ncbi.nlm.nih .gov/pmc/articles/PMC5813653/.

39. See John C. Goodman, "Six Problems with the ACA That Aren't Going Away," *Health Affairs*, June 25, 2015, http://healthaffairs.org/blog/2015/06/25/six-problems-with-the-aca-that -arent-going-away/.

40. Previously published as John C. Goodman, "Simple Solutions to the Worst Problems in Obamacare," *Townhall*, July 4, 2015.

41. See Regina E. Herzlinger, *Market-Driven Health Care: Who Wins, Who Loses in the Transformation of America's Largest Service Industry* (Reading, MA: Basic Books, 1996); and

Consumer-Driven Health Care: Implications for Providers, Payers, and Policymakers, (San Francisco: Jossey-Bass, 2004).

42. Ibid.

43. Previously published as John C. Goodman, "Obamacare's Insurance Exchanges Will Foster a Race to the Healthcare Bottom," *Forbes*, September 25, 2013.

44. Smoking is not a "preexisting" health condition under the ACA.

45. For a more comprehensive look, see chapter 22 from my 2004 book with Gerald Musgrave and Devon Herrick, *Lives at Risk: Single-Payer National Health Insurance Around the World.* Available at http://www.ncpathinktank.org/pdfs/04-130_23_Ch_22.pdf.

46. John Goodman, "How the Left and the Right View the Race to the Bottom," National Center for Policy Analysis, *Health Policy*, September 23, 2013, http://healthblog.ncpathinktank.org/how-the-left-and-the-right-view-the-race-to-the-bottom/#sthash.a; John Goodman, "Study Devastating for Obamacare Backers," Townhall, May 4, 2013, http://townhall.com/columnists/johncgoodman/2013/05/04/study-devastating-for-obamacare-backers-n1586429/page/full.

47. Jayne O'Donnell, "Some Doctors Wary of Taking Insurance Exchange Patients," *USA Today,* October 28, 2014.

48. John C. Goodman, "How Obamacare Made Things Worse for Patients with Pre-existing Conditions," Goodman Institute, Brief Analysis No. 134, March 28, 2020, http://www.goodmaninstitute.org/wp-content/uploads/2020/03/BA-134-Obamacare-Pre-existing-conditions-with-links-for-website-corrected.pdf.

49. See Regina E. Herzlinger, *Market-Driven Health Care: Who Wins, Who Loses in the Transformation of America's Largest Service Industry* (Reading, MA: Basic Books, 1996); and *Consumer-Driven Health Care: Implications for Providers, Payers, and Policymakers,* (San Francisco: Jossey-Bass, 2004).

50. See Regina E. Herzlinger, Who Killed Health Care? America's $2 Trillion Medical Problem-and the Consumer-Driven Cure, (New York: McGraw-Hill, 2007).

51. First three paragraphs previously published as John C. Goodman, "Obamacare's Insurance Exchanges Will Foster a Race to the Healthcare Bottom," *Forbes*, September 25, 2013. Entire section also previously published as John C. Goodman, "Healthcare Solutions for Post-Obamacare America," Independent Institute, Policy Report, November 11, 2014. Pieces also published as John Goodman, "Six Problems with the ACA That Aren't Going Away," *Health Affairs,* June 25, 2015, https://www.healthaffairs.org/do/10.1377/hblog20150625.048781/full/.

52. The only thing that saves the Obamacare exchange is if government subsidies rise, right along with the premiums. That can't happen, however, if the subsidies are capped in future periods.

53. David Maly, "Texas Prepares to Shutter High-Risk Insurance Pool," *Texas Tribune,* October 17, 2013, http://www.texastribune.org/2013/10/17/texas-prepares-shutter-high-risk-insurance-pool/.

54. National Conference of State Legislatures, "Coverage of Uninsurable Preexisting Conditions: State and Federal High-Risk Pools," http://www.ncsl.org/research/health/high-risk-pools-for-health-coverage.aspx.

55. Hadley Heath and Heather Higgins, "Obamacare's Preexisting Problems Need a Pragmatic Fix," *The Hill*, April 23, 2013, https://thehill.com/blogs/congress-blog/healthcare /295587-obamacares-pre-existing-problems-need-a-pragmatic-fix.

56. John Goodman, "Detroit Is Trying to Dump Its Retirees on the Exchange," National Center for Policy Analysis, *Health Policy*, October 18, 2013, http://healthblog.ncpathinktank .org/detroit-is-trying-to-dump-its-retirees-on-the-exchange/.

57. Michael Meulemans, "10% of Large Employers May Drop 2014 Health Benefits," *About.com Insurance*, https://web.archive.org/web/20150907071820/http://insurance.about .com/od/HealthIns/a/In-2014-Ten-Precent-Oflarge-Employers-May-Cease-Health-Benefits .htm.

58. Centers for Medicare and Medicaid Services, "Trends in Subsidized and Unsubsidized Enrollment," August 12, 2019, https://www.cms.gov/CCIIO/Resources/Forms-Reports-and -Other-Resources/Downloads/Trends-Subsidized-Unsubsidized-Enrollment-BY17-18.pdf.

59. Department of Health and Human Services, "Health Plan Choice and Premiums in the 2017 Health Insurance Marketplace," October 24, 2016, https://aspe.hhs.gov/system /files/pdf/212721/2017MarketplaceLandscapeBrief.pdf.

60. Centers for Medicare and Medicaid Services, "Trends in Subsidized and Unsubsidized Enrollment," August 12, 2019, https://www.cms.gov/CCIIO/Resources/Forms-Reports-and -Other-Resources/Downloads/Trends-Subsidized-Unsubsidized-Enrollment-BY17-18.pdf.

61. See, for example, Linda J. Blumberg, John Holahan, Michael Karpman, and Caroline Elmendorf, "Characteristics of the Remaining Uninsured: An Update, Urban Institute," July, 2018, https://www.urban.org/sites/default/files/publication/98764/2001914-characteristics -of-the-remaining-uninsured-an-update_2.pdf.

62. This section adapted from and quoted from John Goodman, "Six Problems with the ACA That Aren't Going Away," *Health Affairs*, June 25, 2015, https://www.healthaffairs.org /do/10.1377/hblog20150625.048781/full/; John C. Goodman, "Obamacare's Impossible Expectations," *Psychology Today*, October 10, 2012, https://www.psychologytoday.com/us/blog /curing-the-healthcare-crisis/201210/obamacares-impossible-expectations.

63. Kimberley S.H. Yarnall et al., "Primary Care: Is There Enough Time for Prevention?," *American Journal of Public Health*, April 2003, 93(4), 635-641.

64. David P. Sklar, "How Many Doctors Will We Need? A Special Issue on the Physician Workforce," *Academic Medicine* 88, no. 12 (2013): 1785–1787.

65. Adam Gaffney et al., "The Effects on Hospital Utilization of the 1966 and 2014 Health Insurance Coverage Expansions in the United States," *Annals of Internal Medicine*, August 6, 2019, https://annals.org/aim/article-abstract/2738920/effects-hospital-utilization-1966-2014 -health-insurance-coverage-expansions-united.

66. Bruce Japsen, "Doctor Wait Times Soar 30% In Major U.S. Cities," *Forbes*, March 19, 2017. Available at https://www.forbes.com/sites/brucejapsen/2017/03/19/doctor-wait-times -soar-amid-trumpcare-debate/#524badb2e740.

67. Louise B. Russell, "Preventing Chronic Disease: An Important Investment, but Don't Count on Cost Savings," *Health Affairs* 28 (2009): 42–45.

68. John Goodman, "Concierge Medicine Taking Off," National Center for Policy Analysis, *Health Policy*, February 8, 2013, http://healthblog.ncpathinktank.org/concierge-medicine -taking-off.

69. John C. Goodman, "For the Vulnerable, Expect Less Access to Care," National Center for Health Policy Analysis, *Health Policy*, November 16, 2011, http://healthblog.ncpathink tank.org/for-the-vulnerable-expect-less-access-to-care.

70. For example, if 100,000 people in Dallas do not use their tax credits in a year to purchase health insurance, and the average credit in Dallas is $5,000, the total in unused tax credits for the year in Dallas is $500 million (100,000 times $5,000). The federal program should compensate for this by apportioning $500 million in financing for the year among the safety-net health care institutions in Dallas that specialize in providing health care for the medically needy without health insurance.

71. This section previously published as John Goodman, "Six Problems with the ACA That Aren't Going Away," *Health Affairs*, June 25, 2015, https://www.healthaffairs.org/do/10.1377 /hblog20150625.048781/full/.

72. Originally published as John C. Goodman and Linda Gorman, 'If the Court Strikes Down Obamacare, How Bad Would That Be?," *Forbes*, April 3, 2019. Available at https://www .forbes.com/sites/johngoodman/2019/04/03/if-the-court-strikes-down-obamacare-how-bad -would-that-be/#5158959e72f7.

73. Lukas Mikelionis, "Trump Administration Backs Total Overturn of Obamacare, Will Support States Challenging the Law," Fox News, March 26, 2019, https://www.foxnews .com/politics/trump-administration-backs-total-overturn-of-obamacare-will-support -states-challenging-the-law.

74. Linda Gorman, "What Are We Getting for Our Obamacare Dollars?," Goodman Institute, Brief Analysis No. 126, August 6, 2018, http://www.goodmaninstitute.org/wp -content/uploads/2018/08/BA-126-What-Are-We-Getting-for-Our-Obamacare-Dollars.pdf.

75. John C. Goodman, "Obamacare Can Be Worse than Medicaid," *Wall Street Journal*, June 26, 2018, https://www.wsj.com/articles/obamacare-can-be-worse-than-medicaid -1530052891.

76. Goodman Institute, "Portable Health Insurance: An Idea Whose Time Has Come," Brief Analysis No. 105, April 6, 2016, http://www.goodmaninstitute.org/wp-content/uploads /2016/04/BA-105.pdf.

77. John C. Goodman, "Donald Trump Takes a Big Step toward Personal and Portable Health Insurance," *Forbes*, June 18, 2019, https://www.forbes.com/sites/johngoodman/2019/06/18 /donald-trump-takes-a-big-step-toward-personal-and-portable-health-insurance/#3ecf24ed 71c1.

78. John C. Goodman and Linda Gorman, "Limited Benefit Insurance," Goodman Institute, Brief Analysis No. 104, April 6, 2016, http://www.goodmaninstitute.org/wp-content /uploads/2016/04/BA-104.pdf.

79. National Bureau of Economic Research, "The Oregon Health Insurance Experiment," https://www.nber.org/oregon/1.home.html.

80. Amy Finkelstein, Nathaniel Hendren, and Erzo F. P. Luttmer, "The Value of Medicaid: Interpreting Results from the Oregon Health Insurance Experiment," *National Bureau of Economic Research*, June 2015, https://users.nber.org/~luttmer/valueofmedicaid.pdf.

81. See KFF State Health Facts at https://www.kff.org/health-reform/state-indicator /waiting-lists-for-hcbs-waivers/?currentTimeframe=0&sortModel=%7B%22colId%22:%22 Location%22,%22sort%22:%22asc%22%7D.

82. Nicholas Horton, "Waiting for Help: The Medicaid Waiting List Crisis," Foundation for Government Accountability, March 6, 2018, https://thefga.org/research/medicaid-waiting-list/.

83. Chris Pope, "Fixing Health-Insurance Markets," *National Review*, May 14, 2018, https://www.nationalreview.com/2018/05/fixing-health-insurance-markets-inteview-mark-pauly/.

84. Jennifer Tolbert et al., "Key Facts about the Uninsured Population," Kaiser Family Foundation, December 13, 2019, https://www.kff.org/uninsured/issue-brief/key-facts-about-the-uninsured-population/.

85. "December 2019 Medicaid & CHIP Enrollment Data Highlights" at www.medicaid.gov.

Chapter 9: The Risk of Becoming Unemployed and Finding No Market for One's Skills

1. "America Is in a Depression. The Challenge Now Is to Make It Short-Lived," *Washington Post*, April 9, 2020, https://www.washingtonpost.com/business/2020/04/09/66-million-americans-filed-unemployed-last-week-bringing-pandemic-total-over-17-million/.

2. Bureau of Labor Statistics, U.S. Department of Labor, Employment Situation Summary, March 6, 2020.

3. Bureau of Labor Statistics, U.S. Department of Labor, Jobs Openings and Labor Turnover Summary–January 2020, March 17, 2020.

4. William B. Conerly, "Unemployment Insurance in a Free Society," National Center for Policy Analysis, NCPA Policy Report No. 274, March 2005, http://www.ncpathinktank.org/pdfs/st274.pdf.

5. Patricia Anderson and Bruce D. Meyer, "The Effects of Unemployment Insurance Taxes and Benefits on Layoffs Using Firm and Individual Data," National Bureau of Economic Research, NBER Working Paper No. 4960, January 1996; Patricia Anderson and Bruce D. Meyer, "The Effects of the Unemployment Insurance Payroll Tax on Wages, Employment, Claims, and Denials," National Bureau of Economic Research, NBER Working Paper No. 6808, November 1998; Frank Brechling and Louise Laurence, *Permanent Job Loss and the U.S. System of Financing Unemployment Insurance* (Kalamazoo, MI: W.E. Upjohn Institute for Employment Research, 1995); David Card and Phillp B. Levine, "Unemployment Insurance Taxes and the Cyclical and Seasonal Properties of Unemployment," *Journal of Public Economics* 53, no. 1 (January 1994): 1–29; Donald R Deere, "Unemployment Insurance and Employment," *Journal of Labor Economics* 9, no. 4 (October 1991): 307–324; Robert H. Topel, "On Layoffs and Unemployment Insurance," *American Economic Review* 73 (September 1983): 541–559.

6. Taken from William B. Conerly, "Unemployment Insurance in a Free Society," National Center for Policy Analysis, NCPA Policy Report No. 274, March 2005.

7. A. Colin Cameron, R. Mark Gritz, and Thomas McCurdy, "The Effects of Unemployment Compensation on the Unemployment of Youth," NLS Discussion Paper, NLS 92-4, 1989; R. Mark Gritz and Thomas MaCurdy, "Measuring the Influence of Unemployment Insurance on Unemployment Experiences," *Journal of Business and Economic Statistics* 15, no. 2 (April 1997); Pierre Yves Cremiéux et al., "Unemployment Insurance and Job Search Produc-

tivity," Human Resources Development Canada, August 1995; Manuel Arellano, Olympia Bover, and Samuel Bentolila, "Unemployment Duration, Benefit Duration, and the Business Cycle," Centre for Economic Policy Research Discussion Paper 1840, March 1998.

8. Bruce D. Meyer, "Unemployment Insurance and Unemployment Spells," *Econometrica* 58, no. 4 (July 1990): 757–782.

9. On Canada, see Pierre Yves Cremiéux et al., "Unemployment Insurance and Job Search Productivity," Human Resources Development Canada, August 1995; and Christian Belzil, "Unemployment Insurance and Subsequent Job Duration: Job Matching vs. Unobserved Heterogeneity," *Journal of Applied Econometrics* (September/October 2001): 619–636. On Europe, see Olivier Blanchard and Justin Wolfers, "The Role of Shocks and Institutions in the Rise of European Unemployment: The Aggregate Evidence," Economic Journal 110 (March 2000): C1–C33. On Spain, see Manuel Arellano, Olympia Bover, and Samuel Bentolila, "Unemployment Duration, Benefit Duration, and the Business Cycle," Centre for Economic Policy Research Discussion Paper 1840, March 1998. And on Sweden, see Kenneth Carling, Bertil Holmlund, and Altin Vejsiu, "Do Benefit Cuts Boost Job Finding? Swedish Evidence from the 1990s," *Economic Journal 111, no. 474* (October 2001): 766-790.

10. Eric M. Engen and Jonathan Gruber, "Unemployment Insurance and Precautionary Saving," NBER Working Paper No. 5252, September 1995; Jonathan Gruber, "The Consumption Smoothing Benefits of Unemployment Insurance," *American Economic Review* 87, no. 1 (March 1997): 192–205; Jonathan Gruber, "The Wealth of the Unemployed: Adequacy and Implications for Unemployment Insurance," *Industrial and Labor Relations Review*, forthcoming. Also Jonathan Gruber, "The Wealth of the Unemployed: Adequacy and Implications for Unemployment Insurance," NBER Working Paper No. 7348, September 1999; Jonathan Gruber and Julie Berry Cullen, "Does Unemployment Insurance Crowd Out Spousal Labor Supply?," *Journal of Labor Economics* 18, no. 3 (July 2000): 546–572.

11. Lawrence H. Summers, "Unemployment," *The Concise Encyclopedia of Economics*. Available at http://www.econlib.org/library/Enc/Unemployment.html.

12. Robert Barro, "The Folly of Subsidizing Unemployment," *Wall Street Journal*, August 30, 2010, https://www.wsj.com/articles/SB10001424052748703959704575454431457720188.

13. Jonathan Gruber and Julie Berry Cullen, "Spousal Labor Supply as Insurance: Does Unemployment Insurance Crowd Out Added Worker Effect?," National Bureau of Economic Research, Working Paper No. 5608, June 1996, https://www.nber.org/papers/w5608.

14. Eric M. Engen and Jonathan Gruber, "Unemployment Insurance and Precautionary Saving," SSRN, NBER Working Paper w2252, September 1995, last rev: February 17, 2002, https://papers.ssrn.com/sol3/papers.cfm?abstract_id=225316.

15. Taken from William B. Conerly, "Unemployment Insurance in a Free Society," National Center for Policy Analysis, NCPA Policy Report No. 274, March 2005, http://www.ncpathinktank.org/pdfs/st274.pdf.

16. Bureau of Labor Statistics, U.S. Department of Labor, The Employment Situation—July 2015, August 7, 2015, Table A: Household Data, Seasonally Adjusted.

17. Bureau of Labor Statistics, U.S. Department of Labor, Databases, Tables, and Calculators by Subject, Labor Force Participation Rate, 1978–2015.

18. Bureau of Labor Statistics, U.S. Department of Labor, The Employment Situation—July 2015, August 7, 2015, Table A-2: Employment Status of the Civilian Population by Race, Sex, and Age; Howard N. Fullerton, Jr., "Labor Force Participation, 75 Years of Change, 1950–98 and 1998-2025," *Monthly Labor Review*, December 1999, Table 1: Civilian Labor Force Participation Rates by Sex and Age, 1950–1998 and Projected 2015 to 2025, 4.

19. Bruce D. Meyer, "Lessons from the U.S. Unemployment Insurance Experiments," *Journal of Economic Literature* 33, no. 1 (March 1995): 91–131.

20. William B. Conerly, "European Unemployment: Lessons for the United States," National Center for Policy Analysis, Brief Analysis No. 475, May 26, 2004.

21. Taken from William B. Conerly, "Unemployment Insurance in a Free Society," National Center for Policy Analysis, NCPA Policy Report No. 274, March 2005.

22. Ibid.

23. William B. Conerly, "Wasting Billions on Unemployment Insurance Overpayments," National Center for Policy Analysis, Brief Analysis No. 458, September 30, 2003.

24. John Hood, "North Carolina Got It Right on Unemployment Benefits," *Wall Street Journal*, July 4, 2014.

25. Ibid.

26. Ibid.

27. Quoted from Jeffrey Dorfman, "Labor Market Data Prove Extended Unemployment Benefits Were Hurting the Recovery," *Forbes*, July 26, 2014.

28. Casey B. Mulligan and Brian Blase, "Congress Can Still Save the Recovery," *Wall Street Journal*, April 7, 2020, https://www.wsj.com/articles/congress-can-still-save-the-recovery-11586279678.

29. Veronique de Rugy, "A Timely Redux for Personal Unemployment Insurance Savings Accounts, Mercatus Center, April 6, 2020, https://www.mercatus.org/publications/covid-19-policy-brief-series/timely-redux-personal-unemployment-insurance-savings.

Chapter 10: The Risk of Plagues, Pandemics, and Other Threats to Public Health

1. This section adapted from John Goodman, "Response to Coronavirus Reflects Trump's Radical Health Reforms," Goodman Institute, Brief Analysis No.136, April 1, 2020, http://www.goodmaninstitute.org/wp-content/uploads/2020/04/GoodmanInstitute-BA-136-Response-to-Coronavirus-with-links-for-website.pdf; John Goodman, "How Would Free Market Health Care Respond to the Coronavirus?," Forbes, March 23, 2020, https://www.forbes.com/sites/johngoodman/2020/03/23/how-would-free-market-health-care-respond-to-the-coronavirus/#4a79cd0c61ff; Marie Fishpaw (Heritage Foundation) and John Goodman, "A Health Plan for President Trump," Goodman Institute, Brief Analysis No. 130, August 15, 2019, http://www.goodmaninstitute.org/wp-content/uploads/2019/10/BA-130-A-Health-Plan-for-President-Trump-web-version.pdf.

2. Thucydides, *The History of the Peloponnesian War* (Penguin Classics, September 30, 1954), https://www.penguinrandomhouse.com/books/292278/the-history-of-the-peloponnesian-war-by-thucydides/.

3. Ibid.

4. Ibid.

5. Ibid.

6. Ole Benedictow, "The Black Death: The Greatest Catastrophe Ever," *History Today*, vol. 55, issue 3, March 2005, https://www.historytoday.com/archive/black-death-greatest -catastrophe-ever.

7. Jeffrey K. Taubenberger and David Morens, "1918 Influenza: the Mother of All Pandemics," *Emerging Infectious Diseases*, vol. 12, no. 1, January 2006, 15–22, https://www.ncbi.nlm .nih.gov/pmc/articles/PMC3291398/.

8. Douglas Jordan, with contributions from Dr. Terrence Tumpey and Barbara Jester, "The Deadliest Flu: The Complete Story of the Discovery and Reconstruction of the 1918 Pandemic Virus," Centers for Disease Control and Prevention, https://www.cdc.gov/flu/pandemic -resources/reconstruction-1918-virus.html.

9. German Lopez, "5 Lessons on Social Distancing From the 1918 Spanish Flu Pandemic," Vox, March 24, 2020, https://www.vox.com/policy-and-politics/2020/3/24/21188121/coronavirus -covid-19-social-distancing-1918-spanish-flu.

10. Edwin Chadwick, *Report on The Sanitary Condition of the Labouring Population of Great Britain*, published in 1842. See Christopher Hamlin, *Public Health and Social Justice in the Age of Chadwick: Britain, 1800–1854*. (United Kingdom: Cambridge University Press, 1998).

11. Christopher Hamlin, *Public Health and Social Justice in the Age of Chadwick: Britain, 1800–1854* (United Kingdom: Cambridge University Press, 1998).

12. Ibid.

13. Ibid.

14. Wikipedia, "Eugenics," last modified May 10, 2020, https://en.wikipedia.org/wiki /Eugenics.

15. Wikipedia, "Buck vs. Bell," last modified April 28, 2020, https://en.wikipedia.org /wiki/Buck_v._Bell.

16. See *The Lynchburg Story,* YouTube, May 1, 2018, https://www.youtube.com/watch?v=51n Rsof66Z0&feature=youtu.be.

17. James H. Jones, *Bad Blood* (New York: The Free Press, 1981).

18. Wikipedia, "1976 Swine Flu Outbreak," last modified May 10, 2020, https://en .wikipedia.org/wiki/1976_swine_flu_outbreak.

19. Ibid.

20. Richard Epstein, "In Defense of the 'Old' Public Health: The Legal Framework for the Regulation of Public Health," SSRN, University of Chicago Law and Economics, Olin Working Paper No. 170, December 2002, https://papers.ssrn.com/sol3/papers.cfm?abstract _id=359281.

21. Ibid.

22. Michael D. Shear et al., "The Lost Month: How a Failure to Test Blinded the U.S. to COVID-19," *New York Times,* March 28, 2020, https://www.nytimes.com/2020/03/28/us /testing-coronavirus-pandemic.html.

23. Ben Elgin and John Tozzi, "Hospital Workers Make Masks from Office Supplies Amid U.S. Shortage," *Bloomberg*, March 17, 2020, https://www.bloomberg.com/news/articles /2020-03-18/hospital-makes-face-masks-covid-19-shields-from-office-supplies.

Chapter 11: Addressing the Risks of Old Age

1. See Andrew J. Rettenmaier and Thomas R. Saving, "Social Security and Progressive Indexing," National Center for Policy Analysis, Brief Analysis No. 520, July 11, 2005. Available at http://www.ncpathinktank.org/pdfs/ba520.pdf. See also Andrew J. Rettenmaier and Thomas R. Saving, "Social Security Reform without Illusion: The Five Percent Solution," National Center for Policy Analysis, Policy Report No. 272, December 17, 2004.,http://www .ncpathinktank.org/pdfs/st272.pdf.

2. Estelle James, "Reforming Social Security: Lessons from Thirty Countries," National Center for Policy Analysis, Policy Report No. 277, June 2005.

3. Estelle James and Augusto Iglesias, "Integrated Disability and Retirement Systems in Chile," National Center for Policy Analysis, Policy Report No. 302, September 1, 2007. Available at http://www.ncpathinktank.org/pdfs/st302.pdf.

4. Estelle James, "Private Pension Annuities in Chile," National Center for Policy Analysis, NCPA Policy Report 271, December 2004.

5. U.S. Social Security system benefits are currently price indexed.

6. Adapted and quoted from Estelle James, Alejandra Cox Edwards, and Augusto Iglesias, "Chile's New Pension Reforms," National Center for Policy Analysis, Policy Report No. 326, March 2010, http://www.ncpathinktank.org/pdfs/st326.pdf.

7. Estelle James, "Private Pension Annuities in Chile," National Center for Policy Analysis, NCPA Policy Report 271, December 2004.

8. This section taken from James et al., "Chile's New Pension Reforms."

9. See Estelle James, Alejandra Cox Edwards, and Augusto Iglesias, "Chile's New Pension Reforms," National Center for Policy Analysis, Policy Report No. 326, March 2010.

10. Adapted from Estelle James, "Social Security Reform around the World: Lessons from 30 Countries," National Center for Policy Analysis, Policy Report No. 253, August 2002.

11. Adapted from Estelle James, "Private Pension Annuities in Chile," National Center for Policy Analysis, Policy Report No. 271, December 2004, http://www.hacer.org/pdf /Chile09.pdf.

12. Estelle James, "Private Pension Annuities in Chile," National Center for Policy Analysis, NCPA Policy Report No. 271, December 2004, http://www.hacer.org/pdf/Chile09.pdf.

13. Estelle James, Alejandra Cox Edwards, and Augusto Iglesias, "Chile's New Pension Reforms," National Center for Policy Analysis, NCPA Policy Report No. 326, March 2010.

14. Kristian Niemietz, "Private Pension Provision: What an Ageing Europe Can Learn from a Latin Tiger," Stockholm Network, 2007.

15. William F. Shughart II, "If Federal Waste Must Increase, Federal Land Holdings Must Decrease," *RealClear Markets*, April 23, 2020, https://www.independent.org/news/article .asp?id=13128.

16. William F. Shughart and Carl P. Close, "Liquidating Federal Assets: A Promising Tool for Ending the U.S. Debt Crisis," Independent Institute, March 6, 2017, revised April

12, 2017, https://www.independent.org/pdf/executive_summaries/2017_03_01_liquidating _federal_assets.pdf.

17. Ibid.

18. Andrew Glass, "President George W. Bush Pursues Social Security Reform, May 2, 2001," *Politico*, May 2, 2018, https://www.politico.com/story/2018/05/02/president-george -w-bush-pursues-social-security-reform-may-2-2001-559632.

19. U.S. Department of Veterans Affairs, Table 1L: VETPOP2016 Living Veterans by Age Group, Gender 2015–2045.

20. Adapted from John C. Goodman, "A Framework for Medicare Reform," National Center for Policy Analysis, Policy Report No. 315, September 2008, http://www.ncpathink tank.org/pdfs/st315.pdf.

21. The following section previously published as John C. Goodman, "A Framework for Medicare Reform," National Center for Policy Analysis, Policy Report No. 315, September 2008, http://www.ncpathinktank.org/pdfs/st315.pdf.

22. John C. Goodman, "A Framework for Medicare Reform," National Center for Policy Analysis, Policy Report No. 315, September 2008, http://www.ncpathinktank.org/pdfs/st315 .pdf.

23. Adapted from John C. Goodman, "A Framework for Medicare Reform," National Center for Policy Analysis, Policy Report No. 315, September 2008.

24. Portions of this section previously published as John C. Goodman, "Paul Krugman Doesn't Have Private Health Insurance," *Health Policy*, National Center for Policy Analysis, December 5, 2012, http://www.healthcarepayernews.com/content/paul-krugmandoesnt-have -private-health-insurance.

25. See, for example, Paul Krugman, "Zombies Against Medicare," *New York Times*, July 17, 2015, http://www.nytimes.com/2015/07/27/opinion/zombies-against-medicare .html.

26. Previous two graphs previously published as John C. Goodman, "Paul Krugman Doesn't Have Private Health Insurance," *Health Policy*, National Center for Policy Analysis, December 5, 2012, http://www.healthcarepayernews.com/content/paul-krugmandoesnt-have -private-health-insurance.

27. John C. Goodman, "Paul Krugman Doesn't Have Private Health Insurance," *Health Policy*, National Center for Policy Analysis, December 5, 2012, http://www.healthcarepayer news.com/content/paul-krugmandoesnt-have-private-health-insurance.

28. John C. Goodman and Lawrence J. Wedekind, "How the Trump Administration Is Reforming Medicare," *Health Affairs*, May 3, 2019, https://www.healthaffairs.org/do/10.1377 /hblog20190501.529581/full/.

29. Ibid.

30. John C. Goodman et al., "Health Care Reform: Do Other Countries Have the Answers?," National Center for Policy Analysis, March 10, 2009, http://www.ncpathinktank .org/pdfs/sp_Do_Other_Countries_Have_the_Answers.pdf.

31. Four previous paragraphs published as John C. Goodman, "Paul Krugman Doesn't Have Private Health Insurance," *Health Policy*, National Center for Policy Analysis, December 5, 2012, http://www.healthcarepayernews.com/content/paul-krugmandoesnt-have-private -health-insurance.

32. This section previously published as John C. Goodman, "A Framework for Medicare Reform," National Center for Policy Analysis, Policy Report No. 315, September 2008.

33. See John Goodman et al., *Lives at Risk*, ch. 24, http://www.ncpathinktank.org/pdfs /livesatrisk/Ch24.pdf.

34. Leslie Foster et al., "Improving the Quality of Medicaid Personal Assistance through Consumer Direction," *Health Affairs* Web Exclusive, March 26, 2003, https://www.health affairs.org/doi/10.1377/hlthaff.W3.162.

35. John C. Goodman, "Making Healthcare Work for American Families: Saving Money, Saving Lives," testimony given before the Energy and Commerce Subcommittee on Health, United States House of Representatives, April 2, 2009.

36. Jim Landers, "Trust Your Doctor to Save?," *Dallas Morning News*, January 9, 2012, http://www.dallasnews.com/business/columnists/jim-landers/20120109-trust-your-doctor -to-save.ece.

37. John C. Goodman et al., *Handbook on State Healthcare Reform* (Dallas: National Center for Policy Analysis, 1997), 179–189.

38. Susan Dentzer, "Reform Chronic Illness Care? Yes, We Can," *Health Affairs* 28 (2009): 12–13.

39. Previously published in John C. Goodman, "A Framework for Medicare Reform," National Center for Policy Analysis, Policy Report No. 315, September 2008.

40. Adapted from http://healthaffairs.org/blog/2011/11/15/a-better-way-to-approach -medicares-impossible-task/.

41. Policy changes previously published as Thomas Saving and John Goodman, "A Better Way to Approach Medicare's Impossible Task," *Health Affairs*, November 15, 2011, https:// www.healthaffairs.org/do/10.1377/hblog20111115.015114/full/.

42. Ibid.

43. Devon M. Herrick, "Concierge Medicine: Convenient and Affordable Care," National Center for Policy Analysis, Brief Analysis No. 687, January 19, 2010.

44. John C. Goodman, "A Framework for Medicare Reform," National Center for Policy Analysis, Policy Report No. 315, September 2008, http://www.ncpathinktank.org/pdfs /st315.pdf.

45. Previously published and adapted from John C. Goodman, "Standing between You and All the Benefits of Telemedicine: The AMA and the Federal Government," *Forbes*, July 9, 2015, http://www.forbes.com/sites/johngoodman/2015/07/09/standing-between-you-and -all-the-benefits-of-telemedicine-the-ama-and-the-federal-government/.

46. Jim Spencer, "Mayo makes case for Medicare reimbursement for telemedicine," *StarTribune,* July 24, 2015, http://www.startribune.com/mayo-makes-case-for-medicare -reimbursement-for-telemedicine/311516651/.

47. Ibid.

48. John C. Goodman, "Will Texas Medicine Return to the Middle Ages?" *Forbes*, May 22, 2015, https://www.forbes.com/sites/johngoodman/2015/05/22/will-texas-medicine -return-to-the-middle-ages/#5af47c9552bd.

49. Jim Spencer, "Mayo makes case for Medicare reimbursement for telemedicine," *StarTribune*, July 24, 2015, http://www.startribune.com/mayo-makes-case-for-medicare -reimbursement-for-telemedicine/311516651/.

50. Ibid.

51. "Landers: Calling on Virtual Medicine to Control Costs," *Dallas Morning News*, July 6, 2015, https://www.dallasnews.com/business/health-care/2015/07/06/landers-calling-on-virtual-medicine-to-control-costs.

52. Adapted from and previously published as John C. Goodman, "What Does Uber Medicine Look Like?," *Forbes*, July 24, 2015, http://www.forbes.com/sites/johngoodman/2015/07/24/what-does-uber-medicine-look-like/.

53. See https://www.doctorsmakinghousecalls.com/.

54. J. P. Newhouse, *Free for All? Lessons from the Rand Health Insurance Experiment* (Cambridge, Mass.: Harvard University Press, 1994).

55. Thomas A. Massaro and Yu-Ning Wong, "Medical Savings Accounts: The Singapore Experience," National Center for Policy Analysis, Policy Report No. 203, April 1996, http://www.ncpathinktank.org/pdfs/st203.pdf; Shaun Matisonn, "Medical Savings Accounts in South Africa," National Center for Policy Analysis, Policy Report No. 234, June 2000, http://www.ncpathinktank.org/pdfs/st234.pdf; Greg Scandlen, "Medical Savings Accounts: Obstacles to Their Growth and Ways to Improve Them," National Center for Policy Analysis, Policy Report No. 216, July 1998, http://www.ncpathinktank.org/pdfs/st216.pdf; John C. Goodman, "Health Savings Accounts Will Revolutionize American Health Care," National Center for Policy Analysis, Brief Analysis No. 464, January 15, 2004, http://www.ncpathinktankorg/pdfs/ba464.pdf; Devon M. Herrick, "Health Reimbursement Arrangements: Making a Good Deal Better," National Center for Policy Analysis, Brief Analysis No. 438, May 8, 2003; and Devon M. Herrick, "Choosing Independence: An Overview of the Cash and Counseling Model of Self-Directed Personal Assistance Services," Robert Wood Johnson Foundation, Fall 2006, http://www.rwjf.org/files/publications/other/Choosing_Independence_final_nov22.pdf.

56. Devon M. Herrick, "Consumer Driven Health Care: The Changing Nature of Health Insurance," *American Journal of Lifestyle Medicine*, forthcoming.

57. Robert H. Brook et al., "The Health Insurance Experiment," RAND Corporation, 2006, http://www.rand.org/pubs/research_briefs/RB9174.html.

58. Ibid.

59. Ibid.

60. John C. Goodman, "A Framework for Medicare Reform," National Center for Policy Analysis, Policy Report No. 315, September 2008, http://www.ncpathinktank.org/pdfs/st315.pdf.

61. Ibid.

62. Jeffrey Brown and Amy Finkelstein, "Insuring Long-Term Care in the U.S.," National Bureau of Economic Research, Working Paper 17451, September 2011.

63. Federal law requires state Medicaid programs to cover at-home care as it relates to health expenses or skilled nursing, but custodial care (assistance with feeding, bathing, dressing, housekeeping, etc.) is optional.

64. Chuck Milligan et al., "Public-Private Partnerships in Medicaid Long-Term Care," Center for Health Program Development and Management, University of Maryland-Baltimore County.

65. In 2011, the national median home value was $169,500. Source: Associated Press, "Home Prices Drop in Nearly Three-Quarters of U.S. Cities," November 10, 2011.

66. A reverse mortgage applicant must be at least sixty-two years of age. The younger a retiree is, the smaller the monthly payout will be. Since almost half of retirees in nursing homes are age eight-five and over, it would be more feasible to require reverse mortgage financing of this older population, since (1) they are the age demographic most likely to need long-term care; (2) they will have access to a greater monthly payout from a reverse mortgage; and (3) they will likely incur the greatest annual medical costs associated with long-term care.

67. Some states currently allow deductions toward state income taxes for premiums paid.

68. Vidhya Alakeson, "International Developments in Self-Directed Care," The Commonwealth Fund's Issues in International Health Policy, February 2010, http://www.common wealthfund.org/~/media/Files/Publications/Issue%20Brief/2010/Feb/1370_Alakson_intl _devel_selfdirected_care_ib_v2.pdf.

69. Bullet points previously published as John C. Goodman, Greg Scandlen, and Devon M. Herrick, "How Entrepreneurs Could Solve Medicare's Problems," National Center for Policy Analysis, Policy Report No. 344, January 2013.

70. Centers for Medicare and Medicaid Services, "Table 12. Number and Percent Distribution of Nursing Home Residents by Length of Time since Admission (in Days) and Mean and Median Length of Time According to Selected Resident Characteristics: United States, 2004," National Nursing Home Survey.

Appendix to Chapter 11: How the Trump Administration Is Reforming Medicare

71. Portions of this appendix were previously published as John C. Goodman, "A Framework for Medicare Reform," National Center for Policy Analysis, Policy Report No. 315, September 2008, http://www.ncpathinktank.org/pdfs/st315.pdf; John C. Goodman, 'How Trump is Reforming Medicare, Part I," *Forbes*, July 8, 2019, https://www.forbes.com/sites/johngoodman/2019/07/08/how-trump-is-reforming -medicare-part-i/#714727c87897; and John C. Goodman, "How Trump is Reforming Medicare, Part II," *Forbes*, July 12, 2019, https://www.forbes.com/sites/johngoodman/2019/07/12 /how-trump-is-reforming-medicare-part-ii/#7257fd5c2c30.

72. John Goodman and Devon Herrick, "Response to Coronavirus Reflects Trump's Radical Health Reforms," Goodman Institute, April 1, 2020, www.goodmaninstitute.org /wp-content/uploads/2020/04/GoodmanInstitute-BA-136-Response-to-Coronavirus-with -links-for-website.pdf

73. U.S. Department of Health and Human Services, U.S. Department of The Treasury, and U.S. Department of Labor, "Reforming America's Healthcare System through Choice and Competition," December 3, 2018, https://www.hhs.gov/about/news/2018/12/03 /reforming-americas-healthcare-system-through-choice-and-competition.html.

74. John C. Goodman, "Lower Cost, Higher Quality Health Care Is Right at Our Fingertips," *Forbes*, July 23, 2018, https://www.forbes.com/sites/johngoodman/2018/07/23/lower -cost-higher-quality-health-care-is-right-at-our-fingertips/#4c516a8a43bb.

75. Steve Bornhoft, "TMH's Telemedicine Program Connects Patients and Doctors in New Ways," *850 Business Magazine*, June 6, 2018, https://www.850businessmagazine.com /tmhs-telemedicine-program-connects-patients-and-doctors-in-new-ways/.

76. Arthur Allen, "A Hospital without Patients," *Politico*, November 8, 2017, https://www .politico.com/agenda/story/2017/11/08/virtual-hospital-mercy-st-louis-000573.

77. John C. Goodman, "Lower Cost, Higher Quality Health Care Is Right at Our Fingertips," *Forbes*, July 23, 2018, https://www.forbes.com/sites/johngoodman/2018/07/23/lower -cost-higher-quality-health-care-is-right-at-our-fingertips/#72492a1c43bb.

78. Centers for Medicare and Medicaid Services, "CMS Proposes Historic Changes to Modernize Medicare and Restore the Doctor-Patient Relationship," press release, July 12, 2018, https://www.cms.gov/newsroom/press-releases/cms-proposes-historic-changes-modernize -medicare-and-restore-doctor-patient-relationship.

79. Centers for Medicare and Medicaid Services, "Information on Medicare Telehealth," November 15, 2018, https://www.cms.gov/About-CMS/Agency-Information/OMH/Down loads/Information-on-Medicare-Telehealth-Report.pdf.

80. John Hsu et al., "Substantial Physician Turnover And Beneficiary 'Churn' in a Large Medicare Pioneer ACO," *Health Affairs* 36, no. 4 (April 2017), 640–648.

81. Thomas Saving and John C. Goodman, "A Better Way to Approach Medicare's Impossible Task," *Health Affairs*, November 15, 2011, https://www.healthaffairs.org/do/10.1377 /hblog20111115.015114/full/.

82. David Muhlestein et al., "Recent Progress in the Value Journey: Growth of ACOs and Value-Based Payment Models in 2018," *Health Affairs*, August 14, 2018, https://www .healthaffairs.org/do/10.1377/hblog20180810.481968/full/?utm_term=Recent+Progress+In +The+Value+Journey%3A+Growth+Of+ACOs+And+Value-Based+Payment+Models+In+2 018&utm_campaign=Health+Affairs+Sunday+Update&utm_content=email&utm_source =Act-On_2018-08-19&utm_medium=Email&cm_mmc=Act-On+Software-_-email-_ -NYC%27s+First+Lady+On+The+Mental+Health+Of+Migrant+Children%3B+Risk+Adjust ment+Litigation%3B+Prices+For+Cardiovascular+Drugs-_-Recent+Progress+In+The+Value +Journey%3A+Growth+Of+ACOs+And+Value-Based+Payment+Models+In+2018.

83. John Bertko et al., "Medicare Advantage: Better Information Tools, Better Beneficiary Choices, Better Competition," *Brookings*, November 27, 2017, https://www.brookings .edu/research/medicare-advantage-better-information-tools-better-beneficiary-choices -better-competition/#cancel.

84. John Goodman, "Is Public Policy Changing the Practice of Medicine?," *Health Affairs*, May 21, 2014, http://healthaffairs.org/blog/2014/05/21/is-public-policy-changing -the-practice-of-medicine/; James C. Capretta, "Replacing Medicare ACOs with a Better Integrated Care Option," Mercatus Center Policy Brief, May 11, 2017, https://www.mercatus. org/publications/healthcare/replacing-medicare-acos-better-integrated-care-option; L&M Policy Research, "Section 1115 Demonstration Monitoring and Evaluation Support," https:// www.lmpolicyresearch.com/index.php/experience/case-studies.

85. Ken Terry, "The MSSP Is No Silver Bullet for Healthcare Cost Control," *The Health Care Blog*, November 19, 2018, https://thehealthcareblog.com/blog/2018/11/19/the-mssp-is -no-silver-bullet-for-healthcare-cost-control/.

86. See https://www.integranethealth.com/.

87. Centers for Medicare and Medicaid Services, "Next-Generation Accountable Care Organization (ACO) Model Fact Sheet." Available at https://innovation.cms.gov/Files/fact -sheet/nextgenaco-fs.pdf.

88. Brent Fulton, "Health Care Market Concentration Trends in the United States: Evidence and Policy Responses," *Health Affairs* 36, no. 9 (September 2017), https://www.healthaffairs .org/doi/10.1377/hlthaff.2017.0556.

89. "The ASC Cost Differential." Ambulatory Surgery Centers, https://www.ascassociation .org/advancingsurgicalcare/reducinghealthcarecosts/paymentdisparitiesbetweenascsand hopds.

90. Centers for Medicare and Medicaid Services press release: "CMS Finalizes Rule that Encourages More Choices and Lower Costs for Seniors," November 2, 2018, https://www .cms.gov/newsroom/press-releases/cms-finalizes-rule-encourages-more-choices-and-lower -costs-seniors.

91. "Hospital Groups Will Sue to Stop Medicare's Latest Site-Neutral Payment Cuts," Advisory Board, November 5, 2018, https://www.advisory.com/daily-briefing/2018/11/05/medicare -rules.

92. Devon M. Herrick, "The Market for Medical Care Should Work Like Cosmetic Surgery," National Center for Policy Analysis, Policy Report No. 349, May 2013, https://www .healthworkscollective.com/wp-content/uploads/2013/06/st349.pdf.

93. Devon M. Herrick, "Medical Tourism: Global Competition in Health Care," National Center for Policy Analysis, Policy Report No. 304, November 1, 2007, http://www .ncpathinktank.org/pub/st304.

94. John C. Goodman, "Will Price Competition Lead to Quality Competition?," *Health Affairs*, April 21, 2011, https://www.healthaffairs.org/do/10.1377/hblog20110421.010444/full/.

95. John C. Goodman, "Why Is There a Problem with Health Care Quality?," *Health Affairs*, March 24, 2011, https://www.healthaffairs.org/do/10.1377/hblog20110324.009787/full/.

96. Jeff Lagasse, "Healthcare Providers Concerned, Unsure How to Address CMS Price Transparency Final Rule," *Healthcare Finance*, November 8, 2018, https://www.healthaffairs .org/do/10.1377/hblog20110421.010444/full/.

97. Robert Pear, "Hospitals Must Now Post Prices. But It May Take a Brain Surgeon to Decipher Them," *New York Times*, January 13, 2019, https://www.nytimes.com/2019/01/13 /us/politics/hospital-prices-online.html?module=inline.

98. Jordan Rau, "Buyer Beware: A Mammogram's Price Can Vary by Nearly $1,000, Study Finds," NBC News, October 13, 2015, https://www.nbcnews.com/health/health-care/buyer -beware-mammograms-price-can-vary-nearly-1-000-study-n440211.

99. Bill Dacey, "Patients Over Paperwork or 'Bait and Switch?,'" *Physicians Practice*, August 21, 2018, https://www.physicianspractice.com/em/patients-over-paperwork-or-bait-and -switch.

100. Council of Economic Advisors, "CEA Report: The Administration's FDA Reforms and Reduced Biopharmaceutical Drug Prices," October 25, 2018, https://www.whitehouse .gov/briefings-statements/cea-report-administrations-fda-reforms-reduced-biopharmaceutical -drug-prices/.

101. Lyndsay Meyer, "FDA in Brief: FDA Highlights Record-Breaking Number of Generic Drug Approvals in October," U.S. Food and Drug Administration, November 9, 2018, https://www.fda.gov/news-events/fda-brief/fda-brief-fda-highlights-record-breaking -number-generic-drug-approvals-october.

102. Avik Roy, "Drug Companies, Not 'Middlemen,' Are Responsible for High Drug Prices," *Forbes*, October 22, 2018, https://www.forbes.com/sites/theapothecary/2018/10/22 /drug-companies-are-responsible-for-high-drug-prices-not-middlemen/#4f2e50d14947.

103. Kula Vera, "Overpaying for Prescription Drugs: The Copay Clawback Phenomenon," University of Southern California Leonard D. Schaeffer Center for Health Policy and Economics, March 12, 2018, https://healthpolicy.usc.edu/research/overpaying-for-prescription -drugs/.

104. Robert Pear, "Trump Signs New Law Aimed at Drug Costs and Battles Democrats on Medicare," *New York Times*, https://www.nytimes.com/2018/10/10/us/politics/trump-health -insurance-drug-costs.html; "Fraud and Abuse; Removal of Safe Harbor Protection for Rebates Involving Prescription Pharmaceuticals and Creation of New Safe Harbor Protection for Certain Point-of-Sale Reductions in Price on Prescription Pharmaceuticals and Certain Pharmacy Benefit Manager Service Fees," *Federal Register*, February 6, 2019, https://www.federal register.gov/documents/2019/02/06/2019-01026/fraud-and-abuse-removal-of-safe-harbor -protection-for-rebates-involving-prescription-pharmaceuticals.

105. Jake Klaisner, Katie Holcomb, and Troy Filipek, "Impact of Potential Changes to the Treatment of Manufacturer's Rebates," *Milliman*, January 31, 2019, https://aspe.hhs.gov /system/files/pdf/260591/MillimanReportImpactPartDRebateReform.pdf.

106. Rachel Sacks, "Trump Administration Releases Long-Awaited Drug Rebate Proposal," *Health Affairs*, February 1, 2019, https://www.healthaffairs.org/do/10.1377/hblog 20190201.545950/full/?utm_campaign=HASU&utm_medium=email&utm_content =Administration+Releases+Drug+Rebate+Proposal%3B+Patient+Safety+Improvement +In+Nursing+Homes%3B+New+Products+Vs++Existing+Product+Inflation+In+Rising +Drug+Costs&utm_source=Newsletter.

107. Carolyn Y. Johnson, "UnitedHealthcare Will Provide Drug Rebates Directly to Members in Some Plans," *New York Times*, March 6, 2018, https://www.washingtonpost .com/news/wonk/wp/2018/03/06/unitedhealthcare-will-provide-drug-rebates-directly-to -members-in-some-plans/.

108. Katie Thomas and Reed Abelson, "How Trump's Latest Plan to Cut Drug Prices Will Affect You," *New York Times*, February 5, 2019.

Chapter 12: Opting Out of Survivor Insurance

1. Estelle James and Augusto Iglesias, "Integrated Disability and Retirement Systems in Chile," National Center for Policy Analysis, NCPA Policy Report No. 302, September 2007, http://www.ncpathinktank.org/pdfs/st302.pdf.

2. Ibid.

3. Ibid.

4. Ibid.

Chapter 13: Opting Out of Disability Insurance

1. Estelle James, "How to Reduce Disability: Lessons from Chile," Brief Analysis No. 719, National Center for Policy Analysis, August 24, 2010.

2. Adapted from Estelle James, "How to Reduce Disability: Lessons from Chile," National Center for Policy Analysis, Brief Analysis No. 719, August 24, 2010, http://www.ncpa thinktank.org/pdfs/ba719.pdf; Estelle James and Augusto Iglesias, "Integrated Disability and Retirement Systems in Chile," National Center for Policy Analysis, Policy Report No. 302, September 2007.

3. Estelle James and Augusto Iglesias, "Integrated Disability and Retirement Systems in Chile," National Center for Policy Analysis, NCPA Policy Report No. 302, September 2007.

4. John C. Goodman et al., *Handbook on State Health Care Reform* (Dallas, Texas: National Center for Policy Analysis, 2007).

5. Estelle James, "How to Reduce Disability: Lessons from Chile," Brief Analysis No. 719, National Center for Policy Analysis, August 24, 2010.

6. Estelle James and Augusto Iglesias, "Integrated Retirement and Disability Systems in Chile," National Center for Policy Analysis, Policy Report No. 302, September 2007.

7. Estelle James and Augusto Iglesias, "Disability Insurance with Pre-Funding and Private Participation: The Chilean Model," in *Funded Systems: Their Role in Solving the Pension Problem* (Santiago, Chile: FIAP, 2008).

8. Quoted from Estelle James and Augusto Iglesias, "Integrated Disability and Retirement Systems in Chile," National Center for Policy Analysis, NCPA Policy Report No. 302, September 2007.

9. The annuity lasts the entire lifetime, thereby providing longevity insurance. The programmed withdrawal has the same lifetime expected present value as the annuity, but payouts are more front loaded and uncertain, and the money may be used up before the person dies. For more details on payout modes see Estelle James, Guillermo Martinez, and Augusto Iglesias, "The Payout Stage in Chile: Who Annuitizes and Why?," *Journal of Pension Economics and Finance* 5, no. 2 (2006), http://www.estellejames.com/downloads/payout-chile.pdf.

10. The typical policy shares the risk between the AFP and the insurer: the AFP covers disability costs for the group up to a contractually agreed-upon maximum (such as 1 percent of wages), while the insurance company takes over once the maximum cost for the group has been reached. If disability costs are below the ceiling, the insurer and AFP share the savings. This limits the risk for the AFP and covers extreme costs.

11. Estelle James and Augusto Iglesias base the breakdown between administrative costs and disability insurance and survivors' insurance on data analysis.

12. To be eligible for disability benefits, a worker must either (1) be working and contributing at the time of the claim, (2) have contributed during the last twelve months and also paid at least six contributions in the year immediately preceding the last registered contribution, or (3) if self-employed, have made at least one contribution in the calendar month before the date of the claim.

13. For example, three years of contributions are typically required in Latin America, and five years are typically required in OECD countries. In the United States, the applicant must have worked in five of the last ten years and cannot be working currently. Organization

for Economic Cooperation and Development, Transforming Disability into Ability (Paris: OECD Press, 2003); Carlos Grushka and Gustavo Demarco, "Disability Pensions and Social Security Reform Analysis of the Latin American Experience," World Bank, Social Protection Discussion Paper No. 0325, December 2003; and Emily Andrews, "Disability Insurance: Programs and Practice," World Bank, Social Protection Discussion Paper, April 1998, http:// info.worldbank.org/etools/docs/library/77186/november2003/readings/disability.pdf.

14. This is true of nondisabled retirees as well. If those on programmed withdrawals exhaust their accounts, the state pays their pension at the MPG level, providing they meet the eligibility requirements. Retirees whose accumulations are not large enough to purchase an annuity greater than the MPG initially must take programmed withdrawals and spend down their accounts. Disabled retirees who don't qualify for the top-up are more likely to be in this situation. See Estelle James, Guillermo Martinez, and Augusto Iglesias, "The Payout Stage in Chile: Who Annuitizes and Why?"; and Alejandra Edwards and Estelle James, "Pension Reform and Postponed Retirement: Evidence from Chile," University of Michigan Research Retirement Center, Working Paper No. 2006-147, December 2006, http://deep blue.lib.umich.edu/bitstream/2027.42/49333/3/wp147.pdf.txt.

15. Emily Andrews, "Disability Insurance: Programs and Practice," World Bank, Social Protection Discussion Paper, April 1998, http://info.worldbank.org/etools/docs/library /77186/novem-ber2003/readings/disability.pdf. Note that different methods of calculating replacement rates may be used for different countries, so these rates are not completely comparable.

16. Estelle James, "How to Reduce Disability: Lessons from Chile," Brief Analysis No. 719, National Center for Policy Analysis, August 24, 2010.

17. Ibid.

18. See Estelle James, Alejandra Cox Edwards, and Augusto Iglesias, "Chile's New Pension Reforms," National Center for Policy Analysis, NCPA Report No. 326, March 2010.

19. Adapted from N. Michael Helvacian, "Workers' Compensation: Rx for Policy Reform," National Center for Policy Analysis, Policy Report No. 287, September 13, 2006.

20. Ibid.

21. Ibid.

22. Ibid.

23. Previously published as John C. Goodman et al., *Handbook on State Health Care Reform* (Dallas, Texas: National Center for Policy Analysis, 2007). A RAND Corporation study concludes that permanent partial disability (PPD) benefits to employees who lose significant time from work replace about 50 percent of the employees' wage loss over a ten-year period. The analysis is based on a comparison of the income of employees who received PPD benefits with their cohorts who were not injured and lost no time from work. See R. T. Reville et al., "An Evaluation of New Mexico Workers' Compensation Permanent Partial Disability and Return to Work," RAND Corporation, 2004.

24. N. Michael Helvacian, "Workers' Compensation: Rx for Policy Reform," National Center for Policy Analysis, Policy Report No. 287, September 2006, http://www.ncpathink tank.org/pdfs/st287.pdf.

25. See Texas Department of Insurance, "Information for Workers' Compensation Nonsubscribers," revised March 2006, http://www.tdi.state.tx.us/consumer/cb007.html.

26. Joseph Shields and D. C. Campbell, "A Study of Nonsubscription to the Workers' Compensation System: 2001 Estimates," Research and Oversight Council on Workers' Compensation, February 2002.

27. John C. Goodman et al., *Handbook on State Health Care Reform* (Dallas, Texas: National Center for Policy Analysis, 2007).

28. Richard Butler, "Lost Injury Days: Moral Hazard Differences between Tort and Workers' Compensation," *Journal of Risk and Insurance* 63, no. 4 (September 1996): 405–433.

29. Adapted from Michael Grabell and Howard Berkes, "Inside Corporate America's Campaign to Ditch Workers' Comp," *ProPublica*, October 14, 2015.

30. Paul O'Donnell, "Dallas Lawyer Leads Push To Slash Workers' Comp Costs – and Employee Benefits," *Dallas Morning News*, October 21, 2015, https://www.dallasnews.com /business/2015/10/21/dallas-lawyer-leads-push-to-slash-workers-comp-costs-and-employee -benefits.

31. Paul O'Donnell, "Dallas Lawyer Leads Push To Slash Workers' Comp Costs—and Employee Benefits," *Dallas Morning News*, October 21, 2015, https://www.dallasnews.com /business/2015/10/21/dallas-lawyer-leads-push-to-slash-workers-comp-costs-and-employee -benefits.

32. Paul O'Donnell, "Dallas Lawyer Leads Push To Slash Workers' Comp Costs – and Employee Benefits," *Dallas Morning News*, October 21, 2015, https://www.dallasnews.com /business/2015/10/21/dallas-lawyer-leads-push-to-slash-workers-comp-costs-and-employee -benefits/.

33. N. Michael Helvacian, "Workers' Compensation: Rx for Policy Reform," National Center for Policy Analysis, NCPA Policy Report No. 287, September 2006.

35. John C. Goodman et al., *Handbook on State Health Care Reform* (Dallas, Texas: National Center for Policy Analysis, 2007).

Chapter 14: Addressing the Risk of Ill Health

1. Section previously published as John C. Goodman, "Applying the 'Do No Harm' Approach to Health Policy," *Journal of Legal Medicine* 28 (2007): 37–52.

2. On what is wrong with Medicaid and what is needed to reform it, see Regina E. Herzlinger, "It'll Take More Than a Band-Aid to Fix Medicaid," *Wall Street Journal*, February 5, 2017, https://www.wsj.com/articles/itll-take-more-than-a-band-aid-to-fix-medic-aid-1486336355.

3. John C. Goodman, "The Universal Health Tax Credit: How Generous Should It Be? What Will It Buy?" Brief Analysis 103, Goodman Institute for Public Policy, April 6, 2016, http://www.goodmaninstitute.org/wp-content/uploads/2016/04/BA-103.pdf.

4. John C. Goodman, "S-CHIP Fiasco," *John Goodman's Health Policy Blog*, October 15, 2007, http://healthblog.ncpathinktank.org/s-chip-fiasco.

5. David M. Cutler and Jonathan M. Gruber, "Does Public Insurance Crowd Out Private Insurance?," National Bureau of Economic Research, Working paper 5082, April 1995, https://www.nber.org/papers/w5082.

6. Section previously published as John C. Goodman, "Applying the "Do No Harm" Approach to Health Policy," *Journal of Legal Medicine* 28 (2007): 37–52.

7. John C. Goodman, "Applying the "Do No Harm" Approach to Health Policy," *Journal of Legal Medicine* 28 (2007): 37–52.

8. This section previously published as John C. Goodman, "Applying the "Do No Harm" Approach to Health Policy," *Journal of Legal Medicine* 28 (2007): 37–52.

9. John C. Goodman, "Saving for Health Care: The Policy Pros and Cons of Different Vehicles," Health Affairs (blog), April 17, 2012, http://healthaffairs.org/blog/2012/04/17/saving-for-heatlh-care-the-policy-pros-and-cons-of-different-vehicles/.

10. Mark V. Pauly et al., "Incremental Steps toward Health System Reform," *Health Affairs* 14 (1995): 125-139; http://www.forbes.com/sites/johngoodman/2016/04/19/roth-health-savings-accounts-what-the-world-needs-now/#b353d796d308.

11. This section previously published as John C. Goodman, "Applying the "Do No Harm" Approach to Health Policy," *Journal of Legal Medicine* 28 (2007): 37–52.

12. See Regina E. Herzlinger, Who Killed Health Care? America's $2 Trillion Medical Problem-and the Consumer-Driven Cure, (New York: McGraw-Hill, 2007).

13. Previously published as John C. Goodman, "Turning the Exchanges into Real Markets," Brief Analysis No. 106, Goodman Institute, April 6, 2016, http://www.goodmaninstitute.org/wp-content/uploads/2016/04/BA-106.pdf.

14. John C. Goodman, "A Workable Safety Net," Goodman Institute, May 9, 2016, http://www.goodmaninstitute.org/wp-content/uploads/2016/05/A-Workable-Safety-Net.pdf.

15. See Regina E. Herzlinger, *Who Killed Health Care? America's $2 Trillion Medical Problem and the Consumer-Driven Cure,* (New York: McGraw-Hill, 2007).

16. This section previously published as John C. Goodman, "Applying the "Do No Harm" Approach to Health Policy," *Journal of Legal Medicine* 28 (2007): 37–52.

17. John C. Goodman, "Applying the "Do No Harm" Approach to Health Policy," *Journal of Legal Medicine* 28 (2007): 37–52.

18. This section adapted from John C. Goodman, "Alternatives to Obamacare," *Forbes*, January 30, 2019, https://www.forbes.com/sites/johngoodman/2019/01/30/alternatives-to-obamacare/#721bcf5861ff; *see also* Sarah Kliff, "Under Trump, the Number of Uninsured Americans Has Gone Up by 7 Million," Vox, January 23, 2019, https://www.vox.com/2019/1/23/18194228/trump-uninsured-rate-obamacare-medicaid.

19. Edward R. Berchick, Emily Hood, and Jessica C. Barnett, "Health Insurance Coverage in the United States: 2017," *U.S. Census,* https://www.census.gov/library/publications/2018/demo/p60-264.html.

20. Jake Thorkildsen, "How Healthcare Sharing Programs Compare to Traditional Health Insurance," *Nerd's Eye View*, March 21, 2018, https://www.kitces.com/blog/healthcare-sharing-program-review-chm-medicare-lhs-samaritan-health-share-plans/.

21. Ibid.

22. Ibid.

23. See https://www.chministries.org/.

24. National Conference of State Legislatures, "Health Insurance Premiums and Increases," December 4, 2018, http://www.ncsl.org/research/health/health-insurance-premiums.aspx; see also https://www.ehealthinsurance.com/resources/guide/individual-health-insurance-cost.

25. See https://www.libertyhealthshare.org/.

26. See https://mpoweringbenefits.org/.

27. See https://bcsf.com/blog/blog/bcs-financial-announces-essentialcare-new-group
-hospital-indemnity-product/, https://www.uhone.com/insurance/supplemental/indemnity
-insurance/what-is-indemnity-insurance, and https://www.cigna.com/employers-brokers
/plans-services/hospital-care.

28. See https://hoorayhealthcare.com/.

29. See https://mytelemedicine.com/.

30. John C. Goodman, "Trump Throws a Life Belt to People Who Buy Their Own Health
Insurance," *Forbes*, August 6, 2018, https://www.forbes.com/sites/johngoodman/2018/08/06
/trump-throws-a-life-belt-to-people-who-buy-their-own-health-insurance/#2f8b3a605d90.

31. John H. Cochrane, "Health-Status Insurance: How Markets Can Provide Health
Security," CATO Institute, Policy Analysis No. 633, February 18, 2009.

32. John C. Goodman, "Alternatives to Obamacare," *Forbes*, January 30, 2019, https://
www.forbes.com/sites/johngoodman/2019/01/30/alternatives-to-obamacare/#721bcf5861ff.

33. See https://s3.amazonaws.com/public-inspection.federalregister.gov/2018-16568.pdf.

34. Quoted from and adapted from John C. Goodman, "Can Obamacare Be Fixed?,"
Psychology Today, March 26, 2014, https://www.psychologytoday.com/us/blog/curing-the
-healthcare-crisis/201403/can-obamacare-be-fixed.

35. Ibid.

36. Karen Branz, "After 4 Years and $1 Billion, the VA and DoD Abandon Plans for a
Fully Integrated HER," Dark Daily, June 14, 2013, https://www.darkdaily.com/after-4-years
-and-1-billion-the-va-and-dod-abandon-plans-for-a-fully-integrated-ehr-614/.

37. Grace Marie Turner, "Oregon's Failed Obamacare Exchange Is a Warning for Other
States," Forbes, March 31, 2015, https://www.forbes.com/sites/gracemarieturner/2015/03/31
/oregons-failed-obamacare-exchange-is-a-warning-for-other-states/#3d84d92225fd.

38. "New Analysis: Half of U.S. Households Eligible for a Tax Subsidy Under the Health
Law Would Owe a Repayment, While 45 Percent Would Receive a Refund," Kaiser Family
Foundation, March 24, 2015, https://www.kff.org/health-reform/press-release/new-analysis
-half-of-u-s-households-eligible-for-a-tax-subsidy-under-the-health-law-would-owe-a
-repayment-while-45-percent-would-receive-a-refund/.

39. Ibid.

40. See https://www.irs.gov/affordable-care-act/corrected-incorrect-or-voided-forms
-1095-a.

41. All quoted material in this section from John C. Goodman, "Can Obamacare Be
Fixed?," *Psychology Today*, March 26, 2014, https://www.psychologytoday.com/us/blog/curing
-the-healthcare-crisis/201403/can-obamacare-be-fixed.

42. Section previously published as John C. Goodman and Linda Gorman, "Limited-
Benefit Insurance," Brief Analysis No. 104, Goodman Institute, April 6, 2016; adapted from
John C. Goodman and Linda Gorman, "Limited-Benefit Insurance: An Alternative to
Obamacare," *Forbes*, September 2, 2015.

43. Sarah Kliff, "7.5 Million Americans Paid Obamacare Fine for Not Buying Health
Insurance," Vox Policy and Politics, July 21, 2015, https://www.vox.com/2015/7/21/9009859
/obamacare-penalty-individual-mandate.

44. John C. Goodman, "Limited-Benefit Insurance," Brief Analysis 104, Goodman Institute, April 6, 2016, http://www.goodmaninstitute.org/wp-content/uploads/2016/04/BA-104 .pdf.

45. On the importance of letting families choose health insurance that meet their needs, rather than the needs of politicians, see Regina E. Herzlinger, "Government Should Get Back to the Basics on Health Care," Manhattan Institute, August 19, 2009.

46. Section previously published as John C. Goodman, "Can Obamacare Be Fixed?," *Psychology Today*, March 26, 2014, https://www.psychologytoday.com/us/blog/curing-the -healthcare-crisis/201403/can-obamacare-be-fixed.

47. Benjamin D. Sommer and Sara Rosenbaum, "Issues In Health Reform: How Changes In Eligibility May Move Millions Back And Forth between Medicaid And Insurance Exchanges," *Health Affairs 2* (2011), 228-236, https://www.healthaffairs.org/doi/pdf/10.1377/hlthaff.2010 .1000.

48. "Roth Savings Accounts," Goodman Institute, May 6, 2016, http://www.goodman institute.org/wp-content/uploads/2016/05/Roth-Health-Savings-Accounts.pdf.

49. Section previously published as John C. Goodman, "Can Obamacare Be Fixed? Part II," *Psychology Today*, April 2, 2014, https://www.psychologytoday.com/us/blog/curing-the -healthcare-crisis/201404/can-obamacare-be-fixed-part-ii.

50. John C. Goodman, "The States Could Reform Obamacare If Only We Would Let Them," *Forbes*, May 29, 2018, https://www.forbes.com/sites/johngoodman/2018/05/29/the -states-could-reform-obamacare-if-only-we-would-let-them/#70b1a5a8522c.

Appendix to Chapter 14: How the Trump Administration Is Reforming the Health Care System

51. A version of this appendix originally appeared as John C. Goodman, "Trump's New Vision for Health Care," *Forbes*, January 14, 2019, https://www.forbes.com/sites/johngoodman /2019/01/14/trumps-new-vision-for-health-care/#7b36cc3b64cb.

52. U.S. Department of Health and Human Services, U.S. Department of The Treasury, and U.S. Department of Labor, "Reforming America's Healthcare System through Choice and Competition," December 3, 2018, https://www.hhs.gov/about/news/2018/12/03/reforming -americas-healthcare-system-through-choice-and-competition.html.

53. Marie Fishpaw and John C. Goodman, "A Health Plan for President Trump," *National Review*, August 1, 2019, https://www.nationalreview.com/2019/08/health-care-plan -transform-dysfunctional-system/.

54. An early advocate for allowing employees to use HRAs to purchase individually owned health insurance is Regina E. Herzlinger. See "The IRS Can Save American Health Care," *Wall Street Journal*, July 1, 2018, https://www.wsj.com/articles/the-irs-can-save-american -health-care-1530477705.

55. See https://atlas.md/wichita/our-fees/.

56. "Executive Order on Improving Price and Quality Transparency in American Healthcare to Put Patients First," The White House, June 24, 2019, https://www.whitehouse.gov

/presidential-actions/executive-order-improving-price-quality-transparency-american
-healthcare-put-patients-first/.

57. Joshua M. Liao and Arnol S. Navathe, "Medicare's Direct Provider Contracting: To Primary Care and Beyond," *Health Affairs*, June 28, 2019, https://www.healthaffairs.org/do/10.1377
/hblog20190626.900740/full/?utm_source=Newsletter&utm_medium=email&utm
_content=Another+Twist+In+Ongoing+ACA+Litigation%3B+Medicare+s+Direct+Provider
+Contracting%3B+Book+Reviews&utm_campaign=HAT+6-28-19.

58. Niran Al-Agba, "CMS Quietly Launches an Offensive against Direct Primary Care," *The Health Care Blog*, February 19, 2018, https://thehealthcareblog.com/blog/2018/02/19
/cms-quietly-launches-an-offensive-against-direct-primary-care/.

59. John C. Goodman, "Lower Cost, Higher Quality Health Care Is Right at Our Fingertips," *Forbes*, July 23, 2018.

60. Ibid.

61. Centers for Medicare and Medicaid Services, "CMS Proposes Historic Changes to Modernize Medicare and Restore the Doctor-Patient Relationship," July 12, 2018, https://www
.cms.gov/newsroom/press-releases/cms-proposes-historic-changes-modernize-medicare-and
-restore-doctor-patient-relationship.

62. John C. Goodman, "Obamacare Can Be Worse Than Medicaid," *Wall Street Journal,* June 26, 2018, https://www.wsj.com/articles/obamacare-can-be-worse-than-medicaid
-1530052891.

63. Katie Keith, "New 1332 Resources; Rhode Island 1332 Waiver Deemed Complete," *Health Affairs*, July 18, 2019, https://www.healthaffairs.org/do/10.1377/hblog20190718.732965
/full/?utm_source=Newsletter&utm_medium=email&utm_content=Why+Narrative
+Matters+Author+Michael+Ogg+Needed+To+Leave+PACE%3B+Section+1332+Waivers%
3B+Growth+Of+Public+Coverage+Among+Working+Families+In+The+Private+Sector&
utm_campaign=HAT.

64. See Regina E. Herzlinger, Market-Driven Health Care: Who Wins, Who Loses in the Transformation of America's Largest Service Industry (Reading, MA: Basic Books, 1996); and Consumer-Driven Health Care: Implications for Providers, Payers, and Policymakers, (San Francisco: Jossey-Bass, 2004).

65. Doug Badger and Edmund F. Haislmaier, "State Innovation: The Key to Affordable Health Care Coverage Choices," *Heritage Foundation*, Backgrounder No. 3354, September 27, 2018.

66. Anna Gorman, "With Chronic Illness, You Are Your Own Best Friend," *Kaiser Health News*, September 7, 2016, https://khn.org/news/with-chronic-illness-you-are-your-own
-best-friend/?utm_campaign=KHN%3A+First+Edition&utm_source=hs_email&utm
_medium=email&utm_content=33922464&_hsenc=p2ANqtz-9etqh2n2nyNS233OwEKy
_zDkHhnijsiNflvfu9IUcW-VbiCpRdkO5nTEy7qGQXuER_8XaKmFreOYjxupFl5DCdg
VEZaw&_hsmi=33922464.

67. John C. Goodman, "Patient Power for Chronic Illness," *Health Affairs*, February 12, 2009, https://www.healthaffairs.org/do/10.1377/hblog20090212.000502/full/.

68. Stephanie Armour, "Trump Administration Moves to Shift Patients' Chronic Illness Costs to Insurers," *Wall Street Journal*, July 17, 2019, https://www.wsj.com/articles/patients
-with-high-deductible-health-plans-to-get-greater-flexibility-11563372139.

Chapter 15: Opting Out of Unemployment Insurance

1. These would probably be nonrecourse loans, so a worker who retires with a deficit account would not be obligated to repay it.

2. Communication from Patricio Eskenazi, University of Chicago graduate student, March 2, 2005.

Chapter 16: Combatting the Coronavirus

1. Portions of this brief analysis can be found at John C. Goodman (with Alfredo Ortiz), "Response to Coronavirus Reflects Trump's Plan to Radically Reform Health Care," *Forbes*, March 17, 2020, https://www.forbes.com/sites/johngoodman/2020/03/17/response-to -coronavirus-reflects-trumps-plan-to-radically-reform-health-care/#43faee311658, and John C. Goodman, "How Would Free Market Health Care Respond to the Coronavirus?," *Forbes*, March 23, 2020, https://www.forbes.com/sites/johngoodman/2020/03/23/how-would-free -market-health-care-respond-to-the-coronavirus/#793b13ef61ff.

2. Paul Blow, "Millions of Chinese, Cooped Up and Anxious, Turn to Online Doctors," *Economist,* March 5, 2020, https://www.economist.com/business/2020/03/05/millions-of -chinese-cooped-up-and-anxious-turn-to-online-doctors.

3. Rajiv Leventhal, "White House: Private Insurers Agree to Cover Coronavirus Testing, Telemedicine Services," Healthcare Innovation, March 5, 2020, https://www.hcinnovation group.com/population-health-management/telehealth/article/21129098/white-house -private-insurers-agree-to-cover-coronavirus-testing-telemedicine-services.

4. John C. Goodman, "Lower Cost, Higher Quality Health Care Is Right at Our Fingertips," *Forbes*, July 23, 2018, https://www.forbes.com/sites/johngoodman/2018/07/23/lower -cost-higher-quality-health-care-is-right-at-our-fingertips/#11dd40f343bb.

5. John C. Goodman and Lawrence J. Wedekind, "How the Trump Administration Is Reforming Medicare," *Health Affairs*, May 3, 2019, https://www.healthaffairs.org/do/10.1377 /hblog20190501.529581/full/.

6. Centers for Medicare and Medicaid Services, "CMS Proposes Historic Changes to Modernize Medicare and Restore the Doctor-Patient Relationship," Press Release, July 12, 2018, https://www.cms.gov/newsroom/press-releases/cms-proposes-historic-changes-modernize -medicare-and-restore-doctor-patient-relationship.

7. Chad Savage, "Trump's New Executive Order: Unleashing HSAs for Direct Primary Care," *Townhall*, August 3, 2019, https://townhall.com/columnists/chadsavage/2019/08/03 /trumps-new-executive-order-unleashing-hsas-for-direct-primary-care-n2551034/.

8. Trace Mitchell and Adam Thierer, "Licensing Restrictions for Health Care Workers Need to Be Flexible to Fight Coronavirus," *Dallas Morning News*, March 23, 2020, https://www .dallasnews.com/opinion/commentary/2020/03/23/licensing-restrictions-for-healthcare -workers-need-to-flexible-to-fight-coronavirus/.

9. John C. Goodman, "Why Not Try Free Market Health Care?," *Forbes*, October 17, 2019, https://www.forbes.com/sites/johngoodman/2019/10/17/why-not-try-free-market -health-care/#7c2301195358.

10. See https://atlas.md/wichita/.

11. Krystle Thornton, "How DPC Doctors Could Start Seeing Medicare Patients," Elation Health, July 24, 2019, https://www.elationhealth.com/direct-care-blog/dpc-seeing -medicare/.

12. Chad Savage, "Trump's New Executive Order: Unleashing HSAs for Direct Primary Care," *Townhall*, August 3, 2019, https://townhall.com/columnists/chadsavage/2019/08/03 /trumps-new-executive-order-unleashing-hsas-for-direct-primary-care-n2551034/.

13. Larry Buchanan, K.K. Rebecca Lai, and Allison McCann, "U.S. Lags in Coronavirus Testing After Slow Response to Outbreak," *New York Times*, March 17, 2020, https:// www.nytimes.com/interactive/2020/03/17/us/coronavirus-testing-data.html?action=click &module=Top%20Stories&pgtype=Homepage.

14. Alec Stapp, "Timeline: The Regulations—and Regulators—That Delayed Coronavirus Testing," *The Dispatch*, March 20, 2020.

15. See https://globalbiodefense.com/tag/emergency-use-authorization/.

16. Robert P. Baird, "What Went Wrong With Coronavirus Testing in the U.S.," *New Yorker*, March 16, 2020, https://www.newyorker.com/news/news-desk/what-went-wrong -with-coronavirus-testing-in-the-us.

17. Jeffrey A. Singer, "Temporarily Unshackled Private Sector Responds to Demand for More Coronavirus Tests," Cato Institute, March 20, 2020.

18. "Biomerica Begins Shipping Samples of 10-Minute Test for COVID-19 Virus Exposure," Biomerica, http://www.biomerica.com/news/biomericacovid19.pdf.

19. See https://www.alivecor.com/, https://www.sonoque.com/s/c3-portable-ultrasound -machine/, and https://xuxastore.com/products/3-in-1-waterproof-usb-endoscope-camera -for-android-mac-pc-5m.

20. Josh Nathan-Kazis, "Aetna Will Waive Copays and Deductibles for Covid-19 Hospitalizations," *Barron's*, March 25, 2020, https://www.barrons.com/articles/aetna-copays -deductibles-covid-19-hospitalizations-patients-51585143836.

21. Bertha Coombs and William Feuer, "The Coronavirus Test Will Be Covered by Medicare, Medicaid, and Private Insurance, Pence Says," CNBC, March 4, 2020, https://www .cnbc.com/2020/03/04/pence-announces-coronavirus-test-will-be-covered-by-medicaid -medicare.html.

22. "2019 Year-End Devenir Research Report," Devenir Research, March 3, 2020, https://www.devenir.com/research/2019-year-end-devenir-hsa-research-report.

23. "IRS: High-Deductible Health Plans Can Cover Coronavirus Costs," Internal Revenue Service, March 11, 2020.

24. Farhad Manjoo, "How the World's Richest Country Ran Out of a 75-Cent Face Mask," *New York Times*, March 25, 2020, https://www.nytimes.com/2020/03/25/opinion /coronavirus-face-mask.html.

25. Nicholas Kulish, Sarah Kliff, and Jessica Silver-Greenberg, "The U.S. Tried to Build a New Fleet of Ventilators. The Mission Failed.," *New York Times*, March 29, 2020, https:// www.nytimes.com/2020/03/29/business/coronavirus-us-ventilator-shortage.html.

26. Jeanne Whalen, "Half a Million N95 Masks Are On Their Way to New York and Seattle, Manufacturer Says," *Washington Post*, March 23, 2020.

27. Andrew Jacobs, Neal E. Boudette, Matt Richtel, and Nicholas Kulish, "Amid Desperate Need for Ventilators, Calls Grow for Federal Intervention," New York Times, March 25, 2020, https://www.nytimes.com/2020/03/25/health/ventilators-coronavirus.html.

28. William McGurn, "Business Makes War on Coronavirus," *Wall Street Journal*, March 23, 2020, https://www.wsj.com/articles/business-makes-war-on-coronavirus-11585004754.

29. Andrew Jacobs, Neal E. Boudette, Matt Richtel, and Nicholas Kulish, "Amid Desperate Need for Ventilators, Calls Grow for Federal Intervention," New York Times, March 25, 2020, https://www.nytimes.com/2020/03/25/health/ventilators-coronavirus.html.

30. Rebecca Ballhaus and Andrew Restuccia, "FEMA Pulls Back from Defense Production Act amid Mixed Signals," *Wall Street Journal*, March 24, 2020, https://www.wsj.com/articles/administration-to-use-defense-production-act-for-first-time-in-coronavirus-pandemic-11585058618.

31. Mark Hallum, "Cuomo Says 'So What' to 'Nationalization' Argument Against Defense Production Act," AMNY, March 2020, https://www.amny.com/coronavirus/cuomo-says-so-what-to-nationalization-argument-against-defense-production-act/.

32. John H. Colchrane, "Flatten the Coronavirus Curve at a Lower Cost," *Wall Street Journal*, March 24, 2020, https://www.wsj.com/articles/flatten-the-coronavirus-curve-at-a-lower-cost-11585067354.

33. Jennifer Vazquez, "New York Starts New Experimental Drug Therapies to Treat COVID-19: Here's What We Know," NBC New York, March 24, 2020, https://www.nbcnewyork.com/news/coronavirus/new-york-starts-new-experimental-drug-therapies-to-treat-covid-19-heres-what-we-know/2341931/.

34. "Chloroquine, an Old Malaria Drug, May Help Treat Coronavirus, Doctors Say," MSN, March 19, 2020, https://www.msn.com/en-us/health/medical/chloroquine-an-old-malaria-drug-may-help-treat-coronavirus-doctors-say/ar-BB110QBP?ocid=spartanntp.

35. Agency for Healthcare Research and Quality, "Off-Label Drugs: What You Need to Know," https://www.ahrq.gov/patients-consumers/patient-involvement/off-label-drug-usage.html; and Katrina Furey, MD, and Kirsten Wilkins, MD, "Prescribing 'Off-Label': What Should a Physician Disclose?," *AMA Journal of Ethics*, June 2016, https://journalofethics.ama-assn.org/article/prescribing-label-what-should-physician-disclose/2016-06.

36. Jeffrey A. Singer, "Coronavirus, Chloroquine, and 'Off-Label' Use," CATO Institute, March 23, 2020.

37. Ellen Gabler, "States Say Some Doctors Stockpile Trial Coronavirus Drugs, for Themselves," *New York Times*, March 24, 2020, https://www.nytimes.com/2020/03/24/business/doctors-buying-coronavirus-drugs.html.

38. Dan Diamond, "FDA Issues Emergency Authorization of Anti-Malaria Drug for Coronavirus Care," *Politico*, March 29, 2020, https://www.politico.com/news/2020/03/29/fda-emergency-authorization-anti-malaria-drug-155095.

39. "HHS Accepts Donations of Medicine to Strategic National Stockpile as Possible Treatments for COVID-19 Patients," U.S. Department of Health and Human Services press release, March 29, 2020, https://www.hhs.gov/about/news/2020/03/29/hhs-accepts-donations-of-medicine-to-strategic-national-stockpile-as-possible-treatments-for-covid-19-patients.html.

40. Noah Weiland and Maggie Haberman, "Oracle Providing White House with Software to Study Unproven Coronavirus Drugs," *New York Times*, March 24, 2020, https://www.nytimes.com/2020/03/24/us/politics/trump-oracle-coronavirus-chloroquine.html.

41. Marie Fishpaw and John C. Goodman, "A Health Plan for President Trump," Goodman Institute, Brief Analysis No. 130, August 15, 2019, http://www.goodmaninstitute.org/wp-content/uploads/2019/10/BA-130-A-Health-Plan-for-President-Trump-web-version.pdf.

Conclusion: Life under a Reformed System

1. John C. Goodman, "How Can We Keep from Going Broke," *Townhall*, March 17, 2012, https://townhall.com/columnists/johncgoodman/2012/03/17/how-we-can-keep-from-going-broke-n1209757.

2. Ibid.

3. Section previously published in large part as John C. Goodman, "A Framework for Medicare Reform," National Center for Policy Analysis, Policy Report No. 315, September 2008, http://www.ncpathinktank.org/pdfs/st315.pdf.

4. For a more thorough examination of modeling of Medicare reform, see John C. Goodman, "A Framework for Medicare Reform," National Center for Policy Analysis, Policy Report No. 315, September 2008, http://www.ncpathinktank.org/pdfs/st315.pdf.

5. Section previously published in large part as John C. Goodman, "A Framework for Medicare Reform," National Center for Policy Analysis, Policy Report No. 315, September 2008, http://www.ncpathinktank.org/pdfs/st315.pdf.

Appendix 1: Ten Things You Need to Know about Medicare for All

1. A version of this section originally appeared at https://www.forbes.com/sites/johngoodman/2018/09/07/what-you-need-to-know-about-medicare-for-all-part-i/#52e31c8773d3 and at https://www.forbes.com/sites/johngoodman/2018/09/11/what-you-need-to-know-about-medicare-for-all-part-ii/#224784f6dae1.

2. Jonathan Michels, Roberta Barnes, and Sydney Russell Leed, "Is This the Year the AMA Finally Joins the Single-Payer Movement?," *STAT*, June 8, 2018, https://www.statnews.com/2018/06/08/american-medical-association-single-payer/.

3. Megan Keller, "Seventy Percent of Americans Support 'Medicare for All' in New Poll," *The Hill*, August 23, 2018.

4. Peter J. Huckfeldt et al., "Less Intense Postacute Care, Better Outcomes for Enrollees in Medicare Advantage Than Those in Fee-For-Service," *Health Affairs* 36, no. 1 (2017), 91–100.

5. John C. Goodman, "Is Public Policy Changing the Practice of Medicine?," *Health Affairs*, May 21, 2014, https://www.healthaffairs.org/do/10.1377/hblog20140521.039122/full/.

6. John C. Goodman, "Standing between You and All the Benefits of Telemedicine: The AMA and the Federal Government." Forbes, Jul 9, 2015, https://www.forbes.com/sites/johngoodman/2015/07/09/standing-between-you-and-all-the-benefits-of-telemedicine-the-ama-and-the-federal-government/#63637a237d3f.

7. John C. Goodman, "What Does Uber Medicine Look Like?" *Forbes*, July 24, 2015, http://www.forbes.com/sites/johngoodman/2015/07/24/what-does-uber-medicine-look-like/.

8. John C. Goodman, "Everyone Should Have a Concierge Doctor," *Forbes*, August 28, 2014, https://www.forbes.com/sites/johngoodman/2014/08/28/everyone-should-have-a-concierge-doctor/#14a399246323.

9. Larry Wedekind, "Power to the Physicians, Not the Hospitals," *NCPA Health Policy Blog*, June 6, 2012, http://healthblog.ncpathinktank.org/power-to-the-physicians-not-the-hospitals/#sthash.SM8zyd1V.dpbs.

10. Ibid.

11. David Muhlestein et al., "Recent Progress in the Value Journey: Growth of ACOs and Value-Based Payment Models in 2018," *Health Affairs*, August 14, 2018, https://www.healthaffairs.org/do/10.1377/hblog20180810.481968/full/.

12. John C. Goodman, "Is Public Policy Changing the Practice of Medicine?" *Health Affairs*, May 21, 2014, http://healthaffairs.org/blog/2014/05/21/is-public-policy-changing-the-practice-of-medicine; James C. Capretta, "Replacing Medicare ACOs with a Better Integrated Care Option," Mercatus Center, May 11, 2017, https://www.mercatus.org/publications/healthcare/replacing-medicare-acos-better-integrated-care-option; and "Section 1115 Demonstration Monitoring and Evaluation Support," *L&M Policy Research* Case Studies, https://www.lmpolicyresearch.com/index.php/experience/case-studies.

13. John C. Goodman, "Obamacare Can Be Worse Than Medicaid," *Wall Street Journal*, June 26, 2018, https://www.wsj.com/articles/obamacare-can-be-worse-than-medicaid-1530052891.

14. Miguel Perez, "UT Southwestern Tops Ranking of Published Research among Academic Medical Centers," *Dallas Morning News*, June 8, 2018, https://www.dallasnews.com/news/2018/06/08/ut-southwestern-tops-ranking-of-published-research-among-academic-medical-centers/.

15. John C. Goodman, "Can the Market Really Work in Health Care?," *Forbes*, May 22, 2018, https://www.forbes.com/sites/johngoodman/2018/05/22/can-the-market-really-work-in-health-care/#51690042787d.

16. Charles Blahous, "The Costs of a National Single-Payer Health Care System," Mercatus Center, George Mason University, July 30, 2018, https://www.mercatus.org/publications/government-spending/costs-national-single-payer-healthcare-system?utm_source=bridge&utm_medium=bridgepost&utm_campaign=medicareforall.

17. Henry J. Aaron, "The impossible (pipe) dream—single-payer health reform," Brookings, January 26, 2016, https://www.brookings.edu/opinions/the-impossible-pipe-dream-single-payer-health-reform/.

18. John C. Goodman, "Was Obamacare Produced by Crony Capitalism?," *Forbes*, August 17, 2015, https://www.forbes.com/sites/johngoodman/2015/08/17/was-obamacare-produce-by-crony-capitalism/#2b39428820e8.

19. Heather Landi, "Physician Survey: EHRs Increase Practice Costs, Reduce Productivity," Healthcare Innovation, October 3, 2016, https://www.hcinnovationgroup.com/policy-value-based-care/news/13027535/physician-survey-ehrs-increase-practice-costs-reduce-productivity; Saurabh Rahurkar, Joshua R. Vest, and Nir Menachemi, "Despite the

Spread of Health Information Exchange, There Is Little Evidence of Its Impact on Cost, Use, and Quality of Care," *Health Affairs* 34, no. 3 (March 2015), https://www.healthaffairs.org/doi/pdf/10.1377/hlthaff.2014.0729; James Fallows, "Electronic Medical Records: A Way to Jack Up Billings, Put Patients in Control, or Both?," *The Atlantic*, March 30, 2014, https://www.theatlantic.com/technology/archive/2014/03/electronic-medical-records-a-way-to-jack-up-billings-put-patients-in-control-or-both/359880/.

20. Mark Litow et al., "Rhetoric vs. Reality: Comparing Public and Private Administrative Costs," Mark Litow and the Technical Committee The Council for Affordable Health Insurance, March 1994.

21. Benjamin Zyher, "Comparing Public and Private Health Insurance: Would a Single-Payer System Save Enough to Cover the Uninsured?," Manhattan Institute, October 1, 2007, https://www.manhattan-institute.org/html/comparing-public-and-private-health-insurance-would-single-payer-system-save-enough-cover.

22. Chris Conover, "The Path to Responsible National Health Insurance Part 1: BernieCare Is Irresponsibility on Steroids," *Forbes*, July 30, 2019, https://www.forbes.com/sites/theapothecary/2019/07/30/the-path-to-responsible-national-health-insurance-part-1-berniecare-is-irresponsibility-on-steroids/#4a0c0f442b96.

23. Chris Conover, "The #1 Reason Bernie Sanders' Medicare-for-All Single-Payer Plan Is a Singularly Bad Idea," *Forbes*, September 28, 2017, https://www.forbes.com/sites/theapothecary/2017/09/28/the-1-reason-bernie-sanders-medicare-for-all-single-payer-plan-is-a-singularly-bad-idea/#2e35c4a15502.

24. Chris Conover, "The #2 Reason Bernie Sanders' Medicare-for-All Single-Payer Plan Is a Singularly Bad Idea," *Forbes*, September 30, 2017, https://www.forbes.com/sites/theapothecary/2017/09/30/the-2-reason-bernie-sanders-medicare-for-all-single-payer-plan-is-a-singularly-bad-idea/#40b39f3c29bb.

25. Chris Conover, "The #4 Reason Bernie Sanders' Medicare-for-All Single-Payer Plan Is a Singularly Bad Idea," *Forbes*, October 6, 2017, https://www.forbes.com/sites/theapothecary/2017/10/06/the-4-reason-bernie-sanders-medicare-for-all-single-payer-plan-is-a-singularly-bad-idea/#632dce81118f.

26. Ibid.

27. John C. Goodman, "Single-Payer Health Insurance: Why Bernie Sanders Just Doesn't Get It," *Forbes*, April 20, 2016, https://www.forbes.com/sites/johngoodman/2015/04/20/single-payer-health-insurance-why-bernie-sanders-just-doesnt-get-it/#47697a51cf13.

28. Andrew J. Rettenmaier and Thomas R. Saving, "Medicare Trustees Report 2010 and 2009: What a Difference a Year Makes," National Center for Policy Analysis, Policy Report No. 330, October 2010, http://www.ncpathinktank.org/pdfs/st330.pdf.

29. Christian Hagist and Laurence J. Kotlikoff, "Health Care Spending: What the Future Will Look Like," National Center for Policy Analysis, Policy Report No. 286, June 2006, http://www.ncpathinktank.org/pdfs/st286.pdf.

30. John Goodman, "What's Wrong with the Health Care Media?" *NCPA Health Policy Blog*, July 18, 2012, http://healthblog.ncpathinktank.org/what's-wrong-with-the-health-care-media/#sthash.WzzEliTh.c3guB05f.dpbs.

31. John C. Goodman, "The Trillion Dollar Surprise in the Budget Deal," *Forbes*, February 22, 2018, https://www.forbes.com/sites/johngoodman/2018/02/22/the-trillion-dollar-surprise-in-the-budget-deal/#5b159a5a8a6d.

32. *2018 Annual Report of the Boards of Trustees of the Federal Hospital Insurance and Federal Supplementary Medical Insurance Trust Funds*, Centers for Medicare and Medicaid Services, https://www.cms.gov/Research-Statistics-Data-and-Systems/Statistics-Trends-and-Reports/ReportsTrustFunds/Downloads/TR2018.pdf.

33. Joseph P. Newhouse, "Assessing Health Reform's Impact on Four Key Groups of Americans," *Health Affairs* 29, no. 9 (2010): 1714–1724.

Appendix 2: What Socialized Medicine Looks Like

1. A version of this section originally appeared as https://www.forbes.com/sites/john goodman/2019/03/05/what-socialized-medicine-looks-like/#4b31a809625b; Sarah Kliff, "Medicare-for-All: Rep. Pramila Jayapal's New Bill, Explained," *Vox*, February 26, 2019, https://www.vox.com/policy-and-politics/2019/2/26/18239630/medicare-for-all-pramila-jayapal -bill.

2. Carmen Chai, "Canada Has Some of the Longest Wait Times to See Doctors, Specialists: Report," *Global News*, February 16, 2017, https://globalnews.ca/news/3251833/canada -has-some-of-the-longest-wait-times-to-see-doctors-specialists-report/.

3. Astrid Guttman et al., "Association between Waiting Times and Short-Term Mortality and Hospital Admission after Departure from Emergency Department: Population-Based Cohort Study from Ontario, Canada," *British Medical Journal*, 2011; 342:d2983.

4. See "'Medicare for All' Proponents Should heed Canada's Health Care Woes," Fraser Institute, (Originally published in the *Wall Street Journal*, April 18, 2019), https://www.fraser institute.org/article/medicare-for-all-proponents-should-heed-canadas-health-care-woes.

5. June O'Neill and David O'Neill, "Health Status, Health Care and Inequality: Canada vs. the U.S.," National Bureau of Economic Research, Working Paper 13429, September 2007, https://www.nber.org/papers/w13429.

6. Henry Aaron, William Schwartz, and Melissa B. Cox, *Can We Say No? The Challenge of Rationing Health Care* (Washington, D.C. Brookings Institution Press: November 21, 2005).

7. Jeremy Sussman and Rebecca J. Beyth, "Choosing Wisely: Five Things Physicians and Patients Should Question," *Journal of General Internal Medicine*, https://www.sgim.org /web-only/choosing-wisely.

8. Bacchus Barua, "Waiting Your Turn: Wait Times for Health Care in Canada, 2017 Report," Fraser Institute, December 7, 2017, https://www.fraserinstitute.org/studies/waiting -your-turn-wait-times-for-health-care-in-canada-2017.

9. Robert J. Blendon et al., "Confronting Competing Demands to Improve Quality: A Five-Country Hospital Survey," *Health Affairs* 23, no. 3 (May/June 2004): 119–135, https://www.healthaffairs.org/doi/pdf/10.1377/hlthaff.23.3.119.

10. *4 Economic Models Ltd. The British Health Care System* (Chicago: American Medical Association, 1976).

11. Peter Townsend and Nick Davidson, *Inequalities in Health: The Black Report* (Harmondsworth, United Kingdom: Penguin 1982).

12. George Davey Smith, Jeremy N. Morris, and Mary Shaw, "The Independent Inquiry into Inequalities in Health," *British Medical Journal* 317, no. 7171 (November 28, 1998), 1465–1466.

13. David A. Alter et al., "Effects of Socioeconomic Status on Access to Invasive Cardiac Procedures and on Mortality after Acute Myocardial Infarction," *New England Journal of Medicine* 341, no. 18 (October 1999): 1359–1367.

14. Sheryl Dunlop, Peter C. Coyte, and Warren McIsaac, "Socio-Economic Status and the Utilisation of Physicians' Services: Results from the Canadian National Population Health Survey," *Social Science and Medicine* 1, no. 1 (July 5, 2000): 123–133.

15. June O'Neill and David O'Neill, "Health Status, Health Care and Inequality: Canada vs. the U.S.", National Bureau of Economic Research, Working paper 13429 2007.

16. John C. Goodman, "Employers Could Slash Their Health Costs Overnight. So, Why Don't They?," *Forbes*, October 2, 2018, https://www.forbes.com/sites/johngoodman/2018/10/02/employers-could-slash-their-health-costs-overnight-so-why-dont-they/#2975bd8c5421.

17. For more on these and other issues, interested readers may want to consult my congressional testimony, delivered with Linda Gorman, Devon Herrick, and Robert Sade. *See* "Heath Care Reform: Do Other Countries Have the Answers? http://www.ncpathinktank.org/pdfs/sp_Do_Other_Countries_Have_the_Answers.pdf

Index

401(k) system, 28, 31, 34, 52, 66, 91, 179
403(b) system, 28

Aaron, Henry, 304
Abbott Laboratories, 281
accidental death benefits, 36
Accountable Care Organizations (ACOs),
    74, 194, 213, 214–18, 295; allowing
    telemedicine charges, 279; incentives
    for quality improvement, 216; popu-
    larity of, 217–18
adjustment of the reduction factor (ARF),
    64
Affordable Care Act (Obamacare): alterna-
    tives to, 39, 43, 255–61, 287; analysis of
    outcomes, 73, 74; community rating,
    40–41, 269; cost of, 18, 57; difficulty
    in enrolling, 144–45; discouraging
    private insurance, 124; disregard for
    individual and family needs, 39–40;
    effect on Medicaid spending, 19–21;
    effects on individuals of different
    ages, 87; encouraging employers to
    hire part-time rather than full-time
    workers, 17; forecasting health care
    spending, 19; and health sharing orga-
    nizations, 256–57; high deductibles
    under, 39, 128, 135, 139, 143, 144, 152–
    53, 155, 192, 203, 205, 258, 260, 266,
    267, 268, 272, 282, 293, 299; how the
    Trump administration is changing,

127–29; and individual insurance, 135;
    inherent unfairness of, 139–40; man-
    dated coverage, 38–39, 46, 138–39, 148,
    150, 152; and Medicare cuts, 21–22,
    189; negative results of, 132, 138–51;
    opportunities for individual choice,
    38–41; penalty for being uninsured,
    123, 248, 266; persisting problems
    in Medicare for all, 299–300; pilot
    programs and demonstration projects,
    194; possible results if court strikes
    down, 152–55; proposals for reform,
    38, 129, 261–69; as social insurance,
    15, 16, 89; unfunded liabilities of, 17,
    288; waivers to, 128. *See also* health
    insurance exchanges
Agomuoh, Obioma, 71
Altman, Daniel, 274
Ambulatory Surgery Center Association,
    219
American Hospital Association, 219
American Medical Association (AMA),
    193, 293
annuities market, 206, 342n9
ARF (adjustment of the reduction factor),
    64
assisted living facilities, 96–98, 289. *See
    also* nursing homes
at-home care, 207, 337n63
AtlasMD, 271, 280
Auerbach, Alan J., 91

automobile insurance, 14, 131
Azar, Alex, 281

baby boomers, 13, 31, 55, 58
Bakken, Earl, 2
Barro, Robert, 162, 166
benefits, 264; accidental death, 36; dental,
    215; eye care, 215; hearing aid, 215;
    lump sum, 25–26, 29; Medicaid,
    13; Medicare, 13, 28, 61–62, 72–74,
    86–88; nontaxed, 123–24; regressive,
    28, 60–63; Social Security, 13, 25,
    83–95; transportation, 215. *See also*
    survivorship benefits
Bevan, Aneurin, 305
Bezos, Jeff, 23, 29
Biggs, Andrew, 94
Biomerica, 281
Black Death, 168
Blahous, Charles, 296
Blase, Brian, 125, 166
Blue Cross, 193, 258, 293
Blue Cross of Texas, 134–35
bond market, 26
Bowles-Simpson deficit reform, 310n10
Britain. *See* United Kingdom
Buck v. Bell, 170
Buffett, Warren, 23, 29
Bulgaria, 51
bundling of services, 198
Bureau of Labor Statistics (BLS), 157
Burns, Scott, 82
Bush, George W., 7, 83, 175, 186

Canada: health care system, 120, 121, 195,
    303–4; inequality in health care,
    305–6; rationing by waiting, 305
cancer, 39, 135, 143, 144, 205, 253, 269, 296,
    304, 305
capitation, 215, 218
CARES Act, 165–66
cash and counseling experiments, 196, 210
cash flow deficits, 58–60

Cassidy, Bill, 129
casualty insurance, 141
cell phones. *See* smartphone apps
Centene, 135, 143
Centers for Disease Control and Preven-
    tion (CDC), 2, 172, 173; testing for
    COVID-19, 281
Centers for Medicare and Medicaid Ser-
    vices (CMS), 19, 98, 146, 213, 271;
    efforts to expand telemedicine, 279;
    payments to ACOs, 216
Chadwick, Edwin, 169
Child Care Assistance, 89
Child Tax Credit, 89, 242
Children's Health Insurance Program
    (CHIP), 95, 124–25, 242, 245
Chile: annuities market, 182–83; disability
    insurance, 108, 225–31; personal retire-
    ment accounts, 179–81; social security
    system, 34; survivor benefits, 223–24;
    unemployment insurance, 46, 274–75
chloroquine, 285–86
Christian health sharing ministries,
    256–57
Christian Healthcare Ministries (CHM),
    256
chronic illness, 211, 272
Churchill, Winston, 170
Cigna, 258, 293
Clinton, William Jefferson "Bill," 83
Close, Carl P., 184
Coburn, Tom, 110
Cochrane, John, 285
communicable diseases, 167–74
communications technology, 213
community health centers, 95
concierge medicine, 118, 198, 271
Conerly, William, 157
Congressional Budget Office (CBO), 13, 18,
    19, 108, 123, 124, 151, 294, 304
Conover, Chris, 298
continuity of care, 126, 283
coordinated care, 216, 294

copays, 68, 139, 144, 219, 221, 232, 259; higher, 38; lower, 244; market determination of, 198; nominal, 141; services with no copay, 150, 196, 259; waiving, 174, 175, 282

coronavirus pandemic, 1–2, 117–18, 157, 172–74, 271; combatting the coronavirus, 277–86; COVID-19 tests, 278, 280–81; effect on telemedicine, 214; in-home treatment, 282; off-label treatments, 285; problems created by government regulation, 172–73; waiving copayments and deductibles for, 174, 175, 282

COVID-19. *See* coronavirus pandemic

Cullen, Julie, 162

Cuomo, Andrew, 285

custodial care, 207, 337n63

Cutler, David, 124, 245

deductibles: high, 39, 128, 135, 139, 143, 144, 152–53, 155, 192, 203, 205, 258, 260, 266, 267, 268, 272, 282, 293, 299; related to the health incident, 256; waiving, 174, 175, 282

Defense Production Act, 285

dental benefits, 215

Department of Health and Human Services (HHS), 172, 212, 281, 286

deregulation: of health care, 284, 286; of paperwork, 220

diabetes, 39, 144, 172, 196, 197, 214, 257, 272, 283

direct primary care, 118, 198, 271, 280

disability and survivors' (D&S) insurance, 223. *See also* disability insurance; survivorship benefits

disability insurance, 5, 15, 16, 17, 31, 35, 43, 45, 85, 131; benefits for women, 230; in Chile, 34, 108, 225–31; effect on labor market, 114–15; eligibility for, 227, 342n12; employer-provided, 115–16; financing, 226–27; as fringe benefit,

116; incentives to game the system, 114; individual purchase of, 115–16; integrating with Medicare reforms, 289–90; integration with workers' compensation, 233; for intellectual disability, 104; for mental disorders, 104–5; minimum pension guarantee, 227; for musculoskeletal diseases, 105–6; newly classified disabled in 1999, 229; opting out of, 225–31; private alternatives to, 45–46, 226, 287; responsibility for fees, 230; Social Security, 103–10; transition to private system, 231; trust fund balances, 59–60; for veterans, 105, 114–15; wage replacement rates, 228

"do no harm" policy, 253

doc-in-the-box clinics, 197

Doctors Making Housecalls, 202–3

Domenici, Pete, 310n10

Dorman, Jeffrey, 165

dual eligibles, 48

Duggan, Mark, 114

dumpers, 145

early retirement program, 77, 237

Earned Income Tax Credit, 89

earnings penalty, 64–65

earnings test, 64

elder law, 99

elderly. *See* retirees

electronic medical records, 69–70, 298

Eli Lilly, 281

emergency care clinics, 197

Emergency Use Authorization (EUA) program, 281, 286

Employee Retirement Income Security Act (ERISA), 233

employers: insurance provided by, 79, 125–28, 130, 245–46; obligation to provide insurance, 110, 112; overpaying for insurance, 133–34; providing long-term care insurance, 208

end-of-life care, 39, 55–56
Energy Assistance, 89
Engen, Eric, 162
enrollment periods, 79, 144, 145, 252
entitlement programs, 25, 89; creating new, 19; for the elderly, 5–6, 7, 27, 45, 56, 59, 93, 97, 177, 206; eligibility for 88, 90; federal, 89; need for reform, 24–25, 27, 30, 97; obligations and costs of, 14, 56. *See also* Medicaid; Medicare; Social Security
entrepreneurs, 151; in the health care sector, 1; in independent doctor associations, 74; political, 50
environmental concerns, 169–70
epidemics, 168; non-communicable, 172. *See also* coronavirus pandemic
Epstein, Richard, 171
equity accounts, 181, 186–87
eugenics, 170
Europe: entitlement spending in, 14; job security in, 157
externalities, 170, 231
eye care benefits, 215

families: as caregivers, 6; as insurance against risk, 5–6
Federal Asset Sale and Transfer Act, 185
Federal Employee Health Benefits Program, 48
Federal Insurance Contributions Act (FICA), 75
federal risk pools, 145–46
Federal Unemployment Tax Act, 158
fee-for-service, 195, 217, 218, 271, 295
Feldstein, Martin, 274
Finkelstein, Amy, 72, 73
fire and casualty insurance, 131
Fishpaw, Marie, 270
fixed-sum tax credits, 240–41, 243–44, 247, 265
Flexible Savings Accounts (FSAs), 130
Flexible Spending Account (FSA), 207, 247

Food and Drug Administration (FDA), 172; Emergency Use Authorization (EUA) program, 281, 286
Ford, Gerald, 171
fraud: in Medicare, 55, 164, 314n3; in Social Security Disability, 109–10
free clinics, 122
free riders, 15, 248
Friedberg, Leora, 64
Friedman, Milton, 60

gag clauses, 221
Gates, Bill, 23, 29
Gawande, Atul, 39
global budgets, 138–39, 305
Gossage, Beverly, 260
government: growth of, 6; implicit debt for social insurance, 17; involved in protection against risk, 6, 11; regulation of insurance by, 15; seizing private pension funds, 51
gross domestic product (GDP), 13, 19
Gruber, Jonathan, 124, 162, 245

Haider, Steven J., 64
Harbaugh, Ken, 114
Heal, 202
health care: in Britain, 62, 120, 303–4, 306; in Canada, 120, 121, 195, 303–6; choice for private or public coverage, 242; choice to insure or not to insure, 239–42; coordinated care, 216, 294; costs of, 120–21; cutting costs in, 301; empowering patients, 272; federal and state policies regarding, 122–26, 130–32; financing and value received (U.S.), 120; government regulation of, 1–3; integrated care, 196, 215, 216, 294; leftwing view of, 73–74; for the medically needy, 329n70; nonprice barriers to, 121–22; as nontaxed benefit, 123–24; overconsuming, 17, 265–66; overinsuring, 265–66; perverse incen-

tives in, 70–72; privatization of, 74;
rationing of, 300; regulation/deregu-
lation of, 284, 286; rising costs of,
56; round-the-clock, 271; socialized
medicine, 303–7; spending on, 138–39;
traveling to obtain, 135–37; waiting
time for, 118–19

health care providers: access to, 40, 296;
assisted living facilities, 96–98, 289;
at-home care, 207, 337n63; bundling
of services by, 198; centers of excellence, 272; community health centers,
95; concierge medicine, 118, 198, 271;
continuity of care, 126, 283; coordinated care, 216, 294; custodial care,
207, 337n63; direct primary care, 118,
198, 271, 280; doc-in-the-box clinics,
197; doctor-patient relationships, 306;
emergency care clinics, 197; end-of-
life care, 39, 55–56; free clinics, 122;
getting the equipment they need,
284–85; independent contractors, 140;
integrated care, 196, 215, 216, 294;
intermediate care centers, 282; limiting rate increases for, 22; new opportunities for, 196–97; nursing homes,
96, 98, 319–20n89; out-of-network,
215, 218; paramedical personnel, 198;
projected increase in productivity,
20–21; reduction in Medicare fees
paid to, 21–22; round-the-clock access
to, 280; urgent care clinics, 259; walk-
in clinics, 36, 38, 70, 189, 197–98

health care reform: to the Affordable Care
Act (Obamacare) 38, 129, 261–69;
held up by special interest groups,
219; making permanent changes, 286;
philosophy of, 44; in the U.S., 118–21

Health City Cayman Islands, 136

health club memberships, 215

health insurance: choice between self-
insurance and third-party, 246–47;
choice for private or public coverage,
244–45, 253; choices in the market for,
247–49; group, 253; guaranteed issue,
248; health-status, 260; increase in
premiums, 152; inducements to use,
243–2424; integration with workers'
compensation, 232; legal restrictions on, 3–4; limited-benefit, 153;
for low-income families, 253; over/
underproviding, 303–4; personal, 270;
portability issue, 153, 270; preexisting condition exclusions, 247, 248;
private, 152; self-insurance, 146, 235,
246–47, 254, 264; short-term, 259–61;
socialization of, 5; tailored to family
needs, 153–54, 266–67; third-party,
254; universal coverage, 119, 144,
250–51, 253, 272

health insurance buyers: choices for, 267–
68; dual eligible, 48; empowerment of,
272; free riders, 15, 248; incentives for,
100, 142, 144–48; jumpers, 145

health insurance exchanges: attracting the
healthy and avoiding the sick, 141,
142, 143, 272, 282; available networks,
141–43; and Blue Cross, 135; community rating, 16, 40, 141–42, 145; cost
of, 248, 256, 269; deregulation of, 250,
261; eligibility for, 124–25, 139, 267;
factors causing death spiral, 145–46;
federal, 262; gaming the system, 145,
146, 148, 250, 253, 269; guaranteed
issue, 145; for high–risk patients,
145–46, 148; HSA option, 130; incentives for buyers, 144–48; incentives
to remain uninsured, 248; increase
in premiums, 145, 147; increasing
demand with no change in supply,
148–51; limited access to physicians,
142–43; for low–income families, 139,
150, 266; online, 262; out–of–pocket
expenses, 141–42, 144, 268; paying
Medicaid rates, 296; perverse incentives in, 249; privatization of, 264;

problems with, 299; problems with overcharging and undercharging, 263; "race to the bottom," 41, 142, 143, 153, 249, 264–65, 272, 282, 299; removing artificial pricing from, 251; removing government risk adjustment, 251–52; removing limited enrollment periods, 252; removing mandates from, 250–51; replacing individual insurance, 249; for retirees, 146, 148; for small businesses, 263; state, 145, 145–46, 262; subsidized and unsubsidized monthly enrollment, 147; tax subsidies for, 138, 139–40, 152, 242, 244–47, 255, 300; technical problems with, 262–63; turning into real markets, 249–54; without perverse incentives, 252–53. *See also* Affordable Care Act (Obamacare)

health insurance plans: as artificial market, 131–32; cost of, 39; covered benefits, 142; eligibility for, 267–68; employer-provided, 79, 125–28, 130, 245–46; employers overpaying for, 133–34; excessive, 123–24; for federal employees, 48; government-run, 72–74; health-status insurance, 40–41, 128–29, 260; incentives for buyers, 142; individual, 135, 253; liberating the marketplace, 197–98, 203–6; limited-benefit, 40, 267; "mini–med," 266–67; network of providers, 142–44; people without, 122–23; personal, 283; portability issue, 125–26, 132; postretirement, 28, 30–31, 146; for pre-Medicare population, 46; premiums for, 142; private, 74, 122–26, 130–32; privatization of, 48; public, 124–25; regulation of benefits, 142; self-insurance, 126, 130–31; short-term, 259–61; for small business employees, 128; special-needs, 265; tax credits for, 46; third-party, 126,

130–31; for vulnerable families, 204–5. *See also* Affordable Care Act (ACA); health insurance exchanges; Medicaid; Medicare

Health Insurance Portability and Accountability Act (HIPAA), 248

health insurance providers: under Affordable Care Act, 142–43; networks of, 264; private administration, 192; public vs. private, 193–95

Health Insurance Retirement Accounts (HIRAs), 205–6; contingent ownership of, 206; investment of funds, 205; management of, 205; options, 206

health maintenance organizations (HMOs), 143, 192, 196

Health Professional Shortage Areas, 200

Health Reimbursement Arrangements (HRAs), 127, 153, 204, 208, 247, 270, 271; excepted benefit, 128

Health Savings Accounts (HSAs), 48, 130, 136, 150–51, 189, 197, 204, 247, 266, 272, 277; and coronavirus treatment, 282–83; in health sharing plans, 258; use to pay HSA fees, 280; and workers' compensation, 232

health sharing plans, 255–58

health status risk adjustment, 251–52

health-status insurance, 40–41, 128–29, 260

hearing aid benefits, 215

heart disease, 144, 196, 214, 269, 272

Helvacian, Michael, 111

Herzlinger, Regina, 304

high blood pressure, 196

Holmes, Oliver Wendall, 170

homeowners' insurance, 14

Hooray Health, 259

hospitalization, alternatives to, 282

hospitals: competition between, 219; plan to reduce Medicare payments to, 21, 22; and price transparency, 129, 219–20

house calls. *See* Uber–type house calls

Housing Assistance, 89
human capital, 63
human resources, 273
Humana, 193, 293
Hungary, 51
hydroxychloroquine, 285–86

illness: cancer, 39, 135, 143, 144, 205, 253, 269, 296, 304, 305; chronic, 211, 272; communicable, 167–74; diabetes, 39, 144, 172, 196, 197, 214, 257, 272, 283; heart disease, 144, 196, 214, 269, 272; high blood pressure, 196; swine flu, 171. *See also* coronavirus pandemic
income inequality, 91–95
indemnity costs, 236
independent contractors, 140
Independent Payment Advisory Board (IPAB), 21, 22, 301
independent physician associations (IPAs), 218
Individual Retirement Accounts (IRAs), 28, 31; government seizure of, 52
insurance: automobile, 14, 131; casualty, 141; deregulation of rates, 237; fire and casualty, 131; health-status, 40–41, 128–29, 260; homeowners', 14; limited-benefit, 40, 153, 258–59, 267; private vs. social, 11; regulated by government, 15; socialization of, 4–5. *See* also disability insurance; health insurance; health insurance plans; life insurance; long-term care insurance; social insurance; unemployment insurance (UI); workers' compensation insurance
IntegraNet Health, 218
integrated care, 196, 215, 216, 294
intermediate care centers, 282

James, Estelle, 179, 223, 225
Jayapal, Pramila, 303
jumpers, 145

Koehler, Darryl, 91
Kotlikoff, Laurence, 64–65, 76, 79, 80, 81, 89, 91
Krugman, Paul, 73–74, 77, 165, 193

labor market, perverse incentives in, 264
Landers, Jim, 201
Leonard David Institute of Health Economics, 143
Levin, Carl, 110
Liberty HealthShare, 256
Lieber, Ron, 116
life expectancy: changes in, 61–62; of the elderly, 72; inequality in, 93
life insurance, 5, 14, 15, 131, 141; as alternative to survivors' insurance, 46; in Chile, 182–83; group, 224
life-cycle accounts, 186–87
lifestyle changes, 38, 39
limited-benefit insurance, 40, 153, 258–59, 267
litigation costs, 236
Liu, Liqun, 30, 75–76, 83–84
LiveHealth, 213
long-term care insurance, 16, 31, 43, 289–90; accessing home equity, 208–9; advantages over Medicaid, 207; creating incentives to purchase, 210; deduction of premiums, 320n101; disadvantages of, 207; employer-provided, 208; expenditures by source, 97; incentives to purchase, 100; under Medicaid, 95–100; opting out of, 48; in other countries, 210; partial privatization of, 48–49; personal accounts for, 211; private, 206–8, 287; public-private partnership programs, 208
Loughran, David S., 64

masks, 284
Matthews, Merrill, 36
Mayo Clinic, 70, 137, 199, 296

McCain, John, 118
McClellan, Mark, 61
McKinney-Vento Homeless Assistance
　Act, 185
MD Anderson Cancer Center, 135, 143,
　296
MediBid, 135, 296
Medicaid, 15, 45, 47, 89; alternatives to, 43;
　analysis of outcomes, 72–73; care for
　low-income patients, 70; complexity
　of, 95–96; coverage for at-home care,
　207, 337n63; coverage for custodial
　care, 337n63; creating less waste
　in, 154; efficiency of, 193; eligibil-
　ity expansion, 123–25; encouraging
　overuse of health care, 17; envisioned
　reductions in spending, 18; evaluation
　of benefits, 13, 72–74; expansion of,
　154; incentives to game the system,
　99–100; inflexible benefits schedule,
　96–97; inflexible eligibility sched-
　ule, 98–99; integrating reforms with
　Medicare, 289–90; limiting patients'
　options, 125; long-term care,16, 43,
　95–100, 206–11; long-term care eli-
　gibility, 208–9; new enrolees due to
　Obamacare, 150; perverse incentives
　in, 100; physicians' reluctance to
　accept, 245; restrictions on hospital
　spending, 138; as social insurance,
　96; unfunded liabilities of, 17, 47,
　288; waiting lists for treatment, 154;
　as welfare program, 96
Medicaid contractors, 143–44
Medicaid long-term care, opting out of,
　206–11
medical records, 144; electronic, 69–70,
　298
Medical Savings Accounts (South Africa),
　204
Medical Savings Accounts (US), 204
medical tourism, 136, 198, 219
medical travel, 135–37

Medicare, 15, 45, 47; "for all," 293–302,
　303; alternate estimate of growth,
　19; alternatives to, 28, 30–31, 43, 287;
　analysis of benefits, 13, 28, 61–62,
　72–74, 86–88; capping growth rate
　for spending, 21; care for the disabled,
　70; care for the elderly, 70; case study,
　19–22; changes under Trump admin-
　istration, 212–22; closing the gap,
　191; complicated benefits structure
　of, 76–78; costs of, 16, 296–97; cuts
　in spending and benefits, 18, 151, 288;
　effect on saving behavior, 17; effects of
　a reformed system, 288–89; efficiency
　of, 193; encouraging overuse of health
　care, 17; and end-of-life care, 55–56;
　fees to providers, 301; hidden costs for
　doctors and taxpayers, 297–99; and
　high-income retirees, 29; innovations
　to, 151, 294–295; as insurance, 24;
　integrating with Social Security, dis-
　ability, and Medicaid reforms, 289–
　90; limiting growth rate of, 19; losses
　to fraud, 55, 164, 314n3; maxing out
　coverage, 98; need to adopt electronic
　medical records system, 69–70; open
　to direct primary care, 271; opposi-
　tion to telemedicine, 200–201; opting
　out of, 48, 188–92, 196–98, 203–6;
　partial privatization of, 48–49; pay-
　ing for telemedicine, 279; payment of
　surgery fees, 219; penalties for delayed
　enrollment, 79; plan to reduce fees
　paid to doctors and hospitals, 21; pri-
　vate administration of, 293–94;
　privatization of, 217, 295; projected
　spending of, 19; proposals for reform,
　87–88, 189–90, 191–92; raising age of
　eligibility, 87; regulation of doctors
　by, 3; regulations on use of telemedi-
　cine, 118, 213; restrictions on growth
　of spending, 138; setting prices for
　services, 67–69, 71; slow to adopt new

modalities, 294; spending from Trustees Report, 21; unfunded liabilities of, 6–7, 17, 19–20, 25, 47, 56–58, 288, 300; value of benefits, 55–56, 89; wrong decisions by, 68

Medicare Actuaries Office, 19

Medicare Advantage (MA) program, 40, 48, 74, 151, 192, 194, 251, 252, 299; fair premiums, 264–65, 269; measurement of quality, 216; private administration of, 293–94; risk adjustment in, 217, 254–55; and telemedicine, 213, 214, 279

Medicare Part A, 79, 215; trust fund balances, 59–60

Medicare Part B, 79, 148, 190, 215, 269; premiums for, 61

Medicare Part C. *See* Medicare Advantage (MA) program

Medicare Part D, 73, 148, 190, 215, 221, 269, 294

Medicare Trust Fund, 19

Medigap, 148, 190, 215, 269

Medisave Accounts (Singapore), 204

Medi-Share, 255

mental disorders, 103–10, 210

mental health care, 95

Merline, John, 109

middle class: high tax rates for, 65; insurance for, 6, 96

Miller trust, 99

Minick, Bill, 233, 233–34

"mini–med" plans, 266–67

minimum essential coverage (MEC), 259

Minute Clinics, 37

Moeller, Philip, 76

monopsony, 69, 295

moral hazard, 15

mortality: effect of health insurance on, 73; of the elderly, 72

MPowering Benefits Association, 257–58

Mulligan, Casey, 166

Munnell, Alicia, 78

Musgrave, Gerald, 136, 136–37

MyTelemedicine, 259

National Bureau for Economic Research, 89, 125

National Center for Policy Analysis, 75

National Health Service, 305

Newhouse, Joe, 301

Nixon, Richard, 118

nonsubscribers, 235–36

nursing homes, 96, 319–20n89; Medicaid coverage for, 96, 98. *See also* assisted living facilities

Obama, Barack, 19, 22, 118, 185, 217, 295, 300

Obama administration, 74, 144–45, 153, 194, 295, 301

Obamacare. *See* Affordable Care Act (Obamacare)

obesity, 172, 196

O'Donnell, Paul, 233

Office of the Inspector General (OIG), 80

O'Neill, Dave, 304

O'Neill, June, 304

online exchanges. *See* health insurance exchanges

Oregon Health Insurance Experiment, 73, 150, 154

Organization for Economic Cooperation and Development (OECD), 94

out-of-pocket expenses, 38, 215, 221, 282

over-the-counter products, 215

pacemakers, 2

Pager, 202

pandemics, 168, 171, 172. *See also* coronavirus pandemic

paramedical personnel, 198

Parente, Stephen, 39

Pareto-optimal change, 44–45, 50–51

PartnerSource, 233, 234

part-time workers, 140, 161

patient billing, 314n3
pay-as-you-go financing, 17, 50, 52, 58, 61, 181, 184
Pence, Michael, 278
Pension Benefit Guarantee Corporation (PBGC), 29
pension benefits, 25, 28, 82–83; private plans, 29
permanent partial disability (PPD), 323n31, 343n23
personal retirement accounts, 177–79; in Chile, 179–81, 188; expected returns for high–wage workers in the US, 187; expected returns for low–wage workers in the US, 186; expected returns for median–wage workers in the US, 186–87; investment options, 181; protecting funds from market volatility, 187–88; transition to, 181, 184–86
phantom billing, 314n3
pharmaceutical companies, and price transparency, 129. *See also* prescription drugs
pharmacies, 278; international, 257
pharmacy benefits managers (PBMs), 221
physician fees: billing by time, 198; equalizing, 218–19; fee-for-service, 195, 217, 218, 271, 295
Physicians for a National Health Program, 295
plagues, 167–68
Poland, 51
Pozen, Robert, 64–65
preexisting conditions, 141, 154–55, 269
preferred provider organizations (PPOs), 143, 192
premiums, 264; risk-adjusted, 192, 254–55
prescription drugs: ending rebates and gag clauses for, 220–22; generic, 220–21; off-label use of, 285–86
preventive services, 148–49, 150, 204–5, 259
price rationing, 37
price transparency, 129, 219–20

privatization: of health care, 74; of Medicare, 217, 295; stealth, 295; of VA system, 188
progressive indexing, 178
Progressive movement, 170
public health: dark side of, 170–72; dawn of, 169–70
public-private partnership programs, 208

Qualified Income Trusts, 99

ratchet effect, 50, 52
rationing by waiting, 149–50, 155, 195, 301, 305–6
Reagan, Ronald, 185
retail clinics, 259
retail outlets, 197
retirees: allowing more control over health care, 210–11; employment for, 162; high-income, 23, 29, 311n7; income of, 93–94; on programmed withdrawal, 343n14; transfer of assets by, 99–100
retirement, 179; age of, 63; expectations for, 31
retirement programs, 5, 85; for local governments, 35; for nonprofit institutions, 35; partial privatization of, 47; personal retirement accounts, 177–79; unfunded liability of, 5. *See also* Social Security
retirement savings, 15, 28, 31
Rettenmaier, Andrew, 30, 56, 75–76, 83–84
reverse mortgages, 24, 208–9, 338n66
risk: adjustments for, 217, 251–52; aversion to, 27, 83–85; avoidance of, 4, 254; different attitudes toward, 24–27, 83; economic, 26–27; freedom to take risks, 4; insurance against, 131–32; market for, 254–55; political, 27; social cost of risk-taking, 15; transfer of, 246
risk pools, 145–46, 154–55, 248; federal, 145–46
risk-adjusted premiums, 192, 254–55

risk-adjustment mechanisms, 144
Rivlin, Alice, 310n10
Roche, 281
Roth Health Savings Accounts, 191, 192, 196, 247, 268–69, 289
Ryan, Paul, 119, 310n10

Samaritan Ministries, 255, 256
Sanders, Bernie, 119, 121, 296, 298, 303
SARS viruses, 285. *See also* coronavirus pandemic
Saver's Tax Credit, 89
Saving, Thomas, 30, 56, 83–84, 197
saving behaviors, 91–93; for retirement, 15, 28, 31; and unemployment insurance, 162
savings accounts, 29
Schieber, Sylvester, 94
self-employment, 180, 243, 265; tax breaks for, 115
self-insurance, 146, 235, 246–47, 254, 264
Sessions, Pete, 129
short-term insurance, 259–61
Shughart, William F. II, 184
Singapore, 34
Skinner, Jonathan, 61
Skype, 69, 117, 173, 196, 213, 214, 277–78, 307
small businesses, 140, 263
smartphone apps, 70, 282, 307
Smith, Thomas, 137
SNAP, 89
social contract, 14
social costs, 76
social insurance, 1, 4, 6; alternatives to government programs, 27–28, 43; benefits not proportional to income, each age group not paying its own way, 48–49; benefits not proportional to income, each age group paying its own way, 47; benefits proportional to income, each age group not paying its own way, 48; benefits proportional

to income, each age group paying its own way, 46–47; in Chile, 34; cost of, 18; design flaws, 16–17; effect on inequality of income and wealth, 91–95; effect on investments, 87–91; effect on saving behavior, 87–91; effect on work, 87–91; feasibility of reform, 49–52; goal of, 6, 28; how it works, 15–17; ignoring individual needs, 16; inaccurate pricing of, 16; as more expensive, 16; opting out of, 43, 44, 45, 287; origins of, 5–7; perverse incentives of, 17; philosophy of, 14–15; postretirement, 28; vs. private insurance, 11; privatization of, 51; proposed new system, 45–49; as protection for society, 23; in Singapore, 34; tax increases to fund, 13; unfunded liabilities of, 17. *See also* Medicaid; Medicare; Social Security
Social Security, 15, 45; ages for claiming benefits, 77; alternatives to, 28–30, 43, 47, 287; alternatives to (Galveston plan), 35–36; bad advice from, 79–82; calculating the value of, 83; complicated benefits structure of, 76–82; cutting benefits, 288; disability insurance, 103–10; and disability spending, 225; early retirement program, 17; and economic risk, 26–27; effect on saving behavior, 17, 76, 95; effects of a reformed system, 288; evaluation of benefits, 13, 25, 83–95; and high-income retirees, 23, 29, 311n7; ignoring individual needs, 16; incentives not to work or save, 63–67; integrating with Medicare reforms, 289–90; and investment portfolios, 26; mismanagement of disability benefits, 103–4; monthly benefits in 2019, 61; number of Americans receiving disability payments, 104; offer of lump sum benefit, 25–26, 29; opting out of,

35, 85–86, 177–81, 184–88; penalties
for working, 102; privatization of, 7,
83–86; progressive nature of benefits,
61, 82–83; proposals for reform, 86,
186; proposed new benefits, 45; rate
of return from, 82–83; reduction in
payroll tax rates, 30; regressive benefit
payments, 28; as retirement insurance, 24; survivors' benefits, 14, 17,
101–2; tax rate required to make foregoing benefits attractive, 86; taxes to
fund, 27; unfunded liabilities of, 6–7,
17, 25, 27, 56–58, 288; value of benefits,
55; value of contract to 21-year-olds in
2014, 84–85; and the very wealthy, 23;
and young workers, 30
Social Security Act, 279
Social Security Administrative Law Judge
(ALJ), 105
Social Security Disability Insurance
(SSDI), 104; eligibility criteria, 106–7;
incentives not to return to work,
107–8; overpayment of benefits, 110;
similarity to unemployment insurance, 108–9; waste, fraud, and abuse,
109–10; years of work required for
disability benefits, 106–7
Social Security Trust Fund, 58; balances
as percentage of annual expenditures,
59–60; reserves, 60
Social Security Trustees, 22
socialized medicine, 303–7
Solman, Paul, 76
Southwestern Medical Center, 135, 143, 296
Spanish flu, 168
Special Needs Plans, 192
specialists, 196, 278
specialization, 144, 272
spending inequality, 92
Standard Comprehensive Plan (SCP), 191
Stapp, Alec, 280–81
State Disability Determination (DDS)
office, 105

state risk pools, 145–46, 154–55
sterilization, forced, 170–71
stock market, 26
Summers, Lawrence, 162
Supplemental Security Income (SSI), 98,
104
survivorship benefits, 35–36, 45, 80–81, 85,
101–2; opting out of, 223–24; private
alternatives to, 45–46
swine flu, 171

TAFCD, 89
tax credits, for health insurance, 46
taxes: on capital gains, 66; double-taxing
savings, 66–67; for entitlement
programs, 25; fixed-sum tax credits,
240–41, 243–44, 247, 265; to fund
Medicare, 298; general revenue,
61; income tax, 61, 63, 65, 89, 123,
246; increases in, 13–14, 56, 288; on
investment income, 65; local tax,
123; marginal tax rate on savings,
67; marginal tax rate on wages, 66;
median lifetime marginal tax rate,
90–91; Medicare payroll tax, 61, 190;
on nonwage income, 65–66; payroll
(FICA), 63, 65–66, 75–76, 80, 102,
123, 178, 188, 243, 246, 273–75; penalty
for being uninsured, 123, 138; rate
required to make foregoing Social
Security benefits attractive, 86; rates
needed to pay for existing federal
programs, 18; reduction in payroll tax
rates, 29; regressive, 60–63; on senior
workers, 63–66; on Social Security
benefits, 65–66; Social Security payroll tax, 60–61, 75, 80, 82, 89; state
tax, 123; subsidies for health insurance
exchanges, 138, 140, 146–48, 151, 152,
240; taxable benefits, 236; on tax-
exempt bonds, 66; for unemployment
insurance, 158, 163–64
Teladoc, 37, 38, 69–70, 200, 201, 203, 213

telemedicine, 3–4, 69–70, 117, 173, 196, 197, 212–14, 218, 259, 277, 307; and ACOs, 279; access to, 271–72; AMA objections to, 199–200; and the coronavirus pandemic, 214; use for diagnosis, 278–80

telephone consultations, 37, 38. *See also* telemedicine

Texas Medical Association (TMA), 200

third-party payers, 195

Thorkildsen, Jake, 256

Thucydides, 167, 169

time costs, 8–9, 37–38, 121, 149–50

Tractica, 201

transportation benefits, 215

trial-and-error principle, 37–38

Trump, Donald J., 134–35, 173–74, 270; changes to Obamacare, 129; executive orders, 4, 271, 286

Trump administration, 22, 126, 153, 173, 218, 219, 222, 260, 280, 283; changes to Medicare program, 212–22; changing Obamacare, 127–29; improvements under, 13; reforming the health care system, 270–73; response to coronavirus, 277

Turner, Grace-Marie, 262

Tuskegee experiment, 171

Uber medicine. *See* Uber-type house calls

Uber-type house calls, 3, 37, 38, 69, 201–3, 294, 307

unemployment, 5; average duration in select OECD countries, 163; duration of, 160; likelihood of reemployment, 161; long–term, 162–63; North Carolina's response to, 164–65; U.S. rate, 157

unemployment insurance (UI), 5, 15, 17, 43, 45; account implementation issues, 275–76; case studies, 164–65; in Chile, 34, 46, 274–75; discouraging job search, 159–62; disincentive

effects of, 159–62; effect on family finances, 162; employment benefits of individual accounts, 275; encouraging inefficiency, 164; encouraging layoffs, 158–59; federal extension of benefits, 165–66; increasing long-term unemployment, 162–63; individual, 273–74; integrating with other reforms, 290; opting out of, 273–76; private alternatives to, 45, 287; problems with, 158–64; for retirees, 162; SSDI as, 108–9; unfair treatment of workers, 163–64

unfunded liabilities, 56–58; of the Affordable Care Act, 17, 288; of Medicare, 6–7, 17, 19–20, 25, 47, 56–58, 288, 300; of Medicaid, 17, 47, 288; of Social Security, 6–7, 17, 25, 27, 56–58, 288

uninsured people, 73, 95, 123–24, 151, 239, 251, 253, 269; choice to remain uninsured, 240–42, 269; numbers of, 148, 155; penalty for being uninsured, 123, 248–49; use of emergency room by, 150, 240

United Kingdom: health care system, 303–4; inequality in health care, 306; private sector medicine in, 306; United Health Service, 62, 120

UnitedHealthcare, 222, 258, 293, 326n26

universal coverage, 119, 144, 250–51, 253, 272

universal tax credit, 261, 263, 264, 268

urgent care clinics, 259

US Preventive Services Task Force, 149

vaccination, 170, 171

ventilators, 284

Verma, Seema, 213, 279

veterans: disability benefits for, 105, 114–15; health care for, 8. *See also* Veterans Health Administration (VA) system

Veterans Health Administration (VA) system, 8, 188; doctors, 8; long-term care program, 210; pharmacies, 8–9;

possible improvements to, 8–9, 36; privatization of, 188; program for mental illness, 210; waiting times, 150

video consultations, 201, 277. *See also* telemedicine

Villarreal, Pam, 96, 108

virtual check-ins, 213, 271, 279

virtual medicine, 212–14, 279

Von Kannon, John, 135–36

wage replacement rates, 237

walk-in clinics, 36, 38, 70, 189, 197–98

wealth inequality, 91–95

weight control, 39

welfare state, 6, 34

wellness exams, 71–72, 148

WellPoint, 193

workers' compensation insurance, 15, 16, 110–14; cost of treatment for back injury, 113; coverage of medical costs, 110; improving, 236–37; inflexibility and perverse incentives, 112–14; integrating with other reforms, 290; integration with disability insurance, 233; integration with health insurance, 232; non-portability of, 113–14; number of treatment days for back injury, 113; opting out of, 231–37; payment for death or dismemberment, 110; private alternatives to, 43, 46, 111–12; replacement of lost wages, 110–11; states opting out of, 111–12; in Texas, 232, 235–36

Yelowitz, Aaron, 125

Young, Richard, 196

Zoom, 69, 117, 196, 214, 278

Zycher, Benjamin, 298

About the Author

JOHN C. GOODMAN is Senior Fellow at the Independent Institute, President of the Goodman Institute for Public Policy Research, and author of the widely acclaimed Independent books, *A Better Choice: Healthcare Solutions for America*, and the award-winning, *Priceless: Curing the Healthcare Crisis*. *The Wall Street Journal* and the *National Journal*, among other media, have called him the "Father of Health Savings Accounts."

Dr. Goodman is often invited to testify before Congress on health care reform, and he is the author of more than fifty studies on health policy, retirement reform and tax issues plus ten books, including *Living with Obamacare: A Consumer's Guide*; *Lives at Risk: Single Payer National Health Insurance Around the World* (with Gerald Musgrave and Devon Herrick); *Leaving Women Behind: Modern Families, Outdated Laws* (with Kimberley A. Strassel and Celeste Colgan); and the trailblazing *Patient Power: Solving America's Health Care Crisis*, which sold more than 300,000 copies. His other books include *The Handbook on State Health Care Reform*, *National Health Care in Great Britain: Lessons for the U.S.A.*, *Economics of Public Policy: The Micro View* (with Edwin Dolan), *Fighting the War of Ideas in Latin America*, and *Privatization*.

Dr. Goodman received his PhD in economics from Columbia University, he has been President and Kellye Wright Fellow in Health Care at the National Center for Policy Analysis, and he has taught and completed research at Columbia University, Stanford University, Dartmouth College, Southern Methodist University and the University of Dallas. In 1988, he received the prestigious Duncan Black Award for the best scholarly article on public choice economics.

He regularly appears on television and radio news programs, including those on Fox News, CNN, PBS, Fox Business Network and CNBC, and his articles appear in *The Wall Street Journal, Investor's Business Daily, USA Today, Forbes, National Review, Health Affairs, Kaiser Health News* and other national publications. Dr. Goodman was also the pivotal lead expert in the grassroots public policy campaign, "Free Our Health Care Now," an unsurpassed national education effort to communicate patient-centered alternatives to a government-run health care system. The initiative resulted in the largest online petition ever delivered on Capitol Hill.

Independent Institute Studies in Political Economy

THE ACADEMY IN CRISIS | *edited by John W. Sommer*

AGAINST LEVIATHAN | *by Robert Higgs*

AMERICAN HEALTH CARE |
edited by Roger D. Feldman

AMERICAN SURVEILLANCE | *by Anthony Gregory*

ANARCHY AND THE LAW |
edited by Edward P. Stringham

ANTITRUST AND MONOPOLY | *by D. T. Armentano*

AQUANOMICS |
edited by B. Delworth Gardner & Randy T Simmons

ARMS, POLITICS, AND THE ECONOMY |
edited by Robert Higgs

A BETTER CHOICE | *by John C. Goodman*

BEYOND POLITICS | *by Randy T Simmons*

BOOM AND BUST BANKING |
edited by David Beckworth

CALIFORNIA DREAMING | *by Lawrence J. McQuillan*

CAN TEACHERS OWN THEIR OWN SCHOOLS? |
by Richard K. Vedder

THE CHALLENGE OF LIBERTY |
edited by Robert Higgs & Carl P. Close

THE CHE GUEVARA MYTH AND THE FUTURE
OF LIBERTY | *by Alvaro Vargas Llosa*

CHINA'S GREAT MIGRATION | *by Bradley M. Gardner*

CHOICE | *by Robert P. Murphy*

THE CIVILIAN AND THE MILITARY |
by Arthur A. Ekirch, Jr.

CRISIS AND LEVIATHAN, 25TH ANNIVERSARY
EDITION | *by Robert Higgs*

CROSSROADS FOR LIBERTY |
by William J. Watkins, Jr.

CUTTING GREEN TAPE |
edited by Richard L. Stroup & Roger E. Meiners

THE DECLINE OF AMERICAN LIBERALISM |
by Arthur A. Ekirch, Jr.

DELUSIONS OF POWER | *by Robert Higgs*

DEPRESSION, WAR, AND COLD WAR |
by Robert Higgs

THE DIVERSITY MYTH |
by David O. Sacks & Peter A. Thiel

DRUG WAR CRIMES | *by Jeffrey A. Miron*

ELECTRIC CHOICES | *edited by Andrew N. Kleit*

ELEVEN PRESIDENTS | *by Ivan Eland*

THE EMPIRE HAS NO CLOTHES | *by Ivan Eland*

THE ENTERPRISE OF LAW | *by Bruce L. Benson*

ENTREPRENEURIAL ECONOMICS |
edited by Alexander Tabarrok

FAILURE | *by Vicki E. Alger*

FINANCING FAILURE | *by Vern McKinley*

THE FOUNDERS' SECOND AMENDMENT |
by Stephen P. Halbrook

FUTURE | *edited by Robert M. Whaples, Christopher J.
Coyne, & Michael C. Munger*

GLOBAL CROSSINGS | *by Alvaro Vargas Llosa*

GOOD MONEY | *by George Selgin*

GUN CONTROL IN NAZI-OCCUPIED FRANCE |
by Stephen P. Halbrook

GUN CONTROL IN THE THIRD REICH |
by Stephen P. Halbrook

HAZARDOUS TO OUR HEALTH? |
edited by Robert Higgs

HOT TALK, COLD SCIENCE | *by S. Fred Singer*

HOUSING AMERICA |
edited by Randall G. Holcombe & Benjamin Powell

IN ALL FAIRNESS |
*edited by Robert M. Whaples, Michael C. Munger &
Christopher J. Coyne*

JUDGE AND JURY |
by Eric Helland & Alexander Tabarrok

LESSONS FROM THE POOR |
edited by Alvaro Vargas Llosa

LIBERTY FOR LATIN AMERICA | *by Alvaro Vargas Llosa*

LIBERTY FOR WOMEN | *edited by Wendy McElroy*

LIBERTY FOR PERIL | *by Randall G. Holcombe*

LIVING ECONOMICS | *by Peter J. Boettke*

MAKING POOR NATIONS RICH |
edited by Benjamin Powell

MARKET FAILURE OR SUCCESS |
edited by Tyler Cowen & Eric Crampton

THE MIDAS PARADOX | *by Scott Sumner*

Independent Institute Studies in Political Economy

MONEY AND THE NATION STATE |
edited by Kevin Dowd & Richard H. Timberlake, Jr.

NATURE UNBOUND |
by Randy T Simmons, Ryan M. Yonk, and Kenneth J. Sim

NEITHER LIBERTY NOR SAFETY | *by Robert Higgs*

THE NEW HOLY WARS | *by Robert H. Nelson*

NO WAR FOR OIL | *by Ivan Eland*

OPPOSING THE CRUSADER STATE |
edited by Robert Higgs & Carl P. Close

OUT OF WORK |
by Richard K. Vedder & Lowell E. Gallaway

PARTITIONING FOR PEACE | *by Ivan Eland*

PATENT TROLLS | *by William J. Watkins, Jr.*

PLOWSHARES AND PORK BARRELS |
by E. C. Pasour, Jr. & Randal R. Rucker

POPE FRANCIS AND THE CARING SOCIETY |
edited by Robert M. Whaples

A POVERTY OF REASON | *by Wilfred Beckerman*

THE POWER OF HABEAS CORPUS IN AMERICA |
by Anthony Gregory

PRICELESS | *by John C. Goodman*

PROPERTY RIGHTS | *edited by Bruce L. Benson*

THE PURSUIT OF JUSTICE | *edited by Edward J. López*

RACE & LIBERTY IN AMERICA |
edited by Jonathan Bean

RECARVING RUSHMORE | *by Ivan Eland*

RECLAIMING THE AMERICAN REVOLUTION |
by William J. Watkins, Jr.

REGULATION AND THE REAGAN ERA |
edited by Roger E. Meiners & Bruce Yandle

RESTORING FREE SPEECH AND LIBERTY ON
CAMPUS | *by Donald A. Downs*

RESTORING THE PROMISE | *by Richard K. Vedder*

RESURGENCE OF THE WARFARE STATE |
by Robert Higgs

RE-THINKING GREEN | *edited by Robert Higgs
& Carl P. Close*

RISKY BUSINESS | *edited by Lawrence S. Powell*

SECURING CIVIL RIGHTS | *by Stephen P. Halbrook*

STRANGE BREW | *by Douglas Glen Whitman*

STREET SMART | *edited by Gabriel Roth*

TAKING A STAND | *by Robert Higgs*

TAXING CHOICE | *edited by William F. Shughart II*

THE TERRIBLE 10 | *by Burton A. Abrams*

THAT EVERY MAN BE ARMED |
by Stephen P. Halbrook

TO SERVE AND PROTECT | *by Bruce L. Benson*

T.R.M. HOWARD |
by David T. Beito and Linda Royster Beito

VIETNAM RISING | *by William Ratliff*

THE VOLUNTARY CITY | *edited by David T. Beito,
Peter Gordon, & Alexander Tabarrok*

WAR AND THE ROGUE PRESIDENCY |
by Ivan Eland

WINNERS, LOSERS & MICROSOFT |
by Stan J. Liebowitz & Stephen E. Margolis

WRITING OFF IDEAS | *by Randall G. Holcombe*

INDEPENDENT INSTITUTE

100 SWAN WAY, OAKLAND, CA 94621-1428

For further information:

510-632-1366 • orders@independent.org • http://www.independent.org/publications/books/